❯ Becoming an
INTERIOR DESIGNER

A Guide to Careers in Design

Second Edition

CHRISTINE M. PIOTROWSKI, FASID, IIDA

WILEY

John Wiley & Sons, Inc.

Published by John Wiley & Sons, Inc., Hoboken, New Jersey.

Published simultaneously in Canada.

For general information about our other products and services, please contact our Customer Care Department within the United States at (800) 762–2974, outside the United States at (317) 572–3993 or fax (317) 572–4002.

Wiley also publishes its books in a variety of electronic formats. Some content that appears in print may not be available in electronic books. For more information about Wiley products, visit our Web site at www.wiley.com.

Library of Congress Cataloging-in-Publication Data

Piotrowski, Christine M., 1947-
 Becoming an interior designer: a guide to careers in design / Christine Piotrowski. — 2nd ed.
  p. cm.
 Includes bibliographical references and index.
 ISBN 978-0-470-11423-0 (pbk.)
 1. Interior decoration — Vocational guidance. I. Title.
 NK2116.P56 2009
 747.092 — dc22

          2008018564

Printed in the United States of America.

10 9 8 7 6 5 4 3 2 1

DISCLAIMER

This publication is designed to provide accurate and authoritative information in regard to the subject matter covered. It is sold with the understanding that the publisher and the author are not engaged in rendering professional services. If professional advice or other expert assistance is required, the services of a competent professional should be sought.

All photographs, documents, and forms are proprietary to the organization, design firm, designer, or author. None of the figures in this text may be reproduced without the expressed written permission of the appropriate copyright holder.

Blackburn
College

Library
01254 292120

Please return this book on or before the last date below

To Martha and Casmier, looking down from above.

With love,

Christine

A truly committed decision is
the force that changes your life.

ANONYMOUS

CONTENTS

PREFACE

The profession of interior design has received a lot of media attention over the years. Network television has portrayed interior designers as characters in major shows and featured them as experts on cable's various home decorating programs. Movies have even included interior designers or decorators as part of the cast. You have no doubt looked at one or more of the magazines related to interior design on the newsstands. The media attention, of course, doesn't necessarily help someone learn all that is involved in pursuing this profession.

This book is about the profession of interior design and the professional interior designer. If you are a student in high school or a postsecondary student who is considering interior design as a career, this book helps you understand what the profession entails. Maybe you have lost interest in your current career and are looking for a way to express your creative side. This book can assist you in understanding how interior design may help you achieve that goal. It will not, however, explain how to establish a practice or actually teach you how to do interior design.

The interior design profession has two broad segments of specialization. Residential interior design, primarily the design of private residences, is the area most familiar to the public. Commercial interior design is the other large segment of the profession. This specialty involves the interior design of businesses such as offices, hotels, stores, restaurants—even airports, sports stadiums, and prisons. Within each of these broad areas, designers might focus on one or more subareas—condominiums and retail stores, for example.

The profession has changed significantly over the last 45 years or so. Here are just some of the ways in which it is different: building and safety codes are emphasized; sustainable design in both residential and commercial interior design has gained importance; the growing complexity of projects and the design process means interior designers must be better educated and trained; licensing and legal responsibilities focus added attention on project management and contract administration; and the aging population has brought an increased awareness of the design of spaces for seniors.

These challenges and others have brought about critical changes in the profession through greater educational preparation, increased technical skills, broader knowledge requirements, and the measurement of professional competency via testing. Thus, today's professional interior designer works in a profession raised to a higher level than that of the stereotypical decorator. Interior design in the 21st century is much more than selecting colors and arranging furniture.

Helping you understand this exciting creative profession and career is the purpose of this second edition. This award-winning book has been revised and updated to include new information on sustainable design, aging in place, and interior design on the global stage, as well as other topics and comments from dozens of additional practitioners at many levels in their career. Numerous new designer profiles with examples of their project work have been added throughout the book.

Additional highlights to the second edition begin in Chapter 1, which provides an overview of the profession of interior design with a brief look at its history and such considerations as licensing, and other general topics. A new section discusses the role of interior designers and poses the question "What do interior designers do?" to dozens of practitioners. Chapter 2 describes the educational requirements of interior designers. A section has been added concerning high school preparation to help younger potential practitioners understand what can be done at that level. Chapter 3 looks at the various environments in which interior designers work. For example, some designers work by themselves from home offices, while others work as team members in large design firms—and everything in between. Note that all the information on job seeking such as résumés and portfolios has been moved to this chapter. Chapter 4 offers insights into the opportunities for various specializations in the field through interviews with practitioners currently working in them. This chapter also includes additional information and comments from designers about the importance of sustainable design and design for seniors. Chapter 5 describes the activities that occur between the inception of a project and its completion. It also discusses working relationships with allied professionals and the project management process. Chapter 6 presents an overview of the business side of the profession. This chapter briefly discusses how interior designers find clients through marketing activities, the importance of contracts in defining proposed services, and how interior designers earn revenue. Chapter 7 is a compilation of comments from practitioners on what they feel is the future of the interior design profession.

Indeed, I think you will find what practitioners have to say interesting and exciting. Included are quotes and commentaries by nearly 100 professionals who are practicing interior design or have been involved in this exciting profession in other ways. Interior designers in many specialties and career stages have provided insights to help you discover what this profession is like. Their responses to questions and points of view comprise a special feature found within and at the end of each chapter. This feature is unique among career books and will help you understand what interior design is like from people doing professional work every day.

The initials that follow the names of many interior designers represent the appellations of professional organizations and are included because attaining professional association membership is an important milestone for professional interior designers, as it is with any design professional. The following list provides a key to identifying these organizations:

AIA—American Institute of Architects

ARIDO—Association of Registered Interior Designers of Ontario

ASID—American Society of Interior Designers

CAPS—Certified Aging in Place Specialist

CID—Certified Interior Designer

CMG—Color Marketing Group

IDC—Interior Designers of Canada

IDEC—Interior Design Educators Council

IES—Illuminating Engineers Society

IFDA—International Furnishings and Design Association

IFMA—International Facility Management Association

IIDA—International Interior Design Association

ISP—Institute of Store Planners

LEED-AP—Leadership in Energy and Environmental Design—Accredited Professional

NCARB—National Council of Architectural Registration Boards

NKBA—National Kitchen and Bath Association

RIBA—Royal Institute of British Architects

RID—Registered Interior Designer

USGBC—United States Green Building Council

If an appellation begins with *F*, as in FASID, the member has earned a fellowship, which is the highest national honor of his or her association. Also note that some designers are required to place their state code before the CID or RID designations. An example is KYCID for Kentucky Certified Interior Designer.

Updated selected references in "Interior Design References" at the end of the book provide further reading on the topics covered in this book. "Interior Designers" in these back pages provides contact information for the various professional organizations and designers mentioned in the text.

I hope you will find this second edition of *Becoming an Interior Designer* a valuable source for learning about the exciting career of professional interior designer. This creative, multidisciplinary profession is a satisfying way to express your talent while providing functional and aesthetic solutions to a client's projects. Because the field offers so many avenues of work, you can find a niche that is stimulating and satisfying to you as it has been for the thousands who have come before you. These are exciting times for the interior design profession. I welcome you to it!

—*Christine M. Piotrowski, FASID, IIDA*

ACKNOWLEDGMENTS

I would like to thank the many interior designers, educators, and other design professionals who have contributed material to this book. Many of them I have known for many years. They graciously shared their insights, experiences, and passions about the profession as well as their project photos and drawings for this book. All these professionals are listed at the back of the book under "Interior Designers."

I also want to thank several people at John Wiley & Sons for their assistance and guidance. Of course, special thanks go to my editor, John Czarnecki, for patiently seeing this book to completion. I want to acknowledge Raheli Millman and Sadie Abuhoff for their assistance on the second edition and Lauren Olesky for her assistance on the first. Lastly, I want to thank my long-time friend Amanda Miller for encouraging me to do this book in the first place.

1 An Introduction to the Interior Design Profession

We spend over 90 percent of our day in interior spaces. Despite this, most people take interiors for granted, barely noticing the furniture, colors, textures, and other elements—let alone the form of the space—of which they are made. Sometimes, of course, the design of the interior does catch our attention. Maybe it's the pulsing excitement of a casino, the rich paneling of an expensive restaurant, or the soothing background of a religious facility.

As you are reading this book, you obviously have an interest in interiors and interior design. It might be because you have always enjoyed rearranging the furniture in your home. Maybe you like to draw imaginative floor plans for houses. It could be that a relative or friend is a contractor and you have been involved in the actual construction of a building in some way. Perhaps you saw a program on television and it inspired you to learn more about the profession.

The interior design profession is a lot more than what you see portrayed on various television programs. The profession of interior design has been defined by educators and professionals. This widely accepted definition is provided to help you understand what the profession is all about:

Interior design is a multi-faceted profession in which creative and technical solutions are applied within a structure to achieve a built interior environment. These solutions are functional, enhance the quality of life and culture of the occupants, and are aesthetically attractive. Designs are created in response to and coordinated with the building shell, and acknowledge the physical location and social context of the project. Designs must adhere to code and regulatory requirements and encourage the principles of environmental sustainability. The interior design process follows a systematic and coordinated methodology, including research, analysis and integration of knowledge into the creative process, whereby the needs and resources of the client are satisfied to produce an interior space that fulfills the project goals.[1]

Professional interior designers are not interior decorators and interior decorators are not professional interior designers, although the public generally does not see any difference. "Interior design is *not* the same as decoration. Decoration is the furnishing or adorning a space with fashionable or beautiful things. Decoration, although a valuable and important element of an interior, is not solely concerned with human interaction or human behavior. Interior design is *all* about human behavior and human interaction."[2]

Although a professional interior designer might provide interior decoration services, an interior decorator does not have the education and experience to perform the many other services of a professional interior designer. A decorator is primarily concerned with the aesthetic embellishment of the interior and rarely has the expertise, for example, to produce the necessary drawings for the construction of nonload-bearing walls and certain mechanical systems that are routinely produced by a professional interior designer.

What Do Interior Designers Do?

Interior design professionals provide the owners of homes and many kinds of businesses with functionally successful and aesthetically attractive interior spaces. An interior designer might specialize in working with private residences or with commercial interiors such as hotels, hospitals, retail stores, offices, and dozens of other private and public facilities. In many ways, the interior design profession benefits society by focusing on how space—and interior environment—should look and function.

The professional interior designer uses his or her educational preparation and training to consider how the design affects the health, safety, and welfare of occupants. Many projects today include careful consideration of sustainable design in the selection of furniture and materials used in the interior. Planning the arrangement of partition walls, selection of furniture, and specifying aesthetic embellishments for the space are all tasks the designer uses to bring the interior to life. A set of functional and aesthetic requirements expressed by the client becomes reality.

In planning a residence or any type of commercial interior, the professional interior designer engages in many tasks using a wide variety of skills and knowledge gained through education and practice. The professional interior designer must consider building and life safety codes, address environmental issues, and understand the basic construction and mechanical systems of buildings. He or she must effectively communicate design concepts through precisely scaled drawings and other documents used in the industry. Another critical responsibility concerns how to manage all the tasks that must be accomplished to complete a project as large as a 1,000-room casino hotel or as small as someone's home. The interior designer must also have the business skills to complete projects within budget for the client while making a profit for the design firm. And, of course, the interior designer selects colors, materials, and products so that what is supposed to actually occur in the spaces can.

This book helps you see clearly what the profession is about and what the real work of interior designers is like in the 21st century. It includes comments from professional interior designers in many specialties, sizes of companies, and areas of the country. These responses are presented to help you get an idea of what working professionals think about the profession. I posed the question "What do interior designers do?" to many of the designers whose work or other comments are in this book. "Problem solving" is a common response, but many other tasks and responsibilities are also mentioned.

What Do Interior Designers Do?

❯ Residential interior designers support their clients in realizing their dreams and creating a home for their family and friends. We research, design, document, and specify the interior architectural finishes, millwork, plumbing, lighting, cabinetry, and interior design details and work closely with the project team (client, architect, and contractor) to implement them. Second, we bring together the complete vision for the project through the design, research, and implementation of the interior furnishings—from all the furniture to the artwork and accessories.
Annette Stelmack, Allied Member ASID

❯ Create environments that support the human condition in whatever activities it chooses, including living, sleeping, working, playing, eating, shopping, healing, or praying. These environments must be safe, accessible, sustainable, and, in many cases, beautiful. But, most importantly they must be functional for the person(s) inhabiting them.
Lisa Whited, IIDA, ASID, Maine Certified Designer

❯ Interior designers create interior environments that are functional, aesthetically pleasing, and enhance the quality of life and culture of the users of the space. In doing so, they have an obligation to protect the health, safety, and welfare of the public.
Jan Bast, FASID, IIDA, IDEC

❯ We influence life patterns by creating healthy and safe environments.
Patricia McLaughlin, ASID, RID

❯ Interior designers solve problems. Our clients come to us with questions, wants, and needs and through design development we answer those questions and provide solutions for those wants and needs—all while protecting the health, welfare, and safety of the public through our knowledge of local and national building codes.
Kristin King, ASID

❯ Interior designers plan and design interior spaces. Interior designers understand how people move through, live and work in, and experience interior space. We consider the specific experiences and functions the space or project must support from the point of view of the user. Our unique understanding of psychological and human factors as well as formal design principles, materials, codes and regulations, and the means and methods of construction inform our diagnosis of user needs and the development of design concepts.
Beth Harmon-Vaughn, FIIDA, Associate, AIA, LEED-AP

❯ They use their creative skills and expertise to create spaces that improve people's environments and make life better. More pragmatically, interior designers gather and analyze information, produce drawings, manage consultant teams, and oversee construction projects.
David Hanson, IDC, RID, IIDA

Private residence: kitchen remodel. Sally Howard D'Angelo, ASID, S. H. Designs, Windham, New Hampshire.
PHOTOGRAPH: BILL FISH

❯ Good question. Interior design is sometimes described as problem solving, but our work is really focused on helping our clients prepare for a future they can imagine but not fully predict. We develop an image that transforms their vision to reality. The vision is from the client's thoughts and business goals.

We take our client's ideas, expressed in business terms, and give them form, make them reality. That reality is something they could have never imagined themselves and when it is right and becomes their vision, we have succeeded with the magic of design. To do so, designers have to understand their aspirations, not merely their needs.
Rita Carson Guest, FASID

❯ Interior designers are problem solvers who must be able to develop a design that fits the client's criteria and budgets. They must be able to take that design concept and make it reality by preparing the necessary drawings, renderings, details, construction documents, specifications, budgets along with the most important part, which is

creativity and visualization. They also must be very strong in communication and, most important, in being listeners.
Lisa Slayman, ASID, IIDA

❯ Depending upon the project, interior designers investigate existing conditions; research work habits and management philosophies; incorporate work and life culture of space users or clients; explore potential solutions that meet functional and aesthetic goals; conform to code and legal constraints; prepare graphic and written materials that communicate the solutions to a wide variety of people—clients, lenders, committees, other design professionals, code officials, and the building industry; and continue building their knowledge.
Katherine Ankerson, IDEC, NCARB Certified

❯ An interior designer serves many roles. A designer is a mentor to clients and others in the profession. We serve as project managers coordinating many trades and making sure that not only we are doing our job correctly, but that others are as well. We inspire interiors as well as lives with our work. Sometimes we do the dirty work that no one else wants to do, but in the end the smile on a client's face and the satisfaction that comes from a completed project makes all the project's challenges worth the time and effort.

Shannon Ferguson, IIDA

❯ We are professionals that offer our clients creative solutions in order for the spaces in which they live, work, play, and heal to function better and be more aesthetically pleasing.

Robert Wright, FASID

❯ We do everything for a space: we think through how the space functions based on who is occupying that particular space, how they are going to live there, work there, and function, and design around those parameters. We coordinate colors, furnishings, fabrics, and everything that goes into the environment.

Laurie Smith, ASID

❯ Interior designers design and create interior spaces, whether residential, commercial, or hospitality. The role of the interior designer is to understand the client's vision and goals for the project and interpret them in the design.

Trisha Wilson, ASID

❯ Good designers provide problem resolution through good design.

Patricia Rowen, ASID, CAPS

❯ Every decision an interior designer makes, in one way or another, involves life safety and quality of life. Some of those decisions include specifying furniture, fabric, and carpeting that comply with fire codes, complying with other applicable building codes, designing ergonomic work spaces, planning spaces that provide proper means of egress, and providing solutions for the handicapped and other persons with special needs. *Universal design* and *green design* are buzz words right now but they have always been and will continue to always be a part of every project. In addition to all of this, we manage projects, with budget, time, and safety in mind.

Donna Vining, FASID, IIDA, RID, CAPS

❯ If they are good at what they do, they create environments that unfold really *meaningful* experiences for their guests.

Bruce Brigham, FASID, ISP, IES

❯ Interior designers take a client's programmatic needs for a space and combine them with creativity and technical expertise to arrive at a customized space unique to their client.

Maryanne Hewitt, IIDA

❯ Interior design is a service industry. A designer must enjoy working with and helping people. Some of the aspects of commercial interior design include research, psychology, art, color, graphics, design, ergonomics, efficiency, and workflow.

Mary Knopf, ASID, IIDA, LEED-AP

❯ They are problem solvers. They need to be able to translate someone else's idea into a new reality. They need to be able to pick up all the puzzle pieces and reconstruct them into another solution—different from what the box said.

Linda Isley, IIDA, CID

❯ In three words: plan, coordinate, and execute. An interior designer is responsible for distilling the client's thoughts, desires, and budget to create a design plan for the project. The designer then coordinates all the elements within the plan and finally is the moving force for the plan's execution.

Greta Guelich, ASID

❯ Interior designers shape the human experience by creating the spaces in which we interact and live.
Darcie Miller, NKBA, CMG, ASID Industry Partner

❯ The easy answer is we create environments that are not only lovely to look at, but are also functional. But actually we are also therapists, accountants, researchers, organizers, shoppers, and sometimes even movers to realize our concept. The interior designer often becomes a family's most trusted friend as major moves, new additions to the family, new hobbies, or any other family change that affects the interior are discussed with the designer—and often we are the first to know.
Susan Norman, IIDA

❯ Interior designers in the corporate world understand corporate culture, how people work, and what corporations need to attract and retain

personnel. Interior designers study the workplace and create environmental solutions that are productive and fitting for the users.
Colleen McCafferty, IFMA, USGBC, LEED-CI

❯ In the course of my 25-plus-year career, I have worked on a variety of projects from small to very large residential projects, hospitals, and healthcare facilities—which are like little cities—numerous corporate offices, a funeral home, a fire/police station, and a yacht. The scope of work has always been varied within each project. Some include all aspects, from initial client contact and proposals, through schematics and budgeting; design development with space planning, furniture arrangement, selection, specifying, and scheduling; finish selection and scheduling; lighting, artwork, and accessory selection and placement; bid documentation and processing; installation; and working with all types of industry professionals, trades, and vendors. I have experienced the retail setting, design studio, architectural firm, and consulting as an independent designer. I have attended multiple trade shows and markets, traveled the world, and met many people in the process. The body of knowledge reflected in the Council for Interior Design Accreditation (CIDA) Standards is very real in its expectations of what interior designers do.
Carol Morrow, Ph.D., ASID, IIDA, IDEC

❯ They solve problems (whether they are spatial, organizational, programmatic, or aesthetic) that affect people's health, safety, and welfare.

Healthcare: rotunda with mural of Hygeia and Panacea (Greek goddesses of prevention and treatment), Scripps Breast Care Center, La Jolla, California. Interior architecture and design: Jain Malkin, Inc., San Diego, California.

PHOTOGRAPH: GLENN CORMIER

Some are great technicians; some are great designers; and a rare few are two or all of these. Some work in large offices; some are sole practitioners. Many work in the residential realm while a large number work in the commercial setting (that includes healthcare, hospitality, retail, or corporate work). Nevertheless all collaborate with other design professionals—including engineers and architects, building service/construction experts, and vendors/suppliers of all types.
David Stone, IIDA, LEED-AP

❯ A good interior designer will listen to the client's needs and try to fulfill them to the best of his or her ability—keeping in mind, of course, function and good design.
Debra Himes, ASID, IIDA

❯ Interior designers help the client improve their space, taking into account the client's needs and culture. The nature of projects vary so much that it is difficult to say.
Jane Coit, Associate Member IIDA

❯ Interior designers incorporate a broad range of skills to plan space that is both functional and aesthetically pleasing. Interior designers must juggle the needs of the client within the constraints of issues such as temporary or leased space, tight budgets, and differing aesthetic tastes. Interior designers provide a specialized knowledge base that includes understanding design elements and principles, space planning, life safety issues, codes, and contract documents.
Laura Busse, IIDA, KYCID

❯ Interior designers create meaningful, aesthetically pleasing environments to enhance the intended human activity within the environment.
Suzan Globus, FASID, LEED-AP

❯ The answer quite honestly depends upon whom and when you ask the question. There are many interior designers who focus upon schematic design and design development phases of work, yet there are many interior designers that place their primary attention upon marketing, branding, or the management of design. Many interior designers work collaboratively with a range of professionals and utilize a range of skills on a daily basis, from computer modeling and rendering skills to sketching or rendering perspective drawings by hand.

Many interior designers select fixtures, furniture, and equipment for their current projects and in the course of doing so, compose and complete material boards. Material boards are used to visualize the range of colors, materials, and furnishings for a project. On the other end of the spectrum, interior designers are immersed in creating interior architecture—often working in collaborative professional environments integrating programmatic, structural, material, and lighting aspects into built form. This is the current professional model in Europe. Regardless of where one finds or sees oneself in the spectrum, most interior designers address design from the perspective of the human body—its size, scale, societal and cultural norms, experiential aspects, and so on.
James Postell, Associate Professor, University of Cincinnati

❯ Through research, development, and implementation, interior designers improve the quality of life, increase productivity, and protect the health, safety, and welfare of the public.
Keith Miller, ASID

❯ As Nancy Blossom's research shows, some are tastemakers, some are place makers, others are trendsetters. With all respect to Robert Ivy, when *we* are at the top of our game, we design holistic spaces that address the spiritual, functional, and life safety needs of our clients. We don't just deal with the finishes and contents of the spaces between the exterior walls. Interior designers need to have an understanding of the context within which they work and understand how their decisions affect structure, site, and infrastructure. All of us deal with the health, safety, and welfare of the public in some way or another through the decisions we make in service to our clients. Even the selection of a simple item like a piece of furniture can have psychological and physiological, as well as code implications. The piece may not project the image that the client wants, it may not support the body properly, and its materials may produce toxic gases in a fire. This, in addition to the larger implications of the interior planning, should give an indication of how far reaching a designer's decisions can be.

Robert J. Krikac, IDEC

❯ Work with clients to create an environment that reinforces and supports their business.

Nila Leiserowitz, FASID, Associate AIA

❯ Create functional, secure living, and working environments that support health, safety, and welfare issues while also raising the quality and enjoyment of life.

Michael Thomas, FASID, CAPS

❯ The interior designer is the bridge between the physical environment and the human in space. Our distinction in the building practice is the wish and capability to help people become more human. And our success is the ability to make these positive connections.

Linda Sorrento, ASID, IIDA, LEED-AP

❯ The interior designer must have a holistic view of any project undertaken. This view comes into play when you see the integration of all the facets and requirements of the project.

An interior designer must have practical and technical expertise, as well as an understanding of the aesthetics, of all elements that make up the interior environment. The designer must understand how people use and respond to these elements. It is not a matter of understanding the individual elements in an interior, but the elements as they interact with each other.

We live, work, and play in a three-dimensional world—spending on average about 80 percent of our time each day indoors.

Interior design deals with the human-built environment. . . . It touches all that we do in both our personal and professional lives. What we see and touch—the environment that surrounds us and how that makes us feel—is most often noticed, and is a direct result of interior design or a lack thereof.

Interior design affects people's lives to a greater degree than any other profession. It affects how we live and move and feel in the built environment—the very quality of our lives.

Linda Elliott Smith, FASID

❯ They are problem solvers foremost. They assess and identify the design problem and they develop the design solution through critical thinking.

Robin Wagner, ASID, IDEC

❯ Interior designers perform a wide range of tasks, so every day is different. From the obvious, like space planning and color selections, to the not so obvious, like personal counseling to late-night photo shoots, there is always something new to do as an interior designer.

Lindsay Sholdar, ASID

> First, what I don't do: I don't design anything alone. I illustrate planning concepts with well-developed graphic representations and discuss how these concepts may improve the performance in an office.
Lisa Henry, ASID

> Interior designers design interior environments that affect the human experience, to establish a clear understanding of place. That is, they create an identity or image for a commercial or private building, to elicit a personal response such as to relax, entertain, have fun, buy product, heal, learn, teach, impress, and so on, or to support a particular task, that is, to create an efficient and ergonomically correct work environment.
Rosalyn Cama, FASID

> In my world, they act as psychiatrists and problem solvers. People need help figuring out how to make their lifestyles fit their residences—and the same goes for their commercial spaces. A designer needs to listen to their clients, their needs, and how they and their families or coworkers use the given spaces. Designs need to provide comfort and functionality—and it is a designer's job to integrate both. Additionally, I feel that my job is to truly make my clients' lives easier. Most people don't want to think about the process of creating the design whether on paper or in true action. I have found that many clients also do not want any part of the construction/deconstruction process either. Therefore, a designer can also take on the role of "go-between" or project manager (to use a more commonly understood phrase).
Marilizabeth Polizzi, Allied Member ASID

> There are a broad range of skills involved in interior design. A designer or firm may specialize in a small segment or cover all the tasks involved. We typically clarify a program defining the constraints and goals for the project, offer and refine creative solutions for the interior space and associated details, make selections for finishes and furnishings, document our findings, create budgets, contract labor, make purchases, and manage the implementation of the project.
Sally Howard D'Angelo, ASID, AIA Affiliate

> For my practice, I spend a great deal of time as a client advocate. I help clients sort through the choices that appear overwhelming, to reach a solution that is practical, interesting, and aesthetically pleasing. I want to find solutions to the problems at hand, whether the problems are large or small. If the problems or things that annoy the user have not been dealt with, the project is not a success. Masking something that is not functioning well by making it pretty is not effective design. Another definition of what designers (at least for myself) do is about 5 percent actual design work and 95 percent project administration and oversight.
Sharmin Pool-Bak, ASID, CAPS, LEED-AP

> The NCIDQ (National Council for Interior Design Qualification) definition is the best example to me of what interior designers do. However, I believe one of the best definitions is in an article by Jill Pable at Florida State University (and her colleague) that discusses the difference between "filled and fulfilling spaces." I believe that interior designers do not fill, but design and create "fulfilling spaces" based on client needs and desires within a given budget and timeline.
Stephanie Clemons, Ph.D., ASID, FIDEC

> Analyze client needs, educate clients, use acquired knowledge to provide solutions that support clients' needs, productivity, strategic plan, and corporate brand.
Terri Maurer, FASID

❭ Interior designers are problem solvers. They provide solutions by addressing such issues as spatial planning, acoustics, and lighting. In addition to creating a functional space, a designer strives to provide an aesthetically pleasing environment for their client.

Teresa Ridlon, Allied Member ASID

❭ If they are doing what I feel they *should* be doing, they work as part of a team with the clients to design spaces that will help the clients lead healthier, happier, safer lives. This goal should be the same whether designing residential or nonresidential spaces. That is the short definition.

Drue Lawlor, FASID

❭ We help create the environments where people live, work, and play.

Melinda Sechrist, FASID

❭ Interior design projects are the design and renovation of interior space within buildings. The interior designer's role is to lead the design process for interior design projects. Interior designers listen to their clients during the programming phase. They bring new research to the design solutions. They create design solutions that meet their clients' needs and exceed their expectations. They document projects for building permit application. They observe construction. Interior designers collaborate with other disciplines throughout the entire project (architects, engineers, lighting designers, vendors, and contractors).

Rachelle Schoessler Lynn, CID, ASID, LEED-AP, Allied Member AIA

❭ Interior designers protect the health, safety, and welfare of the public while creating environments that are appropriate and enjoyable to the occupants of a space.

Alexis B. Bounds, Allied Member ASID

❭ Interior designers create a functioning environment that is aesthetically inspiring. This environment is specific to the client's goals and adheres to all applicable life, health, and safety codes. Green and universal design should be strongly considered.

Carolyn Ann Ames, Allied Member ASID

❭ When it comes right down to it, we're advocates for the end users of a space. We put ourselves in the homeowner's, student's, patient's, customer's, visitor's, or worker's place and create spaces that are safe, comfortable, beautiful, functional, and inviting. Unlike what's shown on TV design shows, design is much more than aesthetics—it's about making better interiors for all of us to inhabit.

Charrisse Johnston, ASID, LEED-AP, CID

❭ Problem solve. We create attractive but functional environments.

Chris Socci, Allied Member ASID

❭ An interior designer is a professional that has the ability through experience and education to create interior environments that serve their end users with functionality and preserve the health, safety, and welfare of the public. Professional interior designers are able to visually enhance spaces. But more importantly, they are able to identify spatial challenges and overcome those obstacles with creative solutions that are developed through researching and observing the physical environments.

Shannon Mitchener, LEED-AP, Allied Member ASID, Associate IIDA

Is Interior Design for You?

Many people think that someone who wants to be an interior designer must be very creative or an artist. It certainly takes creativity to develop plans and design concepts to resolve a client's needs for a professionally designed home environment or commercial space. Few interior designers begin their quest to be part of this profession with innate artistic abilities. These creative or artistic skills are developed through course work and experience, as are the technical skills needed for the development of plans and drawings.

There are many ways to work in the profession as you will see in this book. Not all positions in interior design require a high level of skill in what might be considered artistic endeavors. You may find a place in the profession that uses other skills such as technical mastery of drafting, project organization and management, or the selling skills. The fact that there are many ways in which to work in this profession is an interesting truth for anyone who:

Enjoys solving problems.

Has a concern for details.

Observes interiors and tries to figure out how to change them.

Can comfortably work with a team.

Has creative and artistic abilities and interests.

If you are interested in interior spaces, find yourself wondering about their design, or can think of ways to make them better, that is a strong first step that shows interest in the profession. Reading books about interior design is, of course, another strong indicator of interest. If you are in high school, you can talk to your guidance counselor or a teacher who teaches interior design, drafting, or art classes. You might also want to talk to an interior designer. Contact the local offices of the professional associations and perhaps they can give you the names of designers who teach interior design at a community college or university. Asking questions of those working in the field is a great way to find out if you are really suited for the profession. This book will give you an overview of the profession. You can also visit Web sites to help you learn more about the profession and career opportunities in interior design, such as www.careersininteriordesign.com, a joint effort sponsored by professional associations, educators, and testing organizations. The American Society of Interior Designers (www.asid.org), International Interior Design Association (www.iida.org), and Interior Designers of Canada (www.interiordesigncanada.org) are the largest of the professional associations in the United States and Canada and can be contacted for information that can help you decide if becoming a professional interior designer is for you.

High-End Residential, Construction Remodeling

DONNA VINING, FASID, IIDA, RID, CAPS
PRESIDENT, VINING DESIGN ASSOCIATES, INC.
HOUSTON, TEXAS

What has been your greatest challenge as an interior designer?

❯ Interpreting clients' wishes and giving them what they want and need.

How important is interior design education in today's industry?

❯ It is monumental. If we are to be a profession, we must have a consistent, quality educational program, ever changing and evolving as today's advances move faster and faster.

What led you to enter your design specialty?

❯ My mother was a huge influence. She was my very own Sister Parish, always decorating our home. When I was a teenager, she opened her own antique shop in a small house on the same property as our home.

What are your primary responsibilities and duties?

❯ Everything. When you are the owner, you have all the financial and managerial type of responsibilities and duties as well as being the lead interior designer. In residential, clients want you, and even though my staff teams on all projects, I am heavily involved in most of them.

What is the most satisfying part of your job?

❯ Hearing the clients say they love our work.

TOP LEFT Private residence: master suite. Donna Vining, FASID, Vining Design Associates, Inc., Houston, Texas.
PHOTOGRAPH: ROB MUIR

LEFT Private residence: living room. Donna Vining, FASID, Vining Design Associates, Inc., Houston, Texas.
PHOTOGRAPH: ROB MUIR

What is the least satisfying part of your job?

❯ Depending on others for my end product—so many people are involved, and it is hard to make things happen just like I want them.

What is the most important quality or skill of a designer in your specialty?

❯ Listening skills and teaching clients what is best for them and their lifestyle.

What advice would you give someone who wants to be an interior designer?

❯ Take business and psychology classes and realize that the actual design portion is a small part of the business.

Who or what experience has been a major influence on your career?

❯ My mother was a huge influence. And once I was in the field, the ability to make things beautiful but always functional and durable.

Private residence: dining room. Donna Vining, FASID, Vining Design Associates, Inc., Houston, Texas.

PHOTOGRAPH: ROB MUIR

Design of Active Living and Aging-in-Place Communities

SHANNON FERGUSON, IIDA
PROJECT MANAGER
ID COLLABORATIVE
GREENSBORO, NORTH CAROLINA

What led you to enter your design specialty?

❯ Fate, I suppose. . . . After graduation I received an internship with a North Carolina design firm. When I started with them, they worked primarily with local clients in the healthcare and medical fields. After my internship, I stayed on with ID Collaborative and, as the years have progressed,

we have become more well-known in the senior living and active living communities. After procuring several large projects over the last few years I have had the privilege of progressing my skills in active-living communities and aging-in-place communities across the eastern and southern regions of the United States.

What is the most important quality or skill of a designer in your specialty?

❯ In my opinion the most important quality of an effective designer is being able to listen to your client's expectations and desires and turn them into reality.

How is your specialty different from other specialties?

❯ My specialty is different from others because not only do I deal with people's work environment, but also their living environments. To me a living environment is such a personal space that it can either bring happiness or contribute to sadness and depression. So often you see retirement communities and nursing homes that are depressing and run-down. If you had to live in this every day, I would venture to say that you might be subject to despondency and, in turn, a shortened life span. Therefore, dealing with living environments, especially in the aging population, gives me a responsibility to bring renewed life into the environments that I design.

What are your primary responsibilities and duties in your position?

❯ I serve as a project manager and see projects through from start to finish. Initially, I work with clients to determine their scope of services needed as well as work with them on forming a budget for the project. I work with ID Collaborative's principal on design contracts for projects. Once contracts are approved, I work with the client from schematic design planning into design development through to construction documents and contract administration. Throughout this process, I present interior finish schemes, furnishings, and so on for client approval. We are then able to determine the overall concept for the space, its use, and its character. I work with architects, contractors, and other consultants on all aspects of the project including floor plan layouts, reflected ceiling plans, millwork details, architectural details, building codes, and the like.

Once construction is complete and furnishings are installed, a final punch list is completed with the client and the project is followed through to the very end to be sure the client is satisfied and all work is complete.

What is the most satisfying part of your job?

❯ The most satisfying part of my job is working with the client and assisting them in conceptualizing their thoughts and imaginations and turning them into reality.

What is the least satisfying part of your job?

❯ My least favorite part is the feeling that I have not delivered or captured the true form of the client's concept.

Who or what experience has been a major influence in your career?

❯ My firm as a whole has been a major influence on my career. We have a fantastic group of people who all have different specialties that are remarkable and inspiring to me as a designer.

What has been your greatest challenge as an interior designer?

❯ Education of clients and the community. Many people have a misconception as to what it actually is that interior designers do. After watching all of the shows on Bravo and HGTV, they think that interior designers are flamboyant individuals who swoop into a job, do a quick makeover, and are out of the picture as fast as they came in. These shows do not provide the public with any background information on credentials, requirements for interior design certification, or education, and certainly do not provide the public with an actual picture of what true interior designers do on a daily basis.

GETTING IN

❯ Getting a job in interior design today requires an appropriate education and mastering skills from drafting and drawing to effective communication. It involves learning technical areas of construction, mechanical systems, and codes as well as showing that you have the interest and enthusiasm to work in the profession. Getting in also means knowing what kind of job you want and whether you want to work in a residential or commercial specialty. You also need to consider if you would work best in a small studio, a large multidisciplinary firm, or an intermediate-size practice.

When it comes time to research job possibilities, be sure to do your homework on the companies in which you are interested. If you know something about the company before the interview, you will make a far better impression at the interview. Investigate the style and type of interior design work that the firm does by researching trade magazines and local print media. Look for the firm's Web site and carefully examine as much of it as you can. Talk to professors who know something about the company. Your college placement office might be able to help as well.

You can also find out about possible jobs and about a specific company by researching:

- Department of Commerce articles and reports
- Local magazines and newspapers
- Dun & Bradstreet Reference Book
- Registrar of Contractors
- Board of Technical Registration
- Yellow Pages directory
- Professional association chapters
- Family and friends

You may need two or more versions of your résumé, each specific to a type of design work you are interested in obtaining. For example, you should organize your résumé differently when you apply for a position with a firm primarily engaged in residential design work versus one that specializes in hospitality interior design. The résumé also should be somewhat different if you are applying to a large multidisciplinary firm versus a small firm. The same goes for your portfolio. Showing a commercial firm a portfolio of residential projects could be a waste of time all around. Chapter 3 discusses résumés and portfolios in more detail.

Looking for a job in interior design—whether your first one as you finish school or when you move from one firm to another—is a job in itself. It is important that you go about it in a sensible and organized fashion. The more prepared you are, the more homework you do before you even start your search, the greater your chances of gaining that ideal position. Additional information on the topics related to finding a job can be found in Chapter 3.

Corporate Headquarters, Offices, and Retail Spaces

FREDERICK MESSNER, IIDA
PRINCIPAL, PHOENIX DESIGN ONE, INC.
TEMPE, ARIZONA

What has been your greatest challenge as an interior designer?

❯ There is a fine balance between the activity of design and the need to handle all the business activities that go into the normal day. They are both necessities and constantly in competition for the ten hours per day we seem to feel are required.

What led you to enter your design specialty?

❯ From a young age, I was always interested in how things go together and in drawing. As I learned more about the tools of our trade, I became more interested in how I could manipulate space to affect people. My interest is in commercial design because I believe it has the potential to have great impact.

What are your primary responsibilities and duties?

❯ Design mentor, financial control, strategic planning for the design firm, human resources, design and project management, marketing, and father confessor.

What is the most satisfying part of your job?

❯ Teaching the many aspects of design as well as practicing the same is the reward that is most enjoyed.

What is the least satisfying part of your job?

❯ The challenge of dissatisfied clients due to any number of reasons is a part of the job that can be, at times, very difficult.

What is the most important quality or skill of a designer in your specialty?

❯ The ability to listen and interpret wants and needs with the best possible solution is the mark of a good commercial designer. In the design of office space, it takes knowledge of competing

TOP LEFT Corporate headquarters: entry. Fred Messner, IIDA, Phoenix Design One, Inc., Tempe, Arizona.
PHOTOGRAPH: CHRISTIAAN BLOK

LEFT Corporate headquarters: reception area. Fred Messner, IIDA, Phoenix Design One, Inc., Tempe, Arizona.
PHOTOGRAPH: CHRISTIAAN BLOK

space and construction methods and understanding of the client's sophistication, budget, and taste as well as timelines. The best solution most often is a compromise that blends the most positive aspects of all.

How important is interior design education in today's industry?

❯ It all starts here. This is the opportunity to start building a base that will last a lifetime. Interests and habits that start in school will carry designers into the profession.

Who or what experience has been a major influence on your career?

❯ My involvement with IBD (Institute of Business Designers) and then IIDA (International Interior Design Association) was a link to my colleagues and the profession. It allowed me to gain insight into everyday occurrences with a different perspective. I have also built valuable friendships.

Corporate headquarters: boardroom. Fred Messner, IIDA, Phoenix Design One, Inc., Tempe, Arizona.

PHOTOGRAPH: CHRISTIAAN BLOK

History

As a profession, interior design has a comparatively short history. Architects, artisans, and craftspeople completed interiors before interior decorators began offering their services. Architects created the design of a building's structure and often the interiors. They would engage craftspeople to create and produce the furnishings needed to complete the interior. Other artisans lent their expertise with decorative embellishments and the production of handmade pieces for the interior. Of course, all this was accomplished for the world of the wealthy and mighty—not the average person.

Many historians have credited Elsie de Wolfe (1865–1950) as the first person to successfully engage in interior decoration as a career separate from architecture. At about the turn of the 20th century, de Wolfe established a career by offering "interior decoration" services to her society friends in New York City. "She was an actress and a society figure before she began to remodel her own home, transforming typically Victorian rooms with stylish simplicity by using white paint, cheerful colors, and flowery printed chintzes."[3] Her friends recognized her alternative decor, which was a great contrast to the dark, deep colors and woods of Victorian interiors. She is also believed to be among the first decorators to charge for her services rather than be paid only a commission on the goods she sold to clients.[4]

The door opened for this profession at the turn of the 20th century for several reasons. One was the development of new technologies during the 19th-century Industrial Revolution that helped make possible machine-made furnishings and other products. These mass-produced items were cheaper and more available to the average consumer. As demand for these goods grew, department stores—a new concept in the 19th century—began displaying the new products in their stores, attracting the average consumer. This exposure to new products helped generate interest in the decoration of residences by trained decorators.

The success of the early decorators encouraged many women to seek this avenue of professional and career enrichment. It was, after all, one of the few respectable ways for women to work in the early part of the 20th century. Educational programs were developed to train the early decorators in period styles and to provide the educational background needed to plan interiors. One of the first schools to offer effective training in interior decoration was the New York School of Applied and Fine Arts, now known as Parsons, the New School for Design.

As the profession continued to grow in the major cities, "decorators clubs" were formed in order for the decorators to meet, share ideas, and learn more about their profession. The first national decorators association was formed in 1931 and was called the American Institute of Interior Decorators (AIID)—later to be called the American Institute of Interior Designers (AID). In 1975, the two largest groups of professionals at the time—AID and the National Society of Interior Designers (NSID)—merged to form the American Society of Interior Designers (ASID).

By the 1940s, due to changes in the profession and the built environment industry in general, many individuals working in the field began to call themselves *interior designers* instead of *interior decorators* and to refer to their profession as *interior design* rather than *decorating*. The distinction reflected in these new terms was first applied to those few interior designers working with business clients. In addition, many kinds of new business clients appeared, slowly providing other opportunities for the gradual growth of the commercial interior design profession. Dorothy Draper (1889–1969) is well known for her design of commercial interiors such as hotel lobbies, clubs, and stores. Her influence grew in the 1940s, and she is often identified by historians as one of the first interior designers to specialize in commercial interiors rather than residences.

Of course, numerous influential interior decorators and designers contributed to the development of the profession as we know it today. The names Eleanor McMillen, Ruby Ross Wood, Mrs. Henry Parish II, Billy Baldwin, Florence Schust Knoll, and T. H. Robsjohn-Gibbings are familiar to many practitioners in the field. Architects Frank Lloyd Wright, Mies van der Rohe, and Richard Meier, along with designers David Hicks, Mark Hampton, Michael Graves, and Warren Platner, are just a few of the fine professionals whose talent immeasurably contributed to the growth of the interior design profession in the 20th century. If you would like to learn about the history of the profession in greater detail, you may wish to read one of the books listed in the references.

Commercial: Healthcare

LINDA ISLEY, IIDA, CID
DESIGN DIRECTOR, YOUNG + CO., INC.
SAN DIEGO, CALIFORNIA

What led you to enter your design specialty?

❯ At the time, the banking industry was closing down and I was hired into a firm that specialized in healthcare. My analytical tendencies work well in this field. My strengths are in the technical aspects of design and construction. In healthcare my strengths are utilized.

What is the most important quality or skill of a designer in your specialty?

❯ Being able to listen to the needs of all the "end users" (staff, owners, and patients), and being able to turn those desires into an environment that promotes health and healing.

How is your specialty different from other specialties?

❯ There are many things about the patients you serve that are not documented in the design manuals. You need to be able to interpret the sensitive constraints of fragile health into a solution that is both safe and comfortable.

What are your primary responsibilities and duties in your position?

❯ I project manage the design and documentation of most of the projects in the office. I review all details that are developed in the office for constructability and understanding.

Healthcare: Balboa Naval Medical Center, Pediatric Intensive Care Unit. Linda Isley, IIDA, Young + Co., Inc., San Diego, California. Architect: Ravatt Albrecht.
PHOTOGRAPH: CAMPOS PHOTOGRAPHY

What is the most satisfying part of your job?

❯ The most satisfying is seeing an idea get built.

What is the least satisfying part of your job?

❯ The least satisfying is being described as a "decorator" and not being understood for what knowledge you bring to the design team. Especially when we are relegated to being only the "finish applicators."

Who or what experience has been a major influence in your career?

❯ I have always gravitated to an office that has utilized my abilities to develop elevations and design details. The more experience, the better I became. I spent my first five years out of school in an architect's office doing documentation and presentation work.

What has been your greatest challenge as an interior designer?

❯ Overcoming stereotypes.

Sustainable Design

Watching the news you have no doubt become aware of how our environment is under siege from depletion of resources and climate changes that change the earth and our lives. Did you know that 40 percent of what goes to landfills is construction waste? According to the U.S. Green Building Council (USGBC), buildings consume between 30 and 40 percent of all energy used.[5] The depletion of resources also affects the built environment and the work of many in interior design and architecture. Sustainable design of both residential and commercial interiors will continue to play a very important role in the interior design profession in the 21st century.

The designs, construction methods, materials, and products specified for buildings and interiors all have an impact on the environment as well as the users of buildings. Resources are depleted and landfills become clogged with materials that may never disintegrate. The indoor environment can be harmful to people with allergies. Finding ways to design interior environments and buildings in general is increasingly focusing on sustainable design.

But what is sustainable design? "Sustainable design seeks to meet the needs of the present without compromising the ability of future generations to meet their needs."[6] Concepts in sustainable design in architecture and interior design have emerged since the 1970s though, of course, concern for the environment goes back many more years. Sustainable design is sometimes thought of as green design. Sustainable and green design seeks to create not only designs that utilize materials wisely, but also manufacturing and construction processes that result in as little harm to the environment and the user as possible while meeting the needs of the building's owners and users.

Materials and products specified for interiors also affect the interior environment in another way. Indoor air quality can be harmful to many users of residences and commercial spaces due to the materials that are specified. Toxic fumes referred to as *volatile organic compounds* (VOCs) are emitted from carpeting, paints, wall coverings, and furniture products. These VOCs result from glues used to manufacture furniture, adhesives used to attach carpets to floors and wall coverings to walls, and paint. These fumes are irritants and cause allergic reactions in some individuals.

Sustainable design concepts affect the home as well. For example, homes are built much tighter today, meaning that contractors attempt to keep air leaking in or out of a house to a minimum. This is done to increase the energy efficiency of the house. Unfortunately, the materials used to finish the interior can create VOCs—as can the furniture and furnishing products specified for the residential interior.

The U.S. Green Building Council is a nonprofit organization that has brought architects, contractors, product manufacturers, interior designers, and others in the built environment industry together to find ways to increase knowledge and practice in sustainable design. Their educational programs help all these different entities understand how to design buildings that are healthier for the occupants and save resources. A program developed by the USGBC is the LEED Certification program. LEED stands for Leadership in Energy and Environmental Design. It is a way that building owners and designers can voluntarily create buildings that are healthy and environmentally responsible. "LEED Certification validates a building owner's efforts to create a green building."[7]

There are several books listed in the "Interior Design References" (page 310) that examine sustainable design in interior design. You can also find more information from the USGBC (www. usgbc.org).

Residential: Sustainable Design

ANNETTE K. STELMACK, ASID ALLIED MEMBER
ECOIST, CONSULTANT, SPEAKER,
AND OWNER, INSPIRIT
LOUISVILLE, COLORADO

Sustainable residence: living room, Lake Pines. Annette Stelmack, Allied Member ASID, Inspirit-llc, Louisville, Colorado; formerly with Associates III. Architect: Doug Graybeal, Graybeal Architects (formerly with CCY Architects).

PHOTOGRAPH: DAVID O. MARLOW

What led you to enter your design specialty?

❯ My upbringing as a first-generation American inspired my natural approach to interior design. My family recycled and reused everything. My love for nature and all living creatures was nurtured throughout my childhood and then I too passed this value on to my husband and son. My son enjoys teasing me that I was recycling for the entire office before Denver had the facilities. I would load my car up weekly with the recyclables and deposit them at our local recycling center in Boulder, Colorado. This started more than 20 years ago as my son Bryan is now 25; he was always my assistant on these trips. From the onset, I was continually drawn to organic design forms, finishes, and objects that ultimately led to my area of expertise in the arena of sustainable residential design. I have a deep compassionate caring for our environment and for the future generations of all living species. I am continually inspired by both Mother Earth and her and our children.

What is the most important quality or skill of a designer in your specialty?

❯ Being knowledgeable and literate is vital within all specialties of interior design, including sustainable residential interior design. Initially, I drew from the commercial design sector as they were leading the way in sustainable design. Today, there is an overflowing abundance of information available at our fingertips for all sectors of the market. For environmental resources, I consistently refer to the Internet and books, along with participating in organizations such

Sustainable residence: kitchen, Lake Pines. Annette Stelmack, Allied Member ASID, Inspirit-llc, Louisville, Colorado; formerly with Associates III. Architect: Doug Graybeal, Graybeal Architects (formerly with CCY Architects).

PHOTOGRAPH: DAVID O. MARLOW

as U.S. Green Building Council, ASID, and AIA-COTE. The Internet, books, and networking with like-minded individuals across all sectors of the building industry provide a depth of knowledge and experience that is fundamental in honing and developing our expertise. In tandem with knowledge must be our listening skills. Intuitively listening beyond the words of our clients and team members brings a synergy in our work that transcends the details and, as though by magic, reveals our client's vision. I have found that this brings together exceptional results—from great team chemistry to proactive problem solving to exceeding the client's expectations.

How is your specialty different from other specialties?

❯ Ultimately sustainable, green, eco-friendly design will no longer be a separate set of skills, knowledge, language, or practice. Sustainable design principles and practices are now being incorporated into interior design schools across the country. The Council for Interior Design Accreditation has set forth standards pertaining to

sustainability. Accredited programs must provide education that includes the environmental ethics and the role of sustainability in the practice of interior design.

What are your primary responsibilities and duties in your position?

❯ I was the design director of Associates III Interior Design for over 25 years and an integral member from 1979 to 2006. Associates III is recognized on numerous fronts for their beautiful interiors and earth-friendly design philosophy. I was instrumental in mentoring and coleading this model firm, pioneering the field of sustainable residential interior design with our company vision: *We are environmental stewards with a passion to create nurturing, healthy, and sustaining environments.*

As the design director and a senior project designer with Associates III, I was responsible for managing the design team and overseeing projects, budgets, and deadlines. In addition, I was responsible for business development and departmental management tasks. I also managed projects, leading my teams to the successful completion of the most challenging and largest scale projects taken on by the company. As the environmental leader at Associates III, I formalized and managed the environmental and sustainable efforts on behalf of the firm.

I am also the coauthor of *Sustainable Residential Interiors* (John Wiley & Sons, 2006) with my Associates III friends Kari Foster and Debbie Hindman. Our book clearly and succinctly lays out strategies and tools to meet not only homeowners' needs, but those of the planet.

Over the last two years I have been transitioning out of practicing interior design into my next venture, Inspirit: To Instill Courage & Life. This firm allows me to fuse my passion for environmental stewardship and creativity in order to inspire future generations. I actively teach and mentor sustainability to peers, parents, and students of all ages. My expertise, synergy, and passion for natural and ecological design and responsible living are reflected in all my work. As environmental advocacy and literacy is paramount to me, I'm thrilled to share my expansive knowledge in the arena of environmental sustainability by sharing my passion with all.

I lecture on sustainability and eco-design at building industry events such as "Interiors," the American Society of Interior Designers' annual conference, and other venues. I have been interviewed for *American Architectural Review*, a PBS series spotlighting green design education. And I serve on several committees, including the national ASID Sustainable Design Council and the U. S. Green Building Council—Colorado Chapter.

I am equally moved by others and seek to live by Mahatma Gandhi's inspirational words: "You must be the change you wish to see in the world."

What is the most satisfying part of your job?

❯ The most satisfying part of my job is connecting with people and nurturing relationships. I also love proactively solving problems in addition to mentoring team members' growth and success.

What is the least satisfying part of your job?

❯ As I am now transitioning out of design into my role as an eco-consult, eco-outreach, and eco-education, the part that I won't miss is the lack of perspective that some clients have on the completion of their projects and meeting their unrealistic deadlines. There are other issues more important to the world than whether or not a sofa is going to be delivered at a certain time.

Who or what experience has been a major influence in your career?

❯ In addition to my upbringing, as I already mentioned, attending the EnvironDesign2 conference in 1998 was a pivotal and focused event that fully acknowledged my values and ethics. The experience was emotional and intense. I was moved deeply by William McDonough, Paul Hawken, Sim Van der Ryn, and many others over the course of the weekend conference, and it changed my life for the good. My newfound conviction for environmentally responsible, green building became a motivating force in the firm. I was fortunate to find synergistic alignment with the owner of the Associates III, Kari Foster, who fully supported the next steps of transforming the company. As the environmental leader of the firm, I engaged everyone to identify obvious action steps toward being more environmentally responsible and we used the small successes to build our sustainable practice into an everyday part of our interior design business.

What has been your greatest challenge as an interior designer?

❯ Being patient while the mainstream market—clients, team members, manufacturers, contractors, architects, vendors—begins to recognize the invaluable aspects of integrating sustainable design principles, philosophies, and practices into everything we do. Every decision we make affects the next; it's a chain reaction of good or negative results that directly affects the one and only planet that we live on.

Commercial: Sustainable Design

RACHELLE SCHOESSLER LYNN, CID, ASID, IFMA, USGBC, LEED-AP, ALLIED MEMBER AIA
PARTNER, STUDIO 2030
MINNEAPOLIS, MINNESOTA

What led you to enter your design specialty?

❯ I am a commercial interior designer. I integrate sustainable design thinking into all of my projects. Interior designers have a profound impact on how the indoor environment affects human health.

What is the most important quality or skill of a designer in your specialty?

❯ The ability to collaborate and discover the best sustainable design solution. The ability to brainstorm openly with others in order to explore the possibilities for creating a world generous in resources for the next generations.

How is your specialty different from other specialties?

❯ Sustainable design thinking is integrated into every design specialty. It is not an additional service. It is integrated thinking from the conception of a project.

What are your primary responsibilities and duties in your position?

❯ I am the cofounder of Studio 2030. My business partner David Loehr and I are responsible for all aspects of managing our business. We love to collaborate with our design talent on projects.

Restaurant: Red Stag Supper Club, dining room. A LEED-qualified interior. Rachelle Schoessler Lynn, ASID, CID, LEED-AP, Studio 2030, Inc., Minneapolis, Minnesota.

PHOTOGRAPH: ERIC MELZER PHOTOGRAPHY

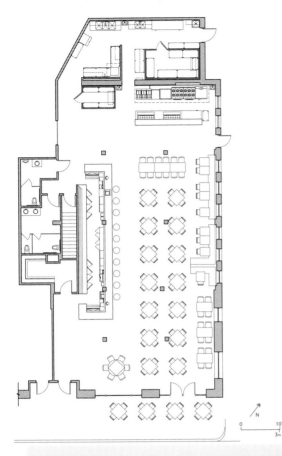

What is the most satisfying part of your job?

❭ The most satisfying aspect of my job is when the client has that "aha" moment. When the client has experienced the project vision in person upon construction completion and when the employees and client respond well to the new environment.

What do you enjoy most about working in the firm you are in right now?

❭ I love working with passionate, talented, smart designers who produce great work for our clients.

What advice would you give to someone who wants to be an interior designer?

❭ Design comes from the soul. This profession is about giving, and the reward is the joy our clients experience.

What is the single most important skill an interior designer needs to be successful?

❭ Passion for great design.

TOP LEFT Restaurant: Red Stag Supper Club, floor plan. Rachelle Schoessler Lynn, ASID, CID, LEED-AP, Studio 2030, Inc., Minneapolis, Minnesota.

LEFT Restaurant: Red Stag Supper Club, bar. A LEED-qualified interior. Rachelle Schoessler Lynn, ASID, CID, LEED-AP, Studio 2030, Inc., Minneapolis, Minnesota.

PHOTOGRAPH: ERIC MELZER PHOTOGRAPHY

What Do You Feel Is the Impact of Sustainable Design on the Profession?

❯ Sustainable design must be environmentally as well as socially and economically thoughtful in order to be truly sustainable. It is the foundation of design for the future.

Beth Harmon-Vaughn, FIIDA, Assoc. AIA, LEED-AP

❯ As an industry, I think that sustainable design is in its early years at this point. I have several clients who have inquired about sustainable products, but very few that actually follow through with them. Part of the reason for this seems to be cost factors and another part is education and time. Currently, these are products and concepts that you have to pursue as an architect or designer. However, in the years to come, I imagine that this concept will become so common that it will be hard not to specify products with recycled content or labeled as "green."

Shannon Ferguson, IIDA

❯ Sustainability is a whole new world. We are used to tearing down and just creating new. For the good of the world, we need to start looking at alternate ways to reuse materials, walls, and furniture, looking for ways to keep materials from the landfill and still give great solutions to the client. This is a time where creativity is really going to challenge our solutions.

Colleen McCafferty, IFMA, USGBC, LEED-CI

❯ Huge! I have been serving as adjunct faculty at several New England schools since 2001. I tell my students that it is a given that they must design for safety (fire and building codes), accessibility (ADA and universal design), and sustainability. We all have an ethical obligation to do everything we can in the design professions to protect the earth for our children and grandchildren. Sustainable design is not a specialty—it is simply a requirement for *all* design.

Lisa Whited, IIDA, ASID, Maine Certified Interior Designer

❯ We are just beginning to feel the impact of sustainability. It is integrated to the design process.

Nila Lesierwotz, FASID, Associate AIA

❯ Green design is not a current fad. It is a philosophical orientation and holds enormous potential for the future of interior design.

James Postell, Associate Professor, University of Cincinnati

❯ Sustainable design is becoming mainstream and clients are beginning to take notice and ask designers to design their spaces with sustainable resources where possible without stressing their budgets.

Interior designers are struggling to find sustainable products at the same time manufacturers are struggling to determine how to transform their manufacturing operations and products to become sustainable. There are no standard means of measurement at this time so the interior designer's biggest challenge is to determine which products are truly sustainable.

Rita Guest, FASID

❯ Sustainable design is something that we all should be practicing in every aspect of our profession and our personal lives. Using materials and products and creating solutions that are sustainable and healthy makes sense for your clientele and the community at large. A sustainable solution should encompass life cycle costs in both real dollars and environmental impact. Designers need to understand the reality of sustainable design in order to remain viable in today's marketplace.

Mary Knopf, ASID, IIDA, LEED-AP

Restaurant: entry. William Peace, ASID, Peace Design, Atlanta, Georgia.

PHOTOGRAPH: CHRIS A. LITTLE

> We have an imperative to correct the spiral of negative influence humans have exerted on our planet, and to make responsible choices that improve the environment, at the very least that do it no further harm.

Katherine Ankerson, IDEC, NCARB Certified

> Sustainable design or rather sustainable lifestyle is more than just a trend, it is a reality which should dictate all aspects of all professions not just interior design. We have a great responsibility to overcome and will once the commitment is made. We *all* just need to commit.

Darcie Miller, NKBA, ASID Industry Partner, CMG

> My hope for our profession is that sustainable design will become the standard and not the exception. As individuals we can make a small difference, but as professionals we have the unique opportunity to educate our clients and the public on the impact of careless design decisions. We can effect change toward sustainability on a much larger scale than most. Our responsibility is to protect the heath, safety, and welfare of not just the public but of the environment as well.

Lindsay Sholdar, ASID

> Sustainable design is a way of life and is here to stay. It affects every aspect of design and the interior and exterior spaces we shape. I think the philosophy and culture of sustainable design has been implemented in our nation so quickly, because (1) our children were taught about it in elementary school and they taught their parents, (2) it makes sense, and (3) we are already seeing the impact of the *opposite of sustainable design* in our atmosphere and environments. Sustainable design aspects should completely permeate all curriculum in interior design education. It should be the only way to design future spaces.

Stephanie Clemons, Ph.D., FASID, FIDEC

> I have always lamented at the category of sustainable design. I think that good design should inherently be sustainable. But currently, it is viewed as a category. Sustainable design is critical, especially as we are stewards of so many materials that go into a job. It is an opportunity for the designer to have a teaching role with clients and educate them on the benefits of sustainable approaches to interior design. Not just the environmental and health benefits, but the

economic benefits of green strategies. It puts a lot of power in the designer's hands to be able to show a financial model of the return on investment. These conversations we have about the financial impact of many different interior design strategies add tremendous value to our clients.

Lisa Henry, ASID

❭ Sustainable design is very important in the industry at the present and is just becoming important to the public as they are made aware of the consequences of their lifestyle choices. In 20 years, the buzz may have faded some, but will grow stronger during the immediate future.

Sally D'Angelo, ASID,
Affiliate Member AIA

❭ Sustainable design affects the health of the earth and the health of my clients. It is my obligation as a professional interior designer and a human being to protect both.

Kristin King, ASID

❭ Within just a few more years, I believe all of our interior design projects will include sustainable, green solutions because we will be more aware of the issues, better educated, and our clients will expect it.

Robert Wright, FASID

❭ Sustainable design is really the responsibility of all of us. We have the opportunity as designers to specify products that will contribute to greener buildings. But we also have the responsibility to really check out the long-term effects of some of the products that we are told are green only to find out they fail sooner and end up in the landfill with worse consequences than a traditional product.

Melinda Sechrist, FASID

❭ In the '80s, it was life cycle design—looking at the cost effects of our interior FFE (furniture, fixtures, and equipment) decisions. Now we must take a broader look at the effects of the choices that we make as the negative impact of human activities on the environment has become clear. Especially in the U.S., where we still consume a disproportionate amount of the world's resources. Sustainability is not a passing fad, but is becoming a necessary mindset for how we go about our lives and the decisions that we make about the built environment. It is becoming more common for students and professionals to be LEED-AP. Clients are beginning to require more sustainability aspects be designed in to their projects not just for the PR, but because it makes good business from a facilities management and financial point of view. With the continuing rise of energy costs, LEED approaches to buildings can have a fast payback of increased first cost and continued operational savings. Sustainable approaches to design can also be used to recruit and retain the best of a generation that lists the environment as a high priority. The impact on design education is clear: sustainability is here for a long time and we need to be preparing our graduates in this area.

Robert J. Krikac, IDEC

❭ We as designers have the opportunity to change the direction of global warming. The buildings and the interiors that we design are major contributors to landfill waste, air quality, water quality and consumption, pollution, energy consumption due to building operations, and energy consumption due to manufacturing of materials required for construction.

Rachelle Schoessler Lynn, CID, ASID,
LEED-AP, Allied Member AIA

The importance of sustainable design is addressed again in Chapter 4.

ETHICAL STANDARDS

❯ The consequences of unethical behavior by politicians, business leaders, sports figures, and many others are widely discussed in the media. Ethical behavior by all members of our society is expected, though not always forthcoming.

Ethical standards help those engaged in a specific profession understand what is considered right and wrong in the performance of the work of the profession. In the case of interior design, ethical standards are guidelines for the practitioner's work relationships with clients, other interior design professionals, employers, the profession in general, and the public.

Interior design professionals who affiliate with a professional association are required to abide by that organization's written code of ethical standards. When they do not, the association may take action against them—and it does not take ethics charges lightly. Designers who remain independent are also expected to conduct their business in an ethical manner, although they cannot be charged with ethics violations. Many unethical actions have legal consequences as well.

Behaving ethically is not hard. Keeping promises made to those you work with and for, only taking work for which you are experienced and capable to accomplish, abiding by the laws within your state regarding the business practice of interior design, and respecting the client and others are not difficult tasks. These are a sampling of what constitutes ethical behavior. What is hard is facing the consequences when one behaves in an unethical manner, regardless of whether one is affiliated with an interior design professional association. You can read the various codes of ethics adopted by interior design organizations by referring to their Web sites (see "Interior Design Resources" on page 297).

Private residence: hall table and mirror. Greta Guelich, ASID, Perceptions Interior Design Group LLC, Scottsdale, Arizona.

PHOTOGRAPH: MARK BOISCLAIR

Education and Research

KATHERINE S. ANKERSON, IDEC, NCARB
CERTIFIED
UNIVERSITY OF NEBRASKA-LINCOLN
LINCOLN, NEBRASKA

What is your design practice or research specialty?

❯ Two areas of interest have driven my research. First, improving teaching and learning in interior design with a particular emphasis on using technology and with strong educational strategies to create interactive animations and simulations. Second, improving the built environment for the aging individual by investigating and creating strategies for a supportive and livable home environment.

What advice would you give to someone who wants to be an interior designer?

❯ This is an exciting and challenging field, where you have an opportunity to affect people's lives through the designed environment. Observe and be curious about everything around you, keep a sketchbook for observations and resulting ideas and thoughts. Develop your interpersonal skills alongside your design skills. Approach every task with excellence in mind. Go beyond—take every advantage to be a leader. Remember that you have a unique set of skills and knowledge that allow you to view problems much differently than most, and do not hesitate to use this uniqueness to contribute back to society in the betterment of the human condition.

What has been your greatest challenge as an interior designer/faculty member?

❯ The greatest challenge of being an interior design educator is also one of the most exciting—to keep current with the profession and issues facing it, and to go beyond knowledge of the immediate to look towards future implications of those issues and what will be facing future interior design graduates.

What is the single most important skill an interior designer needs to be successful?

❯ A passion for the power of design.

Why did you become an educator?

❯ Through all aspects of my life, I have been an educator of sorts. In the office setting, I mentored new professionals; in personal life, I engaged in activities such as coaching that involve teaching young people new skills and teamwork. Education is a natural fit to combine the passion for design with the leadership gifts that I possess. After teaching my first class, I was hooked. The impact we as educators have on the future of the interior design profession, the blossoming of students realizing their potential, the "aha" moments when you see in one's eyes that they "get it"—each of these continue to affect me in a positive and reinforcing manner.

What are a few characteristics of a good student?

❯ A broad curiosity and the willingness to explore and expand their knowledge. An excitement about knowledge and the application of such. Understanding they are in school to learn, that they do not already have all the answers. Being willing to engage in critical discourse about design and other subjects.

Professional Associations

A professional association helps to represent its membership to the general public. An association also provides information and learning opportunities to enhance the membership's practice of the profession. Several associations serve members of the interior design profession in the United States and Canada. Some, such as the American Society of Interior Designers (ASID), serve broad segments of the profession. Others, such as the Institute of Store Planners (ISP), represent specialty designers. The two largest associations in the United States are ASID, with over 40,000 members, and the International Interior Design Association (IIDA), with over 12,000 members. In Canada, the Interior Designers of Canada (IDC) is the national professional association. Seven Canadian provinces also have provincial associations that support local interior designers.

When you become a member of a professional association, you join a network of colleagues with similar interests. Many interior designers are sole practitioners, working by themselves from home offices or small studios. Networking opportunities with members in the local area is a great assistance to these small business owners and a reason many give for joining a professional association.

Chapter and national activities of associations give sole practitioners and designers in larger firms opportunities to obtain and exchange information and gain from peer relationships. Becoming involved in chapter and national committees gives members another opportunity to hone leadership and management skills as well as to form extended networks that develop into valuable resources for both personal and professional growth.

Members of associations are able to take advantage of the services offered by a headquarters staff that analyzes and disseminates large amounts of information that the nonaffiliated designer may not have access to, let alone time to read and absorb. Professional associations also serve as a filter and source of information to help members address issues related to interior design practice, thus helping them remain effective practitioners of interior design.

Association members obtain information via e-mail news flashes, association magazines or newsletters, and mailings, as well as national and regional conferences. In the electronic age, the national association's Web site provides a great deal of important information to interior designers, some of it available only to members. In addition, local chapters throughout the United States and Canada hold member meetings on the local level and provide information via chapter meetings, electronic communications, educational seminars, and newsletters.

Professional association membership conveys a meaningful credential that is important in marketing to potential clients. The prestige this offers helps you compete against individuals who have not obtained the education and other competency qualifications of association members. Acceptance into an association, especially at the highest level of membership termed "professional," means you have met stringent criteria related to education, experience, and competency testing. Becoming a member of an interior design professional association also means you are bound to abide by stated ethical standards and conduct.

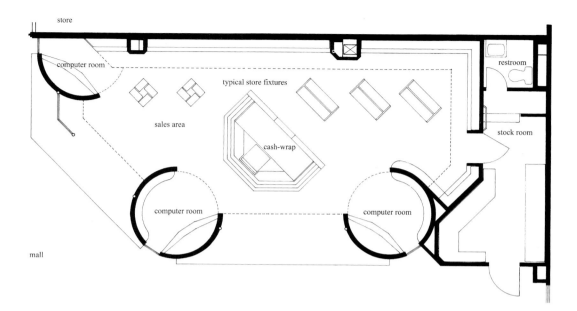

An important responsibility of the associations is to function on behalf of members in relation to government regulation and to national and even international issues. Professional associations have staff departments that research governmental regulations that might affect the professional practice of interior design and the health, safety, and welfare of the public. This information is forwarded so individual state or provincial chapters can inform local members about impending legislation, regulation, and other issues that affect the profession. Individual members also obtain much of this information via mailings and e-mail news flashes.

Retail: floor plan. The Electronics Boutique, Woodbridge Center, Woodbridge, New Jersey. Architect: John Mclean, RA, AIA, John Mclean Architect. White Plains, New York.

Which association is best for you? You alone can answer that question by becoming involved in one. A student in an interior design program can become a student member of the national associations. Upon graduation, the student can advance to the first level of practitioner membership. Although each association provides similar services, the activities of the local chapters often differ; this commonly influences the individual's choice of organization. Attending a few local chapter meetings and getting to know people in them will help you determine which association is right for you.

So you may have an understanding of the qualifications of membership in a professional association, "Membership Qualifications" (see page 34) provides a brief overview of membership qualification for ASID and IIDA. These associations were selected because they are the biggest, in terms of membership, in the United States. Membership qualifications in other associations may vary. "Other Professional Associations" (see page 35) gives short descriptions of some additional professional interior design associations.

CANADIAN INTERIOR DESIGN PROFESSIONAL ASSOCIATIONS

National Association

Interior Designers of Canada (IDC)

Provincial Associations

Registered Interior Designers of Alberta

Interior Designers Institute of British Columbia

Professional Interior Designers Institute of Manitoba

Association of Registered Interior Designers of New Brunswick

Association of Interior Designers of Nova Scotia

Association of Registered Interior Designers of Ontario

Interior Designers Association of Saskatchewan

MEMBERSHIP QUALIFICATIONS

American Society of Interior Designers (ASID)

Professional

Graduation from recognized program of study in interior design.

Educational requirement must meet National Council for Interior Design Qualification (NCIDQ) requirements.

Minimum two years' work experience in interior design.

Completed NCIDQ examination.

Six hours (0.6) continuing education unit (CEU) credits every two years.

Appellation usage (Member Name, ASID).

Allied

Graduation from recognized program of study in interior design.

Minimum two years' work experience in interior design.

Six hours (0.6) continuing education unit (CEU) credits every two years.

Appellation usage (Member Name, Allied Member ASID).

Other membership categories exist for individuals who are not interior design practitioners.

International Interior Design Association (IIDA)

Professional

Graduation from recognized program of study in interior design.

Educational requirement must meet NCIDQ requirements.

Minimum two years' work experience in interior design.

Completed NCIDQ examination.

Ten hours (1.0) continuing education unit (CEU) credits every two years.

Appellation usage (Member Name, IIDA).

Associate

Graduation from recognized program of study in interior design.

Minimum two years' work experience in interior design.

10 hours (1.0) CEU credits every two years.

Appellation usage (Member Name, Associate Member IIDA).

Other membership categories exist for individuals who are not interior design practitioners.

Note: NCIDQ requires a minimum of six years of education and work experience in order to qualify to take the examination. The minimum educational requirement by NCIDQ is a two-year certificate in interior design.

OTHER PROFESSIONAL ASSOCIATIONS

American Institute of Architects (AIA)

Represents the interests of professional architects. Interior designers may be eligible for affiliate membership in a local AIA chapter.

Building Office and Management Association (BOMA)

Members are primarily owners or managers of office buildings. Interior designers who work for firms specializing in large corporate office facilities often belong to BOMA.

Interior Designers of Canada (IDC)

The national association of Canadian interior designers. It deals with issues of national and international interest on behalf of the members of the provincial associations (see "Canadian Interior Design Professional Associations," page 34).

International Facility Management Association (IFMA)

Members are primarily those responsible for the management and/or planning of corporate facilities. IFMA members may work for a corporation such as a large banking institution or a public utility such as AT&T, or be independent facility planners/space planners.

Institute of Store Planners (ISP)

Represents interior designers who specialize in retail stores and department stores.

National Kitchen and Bath Association (NKBA)

Represents interior designers who specialize in kitchen and/or bath design or are retailers of products for kitchens and baths such as cabinet makers.

U.S. Green Building Council (USGBC)

Represents individuals from across the built environment industry working to promote buildings that are environmentally healthy to live and work in. An affiliated program with the USGBC is the LEED (Leadership in Energy and Environmental Design) accreditation program. A designer can choose to be a LEED-Accredited Professional (LEED-AP) by learning and demonstrating a comprehensive understanding of green design and building practices.

Certified Aging-in-Place Specialist (CAPS)

This certification is for individuals who achieve additional experience, technical skills, business knowledge, and customer service skills necessary for working with mature adult clients and others in the aging-in-place segment of the industry.

Note: Many other specialty associations may be of benefit to interior designers, depending on their specialty practice. Some are listed in "Interior Design Resources" (see page 297); others may be found in interior design trade magazines such as *Interior Design, Contract*, and *Interiors and Sources*.

Sustainable Design

LINDA SORRENTO, ASID, IIDA, LEED-AP

DIRECTOR, EDUCATION & RESEARCH

PARTNERSHIPS

U.S. GREEN BUILDING COUNCIL

WASHINGTON, DC

What led you to enter your design specialty?

> My extended family is comprised of artists and engineers extremely close to the natural environment and volunteerism. I began as a fine artist and discovered interior design as it was emerging as a profession. I was fortunate that there is a profession with all the assets to combine my family heritage and purpose.

What is the most important quality or skill of a designer in your specialty?

> The interior designer has a responsibility to improve their skills through continuous learning.

How is your specialty different from other specialties?

> Sustainable design is the basis for all specialties to make decisions for the long term to ensure health and good life for our children and their children.

What are your primary responsibilities and duties in your position?

> I initiate and maintain strategic relationships with key industry organizations and partners to advance the USGBC's mission of sustainable market transformation and its education and research objectives.

What is the most satisfying part of your job? The least?

> I work with an enormous diversity of players in the sustainable built environment and, therefore, open the door for the interior design profession with all sorts of people. Albeit, the least satisfying part of the job is my difficulty in balancing work and life.

Who or what experience has been a major influence in your career?

> Most importantly, Penny Bonda, FASID, who inspired my professional transformation and shift to sustainable design and all the volunteers that I've worked with in this profession.

What has been your greatest challenge as an interior designer?

> The greatest frustration is that the profession continues to be undervalued.

Interior Design Registration and Licensing

In 2008, 24 states, Washington, D.C., and Puerto Rico—as well as the Canadian provinces—had some type of interior design legislation. Another 10 states had legislation pending. Why are interior designers around the country seeking legislation? Regardless of the type of space being designed, the work of those involved in interior design affects the life safety and health of those that use interior spaces. For example, many of the products that are used in an interior give off toxic fumes that can be harmful to many people who have respiratory problems, and many give off toxic fumes when burned. Interior specification of materials and products is done primarily by interior designers, not the architects who design commercial buildings and homes. Having knowledge to select and specify these products goes way beyond only considering the aesthetics of the products.

Beginning in 1982, states began passing legislation to license or register professionals working in interior design. Of course, attempts to regulate interior design practice had been made before. Alabama was the first state to successfully enact legislation affecting interior design. Although legislation varies from jurisdiction to jurisdiction, legislation concerning the interior design profession generally requires specific educational, work experience, and testing requirements in order for individuals to work as, or call themselves, an interior designer. See "Interior Design Registration Laws in the United States" (page 38) for a list of states that have legislation pertaining to interior design work and the type of legislation that has been enacted. Canadian provinces with provincial associations all have some form of legislation.

Legislation can take many forms. In some states, it restricts who may call himself or herself an interior designer. In this case, the legislation is commonly referred to as *title registration*. The legislation regulates what title is affected. In some states the regulated title is *interior designer*. In most others it might be *certified interior designer* or *registered interior designer*. A title act does not limit who may practice interior design, but rather limits the title one may use as a practitioner.

Where such legislation exists, an individual cannot advertise himself or herself as a *registered interior designer* or *certified interior designer* unless he or she meets the education, experience, and examination requirements defined by the jurisdiction. This type of legislation is currently the norm in 18 states and the Canadian provinces.

Some jurisdictions have passed legislation that limits who may practice interior design services as described by a state board of technical registration. If designers do not pursue and meet the requirements set by the state to practice the profession, then they are prohibited from performing the professional services of an interior designer as defined by the state. This type of legislation is called a *practice act*. Generally, interior designers working where a practice act has been established are called *registered interior designer* or *interior designer* depending on the exact language of the law in the jurisdiction. As of 2007, only Florida, Alabama, Louisiana, Nevada, Washington, D.C., and Puerto Rico had enacted practice act legislation.

Within selected jurisdictions, licensing or other registration assures the consumer of interior design services that the person hired for the project has the training, experience, and competence to render professional interior design services. With licensure, problems occurring in the interior design phase are the responsibility of the interior designer; the client has the opportunity to file a complaint with the state board, which can discipline the designer. This protection does not exist where licensing is not in effect. Interior designers use a combination of skills, knowledge, and experience to creatively solve functional and aesthetic problems and meet the needs of the consumer. This is true whether the consumer owns a home or a business facility. It can be argued that no other profession involves as wide a range of technical, aesthetic, planning, and health, safety, and welfare issues as interior design.

INTERIOR DESIGN REGISTRATION LAWS IN THE UNITED STATES

Alabama	Title and Practice	Minnesota	Title
Arkansas	Title	Missouri	Title
California	Self-certification	Nevada	Title and Practice
Colorado	Interior Design Permitting Statute	New Jersey	Title
		New Mexico	Title
Connecticut	Title	New York	Title
Florida	Title and Practice	Oklahoma	Title
Georgia	Title	Puerto Rico	Title and Practice
Illinois	Title	Tennessee	Title
Iowa	Title	Texas	Title
Kentucky	Title	Virginia	Title
Louisiana	Title and Practice	Washington, D.C.	Title and Practice
Maine	Title	Wisconsin	Title
Maryland	Title		

How Important Is Certification by Examination and Licensing of Interior Designers Today?

❯ Passing a qualifying examination and becoming registered or licensed will be the minimum requirements for interior design in the very near future. Nearly half the states in the U.S. and many of the Canadian provinces already have some legislation in place to regulate our profession. Another 10 or so states are currently in the process of getting this type of legislation passed. These two things will become the minimum requirements for those wishing to practice or call themselves "interior designer" in the near future.

Terri Maurer, FASID

❯ As a former regulatory board member and president of NCIDQ, I feel certification by examination and the licensure through the states' regulatory processes is critical to the protection of the public health, safety, and welfare. This ensures that the public can rely on those individuals with certification and licensure as having obtained a certain standard of education and professional experience.

Linda Elliott Smith, FASID

> California licenses interior designers and I think it's very important for the profession.
Jain Malkin, CID

> Critical.
Nila Leiserowitz, FASID

> I would like to see interior designers certified by examination and licensing of professional qualification to represent the rigorous education that we must have. We need to overcome the image that interior designers are nothing more than furniture salesman by the public.
Sandra Evans, ASID

> It becomes more important with each passing year. I believe that in the next couple of decades certification and licensing will become as important and ubiquitous as the CPA (certified public accountant) exam. And because of increased liability related to interior design issues (ADA, mold/air quality, ergonomics, etc.), the general public will begin demanding qualified designers.
Jeffrey Rausch, IIDA

> Critical to continued advancement of the profession through regulation of activities undertaken under the heading of "interior design."
Marilyn Farrow, FIIDA

> Very important. As interior designers we work with lighting, building systems, finish materials, and furnishings that affect the people living and working in the spaces we design. We need to show competence in designing and specifying for interiors spaces beyond the pure aesthetics. It is critical to be aware of the safety of a building's structural materials, the furnishings, and the finishes in respect to one's health and life safety.
Sally Thompson, ASID

> Monumental—the public needs to understand our profession. Examination and licensure assures the public that we are capable of protecting their health, safety, and welfare.
Donna Vining, FASID, IIDA, RID, CAPS

> It is very important to set industry standards that require at least minimum standards of general knowledge. We owe it to ourselves and to our clients.
Michelle King, IIDA

> Very important because of the liabilities that exist in offering professional interior design services. A client is paying for professional service and expects the designer to be accountable for the results.
Leonard Alvarado

> Immensely.
Rosalyn Cama, FASID

> I think certification is vital to the practice of interior design. Until we have certification or legal recognition in all states, we will not have credibility as a professional practice.
Susan Coleman, FIIDA, FIDEC

Note: Additional comments are included in Chapter 6.

ALLIED PROFESSIONS

❯ The interior designer or client, to provide expertise in specific areas of an interiors project, may hire professionals and consultants in allied fields.

Architecture: The profession of designing and supervising the construction of buildings of all types.

Construction: General contractors oversee the tradespersons that are needed to build the project. Subcontractors are hired by the general contractor (or owner of the building) to build certain parts of the project such as framing, plumbing, and the electrical components.

Engineering: The planning and design of various technical aspects of a building or its interior. Types of engineers that might be involved in an interior project include mechanical, electrical, plumbing, heating and ventilation, and structural engineers.

Facility planning: Synonymous with *space planning*. Facility planners often work for client corporations.

Graphic design: The design and development of a wide variety of graphic media for print, film, advertising, books, and other areas of commercial art.

Interior architecture: Many consider this profession synonymous with interior design; however, state boards of technical registration require that the term *interior architect* be used only by individuals who have graduated from a school of architecture or been certified as an architect.

Kitchen and bath design: The specialty design of residential and commercial kitchens and/or baths.

Lighting design: The specialty design of artificial and natural lighting treatments to enhance the design and function of an interior or exterior space.

Space planning: The planning of interior spaces, especially in commercial facilities. Generally, the space planner has less responsibility for the decorative aspects of the interior than the interior designer.

A Career Change Challenge

CHARRISSE JOHNSTON, ASID, LEED-AP, CID
DESIGNER (SPECIALTY: WORKPLACE/
OFFICE DESIGN)
GENSLER
SANTA MONICA, CALIFORNIA

How did you choose which school to attend to obtain your education in interior design?

❭ I was impressed by UCLA Extension Interior Design Program's reputation and instructional quality (the instructors are all practicing professionals) and its flexible class schedule suited my needs. I also liked that it's a postbaccalaureate program and that many of the students were also career changers like myself. What sealed the deal was meeting an inspiring woman who had gone through the program while raising a family, passed the NCIDQ, and become the program's student advisor.

What degrees do you possess?

❭ A professional certificate from the UCLA Extension Architecture and Interior Design Program; an M.B.A. from the Columbia Business School with a dual concentration in management and marketing; and a B.A. from Johns Hopkins University in social and behavioral sciences with a concentration in behavioral biology.

What was your greatest challenge as a student?

❭ Balancing school and family life, I attended school in the evenings while raising two young children. Also, gaining the self-confidence that, even though I'd only used quantitative/analytical skills in my past career (marketing research, strategic planning), I could be as effective a designer as my naturally artistic classmates.

Are you planning to take the NCIDQ exam if you have not already? Why or why not?

❭ I sat for the NCIDQ as soon as I qualified to take it. Passing this exam was important to me personally because it validated years of hard work. It's also important to the profession as a whole because it establishes standards for a still-nascent and often misunderstood profession.

How important do you feel an internship is to a student's educational experience?

❭ Absolutely crucial, no matter what type of design firm or how menial the responsibilities. I had an internship at a boutique hospitality firm where I was relegated to receptionist duty. But, during those three months, I met a ton of sales reps, saw all the presentation boards and proposals, and learned firsthand how the business operated. All of this experience proved valuable later.

How did you choose the firm that you are working for?

❭ Gensler is a legendary firm known for its excellence in all regards. While still a student, I'd met one of the managing principals at an industry conference, and she encouraged me to call her when I was ready to look for a job. I was totally floored and figured that if Gensler would take me, I wouldn't bother looking anywhere else. And, fortunately, that's exactly what happened.

What has been your greatest challenge in your first years of employment?

❭ Again, balancing work with family life. I enjoy my job immensely, and I've been lucky to be assigned to some wonderful projects, so it's often difficult for me to stop working and go home. I'm also committed to ASID (I serve on the national Student Advisory Council) and that takes a lot of time as well. But my kids are great, I work only a mile from home, my office is very family-friendly, and I have a super nanny, so it's worked out very well.

Of course, the other challenge is the low starting salaries. I try not to think about what I'd be making if I'd stayed on Wall Street.

Did you join the student chapter of ASID or IIDA at your school? Why?

〉 My student advisor encouraged me to attend an ASID student chapter meeting because she said it would enrich my education beyond what I was learning in the classroom. One thing led to another and I eventually became a two-term student chapter president.

Why Did You Become an Interior Designer?

〉 Interior design was a degree suggested by my high school principal because I was both artistic and academically strong in math and science. My choices at the time were to become an art teacher or an interior designer. Fortunately, my principal was knowledgeable and wise enough to advise my parents that I should pursue a college degree and not be satisfied with a short-term course.
Carol Morrow, Ph.D., ASID, IIDA, IDEC

〉 I liked the hardware store as a kid. While a business major in college, I decided to add fashion merchandising to make it more interesting and had to take a basic design course as well as textiles. I met a few interior students and figured if they could do it, so could I. So I switched majors and have been at it ever since.
Melinda Sechrist, FASID

〉 I care about people and interior design was the most effective way I could personally contribute to society.
Linda Sorrento, ASID, IIDA, LEED-AP

〉 I have always been interested in space and interior environments and grew up drawing and painting and naturally wanted to major in art in college. My college required that I select a specialty, so I selected interior design. I was still able to take art classes while learning a profession where I could find employment.
Rita Carson Guest, FASID

〉 I had always loved reading floor plans, even as a child. I had worked for several developers—one in the architectural department—and had always been interested in space planning. And then the social worker in me also liked the idea of working with people to create living environments that functioned well.
Jan Bast, FASID, IIDA

〉 I always had an interest in art, design, and manipulating interior space. So, when I was researching a post secondary education, it became apparent that interior design would be a good career choice.
David Hanson, RID, IDC, IIDA

> As a child, buildings, design, and construction always fascinated me. I learned how to draft when I was 14 years old. It was a natural progression to become an interior designer.

Kristin King, ASID

> My passion began as a desire to create better places for people to live and work. I believe that all interior designers share this basic passion. That passion has grown for me to include consideration for how we affect the natural environment in the process. I still focus on interiors, but the choices we make in the process have a significant effect on the larger environment that we all share.

Barbara Nugent, FASID

> It was my childhood dream to improve interior environments. I described my desire to my grandfather, and he said I was describing a career in interior design.

Rosalyn Cama, FASID

> The creation of place has great impact on people. Great place is both aesthetical and emotional.

Nila Leiserowitz, FASID, Associate AIA

> Believe it or not, I'd never heard of interior design as a profession until I was working my husband's way through college at a local university. I worked in the dean's office, where the interior design program was being developed, and the course curriculum came across my desk. I was so impressed with the interdisciplinary approach of the program through art, architecture, interior design, graphic design, and technology that I became interested in pursuing that new major. I found it fascinating that many of the courses focused on various forms of creative problem solving.

Terri Maurer, FASID

> I have always been an artist and was a graphic designer in my first career. However, I wanted to translate my design skills from 2D to 3D. I was led into interior design because I was very interested in the perspective/renderings that had been done for presentations. After taking some drafting classes and courses in perspective, I was hooked on creating the whole environment.

Robin J. Wagner, ASID, IDEC

> I was working in an architectural firm while in school and saw the potential for rapid advancement in commercial interior design. There was a lack of technical knowledge in the field at that time.

Fred Messner, IIDA

> I actually fell into it working for a large design and furnishings firm after high school. I liked it and explored many avenues of industry.

Michael Thomas, FASID, CAPS

> Interior design is an extension of my creative nature and the fulfillment of my desire to be of service to persons who endeavor to enrich their lives through their physical environment.

Sandra Evans, ASID

> I became an interior designer because it was the closest degree I could find to a fine arts degree that my father would fund. At that time, I was interested in all the art classes; but as I began to take interior design labs, I enjoyed the challenge of interpreting a program combined with the complexity of transferring my ideas into a two- or three-dimensional format.

Linda Santellanes, ASID

❯ I'm a registered architect, not a professional interior designer. I suppose you could say I'm a professional interior architect who has a great deal of experience designing interiors.

M. Arthur Gensler Jr., FAIA, FIIDA, RIBA

❯ I didn't plan to become an interior designer. I started out with a degree in psychology and, later, through a circuitous route, discovered this field. This was way before Art Gensler had created the field of corporate office interiors. Healthcare design in those days didn't even exist. In fact, interior design as we know it was taught in only about three schools across the country. At most universities, it was in the home economics department, which was anything but commercial or institutional interior design. It's actually quite an interesting story how I got into the field, but it would take several paragraphs to even scratch the surface. It was, however, quite fortuitous, as I found I really enjoyed it and it brought together many of my talents and abilities. I always had a good head for business, was persuasive and also creative. Those are important prerequisites for this field, especially if one wants to be self-employed.

Jain Malkin, CID

❯ As a teenager I became interested in spaces, particularly my own personal space, and how, with some thought and manipulation of the elements within the space, that environment could take on a totally different feel.

Linda E. Smith, FASID

❯ I started out wanting to become an architect. Lucky for me, the closest architectural school to me was at the University of Manitoba, Canada (100 km away from my hometown). The program offers a master's in architecture and is regarded very highly. The undergraduate degrees offered are environmental studies (three years) and interior design (four years). I chose the interior design program. I knew I would have a solid profession to rely on if I did not continue studying for my masters. (The environmental studies program would provide an undergraduate with a very good foundation to proceed into architecture, but it would not provide a solid degree on its own.)

Once I graduated, I gave myself one year to work in the industry before going back to school for my masters. I have been practicing interior design for 15 years and have no intention of obtaining a master's in architecture.

Jennifer van der Put, BID, IDC, ARIDO, IFMA

❯ At first it was because I wanted to fix up my own house. Then others started asking for my interior design advice and urged me to take it up as a profession.

Greta Guelich, ASID

❯ Even during my education as an architect years ago, the initiation and focus of my design process was with the interior spaces and experiences created for people within the spaces. That bent continued on into practice in both architecture and interior design. As a designer, the ability to shape the settings that people live, work, and play within is a huge responsibility and joy.

Katherine Ankerson, IDEC, NCARB Certified

❯ To provide functional, aesthetically pleasing environments for people to live and work.

Sally Nordahl, IIDA

❯ I always knew that I'd be involved with some type of design, but I had to take a number of art and design classes in college to decide which area was a good fit. I was steered into graphic design by a guidance counselor in college who didn't understand our profession at all. But when I took a job in college working with architectural models, I realized that architecture and design were where my true interests lay.

Suzanne Urban, IIDA, ASID

Sports arena: Ice Lounge, Jobing.com
Arena, Glendale, Arizona. Lisa
Slayman, ASID, IIDA, Slayman
Design Associates, Inc., Newport
Beach, California. Architect: HOK,
Kansas City.

PHOTOGRAPH: ENNIS PHOTOGRAPHY

❯ I have always been intrigued by the built
environment and how space, volume, and
aesthetics affect our well-being and quality of life.
Robert Wright, FASID

❯ On looking back, I can't say for sure that any
one thing swayed me. I always knew that I wanted
to be in an artistic profession, yet there was also
the mechanical side and the what-makes-it-work,
how-was-this-done aspect. I think interior design
found me. Once the decision was made, I have
never regretted nor doubted the choice.
Derrell Parker, IIDA

❯ I wanted to focus on the effect of environment
on personal success.
Neil Frankel, FIIDA, FAIA

❯ The plan has always fascinated me. As a very
young child, I drew house plans for fun. And I had
a high school art teacher who introduced rural kids
to the world of applied art. Everybody assumed a
college-bound rural kid would become a teacher
or home economist. I enrolled in the College of
Arts and Sciences as an art major. A couple of
prearchitecture courses pointed me in the direction
of architecture or interior design. Economics
and circumstances put me in the interior design
masters program at the University of Missouri,
Columbia. I have never been sorry. The intimate
relationship between an interior and the people
who live and work there is fascinating. I truly
believe that when an interior works, people live
better, work better, learn better, and heal better.
M. Joy Meeuwig, IIDA

❯ I considered interior design a perfect place
to blend my artistic abilities with a desire for a
professional career.
Juliana Catlin, FASID

❯ My mother told me I could never make money
being an artist. I still like to create, and this seemed
to be a good avenue for that.
Debra May Himes, ASID, IIDA

❯ I grew up with immigrant parents; my dad was a builder and my mom was a seamstress. It was only natural that I would end up in the building industry, plus a little arm twisting from my parents. From a very young age, I was exposed to residential interiors through my mom's work as a seamstress who provided window treatments, bedding, and pillows to clients. My mother worked for a few interior designers, one who led me to a fantastic, small interior design school in Colorado that was accredited by FIDER (now CIDA). I loved sitting with my dad reading blueprints and going to the construction job sites whenever possible. When I wasn't in the sewing studio helping my mom, I was on the job site with my dad or outside gardening. To this day, I most enjoy problem solving in the field and watching the construction team bring it all together.

Annette Stelmack, Allied Member ASID

❯ I have always loved art and design. When trying to decide how to best put my love of art to use I felt that becoming an interior designer would be the best way for me to share my love and talent with my community. Not only does interior design allow me to use my talents, but it also allows me to create healthier and happier communities for people who live there.

Shannon Ferguson, IIDA

❯ It was a career that would incorporate my interest in science and math and a desire to create. Interior designers at my university were required to have chemistry, biochemistry, and anatomy as it also satisfied prerequisites for textile science.

Linda Isley, IIDA

❯ I became an interior designer after getting a bachelor's degree in fine art and realizing that I enjoy the hands-on and creative nature of the interior design profession. I drew houses as a kid,

rearranged my furniture, and redecorated my room many times. I realized later on what interior designers do and thought that it was the fit for me.

Laurie Smith, ASID

❯ I had the opportunity to go back to college when I was 38. After carefully thinking through my talents and believing my work should be something I loved, I selected a two-year interior design program at the University of California. My husband was serving in the U.S. Navy and we had a three-year tour in Long Beach. I had just enough time before moving again, to complete the program. The state of California was in the midst of interior design legislation at this time, so I began studying for the NCIDQ as I did *not* want to be known as one of the designers who was "grandfathered" in due to this legislation.

Patricia Rowen, ASID, CAPS

❯ My interests and talents in high school included fine arts, math, and music. In looking at career options, architecture came to the forefront. In college I experimented with architecture and fashion design before finding the field of interior design, which seemed like the ideal fit.

Mary Knopf, ASID

❯ As a kid I enjoyed creating floor plans of made-up houses. I have always enjoyed that technical side of design. I guess it came from my mother, who was a seamstress and made bridal gowns without patterns, and my father, who was a tool and die maker. Interior design has always allowed me to help solve the problems of making the interior work for the business. Looking back, it was especially gratifying to work in healthcare and the early days of office systems and help affect the functional working environment of hospitals and office facilities.

Christine M. Piotrowski, FASID, IIDA

> I actually enjoyed art and business. I did not think I could make it as an artist and thought business was a bit boring. I grew up around architecture all my life and I think subliminally it just came to me

Jo Rabaut, ASID, IIDA

> I started out with a liberal arts degree from Williams College. After school I worked for a time as a carpenter and then became a contractor. I taught myself to draw technical drawings by studying and then copying the drawings that I was given to build from. Then I started my own design/build firm. Then one day I said to myself, "I am tired of pounding nails and cutting wood. I know how to do that now. The design part is what I love." So I got myself a temporary job drafting at FORMA, the design division of Westin Hotels. I turned that into a permanent position and began to learn the technical rigors of fine interior design. Then I studied for and passed the NCIDQ. Working on the creation of a complete interior environment from start to finish is what really turned me on to interior design. Now that has evolved into the development of complete, branded environments and "experience" planning—the obvious and necessary evolution of developing great interior design, especially in the retail field in which I work.

Bruce James Brigham, FASID, ISP, IES

> At the time, 1971, the field of interior design was still "unformed." I started in a five-year program as a co-op at the University of Cincinnati, which had Bob Stevens as the head of the department. Bob was an architect, and had the vision to create a department that still stands today as the number-one-rated interior design program in the country. I entered because I naively wanted design and art courses. I got so much more, opening up an entire world that I didn't know existed, gaining exposure to architecture and design, a world that I had not been exposed to before. I also had the pleasure of doing my early co-ops at Herman Miller in Zeeland, Michigan, in the very early days of Systems Furniture, with designers and innovators on site. What a great experience that was, building on what school was teaching me, and what the industry was about to become. At the time of graduation, interior designers were not generally hired by architectural firms, but that soon changed, and the marriage of the interior and exterior soon became an accepted relationship.

Colleen McCafferty, IFMA, USGBC, LEED-CI

> I became an interior designer because it allowed me to express my creativity on a large scale using interactive mediums.

Darcie Miller, NKBA, ASID Industry Partner, CMG

> When I was a child, I would always be working on home furnishings projects like refinishing furniture, making accessories and selling them in the local stationery store, and other art projects. When I started college, I told my parents I wanted to be an interior designer and they discouraged me. They felt I needed to have a degree in business because it would lead me to a more successful place in the workforce. During my studies in junior college, I took a couple of interior design classes as electives and did extremely well. The teacher at that time encouraged me to take it further so, at that time, I changed my major. After I completed all my design classes in that school, I transferred to Cal State Long Beach because it had one of the best interior design programs in the country.

Lisa Slayman, ASID, IIDA

> I enjoy the diversity. Interior design is not dull. You meet fascinating people and work with beautiful items to create an environment that affects people's lives every day.

Susan Norman, IIDA

❯ I wanted to do something with my artistic talents. I took an elective drawing class my first year in college. I was not even thinking of an interior design major. We did perspective drawings, and I was immediately hooked on the caring of interior space and plane through drawing. I began the architecture program the next semester.

Maryanne Hewitt, IIDA

❯ I was always interested in technical drawing and watching my civil engineering father draft. An art teacher in junior and senior high school encouraged that drawing talent and helped me look at architecture schools. In college a professor helped me "see the light" and realize that interior design was where my passion lay. The rest, as they say, is history.

David Stone, IIDA, LEED-AP

❯ I have always had a passion for art, design, and architecture. I wanted to do something creative, but have a job that has many directions.

Jane Coit, Associate Member IIDA

❯ My interest in interior design is broad and comprehensive in scope, but the basis for doing interior design is to make a difference—to make a better world through design.

An attraction of interior design is the brief time span for design ideas to be realized. Most interior projects are conceived and completed within a year, whereas buildings and urban development can take years to complete. Interiors are relatively quick to complete and the satisfaction that results from each project is rewarding.

The primary attraction of the profession is the opportunity to compose and resolve space—down to the details.

In my career as both an educator and practitioner, my central aim has been to better understand the potency and conceptual basis of interior design. For the past 20 years, I have taught interior design students and have worked to develop my design practice. Teaching and practicing are codependent, and in part I became an interior designer because of my love for teaching. I became a teacher for my love of designing.

James Postell, Associate Professor, University of Cincinnati

❯ When I was in junior high, my older sister called from her college dorm to tell me there was a career for me: interior design. Since I can remember, I've been discovered sneaking around parents' friends' houses fascinated at how people use their space. I built dream homes out of blocks for our toy figures, and drew floor plans on notepaper, perplexed at how to put it to scale. In high school I determined that architecture was the more manly profession, and entered a drafting course. Bored out of my mind drawing screws and basic house elevations, I realized my penchant for personal details when a classmate broke my focus, noting the classic paneled door, the window shutters, flower boxes, shrubbery, brick detailing, etcetera. I enrolled in the Interior Design Program at the University of Kentucky and, for the first time in my entire educational career, I felt like I was learning skills that would lead me to my own calling.

I love art and beauty and all their natural and created expressions, but I really love putting those expressions to practical use in environments where people live.

Keith Miller, ASID

❯ I became an interior designer to bridge together my diverse interests and strengths. I enjoy working with people, I am interested in how your surroundings influence your work, I feel compelled and drawn to the creative process, I enjoy numbers and budgets. Finally, I am both a detail-oriented person and a big-picture thinker. As a child I always wanted to be an architect. But after learning more about interior design while completing my first degree in accounting, I felt certain that the emphasis of human interaction within a space versus just the form or function made interior design the better choice.

Laura Busse, IIDA, KYCID

❯ I have always seen my career path as leading toward designing creative solutions. I, as many others, switched professions midlife from a product design and production industry for the mass market to that of interior design in order to work more independently on unique projects designed directly for the individual end user. I was drawn to interior design as a more entrepreneur-friendly field that has the advantage of affording both small and large firms the ability to compete successfully. An interior designer can also balance the time spent on business activities with cycles of intense creativity.

Sally D' Angelo, ASID, AIA Affiliate

❯ I couldn't imagine *not* being an interior designer. I think the idea of being able to improve someone's life by improving their surroundings is very powerful.

Lindsay Sholdar, ASID

❯ I became a designer because it is a unique way to connect the world of visual arts to the world of business.

Lisa Henry, ASID

❯ I "fell" into the career in high school when I took an interior design class. I love the creative yet practical side of the profession. I enjoy the technical aspects of the career (e.g., lighting and computers) as well as the application of psychology and understanding of human behavior. I appreciate how the field must adapt to changing trends yet clearly support the trends that are here to stay (e.g., universal and sustainable design). I love the design process and helping others develop meaningful spaces. It is, and always will be for me, a very fulfilling career.

Stephanie Clemons, Ph.D., FASID, FIDEC

❯ As a young girl, I remember how much I loved to rearrange my bedroom furniture. My mother would take me to the fabric store to select patterns and fabrics for new clothes. I credit her for my ability to visualize. As a teenager I loved the high-style world of fashion design. Dissatisfied with the clothing choices available, I learned to sew and made most of my wardrobe during high school, which provided an excellent education in the knowledge of fabrics. That education continued when I learned to fabricate window treatments, bedding, etcetera for my own residence. I was in my mid-30s when I went back to school to pursue a lifelong love of design.

Teresa Ridlon, Allied Member ASID

❯ Ever since I could hold a pencil I have been drawing floor plans—others "doodled" and I drew plans. Architecture and interiors have always fascinated me, and so it was really inevitable that I would go into interior design. The interest was encouraged by my parents, as we were forever touring homes that were being built as I grew up, and our own home was remodeled several times and redesigned, with the help of an architect and interior designer, both of whom were more than happy to answer my questions and share advice as I grew up.

Drue Lawlor, FASID

Private residence: living room.
Robin Wagner, ASID, IDEC, Wagner-
Somerset Designs, Clifton, Virginia.
PHOTOGRAPH: ROBIN WAGNER

❯ I found a paper I wrote in about fifth grade listing that as my goal. I remember drawing floor plans of homes at that age—with designs that I still wish could be realized today.
Sharmin Pool-Bak, ASID, CAPS, LEED-AP

❯ I will give you the long version. This is the story I share with eighth-graders who are interested in interior design:

I grew up the daughter of an architect and engineer. My father designed our house and had it built in 1966. My parents always gave me great freedom in decorating my room—from painting in whatever color I wanted to allowing me to hang whatever I wanted on the walls. When I was in the seventh grade, I really wanted a loft. The ceilings in our contemporary house were very high. My father said if I drew a plan of what I wanted, he would build it. So I had this wonderful loft space in my room with my mattress up high. It was very cool for a 12-year-old.

I was in high school and not sure what I should study in college. I loved arts and crafts projects, but didn't take art in high school. However, I did take mechanical drafting, and in the summer I worked a little bit in my father's office drafting elevations and floor plans. When I was in high school, I had a science teacher who said I should study forest engineering because it was a field with few women in it and I would make a lot of money. Sounded good to a 17-year-old—tromping around in the woods with a bunch of guys. I entered the University of Maine at Orono and promptly flunked out after one semester. While I was in Orono, however, I decorated my dorm room and won an honorable mention prize for my room. That prize got me to thinking that maybe I could make a living doing what I'd always enjoyed so much, so I entered Bauder College in Atlanta, Georgia, and received an AA in interior design in 1983. I graduated top of my class—proving that once I knew what I wanted to do I could excel at it.

I worked for an office furniture dealer (Herman Miller) for three years. Then, in 1986, when I asked for a raise (I was making $12,000) and was turned down, I decided to start my own company. At the age of 23, I started Lisa Whited Planning and Design, Inc. I kept the company until 2001.

In 1988, realizing I really needed to add to my design education, I entered the Boston Architectural Center, studying architecture. I studied for three years, commuting from Portland, Maine, to Boston (two hours each way) two nights per week. I did not get my degree—but the additional education was invaluable. I also took classes over the years at the Maine College of Art (color theory, etcetera). In 2000, still wanting to add to my education, I entered Antioch New England Graduate School and gained an MS in Organization and Management, graduating in fall 2002.

Lisa Whited, IIDA, ASID, IDEC

❯ I love buildings, the exterior blending with the interior, and bringing them together in a harmonious manner to create a special place to live, entertain your friends and family, work, and, especially, relax.

Kristen Anderson, ASID, CID, RID

❯ At the time I started interior design school in 1981, I was a 30-year-old wife and mother working in a furniture business that my husband and I owned. I was good at helping the customers and thought it would be logical to finish my college degree in interior design rather than in journalism (which is what I was majoring in in the 1960s when I dropped out to get married, as many women did in those days).

As it happened, the FIDER-accredited program at the University of Missouri was powerful. I soon came to understand the true impact designers can have on environments and, therefore, on people (and I'm a people person). I loved every aspect of my education, but I especially loved the people part—the design and behavior classes; the books *Designing Places for People, A Pattern Language, Humanscape, Environments for People* and *Human Dimension for Interior Space*—even the ergonomics part interested me. (Weird, huh?)

Now my life has taken many turns away from the plans I had when I was 30. But I love my work—I love being a professional designer.

Linda Kress, ASID

❯ It was an evolution from birth. I was always drawing, painting, coloring, and making things with my hands. I had a lot of exposure to all types of design, but it was the college program that helped me focus on interior design.

Susan Coleman, FIIDA, FIDEC

❯ By growing up in Japan, I realized that life experiences shape who we are. Everything about my living environment—region, culture, interior dwellings, and so on—influenced the development of my character and how I feel about myself and living. In high school, I specifically realized that I wanted to influence others because I knew well how our environment can affect our motivation and zest for life. I decided to do this through interior design, where I could develop interior environments that enhance motivation and positive experiences for others.

Susan B. Higbee

❯ I have always been interested in art and architecture and decided to focus on the interior environment when I became familiar with this field in college.

Janice Carleen Linster, ASID, IIDA, CID

❯ After reaching a previous career goal as a journalist early in life, I decided the only thing left to do was to write a book and quickly realized I didn't know much about anything other than journalism. I thought I should pursue another interest for the subject of the book and went back to college to study interior design. College led to practicing.

Suzan Globus, FASID, LEED-AP

❯ As a child, I was influenced by my mother and grandmother. Growing up in Miami, I spent a lot of time watching them renovate homes and boats. It was then I realized I could mentally visualize a space in three dimensions. Interior design just seemed to be the natural direction for me.

Sally Thompson, ASID

❯ From a young age, I was always interested in design. I enjoyed art classes and visiting art museums with my parents. I would spend hours with large sheets of paper, drawing entire cities with buildings, houses, and roads. My cities were perfect places to race my matchbox cars. I enjoyed creating my own little world with Lincoln Logs and Legos. My Barbies always had the best-laid-out townhouse on the block. When asked what I wanted to be when I grew up, I would always answer, "an architect." I don't think I really knew what that meant, only that it had something to do with creating the built environment.

I took all the design and drafting classes I could in high school. I was fortunate to have the opportunity to participate in the Georgia Governor's Honors program in Design. My type of artistic talent—more technically oriented—seemed to be the perfect match for architectural design. I entered college determined to get into the School of Architecture and study interior design.

Kristi Barker, CID

❯ I want a career that utilizes both my technical capabilities and creative talents. Interior design is about balancing what is physical and tangible with aesthetic ideals. To me, form and function should be a happy marriage. I also enjoy having new challenges on a regular basis. Each new project offers a chance to approach things differently, to solve a new problem.

Kimberly M. Studzinski, ASID

❯ In 1997, I graduated from Carnegie Mellon University with a Bachelor of Architecture degree. I decided I wanted to work in a more detail-oriented field, so I took a position at a firm that practiced architecture but had interior design as its specialty.

Derek Schmidt

❯ In high school, I was fascinated by the way a building's energy was embedded in its structure. I considered studying architecture, but at that time women were not encouraged to be architects, and I entered a liberal arts program instead. After graduation, I took a series of aptitude tests, and architecture looked like the best career choice, so I enrolled at the Boston Architectural Center. After two and a half years of going to school nights and working days at anything I could get related to architecture, I burned out on school but continued to work. A recession and a move to Denver took me into retail management and human services work. In 1988 I moved back to Boston and got a job with an architect. A vocational counselor advised that, because I loved color and texture and was most interested in how people experienced and used interior spaces, I might study interior design. So back I went to the BAC's interior design program.

Corky Binggeli, ASID

❯ My dad was a contractor and as a kid I worked with him on some of his projects. I thought of becoming an architect but lacked the discipline to study, especially math, while I was in college. I was much more interested in following sports and finding a husband than getting an education. I ended up with an education and married later in my career.

Mary Fisher Knott, CID, RSPI, Allied Member ASID

❯ I had wanted to be involved in the built environment since I was four or five. Of all the things going on, the workers and their tasks fascinated me the most. Being raised in a rural community, I did not encounter much emphasis on the design professions, but I took as many courses as I could that would prepare me for a career in architecture. I say *architecture* because I had no idea that interior design was a profession unto itself. In college I was exposed to the profession of interior design as a career option. When the possibility of a career path in interior design became clear, my academic life became much more exciting, engaging me in a much more passionate manner. After many years working in small architecture firms and then in the interiors group of a large AE (architectural-engineering) firm, I obtained a master's degree and pursued a career in design education. Choosing the education path has allowed me to continue to be a part of the design profession and to give back something to this profession that has provided me such a satisfying career.

Robert J. Krikac, IDEC

❭ My dad and brother are both in the construction business, so I grew up around a construction environment. On top of that, drawing has always been a talent that comes naturally to me. Design is the best mesh of things that I am comfortable with, enjoy, and can earn a living with. I was actually a pre-vet major for two years before design. I switched after realizing it was not stimulating or creative enough for me, so I made the commitment to take on the additional four years of design school. It was certainly worth it.

Alexis B. Bounds, Allied Member ASID

❭ I became an interior designer because of my love of the art field. What blossomed from that was a deep appreciation for the way an interior affects its habitants.

Carolyn Ann Ames, Allied Member ASID

❭ Interior design captures all of my interests—art, business, and science—in one profession. Every day I get to exercise a whole range of skills, so I'm never bored.

Charisse Johnston, ASID, LEED-AP, CID

❭ Because I enjoy working with others and creating beautiful solutions.

Chris Socci, Allied Member ASID

❭ I became an interior designer because I have always been intrigued by architecture and the indoor environments. I always knew I wanted to work in a profession that would allow me to explore both creativity and logic. Once I got in to design school, I soon appreciated and understood the fact that interior designers affect the health, safety, and welfare of the public and users of a space; therefore being able to positively influence an end user through design made this profession even more appealing to me.

Shannon Mitchener, LEED-AP, Allied Member ASID, Associate IIDA

NOTES

1. National Council for Interior Design Qualification. 2008. "NCIDQ Definition of Interior Design." NCIDQ.org, http://www.ncidq.org/who/definition.htm.

2. Charlotte S. Jensen. 2001. "Design Versus Decoration." *Interiors and Sources*, September, 91.

3. John Pile. 2000. *A History of Interior Design* (New York: John Wiley & Sons), 255.

4. Nina Campbell and Caroline Seebohm. 1992. *Elsie de Wolfe: A Decorative Life* (New York: Clarkson N. Potter), 70.

5. U.S. Green Building Council. 2003. *Building Momentum: National Trends and Prospects for High Performance Green Buildings*. (Washington, DC: U.S. Green Building Council) 3.

6. World Commission on Environment and Development. 1987. *The Brundtland Report: Our Common Future*. Oxford: Oxford University Press.

7. Christine M. Piotrowski and Elizabeth A. Rogers. 2007. *Designing Commerical Interiors* 2nd ed.(Hoboken, NJ: John Wiley & Sons), 17.

2 Educational Preparation

There was a time when individuals who had a good sense of color and a knack for rearranging furniture could become decorators. In fact, many of the earliest decorators had very little formal training in the field. There was a reason for that: No real educational programs in interior design or decoration existed before the early part of the 20th century. For anyone wishing to be a professional interior designer in this century, however, a formal education is required. The profession has become too complex to allow minimal educational preparation. In states that certify, register, or license interior designers, formal education is a requirement. In addition, the examination required for licensing and professional-level membership in the associations also requires formal education in interior design.

Interior design education in the early 20th century evolved from the fine arts, home economics, and architecture. One of the most notable early schools where interior decoration courses were offered was the New York School of Fine and Applied Arts, now known as Parsons, the New School for Design. Courses were added there after 1904, when a number of interested students helped encourage the formation of the educational program. Schools of fine art as well as colleges of home economics and architecture gradually added more classes and extensive programs of study. As the profession grew, curriculums became more comprehensive, acknowledging that interior decoration and interior design called for more than developing a sense for color and knowing furniture and architectural styles. Students and employers increasingly realized the importance of formal course work for entrance into the profession.

The profession changed dramatically after the Depression in the 1930s and World War II. Commercial interior designers in particular required more training in building systems and the development of construction drawings. Business and industry in the United States and throughout the world changed in the 1940s and 1950s, creating many specialties in interior design. Professionals working in these areas required even more specialized information to practice effectively.

If your goal is to be known as a professional interior designer capable of designing the interiors of high-end exclusive residences, a casino in Las Vegas, a children's hospital, or any kind of commercial interior, you must obtain formal education. The day of the self-taught decorator is long gone in this serious profession.

Educator

CAROL MORROW, PH.D., ASID, IIDA, IDEC
THE ART INSTITUTE OF PHOENIX
PHOENIX, ARIZONA

What advice would you give to someone who wants to be an interior designer?

❯ Expect to work hard. Most every successful interior designer whom I know is passionate about the field and what they can do to create spaces for people that will please them and solve their problems. If you are creative, artistic, and like to analyze and be exposed to new materials and ideas, I think ID is an ideal career. I have heard this more than once and I say it myself—you will never be bored.

What has been your greatest challenge as an interior designer/faculty member?

❯ Keeping up with all the new requirements and possibilities that technology brings, staying abreast of code and environmental issues, especially with issues of sustainability, and the new LEED certification processes.

What is the single most important skill an interior designer needs to be successful?

❯ Be curious and learn how to research.

What is your design practice or research specialty?

❯ Residential, corporate, and healthcare design.

Why did you become an educator?

❯ It just happened over time. It seemed a logical progression of having worked in many areas of interior design and always having maintained an interest in learning. Moving from one country to another had a lot to do with it as well. Knowledge has no physical boundaries.

What are a few characteristics of a good student?

❯ Creative, curious, critical, persistent.

How do you prepare students for the workforce?

❯ Embed CIDA standards in the curriculum, hire quality faculty who have both academic credentials and industry experience, attend conferences and professional meetings to stay abreast of new developments, and liaise with local professionals and trades.

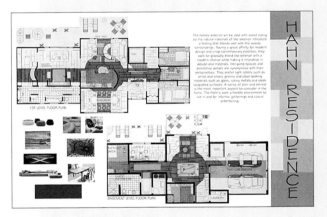

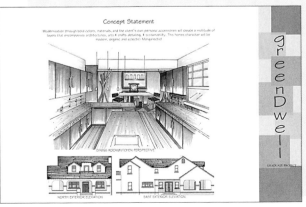

TOP LEFT Floor plans. Work by Jennifer Lossing, student at Department of Interior Design, Art Institute of Phoenix, Phoenix, Arizona.

LEFT Perspective. Work by Jennifer Lossing, student at Department of Interior Design, Art Institute of Phoenix, Phoenix, Arizona.

Educator and Practitioner

ROBIN J. WAGNER, ASID, IDEC
ASSOCIATE PROFESSOR AND DIRECTOR OF
GRADUATES, INTERIOR DESIGN DEPARTMENT
MARYMOUNT UNIVERSITY
ARLINGTON, VIRGINIA
OWNER, WAGNER-SOMERSET DESIGN
CLIFTON, VIRGINIA

What has been your greatest challenge as an interior designer/faculty member?

❯ The greatest challenge as an interior design instructor is teaching to students who do not have a passion about being an interior designer. Some students, not many, just want to get a degree, any old degree—whether to satisfy Mom and Dad or themselves—but have no passion about the field they are studying. If you are going to take the time to get a degree in interior design, do it because it is what you really want to do, or at least what you want to do at that time. (We all go through changes in life.) There is nothing harder than trying to motivate someone who does not care about design and is not passionate about his or her work.

What is the single most important skill an interior designer needs to be successful?

❯ The ability to critically think.

Why did you become an educator?

❯ I ask myself that question all the time. As an educator, there is more to your job than just teaching in the classroom; however, the energy and new challenges that occur in the classroom are what keep me teaching. I began as an adjunct teaching a class on perspective, rendering, and presentation skills because of my graphic background. But I came away with learning so much about myself as a designer and as a person through my students. I have been hooked ever since.

How do you prepare students for the workforce?

❯ Students who take core classes get a thorough training in interior design expectations; but most of all I feel the in-class critiques with professionals is the best preparation for students on helping them to present themselves, present their work, and defend their design choices.

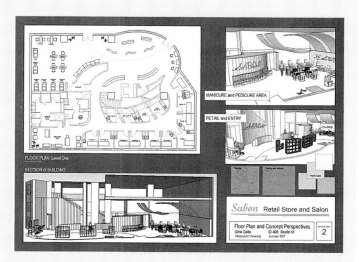

Project presentation board. Work by Gina Gallo, student at Marymount University, Arlington, Virginia.

Private residence: dining room. Robin J. Wagner, ASID, IDEC, Wagner-Somerset Designs, Clifton, Virginia.

PHOTOGRAPH: ROBIN WAGNER.

What are a few characteristics of a good student?

❯ They should be passionate about design and their ability to create and express themselves, willing to explore design solutions and take risks, and able to take constructive criticism about their design choices.

Your design specialties include residential, educational spaces, and retail. What led you to enter your design specialties?

❯ I first got into educational facilities with a graphic design job for signage. The school system found out I also did interior design work. I was very interested in taking on educational facilities because my kids have learning disabilities. My research into my children's disabilities led me to wanting to create environments responsive to children's needs.

Retail design has become an area I have lately gone into. The research and behavioral mapping studies done on how people shop have become an interest to me, and their application to retail design. Additionally, design components of retail draw on my graphic design background.

What is the most important quality or skill of a designer in your specialties?

❯ Several skills are required—but the most important are to be able to identify the design problem, assess the needs of the design problem, and to solve the design problem with an aesthetic, functional, safe, and effective design solution.

High School Preparation

Most design firms require entry-level designers to have a degree in interior design. It is increasingly important that the degree be a four-year degree from an accredited interior design program. Some firms will hire individuals with a two-year degree in interior design, especially if they have a previous degree in some other field. Fewer and fewer major interior design firms are hiring individuals to work with clients and complete design work involving planning and specification of the interior when the person has only a two-year degree—or no degree at all.

The high school student interested in interior design as a career should be planning on academic course work that will allow her or him to gain admittance to a university or college. The college preparatory program at your high school prepares you to enter a college. High schools also offer other courses that will be of value to you in the profession such as drafting and art classes. The additional language, math, and science classes will be very important to the requirements in a college interior design major. Taking advanced placement (AP) classes in the general studies areas of English, math, and sciences gives you some college credit. These AP classes help to reduce some of the course burden in college or give you the opportunity to take elective classes that might not normally fit into your college schedule.

Drafting and AutoCAD classes are very important and will be required in the college program; they are offered at many high schools. Art and sketching or drawing classes will help develop the artistic and creative side a future professional needs. An art class such as sculpture or ceramics can help develop your three-dimensional sense of design. You might even try to squeeze in a general business class, as business topics will likely be required in college.

The mathematics and science requirements in college will vary based on whether the college program offers a bachelor of arts or a bachelor of science. Colleges that offer a bachelor of science in interior design often require more math and science than those that offer a bachelor of arts. In that case, more language classes are common.

Become a better observer of the interior environment and the objects that are placed in interiors. When you visit a new restaurant or hotel with your parents, look at how the interior was designed, the way space is used, how traffic flows, and the colors that are used. Make a point of visiting museums and historic sites to learn more about the fine and decorative arts. And, of course, try to interview interior designers, architects, or others in the industry.

Commercial Offices and Tenant Improvement

SUSAN HIGBEE
DIRECTOR OF INTERIOR DESIGN,
GROUP MACKENZIE
PORTLAND, OREGON

What has been your greatest challenge as an interior designer?

❭ I think initially, it was establishing a role that was accepted and recognized in the industry as essential to the architectural design process. Our culture here is that architecture and interior design is an integral process. Our best successes are produced when we have a collaborative team working on a project.

What led you to enter your design specialty?

❭ I have worked in all aspects of interior design, but I have seen the greatest challenges and rewards in commercial interiors. It is a very fast-paced industry with many different project types. Clients are not involved so much on a personal level and hire you for your expertise and direction to lead them through the process. It is exciting every single day.

What are your primary responsibilities and duties in your position?

❭ I am currently the director of interiors at Group Mackenzie. I direct a staff of seven interior designers. I also manage larger teams that consist of a multidisciplined group of architects and engineers, depending on the nature of the project. My primary departmental responsibilities include management of workload distribution, team collaboration, team performance and efficiency, quality control of work output, quality of design, fiscal performance, and staff development.

As a senior leader in the firm, I am also responsible for business development for interior design and space planning/tenant improvement projects.

Corporate: employee café, Regency Blue Cross Blue Shield of Oregon. Susan Higbee, Group MacKenzie, Portland, Oregon.

PHOTOGRAPH: SERGIO ORTIZ

What is the most satisfying part of your job?

❭ Satisfying the client is the most rewarding part of my job. It brings great pleasure to gain the confidence of a client, and to meet their needs no matter what the challenge brings.

What is the least satisfying part of your job?

❭ I do not enjoy anything that compromises the ability to provide this service.

What is the most important quality or skill of a designer in your specialty?

❭ I think it is most critical to be skilled at listening and understanding the functional requirements for a project. A commercial project will have many functional requirements that must be met to be successful operationally. It is our job to provide innovative, aesthetic environments while meeting the functional requirements. If this is done poorly, businesses loose efficiencies. If done well, businesses can see increased efficiencies as well as improvement in morale, worker productivity, and so on.

Who or what experience has been a major influence in your career?

❭ Growing up overseas in Japan played a significant role in influencing my career. It was the upbringing in different cultures that made me aware that everything in your environment shapes who you are.

TOP Corporate: office lobby, Krause IV office building. Susan Higbee, Group MacKenzie, Portland, Oregon.
PHOTOGRAPH: RANDY SHELTON

ABOVE Corporate: office lobby, Waggener Edstrom office. Susan Higbee, Group MacKenzie, Portland, Oregon.
PHOTOGRAPH: RANDY SHELTON

Choosing an Educational Program

Choosing the educational program that is right for you is a highly individual process. One of the key determinants in this decision is your goal in the profession. For example, if your goal is to work in a large commercial interior design or architecture firm, you must complete a four- or five-year baccalaureate program. If you would rather work in a smaller firm or already have a bachelor's degree in another area, a two-year community college program might yield many excellent job opportunities that satisfy your goal.

One factor in choosing an educational program is whether it meets the requirements you need to qualify for the National Council for Interior Design Qualification (NCIDQ) examination. States and provinces that license interior designers require the NCIDQ exam for licensure. If the program you are considering does not meet the minimal educational requirements established by your state or province and by NCIDQ, you will not be allowed to take the exam. This could limit your role in the interior design profession even if your jurisdiction does not have interior design legislation at this time. More states are regulating the practice of interior design all the time, and the NCIDQ examination will most likely be the primary licensing tool in these states as well. Additional information on the NCIDQ examination is provided in this chapter.

Another factor to consider in choosing your educational preparation is the faculty. The background and experience of those teaching the classes is important. A strong faculty whose members have practice backgrounds is vital. In four- and five-year schools, one or more of the faculty may be oriented to research rather than practice. These teachers provide valuable instruction in lecture classes such as design theory and history of furniture. Both practitioners and research-oriented faculty are important to the program.

Some faculty members work at the institution full-time, providing classroom instruction, academic and career advising, and administration of the program. Schools often utilize part-time faculty members who work full-time as professional interior designers and teach one or two classes. One learns from both kinds of faculty members. Full-time faculty are more common in four- and five-year programs, and part-time teachers are commonly used in community colleges. Of course, four- or five-year programs also have some part-time teachers to fill certain teaching slots, just as community college interior design programs can have one or more full-time faculty members. The background, design interests, and teaching schedule of the faculty may be important considerations for you when choosing a program.

Whether or not the program is accredited by the Council for Interior Design Accreditation (CIDA, formerly FIDER) is another important factor to consider when selecting an interior design program. Accreditation from CIDA means that the curriculum, faculty, facilities, and support of the school's administration meet standards accepted by the profession. Some states require that interior designers who practice in the state have graduated from a CIDA-accredited program.

An additional consideration is the location of the school. A college located in a large urban area has an advantage of giving students the opportunity to visit local museums, design firms, and project locations within easy reach of the school. It is likely to be a larger school with a larger group of students in the program. That can be positive as this larger group of peers gives students more opportunity to meet new people. It can also be a disadvantage of sorts as the competition for entry into classes might be greater. A smaller college may help the shy student gain confidence with a smaller group of peers. Of course, a smaller college will offer trips as well to urban centers for class assignments or even study tours.

Investigate the curriculum and faculty, visit the facilities, and even ask for names of graduates who might talk to you about the preparation they received. Talk to potential employers as well to find out what kind of educational preparation they require of entry-level employees. All this research will help you determine the right academic program for your goals and needs.

How Did You Choose Which School to Attend to Obtain Your Education in Interior Design?

> I sought a state school that was FIDER- (now CIDA) accredited. I was lucky to live in Missouri and graduated from one of the first FIDER-accredited programs. I have master's degrees in Business and Marketing and am working on a Ph.D. in Design.

Beth Harmon-Vaughn, FIIDA, Associate AIA

> I attended the University of Texas in Austin, Texas. I received a Bachelor of Science with a major in Interior Design from the School of Architecture.

Trisha Wilson, ASID

> I only wanted to attend a school that was FIDER-accredited. I went to Kent State University and received a Bachelor of Arts degree in Interior Design.

Kristin King, ASID

> I made sure at the time that I chose one of the best interior design schools in the country to obtain my degree. I have a Bachelor of Arts degree in Interior Design.

Lisa Slayman, ASID, IIDA

> I have a degree from Washington State University, which was a FIDER-accredited school. I chose WSU because it was far enough away from home that I felt independent and, once I started in the program, I realized that it was run by professionals. I am not sure I understood that at the time, but I really appreciate that fact now that I have been practicing almost 30 years.

Melinda Sechrist, FASID

> I have a B.S. in Home Economics with an emphasis in interior design from a state university in Texas. To be honest, I chose that school because of a full scholarship offered to me. I did not immediately know that I wanted to study interior design. I did receive a very good interior design education from the school's FIDER-accredited program.

Robert Wright, FASID

> My decision was based on a school that was accredited, a decent location to where I was living, and size of the school. (I did not want to go to a large school and be in large studio classrooms.) I have a bachelor's in Interior Design and a Master of Arts in Interior Design.

Robin Wagner, ASID, IDEC

❯ It was important to me to find an education with a bachelor's degree and when I researched schools, I found out about FIDER-accredited schools, so that helped to narrow down my choices. I have a bachelor's in Interior Design.
David Hanson, RID, IDC, IIDA

❯ I chose the best Colorado program in 1977 that was FIDER-accredited and received a bachelor's in Interior Design from its four-year program. Unfortunately, the program no longer exists, but there are other programs available that are outstanding.
Annette K. Stelmack, Allied Member ASID

❯ At the time I received my degree, there were limited choices in San Diego to study interior design; I chose to attend San Diego State University.
Jan Bast, FASID, IIDA, IDEC

❯ I have an Associate of Art in Interior Design from Bauder College (Atlanta, Georgia) and a Master of Science in Management and Organization from Antioch New England Graduate School (Keene, New Hampshire). Along the way I also studied architecture at the Boston Architectural College. I was very young when I started school in Atlanta in 1981. I did not know what to look for in a school or much about the profession. I just "went for it" and thought that escaping Maine to a big city in the South would be exciting. Looking back, knowing what I know now, I definitely would have sought, at minimum, a CIDA-accredited, four-year interior design program.
Lisa Whited, IIDA, ASID, Maine Certified Interior Designer

❯ I selected the program based on my geographical area. I am a "mustang"—I've worked my way to professionalism with two years of general college study, a certificate in interior design, and a lot of hard work.
Patricia Rowen, ASID, CAPS

❯ I was fortunate enough to be living in Chicago when I decided to pursue a degree in interior design and had many choices. I chose Harrington Institute of Interior Design after talking to firms, instructors, and looking at the work the students completed. Their reputation and their being a FIDER-accredited program were all important factors. I have an associate's degree in Interior Design from Harrington and a bachelor's in Art from Western Michigan University
Laurie Smith, ASID

Lodging: lobby, The Palace of the Lost City, Sun City, South Africa. Trisha Wilson, ASID, Wilson Associates, Dallas, Texas.
PHOTOGRAPH: PETER VITALE

> When I entered college, I knew that I wanted to major in interior design. I attended Appalachian State University (which was not FIDER-accredited at the time), but had a great reputation for the interior design department. Due to family constraints, this was my best option for an interior design education. The school is currently under review for accreditation, and I can attest to the validity and success of the students that their program produces. I graduated magna cum laude from ASU with a Bachelor of Science in Housing and Interior Design. I also have a minor in Business.

Shannon Ferguson, IIDA

> CIDA was not an option when I was choosing a school with interior design. I did not want to attend an interior design program housed in the home economics department. I found two located in the art departments of universities, one with a B.A. major and an art history minor; I chose that one.

Patricia McLaughlin, ASID, RID

> I did not start out in interior design. I started out in chemistry and then transferred as the pieces fell in place. If I had gone to U.C.–Berkeley for chemistry—I may have been an architect by now. Fortunately for me, Virginia Tech was FIDER-accredited. And so was SDSU (San Diego State University) when I transferred.

Linda Isley, IIDA

> I didn't. Because I did not know then that what my passion would lead me to was interior design and brand development. I got a four-year liberal arts degree in fine art and architectural history. I had to do the rest myself . . . so I know how important a good interior design education can be.

Bruce Brigham, FASID, ISP, IES

> It was a bit by accident. I decided to attend the University of Nebraska–Lincoln to major in journalism with a minor in home economics. My goal was to write for a women's magazine. At that time, the home economics department required you to take classes in all the disciplines. Early on when I took the first interior design class, I knew I would drop the journalism and go for the degree in interior design.

Susan Norman, IIDA

> I grew up in Iowa, thus Iowa State University was a natural selection.

Carol Morrow, Ph.D., ASID, IIDA, IDEC

> I was very fortunate in my selection of schools. Since I started out seeking an architectural degree, I sought recommendations from an architect and studied the four schools that he recommended. When I decided to pursue an interior design degree, it was pure luck that I ended up selecting an accredited program. I hold a Bachelor of Arts degree in Interior Design. I recommend that aspiring students look for a four-year program and certainly one that is accredited. In addition, students should look for schools that offer a wide range of math, science, and business classes.

Mary Knopf, ASID

> Probably not a good question for me. I went to my college to swim competitively. Once I realized what I really wanted to do, I did not want to change schools. I supplemented with classes at the College for Creative Studies in Detroit, Michigan, and decided to dive into my first job. Take the NCIDQ as soon as possible. I have a Bachelor of Arts from Central Michigan University.

Jo Rabaut, ASID

Hospitality: Hidden Valley Country Club, Reno, Nevada. M. Joy Meeuwig, IIDA, Interior Design Consultation, Reno, Nevada.

PHOTOGRAPH: PERSPECTIVE IMAGE, SEATTLE, WASHINGTON

❭ For me I chose the "family school" and I was lucky in that it had an excellent program of design. I hold a Bachelor of Interior Design from the School of Architecture.
Charles Gandy, FASID, FIIDA

❭ There was not much magic to it in 1971. In a sense I got lucky in going to the University of Cincinnati: It had the program that I was looking for, did it better than anyone else, and I didn't have to look out of state.
Colleen McCafferty, IFMA, USGBC, LEED-CI

❭ I have a B.A. in Foreign Languages with a focus in French and a minor in Art. I also have a certificate in interior decorating, which helped me obtain my current position. I chose the school from which I received my certificate in interiors because it fit my lifestyle at the time and met the need. The curriculum was correspondence studies and allowed me to study at home while spending time with my newborn son. I was also not interested in obtaining another B.A. or to pursue an M.F.A. in this field.
Darcie Miller, NKBA, ASID Industry Partner, CMG

❭ I was fortunate to have started in a university that had an architecture program and an interior design program. When I realized interior design was where my passion lay, I was able to transfer between programs. I also chose my school because it was a large, "full-service" institution and it was *not* in my hometown backyard. While the exact title of my degree is no longer available, it is a Bachelor of Science in Design with a major of Interior Architecture. The equivalent offered today by the university (it is still one of the top-ranked programs nationwide) is a B.S. in Design, Interior Design degree.
David Stone, IIDA, LEED-AP

❭ I have a Bachelor of Science degree from Northern Arizona University. At the time I attended that university, Phil Bartholomew was in charge of the department. He also felt very passionate about the importance of the interior design field and was a great mentor.
Debra Himes, ASID, IIDA

❭ The quality of the program and the location of the school. I have a bachelor's in fine arts and a bachelor's in business.
Donna Vining, FASID, IIDA, RID, CAPS

> For my B.S. in Design, I thought I wanted a school of architecture, but found interior design as a specialty after coming to the university. For my M.S. in Design, I needed a program that could allow me to continue working and living with my family without relocating. Arizona State University was the institution for both degrees. It had a strong national reputation as a program of excellence due to its excellent faculty and facilities.

Robert J. Krikac, IDEC

> I come from a long line of (University of Florida) Gators, but primarily I followed love. My high school sweetheart (actually my whole-life sweetheart—we met in third grade) was a diehard Gator who wouldn't consider any other school. We both applied only there and we both were accepted. We'll be married 13 years this year.

Maryanne Hewitt, IIDA

> Location and FIDER accreditation were the main factors in selecting a school. I graduated with a Bachelor of Science degree.

Greta Guelich, ASID

> When I attended college in 1976, I based the decision of where to go to school upon my desire to secure an education that offered a curriculum in design, which was deeply embedded in the humanities, but also one that was taught as an applied craft. After receiving an undergraduate degree in architecture from Rice University, I pursued a graduate degree from the University of Pennsylvania for the depth and breadth of theory and the opportunity to study in Paris and Venice during my last semester of graduate school.

James Postell, Associate Professor,
University of Cincinnati

> I liked Northern Arizona University for its size, geography, and character. I was an undecided major going in so interior design was not a part of my university choice decision.

Jane Coit, Associate Member IIDA

> I was very fortunate in my excessive ignorance entering my freshman year of college right after high school. I stumbled into an excellent CIDA-accredited interior design program at the University of Kentucky in Lexington—my hometown at the time—and received a Bachelor of Arts degree in Housing and Interior Design.

Keith Miller, ASID

> After completing a bachelor degree in accounting at the largest university in my state, I elected to take interior design courses at the same university, as it was FIDER-accredited. I learned about the program and found that the faculty was very talented with diverse backgrounds and all of my business credits transferred, enabling me to pursue a master's degree upon completion of a portion of the design requirements. I have many colleagues in the design industry who complete two-year technical programs. I am very confident in their design skills, but two-year programs do not allow for the diversity that a four-year program has. While many students balk at math, writing, or communication courses, they are necessary and useful in the real world.

Laura Busse, IIDA, KYCID

> I looked for a school with a good reputation for turning out great designers and one that was FIDER-accredited. What degree do I possess? I have a B.F.A. in Interior Design.

Linda Elliott Smith, FASID

> Education is critical to readying the profession to meet the market needs. The interior design profession must embrace the importance of research and education to secure its position in the industry.
Linda Sorrento, ASID, IIDA, LEED-AP

> Had I known then what I know now, I would have only considered schools accredited by CIDA and known for a faculty that practices professionally. Through blind luck, I ended up at what was then FIDER-accredited San Diego State University, where I earned my bachelor degree in Art with an emphasis in Interior Design. I learned from very talented instructors who gave students every opportunity to acquire the tools it would take to be successful in the industry.
Lindsay Sholdar, ASID

> I already had an undergrad degree—with the plan to go in a much different direction. When I finally realized where I belonged, I looked into credible programs in the area that would allow me to utilize my existing credits and make it so I wouldn't have to go to school for another eternity. Scottsdale Community College allowed me to accomplish all I set out to do, a B.A. in Political Science and an A.A.S. in Interior Design.
Marilizabeth Polizzi, Allied Member ASID

> We could only afford the community college and state university programs. The schools were close to home, had good basic programs and fine reputations for the courses offered. I have an A.A. degree in Education and a B.A. degree in Art.
Mary Knott, Allied Member ASID, CID, RSPI

> In 1971 it was a hit or miss how to choose a program in interior design, as guidance was not clear. I happened to figure out that an undergraduate degree would come from a land grant college and so I attended the University of Connecticut where I earned a Bachelor of Science degree in Interior Design and Textiles from the School of Home Economics. In 1975, when I graduated, accreditation programs were just beginning to set the standard. I have continued my education through a number of venues, but primarily through the nonprofit organizations that I have come to lead, ASID (American Society of Interior Designers) and the Center for Health Design.
Rosalyn Cama, FASID

> It wasn't necessarily thought out. Associate in arts.
Michael Thomas, FASID, CAPS

> At the time, I sought out a four-year degree. I have a B.S. in Interior Design.
Nila Leiserowitz, FASID, Associate AIA

> I went to school at Georgia State University so that I could stay at home and work my way through college. It was the university with the best reputation for my major in Atlanta.
Rita Carson Guest, FASID

> I was lucky enough to live in a state with a very highly rated interior design program. Iowa State University's interior design program was going through FIDER accreditation when I was there, and has continued that format. The interior design program was one of the few in the country at that time located in the College of Design. We had much interaction with other design disciplines—architecture, graphic arts, even textile design. I have a B.S. in Interior Design from Iowa State University and a Master of Fine Arts in Scene Design/Technical Theater from the University of Arizona.
Sharmin Pool-Bak, ASID, CAPS, LEED-AP

❭ I went to Michigan State University for my bachelor's because one, it was FIDER-accredited even in 1975; two, near to where my family lived; and three, a fantastic university. I went to Utah State University for my master's and Colorado State University for my doctorate because of the same reasons above. Interestingly, all have been land grant universities.

Stephanie Clemons, Ph.D., FASID, FIDEC

❭ I selected the New York School of Interior Design initially because it offered a one-year program, which I felt would give me enough insight into the profession to decide if I wanted to make a career change. It did, and I did. Having already been awarded an undergraduate degree in an unrelated field, I obtained a postbaccalaureate major in Fine Arts, Interior Design by attending classes at night at a university closer to home, where I was working and raising a baby. The choice was based on what worked with my lifestyle as well as what would give me a foundation to pursue a professional path.

Suzan Globus, FASID

❭ I have two undergraduate degrees in different design fields, the second of which is in interior and environmental design. I took additional courses in architecture and business for several years and eventually took an M.B.A. in Leadership. For my interior design degree, I sought out a FIDER-accredited school in my area on the advice of an architecture professor. My next priorities were: within commuting distance, friendly to nontraditional students, and a good reputation within the design/build industry.

Sally D'Angelo, ASID, AIA Affiliate

❭ Initially I began my education at a university that offered a five-year interior design program. This particular program was oriented more toward commercial design. My desire was to work in the residential design industry; therefore, I transferred to a local community college. After three years, I received an Associate of Applied Science degree in Interior Design.

Teresa Ridlon, Allied Member ASID

❭ I hold a Bachelor of Arts degree in Interior Design from Kent State University in Ohio. I worked at Kent State while my husband finished his degree when I decided to begin my work in their interior design program. The program took an interdisciplinary approach that included interior design, art, technology, and architecture, which I thought was an excellent way to look at interior design.

Terri Maurer, FASID

❭ I graduated from Iowa State University with a Bachelor of Fine Arts degree in Interior Design.

Rachelle Schoessler Lynn, CID, ASID, LEED-AP, Allied Member AIA

❭ I earned a master's degree from Washington State University. This is the only school in Washington that offers such a degree and the undergraduate program is accredited and has an excellent reputation.

Leylan Salzer

❭ I looked for a FIDER- (now CIDA) accredited interior design program.

Lisa Henry, ASID

COUNCIL FOR INTERIOR DESIGN ACCREDITATION

CIDA, the Council for Interior Design Accreditation—formerly the Foundation for Interior Design Education Research (FIDER)—is a private, not-for-profit organization whose purpose is to lead the interior design profession to excellence by setting standards and accrediting academic programs. Founded originally in 1970, it is the recognized body for accrediting interior design educational programs in the United States and Canada. According to CIDA, the educational standards required by the council "are used to evaluate interior design programs that prepare students for entry-level interior design practice and position them for future professional growth."[1]

An interior design program that receives CIDA accreditation offers interior design–related course work that develops knowledge, skills, and abilities in design fundamentals, the design process, space planning and furniture planning, building systems and interior materials, regulations and standards that affect interior design. Accredited programs also offer classes in business and professional practice, communication, and professional ethics and values. In addition, four-year accredited programs include a minimum of 30 semester credit-hours of liberal arts, sciences, and humanities courses. The exact mix of classes is left to the individual school as long as student learning demonstrates achievement of the accrediting standards (see "Council for Interior Design Accreditation Professional Standards, 2006," facing page).

Academic accrediting standards for interior design programs are maintained through research into the field of interior design and building community consensus regarding requirements to enter the profession. CIDA maintains a close relationship with the major professional associations and the NCIDQ through representation on the board of directors. Many state regulatory bodies governing use of the title or practice of interior design refer to CIDA in their educational requirements.

Over 100 CIDA-accredited programs are taught in the United States and Canada. For more information about CIDA, visit the council's Web site at www.accredit-id.org. Contact information is included in "Interior Design Resources" (see page 297) and interior design programs that currently hold CIDA accreditation are listed in "CIDA-Accredited Interior Design Programs in the United States and Canada" (page 299).

COUNCIL FOR INTERIOR DESIGN ACCREDITATION PROFESSIONAL STANDARDS, 2006

A complete, detailed definition of each of these professional standards can be obtained from the CIDA Web site (www.accredit-id.org).

1. **CURRICULUM STRUCTURE:** The curriculum is structured to facilitate and advance student learning.

2. **PROFESSIONAL VALUES:** The program leads students to develop the attitudes, traits, and values of professional responsibility, accountability, and effectiveness.

3. **DESIGN FUNDAMENTALS:** Students have a foundation in the fundamentals of art and design, theories of design, green design, and human behavior, and discipline-related history.

4. **INTERIOR DESIGN:** Students understand and apply the knowledge, skills, processes, and theories of interior design.

5. **COMMUNICATION:** Students communicate effectively.

6. **BUILDING SYSTEMS AND INTERIOR MATERIALS:** Students design within the context of building systems. Students use appropriate materials and products.

7. **REGULATIONS:** Students apply the laws, codes, regulations, standards, and practices that protect the health, safety, and welfare of the public.

8. **BUSINESS AND PROFESSIONAL PRACTICE:** Students have a foundation in business and professional practice.

9. **FACULTY:** Faculty members and other instructional personnel are qualified and adequate in number to implement program objectives.

10. **FACILITIES:** Program facilities and resources provide an environment to stimulate thought, motivate students, and promote the exchange of ideas.

11. **ADMINISTRATION:** The administration of the program is clearly defined, provides appropriate program leadership, and supports the program. The program demonstrates accountability to the public through its published documents.

12. **ASSESSMENT:** Systematic and comprehensive assessment methods contribute to the program's ongoing development and improvement.

Four-Year Educational Preparation

A four-year degree with a major in interior design is highly recommended by most employers, especially the larger firms. A four-year bachelor's degree offers you the opportunity to take the largest number of interior design and related major classes plus obtain a strong overall liberal arts background. The breadth of classes that train students in the technical skills and knowledge areas are more available in a four-year program.

The majority of degree programs in interior design are found in departments of interior design, fine arts, architecture, and human ecology. Depending on the college, university, or professional school and the department in which the program is located, the four-year degree can be a Bachelor of Science, Bachelor of Arts, or Bachelor of Fine Arts. Several institutions offer a five-year bachelor's degree in interior design. These programs are most commonly associated with a college of architecture.

It is important to note that some schools offer programs that require three years of concentrated study for a bachelor's degree. This is most common at a professional school, where the student is required to attend classes full-time for the full year. This allows the student to graduate in three years rather than the traditional four years. Breaks, of course, between sessions are scheduled.

The number of semester or quarter credits required varies by institution. A four-year program commonly includes at least 120 semester credits, of which 60 or more are interior design–related. These numbers match the NCIDQ's qualification requirements in education at this time.

Let's look briefly at the type of course work you might experience in a typical four-year major in interior design. These programs all begin with a large dose of liberal studies classes in the first year. A few introductory classes in interior design and design theory, beginning drafting, whether manual or computer-aided drafting (CAD), and perhaps a basic art studio may be required during the first year.

The second year includes additional liberal studies classes as well as more intense interior design classes. This may be the point where you have the opportunity to expand on CAD skills and take classes in programming, furniture or architecture history, perhaps media classes to learn rendering, and other basic technical or art classes. Elective hours in business, fine art, or other areas of interest may also be taken.

Many schools require a portfolio of work to be presented for entry into the third and fourth year (sometimes referred to as *professional-level classes*). This is because some schools only allow a limited number of students to be admitted into the last two years of classes while a great number of students apply. If this is the case, you submit examples of design and art work completed in the early classes as well as evidence of overall academic performance. For example, it is common that a portfolio required for entry into the professional-level classes would include examples of the student's two- and three-dimensional design projects, drafting examples, any project assignments showing space planning concepts and development, and other examples of work accomplished during the first two years of academic training. In addition, the portfolio admission process also requires transcripts and an essay focused according to the instructions of the particular college program.

The third year is when the real interior design work begins. You are finally in major studio classes, where you produce floor plans, furniture layouts, and other basic design documents for small residential or commercial spaces. The third year is when the basic skills and theory classes are combined in studio classes that require design solutions commonly addressed by interior designers. Other design classes likely include technical classes related to materials, building structure, codes, and mechanical systems. Upper-level liberal studies classes and electives in other areas of interest to the student, or required by the university, are common in addition to the interior design and related major courses in the third year.

Classes in the fourth year are advanced studios that challenge you to plan and design larger complex spaces. Some schools have very specialized studios at this level, allowing a student to gain experience in a particular design specialty such as hospitality, corporate offices, residential, or various types of institutional spaces. Advanced classes in such areas as lighting design, business practices, and research are also required in the fourth year. Depending on the program, a senior thesis project or culminating project might be required. The fourth year also includes discussions about and development or refinement of your portfolio, résumé, and job-hunting skills. The last of the liberal studies and elective classes are also part of the fourth-year program.

If the school requires a fifth year of studies, this year is typically focused on an extensive special project investigated and developed over the year. It is sometimes called a *thesis project*, though it is not the same as a thesis produced in a master's degree program. The fifth year also allows students to take additional elective courses that prepare students to achieve professional goals.

Many schools require an internship experience. This is an important opportunity for you to work for several weeks or up to a full semester in an interior design firm. Through the internship, you discover how to connect what you learned in classes and studios to the working world. The internship is usually taken after the end of either the third year or fourth year of classes. When is the best time? That varies with each student's overall performance in the first three years of course work as well as with the policies of the institution.

Educator

DENISE A. GUERIN, PH.D., FIDEC, ASID, IIDA
UNIVERSITY OF MINNESOTA
ST. PAUL, MINNESOTA

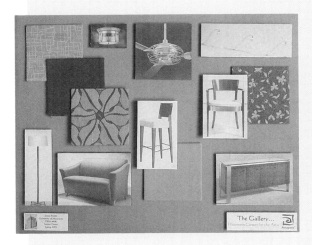

TOP Project sample board. Work by Jamie Smith, former student at Department of Design, Housing, and Apparel, University of Minnesota, St. Paul, Minnesota.

ABOVE Perspective. Work by Jamie Smith, former student at Department of Design, Housing, and Apparel, University of Minnesota, St. Paul, Minnesota.

What is the purpose of your design program?

❯ To teach the relationship between design and human behavior and how to provide design solutions to support human behavior and needs.

What advice would you give someone who wants to be an interior designer?

❯ Be prepared for labor-intensive projects that stimulate you to reach beyond your knowledge. Shadow interior designers from several areas of specialization (hospitality, healthcare, residential, corporate, etcetera) and interview them so you have a good understanding of what an interior designer does. Do this before you make up your mind to be an interior designer.

What are a few characteristics of a good student?

❯ Passion for design, good time management, curiosity about the world, and critical thinking ability.

How do you prepare students for the workforce?

❯ We prepare students to be the leaders of the profession. We do this with a heavy emphasis on research and theory. Students study the relationship of design and human behavior and how to identify and solve problems within this framework. In addition to course work and internships, we use a one-semester thesis project as a bridge between academic life and the work world.

What is the single most important skill a designer needs to be successful?

❯ Communication skills: oral, written, drawing/ sketching, and drafting.

Why did you become an interior designer?

❯ To work with people and improve their environments so that they function better. Remember, that was more than 30 years ago.

How important is certification by examination and licensing of interior designers today?

❯ I believe it is mandatory for all qualified interior design practitioners to be NCIDQ certificate holders and licensed, registered, or certified if their jurisdiction has this regulation. With the appropriate education and experience, interior designers can sit for the NCIDQ exam whether or not their jurisdictions are regulated. This is one way to improve the profession. Then, if it is possible to gain legal recognition in their jurisdiction of practice, interior designers must take the responsibility to do that in order to show that they are able to protect the health, safety, and welfare of the public.

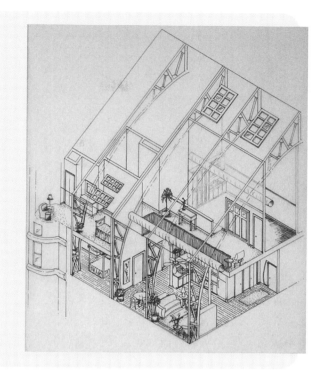

Perspective. Work by Jamie Smith, former student at Department of Design, Housing, and Apparel, University of Minnesota, St. Paul, Minnesota.

Educator

TOM WITT

ARIZONA STATE UNIVERSITY

TEMPE, ARIZONA

What is the purpose of your design program?

❯ The purpose of our program is to prepare verbally and analytically competent leaders for the profession.

What advice would you give someone who wants to be an interior designer?

❯ Spread your education as broadly across the university curriculum as you possibly can—art, music, writing, chemistry, biology, and philosophy.

Perspective. Work by David Hobart, former student at School of Design, Arizona State University, Tempe, Arizona.

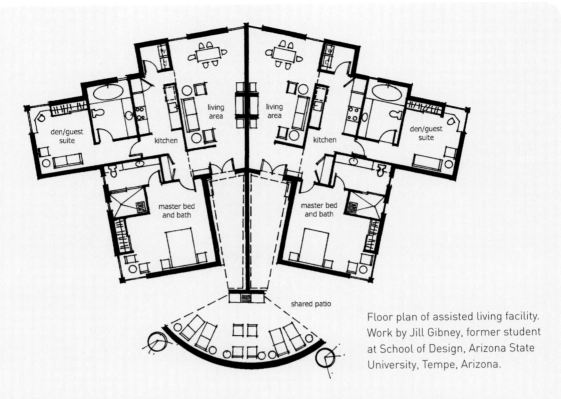

living area

living area

den/guest suite

kitchen

kitchen

den/guest suite

master bed and bath

master bed and bath

shared patio

Floor plan of assisted living facility. Work by Jill Gibney, former student at School of Design, Arizona State University, Tempe, Arizona.

What are a few characteristics of a good student?

❯ Self-motivated and directed; a creative, critical, and analytical thinker interested in both art and science.

How do you prepare students for the workforce?

❯ We have a faculty involved in both research and practice. Projects are grounded in the practice of the profession; and professional architects and interior designers are engaged regularly as consultants, as are practitioners of allied professions. The students are required to complete a summer internship under the direct supervision of a master designer.

What is the single most important skill a designer needs to be successful?

❯ To be successful, the professional interior designer needs to be a critical, analytical thinker.

Why did you become an interior designer?

❯ I love architecture and believe that interior design is the most intimate form of architecture, that is, has the greatest potential for improving the lives of people.

How important is certification by examination and licensing of interior designers today?

❯ At the present time, registration does not seem very important. But registration is the next logical step in the evolution of the profession. The importance of registration is increasing, with more and more interior designers doing ever more complex projects and working in teams with architects and engineers. Increasing liability issues and the potential impact of this work on the health, safety, and welfare of the users will mandate registration.

The Importance of Internships

An internship experience is the student's opportunity to work for a concentrated period in a practitioner's studio or office while often receiving academic credit for the work. Often, each student's adviser or another faculty member arranges the internship with input from the student. Most schools involve students in setting up their internship to give them valuable job-interviewing experience.

Each internship is different and in many cases can be structured to meet at least some of the future professional interests of the student. Depending on the actual office needs and the student's requirements and interests, the intern might spend time:

Assisting designers in researching products for specifications.

Preparing sketches.

Drafting floor plans or other drawings needed for construction documents.

Meeting with clients and the practitioner designer.

Attending meetings or presentations by vendors and suppliers.

Not every student gets the opportunity to actually work on portions of projects. Some may serve as a strong support person to a senior designer, helping make product specification decisions and developing specification documents. Other offices give students the opportunity to prepare drawings—always under the supervision of a professional designer.

In general, the larger the design firm, the more structured the internship. Students may spend a portion of the internship doing what many consider to be "grunt work," such as filing catalogs and samples in the design library; visiting showrooms to search for appropriate samples; or drafting small details needed in construction drawings. As mundane as these tasks may appear, they are a part of the profession. Gradually, the student may be allowed to sit in on client interviews, draft more important parts of the construction documents, and have more direct interaction with the senior designers in the firm.

It is important for the student and the faculty members responsible for supervising the internship experience to carefully discuss and evaluate the student's abilities and career interests before determining an internship location. Although any internship experience teaches the student valuable lessons about actual professional work, one established to closely support the student's goals and current skills will be most valuable to his or her overall educational preparation.

Two-Year Associate Degree

Not everyone wishes to spend four or five years in school pursuing a bachelor's degree in interior design. Perhaps you already have a degree in another field and have decided to change careers and enter the interior design industry. The two-year degree offered by community colleges and some professional schools is referred to as an associate degree. Depending on the number of interior design classes, a two-year associate degree in interior design is acceptable to studios and retail stores that hire sales associates as well as interior designers. Generally, a two-year degree without some sort of bachelor degree is not sufficient to obtain employment with large interior design or multidisciplinary firms. Of course, some firms might hire an individual with a two-year associate degree in interior design and several years of full-time work experience in design or a related field.

At this time, two-year programs should require at least 40 semester credits or 60 quarter credits of interior design–related course work in order to qualify for the NCIDQ exam. Not all two-year programs offer this amount of course work. Remember that states and provinces that legally register or certify interior designers unanimously require the NCIDQ examination for licensure. However, a jurisdiction may require a four-year degree for legal registration or that the program is accredited by the Council for Interior Design Accreditation. Two-year programs that are currently accredited by CIDA are likely to lose accreditation unless they meet specific requirements of CIDA when their accreditation is subsequently reviewed. Thus, it is important to check with your appropriate state or provincial registration agency, school, or NCIDQ, as the educational requirement to take the exam can change.

During the first year, introductory interior design classes such as basic design, color theory, history of furniture, textiles, and drafting are required. Most two-year programs require a number of liberal studies classes, especially English, mathematics, science, and other liberal studies classes or electives. The emphasis is, however, on preparation in the major.

The second year emphasizes such classes as

BY THE NUMBERS

According to the CIDA, approximately 115 baccalaureate programs are accredited in interior design and an additional 15 preprofessional programs that are nonbaccalaureate programs are CIDA-accredited. As of 2003, preprofessional level programs are no longer accredited by the council. Those that are will have to seek accreditation at the professional level of curriculum when it is time for them to renew accreditation. An estimated 20,000 students are enrolled in the accredited programs. Courses are taught by an estimated 500 full-time, 350 part-time, and 800 adjunct faculty members. Interior design education has been a fast-growing program at many schools. There is no accurate estimate of how many students enroll annually beyond the figures estimated by CIDA; it is likely to be several thousand. Many other schools offer some kind of interior design program. These range from a few classes meant for students interested in working in a retail store as a sales associate to strong two-year associate and baccalaureate programs that might prepare students to work in interior design firms.

CAD, space planning, business practices, studio projects in residential and commercial interiors, and materials. Elective courses that allow the student to develop additional skills in space planning and furniture specification through project problem solving are encouraged or required. Of course, most programs also require students to study building and safety codes and mechanical systems. Furthermore, most two-year programs require students to complete an internship.

Students who have completed a two-year associate degree program can transfer to many four-year bachelor degree programs in interior design. The four-year program may require additional course work in liberal studies or other preprofessional courses that were not a part of the two-year program. It is quite common to require transfer students to submit a portfolio of work to evidence skill mastery or overall performance in interior design classes.

In recent years, many two-year associate degree programs developed special programs called "two plus two." What this means is that the student can take classes in the interior design major at a community college for the first two years and, after admittance, complete the last two years through a special program at an in-state university that offers a four-year degree program in interior design. Sometimes the classes in the last two years are also offered at the community college through televised instruction, the Internet, or classes held on the community college campus taught by instructors from the university program. This option gives flexibility to students who cannot go to another campus that may be remote from family or work obligations.

Teaching as a Career Option

LEYLAN SALZER, M.A.
WASHINGTON STATE UNIVERSITY
SPOKANE, WASHINGTON

Why did you become an interior designer?

❯ I was looking for a career that I could love. Interior design provides both challenge and excitement. Each project is a complex design problem that requires research, teamwork, and creativity. These are all things that I enjoy and am driven by.

How did you choose which school to attend to obtain your education in interior design?

❯ I earned a master's degree from Washington State University. This is the only school in Washington that offers such a degree and the undergraduate program is accredited and has an excellent reputation.

What was your greatest challenge as a student?

❯ I made the transition from business to interior design. It was difficult to change my thought process from strictly analytical to analytical and conceptual. Once I made this transition, I think it was a great benefit to have both skills.

What is the most satisfying part of your educational experience? The least?

❯ Finding a profession that I am passionate about is by far the most satisfying part of my educational experience. I spent long hours in studio, yet I wanted to be there because I felt strongly about producing quality work.

How important do you feel an internship is to a student's educational experience?

❯ An internship is critical. There is a huge gap between academia and the profession and an internship is a great way to fill that gap. You can make it through four years of school without seeing a set of construction documents. Yet this is a significant aspect of the job. Basic knowledge of construction documents would make a student much more marketable when looking for employment.

What are your goals for your career over the next 5 to 10 years?

❯ My goals have recently changed. I was on track for a project manager position and now I am back in academia teaching interior design. If I decide to pursue a teaching career, my goals for the next 5 to 10 years will be to gain associate professor status and focus on defining how students can use computer technology to strengthen rather than dilute the creative process.

What advice would you give to someone who wants to be an interior designer?

❯ To be successful in this profession you must be passionate about your work. It is a demanding job that requires full commitment. It is much easier to remain committed if you feel strongly about your work.

Who or what experience has been a major influence in your career?

❯ Every project influences me in a different way, which is why this profession is so great. Each new job and team I work with brings a new set of issues that need to be solved, providing me with endless opportunities to learn.

Postgraduate Education in Interior Design

Postgraduate education in interior design is important to many people in this profession. Most individuals who seek a postgraduate degree (master's or doctorate) do so because they are interested in teaching. Of the approximately 50 institutions offering postgraduate degrees in interior design, 8 have a Ph.D. (doctoral) program. A list of institutions that offer postgraduate studies in interior design can be obtained from the Interior Design Educators Council (IDEC) Web site at www.idec.org. Contact information for the IDEC is included in "Interior Design Resources" (see page 297).

Education at the postgraduate level is generally oriented to research. The focus is on a thesis or a doctoral research effort in subject areas such as human factors, the history of decorative arts, and environmental design. Most programs allow for an individually designed program that may also include areas of practice such as facility planning and design, lighting design, design for special populations, and professional practice.

Some practitioners are interested in moving up the ranks in the larger design firms and seek a master's degree in business administration or organizational management rather than interior design. These business-focused degrees in management, marketing, and organizational behavior from colleges of business provide the in-depth background the largest design firms often find valuable for their highest-level design and management staff.

Educator

ROBERT J. KRIKAC, IDEC
WASHINGTON STATE UNIVERSITY
PULLMAN, WASHINGTON

What is your design practice or research specialty?

❯ Perception and communication—specifically, freehand sketching.

What has been your greatest challenge as an interior designer and faculty member?

❯ The shift from projects to academic scholarship—publication and creative endeavors. From being in practice so many years, I find it easier to execute projects that involve making things (drawings, models, project-related documents)—easier than traditional research and writing. I am lucky to have an administration that supports and recognizes creative scholarship as well as colleagues who are excellent scholars in the traditional sense of the word.

Why did you become an educator?

❯ Because after 20 years of practice, I saw that I had a wealth of information to contribute back to the classroom, and teaching inspired me. The firm that I was working for at the time was closing its Phoenix office, and I saw it as an opportunity to make a lateral move within the profession. It cost me everything that I had at the age of 40 to go back to school for my M.S. degree so that I could teach at a university. But it was worth it. I now have the best job I've ever had. I get to mentor the future practitioners of my profession, and I have the freedom to pursue the research and creative endeavors that interest me.

What advice would you give someone who wants to be an interior designer?

❯ Make sure there is something about this profession that is your passion. Some days, it will be the only thing that can get you out of bed to face another day in the office.

What is the single most important skill a designer needs to be successful?

❯ *Flexistence*, a combination of flexibility, necessary to deal with the ever-changing nature of design projects, and persistence, required to bring a project to fruition.

What is the purpose of your design program?

❯ The purpose of our program is to develop critically thinking graduates who have the necessary skills to identify and creatively solve design problems.

What are a few characteristics of a good student?

❯ Passion about the work combined with the understanding that critical statements are about the work itself. An understanding that the professor is a guide, not an answer source, that the answers must come from the student's investigation and exploration of the issues. Flexistence.

How do you prepare students for the workforce?

❯ In general, by instilling in them the need for passion and curiosity about the built environment. Specifically, through a range of interdisciplinary course work in project types; aspects of theory, history, and practice; experiential learning programs; travel; and interaction with practitioners. Our faculty members have a great deal of practice and academic experience and can relate classroom experiences to aspects of practice. They are able to show the students at all levels of the program how the material being covered is utilized by the profession.

How important is certification by examination and licensing of interior designers today?

❯ These two steps are crucial if interior designers are to become respected as professionals.

NCIDQ Examination

The National Council for Interior Design Qualification (NCIDQ) is a private, not-for-profit corporation founded in 1974. Its primary purpose is to develop and administer the NCIDQ examination used to provide credentials to professional interior design practitioners. The NCIDQ exam is the professional competency examination most accepted by state and provincial regulatory agencies where practice regulation and licensing exist as an indicator of minimal professional competency. The examination is also required by the ASID, IIDA, IDEC, and IDC professional associations in order for members to advance to the highest level of membership.

By utilizing a standardized examination that is broadly accepted, it is easier for interior designers to be afforded licensure reciprocity. What this means is that if an interior designer is licensed (or registered or certified) in one state, he or she will most likely be able to practice in other states as well since all jurisdictions that currently have legislation accept the NCIDQ examination as part of the licensure criteria. Reciprocity, however, is up to each state and is not automatically granted.

Why is a highly respected and broadly accepted professional competency examination important? One criterion of any profession is the administration of an examination that tests professional competency. Architects must pass the Architect Registration Examination (ARE) to be a licensed architect; attorneys must pass the bar exam; doctors must pass medical board examinations; and accountants must pass an examination to be a certified public accountant. For the interior designer, passing the NCIDQ examination is a similar professional milestone.

Although continually updating and administering the examination is the NCIDQ's primary mission, it has other responsibilities to the interior design profession. Through research and discussions it helps in identifying public health, safety, and welfare issues; assists in defining, researching, and updating the body of knowledge required of the profession; and analyzes the performance of exam candidates. In addition, the NCIDQ is responsible for records maintenance on certificate holders, records continuing education credits taken by practitioners, and works with authors to develop single-topic monographs.

The current examination is an intensive two-day, three-part test consisting of multiple-choice questions and practicum sections. The multiple-choice sections test the candidate's knowledge about practice issues in all sections of the design process. The practicum sections require the candidate to produce a design solution and create a floor plan and other common design drawings or documents.

To take the examination, candidates must have essentially six years of combined education and work experience, including at least two years of interior design study. By January 1, 2009, candidates will be required to have three years of interior design education and essentially three years of work experience—"essentially" because the work experience requirement is now stated in terms of hours of work experience rather than full-time work over the course of continuous years. This was done to accommodate the changing manner that students attend school and work after graduation. As of January

1, 2008, candidates who begin to accrue the hours of work experience needed to qualify for the exam are required to complete that experience under the direction of an NCIDQ certificate holder, a licensed or registered interior designer, or an architect who offers interior design services. Of course, requirements can change and you should address your specific questions on your qualifications to the NCIDQ.

Programs and materials are available to help candidates prepare for the examination. A study guide including practice practicum sections is available from NCIDQ. The ASID offers a program called Self-Testing Exercises for Preprofessionals (STEP). This is an intensive weekend study program—open to any examination candidate regardless of association affiliation—covering both the practicum and multiple-choice sections of the examination. Some community colleges offer study workshops.

Completing the NCIDQ examination should be a goal for all professional interior designers, whether they work in a state or province with licensing legislation or wish to affiliate with a professional association. The exam is a measure of competence that, in conjunction with your design education, indicates to potential clients that you are a professional.

THE NCIDQ INTERIOR DESIGN EXPERIENCE PROGRAM (IDEP)

A program developed by NCIDQ several years ago is the Interior Design Experience Program (IDEP). It is a monitored plan that strives to ensure a validated range of experiences for an entry-level designer. Not all entry-level designers receive a broad range of experiences during their first year or two since work assignments are made relative to the needs of the design firm. When a graduate and a design firm agree to participate in the IDEP program, the entry-level designer gains the agreed-upon broad experience that also helps the individual be prepared for the NCIDQ examination. It is not required in order to qualify to take the examination, however.

According to the NCIDQ, "IDEP . . . provides a structure for the essential transition between formal education and professional practice, recognizing the differences between classroom and workplace."[2] Participants, of course, work with their supervisor or boss at the place of employment. They also locate a professional designer who mentors the individual during the program. That mentor is not the participant's boss or even someone at his or her place of work. The mentor can provide valuable career advice in a neutral atmosphere of trust.

There are several requirements for participating in the IDEP program. It is important for you to review these requirements and discuss the program with your college adviser and any potential employers prior to graduation. Information on the program can be obtained from the NCIDQ Web site at www.ncidq.org.

Continuing Education

As with any profession, interior designers must keep up with the latest advances in technology, business practice, regulations, and information on the design specialties in which they work. One way this is done is by taking *continuing education unit* (CEU) seminars and workshops. Some jurisdictions require a certain number of CEUs in order for practitioners to renew their license or certification. Both ASID and IIDA require CEU credits for continuation of a practitioner's status in the organization.

CEU seminars and workshops are of varying lengths depending on the topic and outline (see "Continuing Education Units," facing page). Seminars can be as short as one hour, which earn participants .10 CEU credits. For example, the interior designer can take a seminar on a specific aspect of marketing for one hour. Another workshop on a broader topic in marketing might last for three hours and be worth .30 CEU credits. An all-day workshop on working with markers as a method of doing renderings, for example, could be worth from .60 to .80 CEU credits.

An individual can participate in a continuing education seminar or workshop in several ways. Professional associations offer many of these programs at their national meetings. Local chapters schedule seminars of interest to the local membership. Major trade markets such as the NeoCon conference and trade show in Chicago in June and Baltimore in October offer numerous continuing education seminars. Correspondence courses enable interior designers who cannot travel to study at their convenience. Practitioners can also obtain classes via the Internet through private seminar providers.

These seminars are taught by interior designers, architects, educators, and industry members. The programs are reviewed by an independent organization, the Interior Design Continuing Education Council (see the box on facing page for more information).

Upon completion of the seminar, the designer participant completes forms that are forwarded to NCIDQ. Registering the completion of classes is

Private residence: living room. Charles Gandy, FASID, FIIDA, Charles Gandy, Inc., Atlanta, Georgia.
PHOTOGRAPH: ROGER WADE

especially necessary for designers who work in jurisdictions that require a certain number of CEUs per year to retain legal registration. Some employers require employees to register the course completion to obtain reimbursable funding.

Designers can take college-level classes to upgrade skills or add new knowledge areas. For example, it is not unusual for practitioners to take college-level business classes to obtain a master's degree or simply to increase their knowledge in specific areas of business. College-level classes might not be eligible to receive CEU credits, however.

CONTINUING EDUCATION UNITS (CEU)

Seminars are approved by the Interior Design Continuing Education Council (IDCEC). Core members of the Council are:

American Society of Interior Designers

Interior Designers of Canada

Interior Design Educators Council

International Interior Design Association

Representatives of the organizations review proposed seminars to ensure that they meet the standards and needs of the interior design professional. In this way, seminars and workshops at various skill and knowledge levels, given by experienced speakers, are the only programs that receive IDCEC approval. A large number of seminars have been approved since each member organization might have its own list of approved seminars. However, an interior designer may receive credit for the seminar regardless of the IDCEC organization that has offered the program. Seminars emphasize knowledge, skills, and competencies in a wide range of interior design practice knowledge.

Specific courses are approved in the areas of:

- Theory and creativity
- Interior design (such as design process, universal design, and space planning)
- Interior design education
- Design specialties
- Technical knowledge (such as lighting, acoustics, and textiles)

- Codes and standards
- Communication systems
- Business and professional practice
- Ethics
- History and culture

Educator

DENNIS MCNABB, FASID, IDEC
HOUSTON COMMUNITY COLLEGE SYSTEM
CENTRAL COLLEGE
HOUSTON, TEXAS

What is the single most important skill a designer needs to be successful?

❯ Communication.

What advice would you give someone who wants to be an interior designer?

❯ Do your homework concerning all aspects of the profession.

What is the purpose of your design program?

❯ To train the individual in as short a period of time as possible to become employed.

What are a few characteristics of a good student?

❯ Organization, focus, and determination.

How do you prepare students for the workforce?

❯ Provide them the technical skills needed to become employed in the profession.

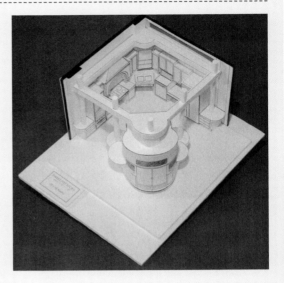

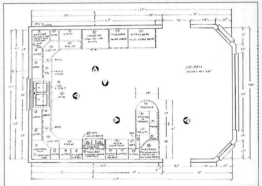

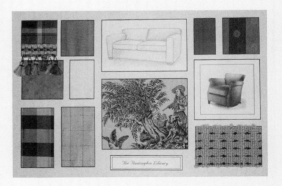

TOP RIGHT Model of barrier-free kitchen. Work by Bev Newman, Allied Member, ASID, former student at Houston Central Community College, Houston, Texas.

CENTER RIGHT Floor plan. Work by Bev Newman, Allied Member, ASID, former student at Houston Central Community College, Houston, Texas.

BOTTOM RIGHT Sample board. Work by Bev Newman, Allied Member, ASTD, former student at Houston Central Community College, Houston, Texas.

How important is certification by examination and licensing of interior designers today?

❭ I have mixed feeling about this question, but would have to say that for many aspects of interior design it is vital for the future of the profession.

Why did you become an interior designer?

❭ I have always wanted to create. I found early on that my talents led me to interior design. I have always had a passion for creating environments where people felt nurtured and appreciated the space.

Educator

SUE KIRKMAN, ASID, IIDA, IDEC
HARRINGTON INSTITUTE OF INTERIOR DESIGN
CHICAGO, ILLINOIS

What advice would you give someone who wants to be an interior designer?

❭ Find a very good school that specializes in curriculum based on industry needs and whose faculty comprises professionals in the field who have academic credentials.

What is the single most important skill a designer needs to be successful?

❭ Attention to and understanding of human behavior and people's needs and wants. The designer needs to be able to listen carefully, interpret the real needs and concerns, and then solve the issues.

What is the purpose of your design program?

❭ To educate students with a body of knowledge and level of experience that prepares them for above-entry-level positions in the design industry.

What are a few characteristics of a good student?

❭ Focus and good class preparation. Attention to detail in all things. Strong time management skills combined with team and individual skills.

How important is certification by examination and licensing of interior designers today?

❭ Because we deal with health and safety issues and issues that affect the human condition—how we move, feel, understand, function, and so on—it is important that interior designers have the education, experience, and training necessary to make those decisions.

Experimental design: steel table. Work by Pawel Witkowski, student at Harrington Institute of Interior Design, Chicago, Illinois.

Experimental design: double lounge chair with table. Work by Natalie Schebil, student at Harrington Institute of Interior Design, Chicago, Illinois.

How do you prepare students for the workforce?

❯ All students are required to take a minimum of 300 hours of approved internship along with a practicum course that works through job issues such as goal setting, preparing for the NCIDQ, professional organization, employment issues (sexual harassment, job interviewing, résumés, and working with clients). Students also take a portfolio class, which helps them define and refine their portfolio and customize it with technology.

Why did you become an interior designer?

❯ To use my creative response to interior space in a unique way; to solve problems for the client so as to enhance their use of an interior space; to fulfill a natural curiosity about how space is used.

Educator

STEPHANIE A. CLEMONS, PH.D., FASID, FIDEC
COLORADO STATE UNIVERSITY
FORT COLLINS, COLORADO

What has been your greatest challenge as an interior designer and faculty member?

❯ I love teaching very, very much. My students are absolutely fantastic and are amazingly caring individuals who work hard and design fulfilling spaces. They truly care about people, this earth, and future generations when they design. My greatest challenge has been working within the politics of a university setting. It is somewhat of a conundrum that creative designers position themselves in a hierarchical, structured setting. I've always chuckled at that fact.

Why did you become an educator?

❯ I think—like 99 percent of current design educators—that I fell into the career through a back door. I had practiced design (and enjoyed it very much), and had passed the NCIDQ, when the nearby university asked me to teach a design class. I loved using my creativity to shape how to better deliver information to the students. Each student has a different, three-dimensional story. I found that I enjoyed advising as much as teaching. I also discovered that teaching students is a real "high" for me. When we connect in a classroom, jointly enjoying the learning process and the topics under discussion, it is hard for me to "come down" for hours. My students are fantastic and their enthusiasm is infectious.

What is your design practice or research specialty?

❯ My research specialty is infusing interior design content into the K–12 grade levels.

What are a few characteristics of a good design student?

❯ Hardworking, caring about details, good communicator, creative, person of integrity, ethical, ability to visualize in three dimensions, team oriented, enjoys people.

How do you prepare students for the workforce?

❯ We offer our students the best education and resources we can provide, share the values of the profession, connect them with the top, networked design professionals in our nation, encourage them to take risks and reach out toward life rather than waiting for it to come to them.

What is the single most important skill an interior designer needs to be successful?

❯ Given that they can design, the skill of clear communication is essential. Graphic, oral, and written communication skills are critical.

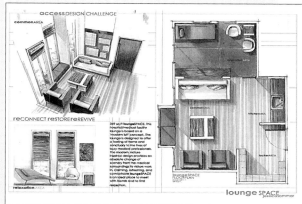

TOP RIGHT Three-dimensional computer drawing. Work by Joshua Brewinski, student at Department of Design and Merchandising, Colorado State University, Fort Collins, Colorado.

CENTER RIGHT Project drawings. Work by Jessica Sommer, student at Department of Design and Merchandising, Colorado State University, Fort Collins, Colorado.

BOTTOM RIGHT CAD image. Work by Sarah Fogarty, student at Department of Design and Merchandising, Colorado State University, Fort Collins, Colorado.

Commercial, Hospitality: Food and Beverage

CORKY BINGGELI, ASID
PRINCIPAL, INTERIOR DESIGNER
CORKY BINGGELI INTERIOR DESIGN
ARLINGTON, MASSACHUSETTS

What has been your greatest challenge as an interior designer?

❭ Because I have my own, one-person firm and work from a home office, I miss out on the exchange of information, feedback on design, and peer support that a larger office provides. After the BAC (Boston Architectural Center), I brought together a small group of designer friends to exchange job leads and talk about our work. I still keep in touch with these folks, and I also benefit from membership in ASID, which gives me a wide network of design relationships. I have also developed a close relationship with another designer, Christina Oliver, ASID; we share sources, sometimes do projects together, occasionally refer clients to each other, cover for each other on vacations, and generally enjoy our friendship and mutual support.

What led you to enter your design specialty?

❭ While I was at BAC, I became interested in restaurant design. Soon after leaving, I interviewed with someone who was opening a restaurant and wanted a student designer to do the design for free. I got the job, but also insisted on a modest fee. The project—the Iguana Cantina in Waltham, Massachusetts—was a success, and got quite a bit of publicity, mainly because of the 28-foot-long robotic iguana that I built with three of my friends. This led to other projects for the same and for other clients, and I was on my way.

What are your primary responsibilities and duties in your position?

❭ I pretty much do everything from marketing to designing, construction drawings, bookkeeping, and filing. My husband, Keith Kirkpatrick, helps me with a sideline, scheduling local artists to show their work at several of my client's restaurants. I teach one course per term, either at Wentworth Institute of Technology or at Mount Ida College. I have also written a book. *Building Systems for Interior Designers* (John Wiley & Sons, 2002).

What is the most satisfying part of your job?

❭ I love the types of projects and the clients with whom I get to work. They are mostly entrepreneurial owner/operators of restaurants, hair salons, and fitness centers, as well as hotel people. My relationships tend to be one-on-one with decision makers, and most of my clients are high-energy people who work hard and truly like other people. The projects tend to be creative, high visibility, and fast turnaround. Although I like

Retail: Linear Aveda Salon & Spa, Boston, Massachusetts. Corky Binggeli, ASID, Corky Binggeli Interior Design, Arlington, Massachusetts.
PHOTOGRAPH: GREGG SHUPE

working with people, I also need a lot of quiet time by myself, and the balance between client contact and the isolation of my design office is just right. And I get to pet my cat during breaks.

What is the least satisfying part of your job?

❯ The least satisfying part is sometimes having too much work and sometimes having not enough, or having clients be slow about paying. It is not fun to nag people for money.

What is the most important quality or skill of a designer in your specialty?

❯ Listening to what the clients say, both verbally and nonverbally, about their priorities and concerns. Although I am always happy to follow my own creative muse, I try to get my ego out of the way and really find out what the client is trying to achieve. I don't always go in exactly the direction a client might expect—they are paying me for my expertise and experience—but I do pay close attention to their conceptual and business concerns, and I explain my work in that light. Their business success is the basis of my future work, so I respect their perspective and budget.

Who or what experience has been a major influence in your career?

❯ I have known quite a few architects and designers who have their own firms, and find that they spend most of their time getting new work, massaging clients, managing employees, and administering their offices, while the actual design work gets done by someone else. Knowing that I wanted my own business, I was determined to structure it so that I would be doing my own design work. I have had employees before in other types of work, and I know I don't like hiring, managing, and firing people. I could possibly make more money working for a large firm, and could definitely take on larger projects as part of a larger team, but I prefer the flexibility and independence that comes with my do-everything approach.

Retail: Linear Aveda Salon & Spa, Boston, Massachusetts. Corky Binggeli, ASID, Corky Binggeli Interior Design, Arlington, Massachusetts.
PHOTOGRAPH: GREGG SHUPE

Hospitality: Appetito Restaurant, Boston, Massachusetts. Corky Binggeli, ASID, Corky Binggeli Interior Design, Arlington, Massachusetts.
PHOTOGRAPH: DOUGLAS STEFANOV

How Important Is Interior Design Education in Today's Industry?

> For a commercial or residential designer, a college degree is a must in today's market. With technology, global competition, and an international marketplace the skill sets provided by an accredited school are mandatory. We are moving faster than any of us thought possible and designers must stay abreast of the changes in technology and continue to understand the latest research and building code issues.
Mary Knopf, ASID, IIDA, LEED-AP

> Very, very, very important, and the right education too. Making sure it is CIDA-accredited and that you get a balanced knowledge of contract design, building and life safety codes, the latest technology, and a strong foundation in critical thinking.
Robin Wagner, ASID, IDEC

> Education for the interior designer is imperative today. No interior designer is hired by my firm for any position if they do not have or are not working on a degree in this field. I personally have a Bachelor of Science degree in this field, am NCIDQ-certified, have my specialty contractor's license for both residential and commercial, and take continuing education courses each year.
Debra Himes, ASID, IIDA

> Interior design education is very important. You need to learn all of the basics in college.
Rita Carson Guest, FASID

> I would not be a partner in an architecture firm without my interior design education. Design is complex, and it involves critical and analytical thinking.
Sandra Evans, ASID

> It is absolutely critical, and you've got to get it any way you can. I am a firm believer in ID education—formal, that is. But after that basic foundation (and then some experience and an NCIDQ certificate), you need to work with good mentors. Experience, experience. Practice, practice.
Bruce Brigham, FASID, ISP, IES

> Issues that designers deal with and the knowledge base required to understand them are growing. The complexity of the issues we work with is also increasing; therefore, a baseline of education is extremely important so you can hit the ground running. Education also gives you time to define a working style and methods of approaching the creative process.

I also cannot stress enough the importance of continuing education for all designers. Our knowledge base becomes obsolete at an ever-increasing rate. It must continue to evolve.
Sari Graven, ASID

> Education is very important. And continuing education is a must to ensure the professional is providing clients with the most up-to-date information. I cannot imagine the building industry without professional interior designers.
Jennifer van der Put, BID, IDC, ARIDO, IFMA

> Education is critical to readying the profession to meet the market needs. The interior design profession must embrace the importance of research and education to secure its position in the industry.
Linda Sorrento, ASID, IIDA, LEED-AP

❯ Education is more important than ever because the profession, and especially my specialty of healthcare, demands great technical knowledge as well as excellent communication and CAD skills.
Jain Malkin, CID

❯ As an educator, my bias is toward a CIDA-accredited interior design program education. It sets up the entry-level interior designer for success.
Stephanie Clemons, Ph.D., FASID, FIDEC

❯ Tremendously important. It's very labor intensive and expensive to train people. If a design firm has a choice of applicants for a position, they will choose the talented person with the best base of skills, knowledge of codes and materials. A good education saves training time and makes that person more immediately productive. The better the knowledge base, the more it gives a young designer an edge.
Sally Howard D'Angelo, ASID,
Affiliate Member AIA

❯ Education is the backbone of our industry.
Robert Wright, FASID

❯ Vital. It is imperative that we support accredited design programs and steer interested individuals toward CIDA schools. Decorators, specifiers, and would-be "designers" dilute the design world and bring down the field of interior design. We only hired designers with a comprehensive education that met CIDA standards. It just shouldn't be any other way. Get out there and get educated from an accredited interior design program. It made a world of difference in my life.
Annette Stelmack, Allied Member ASID

❯ Unfortunately, not important enough—it lost its role when we substituted space planning for design.
Neil Frankel, FAIA, FIIDA

❯ An interior design education in today's industry is crucial. I believe a structured education is essential to attaining a personal goal of advancement and to aiding in your credibility to others.
Linda Santellanes, ASID

❯ I can't stress the importance of qualified education to the future of the industry enough.
David Hanson, RID, IDC, IIDA

❯ Education provides us with knowledge and, hopefully, helps us develop wisdom. Education gives us the tools to be flexible—adaptable—able to meet new challenges and take advantage of

Restaurant: banquette. William Peace, ASID, Peace Design, Atlanta, Georgia.
PHOTOGRAPH: CHRIS A. LITTLE

new opportunities. That is what survival in today's industry is about.

M. Joy Meeuwig, IIDA

> Changing technology and today's fast-paced business climate have made it important to be educated in order to bring the very best products, techniques, and principles to clients.

Beth Kuzbek, ASID, IIDA, CMG

> Very important, with today's focus on licensing the professional, but as important is the quality of the education. *Professional* is a title. It's the knowledge or expertise the person has that differentiates between the professional and the decorator. A decorator's primary focus is on enhancing the aesthetics of an environment with colors, textures, and finishes. A professional interior designer does that and much more in the area of workplace productivity, safety, and efficiencies. The professional affects how people work.

Leonard Alvarado

> The ability to acquire basic knowledge skills lays the foundation to building a full career. Formal education in accredited interior design–focused programs is the only way to obtain this foundation. Without it, I do not believe that you can become a competent, qualified interior designer, no matter what your intended specialty is, or innate talents are.

David Stone, IIDA, LEED-AP

> Education is paramount—and to be able to apply the skills learned. Those who learn through experience may learn one task well but will not become innovative problem solvers. They only learn to become solution appliers—repeating responses learned from experience.

Linda Isley, IIDA

> Essential—not many more years are left for the nonprofessionals who just hang out their shingle. The public is becoming more and more aware that real designers have a design education.

Linda Kress, ASID

> Extremely important. I tell all students that, at minimum, they *must* graduate from a FIDER-accredited school with a bachelor's degree in interior design. An associate degree does not cut it anymore. (And I told this to students before I entered my current job in education.)

Lisa Whited, IIDA, ASID, IDEC, Maine CID

> Interior design education is very important to our industry and profession. The profession is demanding more and better prepared entry-level professionals with the expectation for significant internships, a worldview that has been informed by travel abroad, and a solid foundation of general educational studies as well as knowledge and application of design theory and principles.

Beth Harmon-Vaughn, FIIDA, Associate Member AIA, LEED-AP

> Extremely important; it is the future of design. The collaboration of all design disciplines starting in the early stage of design education will elevate our status with the public.

William Peace, ASID

> I believe it is very important. Fewer jobs are available in this economy, so competition among individuals pursuing jobs is very high. A solid, strong education is essential, with emphasis on both design and technical skills.

Susan B. Higbee

> The body of knowledge is growing so rapidly that I can't imagine it will be long before design services offered by people without education will not be valued.

Suzan Globus, FASID, LEED-AP

❯ Interior environments provide more than just shelter. Design is both life-enhancing and capable of being a healing art. As designers, we have the ability to design the stresses and irritations out of people's lives. The aesthetics are always important, and design education enhances our ability to create peaceful, functional spaces while attending to the philosophical and environmental safety issues facing us today.

Sally Thompson, ASID, Affiliate AIA

❯ I believe a minimum of four years is essential, as is ongoing education throughout our careers.

Janice Carleen Linster, ASID, IIDA, CID

❯ Education is imperative for the survival of the profession. Our responsibility as professionals is to protect the health, welfare and safety of the public. Understanding this starts through education. I am also an adjunct instructor at a university teaching interior design. That is how important I feel education is to our industry.

Kristin King, ASID

❯ The knowledge gained through structured interior design education is invaluable as the basis for any practitioner. However, because the interior design profession continues to evolve and expand, the interior design practitioner's education must not stop at graduation. With sources, processes, and code requirements in a constant state of evolution, the interior designer must make a commitment to lifelong education.

Linda Elliott Smith, FASID

❯ Education is of the utmost importance. Competition is fierce, and the better prepared one is, the more successful one will be. Education is another ticket in the lottery. The more tickets you have, the better your chances are to win.

Charles Gandy, FASID, FIIDA

❯ Interior design education is extremely important. This complicated profession has many aspects far beyond aesthetics. Codes, materials, workflow systems, controlling costs, and just the actual process of implementing a design complicate the process far more than ever before. Therefore, a good design education is a critical foundation for any person's success as an interior designer today.

M. Arthur Gensler Jr., FAIA, FIIDA, RIBA

❯ It is monumental. If we are to be a profession, we must have a consistent, quality educational program, ever changing and evolving as today's advances move faster and faster.

Donna Vining, FASID, IIDA, RID, CAPS

❯ Educating designers is crucial to the evolution of our profession in the next generation of designers. We finally are licensed in many states and have begun on the true path to professionalism. But we must forever shut the door on the uneducated designer's ability to design projects, especially commercial projects. The health, welfare, and safety of the public are at stake daily in the decisions we make, and uneducated designers undermine the credibility of our profession.

Juliana Catlin, FASID

❯ I think it is extremely important. Education gives you the grounding and building blocks for your career.

Laurie Smith, ASID

❯ Extremely! As mentioned already, the interior design industry is continually working on licensing, which is going to make qualifications stricter for designers in the years to come. Without proper education it is very difficult for young professionals to get a start in the field and increasingly difficult to achieve NCIDQ certification.

Shannon Ferguson, IIDA

> Important, but the professional societies need to build stronger bridges between them.
Michael Thomas, FASID

> It's extremely important to be educated and considered a professional. There have been too many people that have called themselves designers who have made horrible decisions and financially taken advantage of people. They have really affected the image of the profession.
Lisa Slayman, ASID, IIDA

> We need to increase our credibility by showing that interior designers "mean business" and have the education that supports the respect we should be getting.
Linda Isley, IIDA, CID

> It is critical to setting high standards for our profession. The passage of the NCIDQ exam is a must.
Patricia Rowen, ASID, CAPS

> Very. I also think the internship programs are so beneficial. I even volunteered to clean the offices of an architectural firm while at school.
Jo Rabaut, ASID, IIDA

> It's imperative. That's why CEUs are important to continue your education. The field is constantly changing and you need to keep current. I also go to home furnishing markets and K/BIS (the Kitchen/Bath Industry Show) to view current trends and products on a regular basis.
Susan Norman, IIDA

> Though somewhat responsive to industry and marketing demands, interior design education is critically important. The influence that interior design education has upon industry is not apparent in the short view, but over that long term, the influence that education has over practice is substantial.
James Postell, Associate Professor, University of Cincinnati

> I can't say enough that education is of most importance. Schools that go beyond to incorporate architecture and even industrial design into the program, along with a co-op experience, can set a firm foundation for a student's future.
Colleen McCafferty, IFMA, USGBC, LEED-CI

> I believe it creates a strong background for new designers. I probably would not consider a new candidate without a degree in interior design or architecture.
Jane Coit, Associate Member IIDA

> Critical. As technological data expands, so also does the client's need for professional expertise expand.
Marilyn Farrow, FIIDA

> Interior design education has changed in the last decade, but is not changing fast enough. In the real world, there are multiple perspectives and personality conflicts. Design students must learn to appreciate another point of view, be able to follow a plan, lead a team, resolve a dispute, or persuade the group to adopt an idea. These are skills that are difficult to teach and learn at the university level. While it is increasingly challenging to incorporate all aspects of design education into a four-year design education, business skills and classes are severely lacking from most programs. I make this statement having completed degrees in both the business and design. The following skill sets cross both degrees, but I believe show the need for business skills in the design world:

Design and creativity: Conceptualizing, problem solving, and marketing.

General business: Evaluating products and materials, making comparisons, performing punch lists and inspections, resolving ethical dilemmas, and acquiring technical computer skills such as Microsoft Excel, PowerPoint, and database management systems.

Accounting: Fee tracking, record keeping, bidding, budgeting, and cost estimating.

Public interaction: Communicating, presenting, marketing, and branding.

Management: Coordinating projects, supervising employees, understanding assets and liabilities, making thoughtful decisions, and saving the firm (and clients) money.
Laura Busse, IIDA, KYCID

❯ Designers make decisions every day that, if uninformed, can endanger the safety of the public. That makes a formal, college level education critical and an ongoing commitment on the part of the designer to continue learning throughout a career paramount.
Lindsay Sholdar, ASID

❯ More than ever industry is looking for trained interior designers. My background as an educated professional designer was the key to working at Knoll.
Lisa Henry, ASID

❯ Critical for two reasons: In order for the interior designer to be licensed, we need to analyze the current curriculum and the shortage of interior design educators.
Nila Leiserowitz, FASID, Associate Member AIA

❯ Education is more important than ever before in my eyes. As the specialization continues, designers will be required to be true "experts" in that area.

So many segments interact in any one project, products are evolving at a frenetic pace, and the knowledge of the public is increasing their level of expectation. Education also sets a standard for ethical and business practices. The public is not afraid to litigate, if they feel wronged.
Sharmin Pool-Bak, ASID, CAPS, LEED-AP

❯ With today's competition in the design industry, education is a valuable asset that a designer cannot afford to forgo. Today's information-savvy client has a high level of expectation which many times requires a designer to possess specific credentials. These credentials are available only through a learning institution offering a design certificate or degree.
Teresa Ridlon, Allied Member ASID

❯ Education is imperative. We look for designers that have graduated from CIDA-accredited programs or similar, and we have a preference for interior designers with no less than a four-year professional degree in interior design. Interior designers are required to provide documentation stating completion of approved college degree programs when applying for licensure to practice in certain states in the U.S. We look for designers that are qualified to take the NCIDQ exam and gain licensure in Minnesota—or have already accomplished both of these. In addition, we look for interior designers that have passed the LEED exam.
Rachelle Schoessler Lynn, CID, ASID, LEED-AP, Allied Member AIA

NOTES

1. Council for Interior Design Accreditation. 2006. "Professional Standards." http://www.accredit-id.org/profstandards.html.
2. National Council for Interior Design Qualification. 2008. "What is IDEP?" http://www.ncidq.org/idep/idepintro.htm.

3 Where the Jobs Are

Interior designers work in many different environments. Some work for a small firm with just a few others. Many designers find working in a larger interior design firm has advantages. You might even desire to join a retail store as a sales associate or designer. Although it is impossible to know for sure, a large percentage of interior designers are self-employed and work for themselves. One of the wonderful things about the interior design profession is that it offers many choices to suit many interests and abilities.

The work environment you choose should be one that will satisfy your interests and suit your personality. Many interior designers begin their careers in small firms, where they have the opportunity to learn about project and business management. Others prefer working in larger firms. They know that they might be small fish in a big sea, but the experience they receive will be valuable. Perhaps you hate to sell but love to design. In that case, small studios, which depend on the sale of merchandise for the bulk of their revenues, might not be a wise choice.

If interior design is your second career, you may feel more comfortable working on your own once you have gained some real-world experience by working for someone else. However, the opportunity to work as a sole practitioner should be approached somewhat cautiously. Because of the complexity of the interior design profession, it is unwise to begin a solo practice until you have experience. Working for someone else for a while helps you learn about the business side of the profession while you gain experience in design and working with clients. Additional information about business and project management is discussed in later chapters.

The options discussed in this chapter are by no means every conceivable work environment for the interior designer. These are both the most common types and the places that most entry-level interior designers find their first employment. By considering these options and the design specialties discussed in Chapter 4, you may find the combination that fits your goals as you begin your career as a professional interior designer.

INTERIOR DESIGN AND THE ECONOMY

Interior design has a major impact on the economy and has seen substantial growth. *Interior Design* magazine surveys the 100 largest design firms each year. This research report was started in 1978 and is reported in the January issue of the magazine. The survey results show much information concerning the giants and the impact of interior design and the work of these large design firms on the economy. The 2008 article compares information from the first report in 1978 and the present. For example, in 1978 the median value of goods and services was $10 million whereas the 2008 value is $289 million.[1] The current group of 100 firms reported total professional fees of over $2.4 billion and nearly 11,000 members of the design staff.[2] Compare this to the January 2003 issue, where the giant 100 firms reported total professional fees of nearly $1.4 billion.[3]

In addition to those who work at the large design firms, there are many small interior design businesses with five or fewer employees, and sole practitioners.There are also many interior designers working in allied areas of the built environment industry such as salespeople in retail specialties such as furniture or lighting fixture stores. Given so many ways to practice in this field, it is easier to gauge their numbers by how many interior designer practitioners are affiliated with recognized associations. Even that number is not accurate, however, as many professional interior designers choose to stay unaffiliated.

According to the U.S. Department of Labor Bureau of Labor Statistics (www.bls.gov), the occupation label *interior designer* represented over 50,000 jobs in late 2005 compared to 30,000 in 2001.[4] The ASID reports that approximately 55,000 interior designers practice in the United States.[5] The median annual earnings for interior designers as reported by the Bureau of Labor Statistics were $47,000 in 2005. The lowest 10 percent earned less than $23,800 and the highest 10 percent earned over $75,800.[6] The statistics presented in the January 2008 "Interior Design 100 Giants" issue of *Interior Design* were higher. The median annual salary for principals and partners was $142,000, designers $65,000, and other billable design staff made $48,000. [7]

Notes

1. Judith Davidson. 2008. "30 Years—Interior Design Giants." *Interior Design*, January, 118.

2. Davidson, 2008. "30 Years—Interior Design Giants," 118–162.

3. Judith Davidson. 2003. "Interior Design Giants." *Interior Design*, January, 139–158.

4. U.S. Department of Labor, Bureau of Labor Statistics. 2007, May. Occupational Employment Statistics: Occupation Identification number 27-1025. www.bis.gov.

5. American Society of Interior Designers (ASID). 1998. ASID Fact Sheet: Economic Impact of the Interior Design Profession. Washington, D.C.

6. U.S. Department of Labor, Bureau of Labor Statistics, 2007, May. Occupational Employment Statistics: Occupation Identification number 27-1025.

7. Davidson, 2008. "30 Years—Interior Design Giants," 162.

Light Commercial and Residential

SALLY HOWARD D'ANGELO, ASID, AFFILIATE AIA
PRINCIPAL, S. H. DESIGNS
WINDHAM, NEW HAMPSHIRE

What has been your greatest challenge as an interior designer?

❯ It's a wide-open field with many specialized possibilities, all of which take many years to learn. The greatest challenge for me is to decide on that specialty. The desire to explore new types of challenging projects in different specialties causes me to continually reach. This keeps my creative juices flowing, but the design process is not as systematized and, therefore, less profitable. The more practical course requires a designer to develop expertise and efficiency in a specialized area of work. Owning my own firm allows me to control the mix. I try to do a little of each.

What led you to enter your design specialty?

❯ I like to assess the problem, design the solution, and implement the design. I chose to run my own business because I wanted to follow the project straight through, from contract to final payment. In order to control the whole process, I take on small to medium-size projects that can be easily managed from start to finish. I like the efficiency of commercial design process because the budget and time frame are exact and decisions are made quickly. Functionality and increased productivity are often the main objective, with a change in image as the exciting by-product. I also like to work with residential clients who want to realize a better solution to an existing problem and are personally involved. Those are slower projects that require a large amount of client input but result in creative, synergistic solutions.

Teacher's lounge: Central Catholic High School, Lawrence, Massachusetts. Sally Howard D'Angelo, ASID, S. H. Designs, Windham, New Hampshire.

PHOTOGRAPH: BILL FISH

TOP Private residence: master bath remodel. Sally Howard D'Angelo, ASID, S. H. Designs, Windham, New Hampshire.
PHOTOGRAPH: BILL FISH

LEFT Nesmith Library: Children's Theater, Windham, New Hampshire. Sally Howard D'Angelo, ASID, S. H. Designs, Windham, New Hampshire.
PHOTOGRAPH: BILL FISH

What is the most satisfying part of your job?

❯ Presenting a creative and functional solution to a client who could have never thought of that possibility before is worth all of the work. I am the momentary hero.

What is the least satisfying part of your job?

❯ I get the least satisfaction from a cookie-cutter design. It takes time to develop a really creative solution, and sometimes I am not given that time. It's hard to discipline myself to stop designing.

What is the most important quality or skill of a designer in your specialty?

❯ As a small business owner, assuming you are already a talented designer, you have to enjoy people and constantly be willing to get involved with them. Whether working in the commercial or residential market, you need to be cognizant of the client's ultimate goal for the project, how it will add value to the business or home and improve the lifestyle of the family or function of the business. You need to solicit and document that goal and design toward that end.

Who or what experience had been a major influence in your career?

❯ My professional association, ASID, has played a major role in my professional development. It gave me extensive education and training in all areas of the business and design world. I've traveled throughout the country, served on many boards of directors, and discussed topics of every kind on behalf of the association. The more involved I became, the more I got out of it. It opened many doors to me throughout my career, and I've met talented associates of every kind who took the time to help and mentor me.

Career Decisions

There are many decisions you will face as you begin determining where you want to work in the profession. Deciding to work in residential or commercial interior design—and any specific specialty—is one career decision. Are you interested in the design of private residences or maybe hotels, hospitals, libraries, offices, or facilities for senior living? Although the process of designing these different spaces is the same, the requirements to create a functional interior for each are different and will affect this aspect of your career decision.

The type of firm you wish to work at is another decision that you must make. Some firms are unlikely to be open to entry-level designers. Others will welcome them to their staff. Before looking at specific work environments, let's discuss general factors you should consider.

One of these general considerations is the size of the company. First are sole practitioners, working alone or with an assistant. A sole practitioner may occasionally utilize a student intern and some do find a part-time assistant helpful. Next are the small firms—those with 10 or fewer total employees. Medium-sized firms have between 10 and 25 employees. Large interior design firms have between 25 and 50 employees. Multidisciplinary firms that offer a combination of interior design, architecture, engineering, and landscape architecture services may have well over a hundred employees.

There are certain advantages in working for a small- or medium-sized firm. These kinds of firms generally can give you a broader range of experiences, especially at the beginning of your employment, than any type of large firm can. Employees of small- or medium-sized firms handle many parts of a project because fewer people are available in the company to take on the responsibilities. The owner or principal of the firm may involve you in projects quickly, giving you experiences you might not have expected at once. Naturally, this means that the skills you bring to the firm need to be of high quality.

Large firms can offer broad experience, but at a distance. In a very large firm, it is not just a cliché that all you may get to do for the first year is some small, repetitive task such as selecting materials palettes. In a large firm, it takes more time for the entry-level designer to be given major project responsibility unless the individual has exceptional talents or experience. In some large firms, entry-level designers are not hired at all or work only as assistants to senior interior designers. The pressure to be productive and generate a large number of billable hours can be stressful for entry-level interior designers working in firms where this is critical to the performance evaluation of the design professional staff.

Compensation options are another general consideration. Compensation is not high in interior design in comparison to many other professions. The information in "Interior Design and the Economy" (page 100) clarifies this important issue. If the firm generates revenue by charging for services, the interior design staff is generally paid a set salary. An interior design firm that also sells furniture or a retail store with an interior design department often pays designers based on commission or possibly some combination of a small salary plus commission. This means you are paid based on the amount of furniture and other products you sell to the client rather than a salary. Being paid a commission provides the opportunity for higher total personal income than when paid a salary. Commission compensation comes with a risk; that is, you must continually sell merchandise in order to earn that commission. It takes time for many people to gain sufficient skills in selling to clients in order to make commission compensation actually beneficial.

Small firms can have their disadvantages. The compensation can be lower. This means the pay as well as employee benefits such as healthcare, retirement, profit-sharing, and the like, may be less or nonexistent. A small firm may not be able to pay for your NCIDQ and other professional association fees and dues—even though they encourage employees to take the exam and hold memberships. Larger firms encourage their employees to take the NCIDQ examination and often pay for continuing education seminars and workshops. Depending on many factors, the design reputation of a small firm generally remains close to home and may also mean limited travel opportunities for work in a different location.

Keep in mind that you must learn what it is like to work in whatever type of firm and specialty you enter. This is often referred to as paying your dues—which is different, of course, from paying dues to an association. Regardless of size, most firms will not let an entry-level designer work alone with a client. You must be patient, learning and gaining experience so that your employer will grow comfortable with turning you loose with a client.

As you plan your professional goals, keep in mind that you need to look for compatible colleagues and the opportunity to learn and grow to keep motivated. If you want to gain a quick reputation or work for a prestigious firm, you need to plan your work experiences to carefully build skills that will be favored by the large multidisciplinary firms. If your goal is to have your own small practice one day, many types of firms and specialties will be appropriate work environments in which you can acquire skills and knowledge to help you when you open yours. As you discover what you want from the profession, you can determine where to go for a position that will lead you toward your ultimate goals.

Finding a Place in Commercial Interior Design

SHANNON MITCHENER

LEED-AP, ALLIED MEMBER ASID, ASSOCIATE IIDA

GRADUATE, UNIVERSITY OF AKRON

DESIGN SPECIALTY: COMMERCIAL INTERIOR DESIGN

MATRIX A.E.P

TULSA, OKLAHOMA

How did you choose which school to attend to obtain your education in interior design? What degrees do you possess?

❯ I made my school selection based first and foremost on whether or not it was a FIDER/CIDA-accredited program. The Colorado State University (CSU) design program also incorporated construction classes through the construction management program (one of the top-ranked programs in the nation). I felt this was a very important element in my education in order to understand the logic of the built environment. Their design program also integrated diligent hand-sketching, technical training in CAD and 3D software, extensive research in classes to understand the programming side of design, as well as outreach experiences, which made it easy for me to select CSU. I graduated cum laude in May 2006 with a Bachelor of Science in Interior Design.

What was your greatest challenge as a student?

❯ I know one of my greatest challenges as a student was construction detailing, especially custom-designed millwork, custom walls, and water features. These architectural features were designed through creative vision alone, no budget restrictions or material limitations. It is very challenging as a student to look at a "Graphic Standards" detail, understand how a typical would be built in reality, and then attempt to customize those details without truly knowing the

components necessary to carry out your vision. This is a process that I have found to be much easier in a collaborative work environment.

How did you choose the firm that you are working for?

❯ I have always been set on working for a full-scale firm that blended architects, designers, and engineers together in a collaborative setting. I am interested in every aspect of the built environment and I have been very fortunate to work with experienced professionals in virtually every avenue of design. I have learned so much by having the opportunity to ask questions about any discipline I don't understand. I learn something new every day, and I appreciate the knowledge that my coworkers can teach me.

What has been your greatest challenge in your first years of employment?

❯ My greatest challenge as a young designer has also been the thing I love most about my job. With each project, we are challenged to satisfy actual clients. During school, our assignments provided us with a proposed programming checklist, if you will, and for the most part, if we were satisfied with the outcomes and met each requirement outlined in the program, our project was a success.

Being able to truly interpret a client's programming requirements is vital. Oftentimes, our client thinks they know what they need, but once we look at a certain function they are trying to accomplish, a completely different solution can be developed for them, which may work much better than what they had before. There are also many times when their program is a wish list that cannot be accommodated due to budget limitations or spatial constraints. It is our job to look outside the outline of a program and accommodate their needs in creative ways through the function they need, rather than items they request, and I learn this each passing day on a project.

Are you planning to take the NCIDQ exam if you have not already? Why or why not?

❭ Yes, I am planning on taking the NCIDQ within the next year or two. I feel as young professionals in this field, the NCIDQ provides us with a sense of achievement no one else can claim unless they themselves have passed the exam. This allows not only other professionals, but the public as well, to realize our line of work requires education, experience, and skill that not everyone possesses.

Did you join the student chapter of ASID or IIDA at your school? Why?

❭ Yes, I was extremely active in both the CSU student ASID chapter and the state ASID chapter. I joined the student chapter in my freshman year and became a publicity chairperson at that time, which lasted through my sophomore year. In my junior year, I was the 2006 ASID Student Rep to the Board of Colorado, as well as a Committee Chairperson for the Colorado Chapter's community service project and the Student Affairs committee. ASID will continue to serve as a vital connection for me as I continue my journey as an emerging professional in the field of design. More recently, I have joined the Texas–Oklahoma chapter of IIDA, which has allowed me to get involved with community efforts and networking opportunities, which I am extremely excited to continue.

As a student, both organizations are wonderful to get involved with, and I owe both the Colorado ASID chapter and National ASID chapter headquarters many thanks for their contributions to my design journeys thus far.

How important do you feel an internship is to a student's educational experience?

❭ It's extremely beneficial. My internship allowed me the opportunity to learn how to do design work on actual projects and real budgets, as well as work in a collaborative environment with both architects and engineers. This taught me a tremendous amount about the design process, mechanical systems, constructability, and the list goes on. It also allows students the chance to experience various areas of design and select the specialization they may want to pursue. My internship was also the first time I was exposed to current product materials, finishes, furniture, and fixtures. Many interns will be responsible for the materials library, which is a task I was grateful for, among many others. It allowed me the opportunity to meet reps in the industry and gain new product information that is typically not given in many school settings. The networking I established during my internship was also the key in landing me my first and second job.

Independent Design Firms

An independent interior design firm—also called a *studio*—is probably the most common type of work environment open to the interior designer. In this situation, the owner or owners are free to focus on any specialty, providing design services while specifying and perhaps selling products to their chosen client target market. Independent firms can be of any size, from a sole practitioner working alone to a very large company with numerous employees. They can be highly specialized, working with only one type of client such as high-end residential interiors, or a generalist, providing services to two or more design specialties, such as a firm that does small hotels and restaurants and also designs office spaces.

These firms often conduct business as a *designer/specifier*—that is, they plan and specify the merchandise for the project, but do not sell the goods to the client. The designer/specifier provides the interior design services described in all phases of the design project process discussed in Chapter 5 except for many of the tasks in the contract administration phase. Clients of such firms may buy the goods themselves from independent suppliers or use a competitive bid process to purchase the needed goods and installation services.

Other independent design firms choose to sell merchandise as well as provide interior design services. Commercial interior designers tend to be of the designer/specifier type; residential interior designers commonly sell merchandise to their clients as well as provide interior design services. The difference affects many aspects of the organization and management of the firm, regardless of its size, and it very well may affect your choice of work environment. For example, it is very important for designers in the designer/specifier work environment to bill as much as 90 percent of their work time to clients since the revenue for the firm comes primarily from fees.

Working for a small independent interior design studio, with a limited number of employees, has an important advantage: You are generally given more direct project responsibility faster than your entry-level colleagues who work in larger firms. Of course, entry-level interior designers always work under the direction of the owner in a small firm, as do entry-level designers working in a large firm. Depending on the reputation and experience of the owner, projects in a small independent firm might not be as large and exciting as those that come to large firms. Others would argue that working in a small firm specializing in high-end residential interiors, for example, can be very exciting if the firm is consistently able to obtain large projects. Whether the projects are large or small, small firms are great places to gain experience.

It is important to make note that the owner (of a small firm) or the design director (in larger firms) is instrumental in determining what goes out the door. The project work done by other designers is often scrutinized and reflects the owner's personal style or style developed by the firm. Understanding this work environment issue is important because your design ideas can be vetoed by senior designers, which can be difficult for designers who want to decide the concepts and solutions of a project.

For a designer/specifier firm, the interior design staff is commonly paid a set salary. Some of the compensation for interior designers working in a firm that also sells merchandise results from commission on the goods sold to the client. If you are paid a salary, you are paid that set amount regardless of the hours you work. If a commission is paid as part of your compensation, then the amount paid will vary quite a bit from paycheck to paycheck. More income can be generated from a commission-based compensation package. However, more risk is entailed. It will take time to develop selling skills and a client base to reach an effective commission level that matches a straight salary.

Independent design firms of any size look for employees with experience and education in the overall design process. Background in the specialty of the design firm (hospitality projects, for example) is also valuable. Experience with CAD, the ability to handle multiple tasks, and an understanding of project management are additional skills expected in any size independent design firm. Depending on the size of the firm, it may take up to two years or more in order for you to be given full project responsibility.

High-End Residential and Commercial

ROBERT WRIGHT, FASID

OWNER, BAST/WRIGHT INTERIORS, INC.

SAN DIEGO, CALIFORNIA

Private residence: entry. Robert Wright, FASID, Bast/Wright Interiors, San Diego, California.

PHOTOGRAPH: BRADY ARCHITECTURAL PHOTOGRAPHY

What is the most important quality or skill of a designer in your specialty?

❯ Listening with a sixth sense and correctly interpreting the client's needs. It is difficult for some clients to communicate when it comes to an area so subjective and personal as aesthetics and design.

What has been your greatest challenge as an interior designer?

❯ I challenge myself and my design staff to always place the client's needs front and center. Have we listened? Have we responded with the right solution? Have we exceeded the initial project goals? I want a satisfied client.

What led you to enter your design specialty?

❯ An evolution in my career brought me to the residential specialty. Residential interior design allows me to tap into my client in the most personal way. I know that a well-functioning and aesthetically pleasing home can change one's outlook on all aspects of life.

What are your primary responsibilities and duties?

❯ I own the design firm. I am responsible for overseeing the administrative operations as well as knowing what is happening with all of the client work. The majority of my days are spent dealing with the client. I spend a lot of time on the telephone and on the freeways.

Who or what experience has been a major influence on your career?

❯ Several people have had a major influence on me. My first boss, Hester Jones, taught me 80 percent of what I still do today. This includes all aspects of business as well as how to work with people and how to put together a proper design presentation. She exposed me to ASID, which has been the common thread throughout my career. My second job, with Nevelle Lewis and Associates, exposed me to design refinement and project management. I also had the highest respect for my boss, Larry Herr, at Parron Hall Interiors. He held all his employees in the highest regard with the utmost in respect.

I started my career in Houston, Texas, during the late-1970s oil boom. Internationally known architects and designers were all doing projects in Texas. I was exposed to the best of design at a very good time in my career.

Travel is imperative, too. I make it a point to travel for both business and pleasure. Everywhere I go contributes to design details that can be incorporated into projects. A good designer needs to make it a point to go to markets and seminars to stay aware of what is happening in our industry.

What is the most satisfying part of your job?

❯ It is twofold—seeing a project finish with both an incredibly pleased client and a healthy profit margin.

What is the least satisfying part of your job?

❯ When I do not have a good balance between client work and administrative duties as an owner of the firm.

TOP Commercial headquarters: typical workstation. Robert Wright, FASID, with Kellie McCormick, ASID, Bast/Wright Interiors, San Diego, California.
PHOTOGRAPH: BRADY ARCHITECTURAL PHOTOGRAPHY

ABOVE Commercial headquarters: office park. Robert Wright, FASID, with Kellie McCormick, ASID, Bast/Wright Interiors, San Diego, California.
PHOTOGRAPH: BRADY ARCHITECTURAL PHOTOGRAPHY

What Motivated You to Start Your Own Design Firm?

> At the time I began my own firm, I had been in a partnership, following a number of experiences working for several types of design entities. I became pregnant, the partnership ended, and I was faced with the opportunity to work on my own. The timing was right for me because I could spend time with our son during his early years. Given my experience in building and managing the partnership, I had the tools and skills to begin building my own business.

Terri Maurer, FASID

> When I first began design classes, I knew I would start my own design firm and felt it was only a matter of time and experience before I actually set the wheels in motion. It was just an innate desire to build something that would be successful.

Greta Guelich, ASID

> I basically like to build things, and working for someone else did not offer that opportunity. Also, running my own design firm allowed the flexibility I needed to raise my family.

Debra Himes, ASID, IIDA

> I became my own boss because I had to move from state to state because of my husband's career opportunities. It is difficult to develop seniority at a firm while moving around but easy to gain varied experience that facilitates development of comprehensive knowledge beneficial to a consulting practice.

Marilyn Farrow, FIIDA

> One of the wonderful aspects of interior design is our ability to evolve professionally. For many years, I was an employee in firms from small to international. I have now decided to be a sole practitioner and have opened my own design firm. Although I still team with others when needed, I am enjoying the freedom of being self-employed at this point in my career. Isn't it wonderful that we have so many opportunities in so many specialties—healthcare, hospitality, retail, corporate, residential, government—as well as in the formatting of our business?

Barbara Nugent, FASID

> I started my own firm for two reasons: In 1968, there wasn't a design firm in my market that allowed a designer to provide professional services rather than purvey a product, and I wanted to be able to integrate my professional life with my family life.

M. Joy Meeuwig, IIDA

> I started my own practice in the interest of seeking new opportunities. I wanted to be able to move beyond the safety of employment at a thriving firm and steer my own course toward success. I wanted to leverage my unique set of skills and have the ability to take projects that I felt stretched my ability and made me a better designer, businesswoman, and member of a profession with which I am proud to associate.

Lindsay Sholdar, ASID

> I never wanted to be a business owner.

Beth Harmon-Vaughn, FIIDA, Associate AIA, LEED-AP

> What motivated me to start my own design firm was the opportunity to design what I wanted to design, to have some control over my environment, to have some flexibility, and to receive some tax relief and company benefits.

Linda Santellanes, FASID

> I was motivated to start my own firm after being laid off several times. I observed how volatile the large firms can be. I decided that I wanted creative control over projects and the flexibility that owning your own firm allows. It is the thinking that "I can do it better than others" and that you have the confidence to make it happen.

Laurie Smith, ASID

> Creative freedom, accountability, income, being nimble as a designer.
Kristin King, ASID

> We moved to a rural county in Michigan of approximately 50,000 people. I needed to create my own work to be employed in this area of the state.
Patricia Rowen, ASID, CAPS

> As with many designers, I turned to interior design from a prior career that no longer suited my needs. My choice of business ownership was partly a result of my semirural location and family situation and partly a desire to control my own choice of projects and a need to control my own time.
Sally Howard D'Angelo, ASID, Affiliate Member AIA

> I was looking for a change in employment and rather than move to a different firm, I decided it was time to try to having my own business.
David Hanson, RID, IDC, IIDA

> The residential designer who took me on as an intern strongly encouraged me to step out and do it. As strenuous as it is—and it is greatly strenuous—it tapped into an unknown entrepreneurial drive for independence I never thought I had. It completely changed me into a person of great faith in provision and fulfillment beyond my own capacity.
Keith Miller, ASID

> Ah—the desire for freedom, mostly. I knew I could do it—and had financial backing—and felt it was time for me to work the days I wanted, the hours I wanted, and create the designs with my name on it where I wanted, when I wanted, how I wanted. Yes, it's all about me.
Marilizabeth Polizzi, Allied Member ASID

> Probably independent nature.
Drue Lawlor, FASID

> Freedom and responsibility to design motivated me to start my own design firm.
James Postell, Associate Professor, University of Cincinnati

> I thought it would be fun. I thought that was the natural progression for me personally. I had worked in a retail setting and left it to move to a design studio setting. For me, the studio was basically a sole practice with my income going to support someone else's studio. The particular situation I was in did not have much support in the way of office staff, assistant, and the like. There was purchasing and an inventory of samples, but in my mind that did not, and still does not, offset the fact I was required to do all the functions I do in my sole practice.
Sharmin Pool-Bak, ASID, CAPS, LEED-AP

> While working at a kitchen showroom, I was given the opportunity to complete the design and accessorizing of a Viking appliance distributorship. After solely designing kitchens for four years, my passion for doing complete residential projects was ignited. Before venturing out on my own, I decided to work for an interior design firm. I did not always embrace their design philosophy; therefore, after a few months and with the encouragement of prospective clients, I decided to start my own practice. I've been in business now for five years and have been very fortunate in that all of my work is referral-based.
Teresa Ridlon, Allied Member ASID

> My kids. I needed more flexibility than what a traditional firm could offer.
Maryanne Hewitt, IIDA

> Being in charge and total control of every aspect of the business.
Sue Norman, IIDA

Architectural Offices

Many architectural firms offer interior design services to their clients. The larger the firm, the more likely it has an interior design department. In most cases, the interior designers work on projects related to the work of the architectural firm. In a larger architectural office, interior design services are often a separate service offering. This means that projects may be obtained without a connection to the architectural department.

Interior design positions in architectural offices vary with the size of the firm. Interior designers seeking direct project responsibility are likely to find that architectural offices require at least a few years of professional experience before hiring an interior designer for the staff. It is, of course, always possible that an individual with exceptional talent can obtain an entry-level position with a small- to medium-sized architectural firm. The large multidisciplinary firms more often hire experienced designers to be in charge of projects. When they hire entry-level designers, the hiring is often offered as an assistant to the senior designers. Assistants commonly are involved in materials specification, drafting various project details such as cabinet drawings, or other portions of a project. They can also be involved in preparing necessary paperwork and otherwise supporting senior designers while learning the actual work of the designers at the firm. Of course, the entry-level designer is expected to work as a member of a team, know CAD, and be able to handle multiple tasks.

In both architectural and interior design firms, senior designers—also called *project designers*— create the ideas and direction of the whole project. A senior interior designer also supervises other designers, leading a team to complete all the documents necessary for a project. The senior designer is also the primary contact with the client—attending meetings, taking phone calls, negotiating concepts, and generally keeping the client informed of the progress of the project. If you begin working in an architectural firm, you will be given project design responsibility and the opportunity to work directly with clients only after you have proven your design and project management skills. Once again, depending on the size of the firm, this may take two or more years.

The architectural firm most commonly generates revenue from services only. For this reason, the productivity of an interior designer is very important. It is common for designers in an architectural firm to be responsible for billing 90 or even 100 percent of their time. Being slow and methodical—as an entry-level designer might be—is not considered productive. Because revenues come from billable hours and services, designers are commonly paid a salary. Depending on the firm, additional benefits might include health insurance, payment of professional dues, and reimbursement for continuing education seminars.

Commercial Banking, Education, Healthcare, and High-End Residential

SANDRA EVANS, ASID

PRINCIPAL, KNOELL & QUIDORT ARCHITECTS

PHOENIX, ARIZONA

What has been your greatest challenge as an interior designer?

❯ My greatest challenge as an interior designer is to write a program that interprets my clients' needs and dreams. After the program is written, the challenge is to educate them with sensitivity to the budget and their own knowledge or lack thereof concerning appropriate interior design for the project.

What led you to enter your design specialty?

❯ The roots of architecture at our firm are in residential design. While a great many of our projects are in commercial, banking, educational, healthcare, and industrial facilities, we still are extremely involved in private residences.

What are your primary responsibilities and duties?

❯ They involve space planning, establishing a concept (style, period, color), designing furniture, specifying furnishings and finishes, and coordinating efforts between the owners, contractors, and vendors.

What is the most satisfying part of your job?

❯ The most satisfying part of my job is when clients tell me my work has had a profound effect on their lifestyle.

What is the least satisfying part of your job?

❯ The least satisfying part of my work is selecting accessories and designing window coverings.

What is the most important quality or skill of a designer in your specialty?

❯ The most important quality of a designer is to listen to the clients and keep an open mind regarding their opinions about what they want

Private residence: living room. Sandra Evans, ASID, Knoell & Quidort Architects, Phoenix, Arizona.

PHOTOGRAPH: JIM CHRISTY

Private residence: great room and kitchen. Sandra Evans, ASID, Knoell & Quidort Architects, Phoenix, Arizona.

when it does not relate to the architecture. Diplomacy requires knowledge and patience. I try to educate my clients without insulting their aesthetic sensibility. For example, in designing liturgical furniture, it is critical to create elements that are dynamic to celebrate the worship service.

Who or what experience has been a major influence on your career?

❯ My experience with Knoell & Quidort Architects, and especially the work and integrity of Hugh Knoell and Phil Quidort, has been the inspiring and major influence on my career.

Retail Design

JOHN MCLEAN, RA

PRINCIPAL AND DESIGN DIRECTOR

JOHN MCLEAN ARCHITECT/

ARCHITECTURE & INDUSTRIAL DESIGN

WHITE PLAINS, NEW YORK

What has been your greatest challenge as an interior designer?

❯ Retail design is a challenge because it involves skill and talent in three primary areas of human endeavor: quality, cost, and schedule. Retail design is programmatically comprehensive. It involves the integration of architecture, spatial composition,

lighting, display and store fixture design, point-of-sale graphics, and graphic and store signage design.

Because I am also an industrial designer, I am educated to design and think in terms of mass production/prototypical design solutions. These design solutions often are then related to a variety of sites, such as shopping malls, strip malls, small town/urban storefronts, and boutiques. Keeping this variety in mind, a dynamic frame is created through which I enter to meet these challenges.

Why did you become an interior designer?

❯ It is a natural outgrowth of my architecture and industrial design practice. I view projects holistically. This type of design is best called

Commercial retail: The Electronics Boutique, Woodbridge Center, Woodbridge, New Jersey. John Mclean, RA, AIA, White Plains, New York.

comprehensive design. The comprehensive design approach gives all aspects of the space program the look of a natural flow and fit—that is, from architecture to the interior design to the landscaping.

What led you to enter your design specialty?

❯ Store design has been part of my psyche since childhood. The purpose of retail design is to entice or seduce a person to enter the store and then to create an atmosphere conducive to "yes" in making a purchase.

I remember the Bohack supermarket storefront design of my childhood. The façade was constructed of cream-colored porcelain enamel metal panels with the name Bohack in red, raised in relief, on the panels. Of historic note is the fact that Gordon Bunschaft of SOM designed this store.

Supermarkets did not have a general reputation for design quality prior to the 1980s. Therefore, when the opportunity arose for the office that I was formerly associated with to design a supermarket, I was already primed to meet the challenge. I am proud to be credited with heading this team.

Commercial retail: The Electronics Boutique, Woodbridge Center, Woodbridge, New Jersey. John Mclean, RA, AIA, White Plains, New York.

What are your primary responsibilities and duties?

❯ I am the principal in charge and director of design.

What is the most satisfying part of your job?

❯ The most satisfying part of my professional life is having the opportunity to use the creative talents for which I have been trained. Being able to successfully meet the challenge presented by a project is a great reward.

What is the least satisfying part of your job?

❯ The best way to answer this is to acknowledge that good design has to be supported by economic viability. It is very important, therefore, for a professional to treat his or her practice as if it is an ongoing project where the parameters of quality, schedule, and cost are balanced.

What is the most important quality or skill of a designer in your specialty?

❯ The most important quality and skill expressed by a designer should be to constantly strive

to bring a fresh point of view to each project. Prototypical design can translate into variations on a theme rather than static repetition. This was the practice I followed in creating the Electronics Boutique stores. The result was distinct but recognizable store designs.

Who or what experience has been a major influence in your career?

❯ Frank Lloyd Wright, who taught that design matters in the life of a person and a community; Mies van der Rohe, who practiced as a comprehensive designer of commercial environments and brought the aesthetics of architecture and design to the corporate world; Eero Saarinen, who kept the principles of the modern movement alive and showed that there is more than styling in linking architecture and design; and Louis Kahn, for his poetic approach to design.

Furniture Retailers

Another common work environment for the interior designer is the furniture retailer. Many furniture retailers sell furniture to the consumer such as Ethan Allen, Inc., and through department stores such as Macy's. Department stores may also have interior designers working out of the furniture department. Those that sell the high-priced, high-quality products directly to the residential consumer make available interior designers to assist the consumer with needed design services. This is an attractive work environment for many professional interior designers interested in the residential specialties. Job opportunities in the interior design departments of department stores and other furniture and specialty stores are excellent places for the entry-level designer to get started in the profession. For the most part, however, entry-level individuals will work as assistants to more experienced designers in the furniture or specialty store.

Experienced interior designers working in a retail furniture store or in some department store environments generally have assistants who are entry-level interior designers. Because few retailers are willing to let young, inexperienced interior designers work with clients, these design assistants help the senior designers produce sketches, draft floor plans, and develop color schemes. In this way, they learn valuable lessons about the work expected of designers in furniture stores and working with clients. Interior designers in large retail and department stores also have access to office assistance for help with some of the paperwork.

In many ways, the interior designers in stores function like small studios or even sole practitioners. The goal of the interior designer working in the retail store, however, is to sell the products offered by the store rather than items otherwise available in the market. In some companies, the designer cannot sell anything other than what is normally handled by the store. This is an important difference between working in an independent interior design studio and working in a retail furniture store.

Compensation is commonly by means of a small salary, with the bulk of compensation being paid based on commission related to the sale of merchandise. Many retailers do not charge a design fee for interior design services, so the entire revenue generated by the design staff is based on the sale of merchandise. For an interior designer to succeed in this work environment, she or he should be comfortable with recommending purchases. Because interior design assistants are generally not responsible for selling merchandise, they are compensated by some salary and perhaps a small commission.

Law office: Alston & Bird LLP, hallway. Rita Carson Guest, FASID, Carson Guest, Inc., Atlanta, Georgia.
PHOTOGRAPH: GABRIEL BENZUR

Working for a Manufacturer

LISA HENRY, ASID
ARCHITECTURE AND DESIGN MANAGER
KNOLL, INC.
DENVER, COLORADO

What led you to enter your design specialty?

❯ At Knoll I am connected to an incredible legacy of Florence Knoll's Planning Unit, which laid the foundations for modern office planning in the 1950s. I walked into my first Knoll office in 1997 and knew immediately there was something remarkable going on. The horizontal planes, the grid, the refined details in the furniture, the counterpoint of the furniture to the architecture, with the furniture subservient in a wonderful way in supporting the architecture. It was a Siren's call!

What is the most important quality or skill of a designer in your specialty?

❯ Continuous learning is the most important quality I have discovered. The changes that are happening in the world in general, in business in particular, and in interior design specifically require a designer to never stop learning. Reading about global, demographic, economic, and technology issues, to name a few, is necessary to present meaningful and relevant ideas to a client.

How is your specialty different from other specialties?

❯ We are not a traditional design practice. We study companies and then make decisions about what gaps exist in their office furniture and office environment requirements. Then we contract with the most innovative designers to design the pieces using the Knoll visual vocabulary as a background.

What are your primary responsibilities and duties in your position?

❯ I keep my finger on the pulse of designers and architects and connect them to Knoll and connect Knoll's resources to them.

What is the most satisfying part of your job?

❯ I love working on a wide array of projects in development at any time. I also particularly enjoy connecting people to one another. For example, designers who are looking for jobs or students who are looking for that internship or first job often call me. Because of the work I do I know many different design firms and the type of work they do. I can help match a searcher's interest with the right firms.

What is the least satisfying part of your job?

❯ When I pour my heart and soul into trying to win a project for our company and we lose. I honestly feel disappointed because I know there was something we did not communicate that could have made the difference.

Who or what experience has been a major influence in your career?

❯ One of my instructors in school said to never say no to an opportunity that presents itself. I read that to mean that I would learn from stepping up to a leadership or business opportunity even though it might seem that it was not the best time or there was another reason *not* to do it. I learned to say yes and find a way to do it well. As a result, I learn a lot and regret little.

What has been your greatest challenge as an interior designer?

❯ My greatest challenge is poring over the amazing amount of new information to keep ahead of the learning curve and then deciding what area is really important to be aware of, competent in, and a master of.

Office Furnishings Dealers

Office furnishings dealers are retailers that specialize in selling products for offices—sounds obvious, doesn't it? The name for this type of company came about as stores dealing with office products began to focus on selling furniture made by one or two specific furniture manufacturers such as Herman Miller, Inc., Haworth, Inc., and Steelcase, Inc. They became dealers by making special arrangements with one or more manufacturers based on the large volume of furniture they sold. Office furnishings dealers focus on specifying and selling those products with which they have the dealership arrangement, but they sell many other kinds of furniture and products appropriate for offices and similar commercial interiors.

Many of these companies have interior design departments. Projects primarily involve corporate offices and professional offices for financial institutions, law firms, medical office suites, and the like. These designers rarely design restaurants, hotels, retail stores, or private residences. Interior designers primarily work on projects brought to the company by the furniture sales staff. Sometimes the interior design departments of the large dealers also seek projects that are not initially obtained by the in-house sales staff.

Office furnishings dealerships provide excellent work environments for entry-level interior designers. You can learn a lot about how to space-plan and design, work with clients, and be part of a team. This work environment is often used as a stepping-stone to many of the interior design and architectural firms that specialize in other areas of the commercial interior design. Important employment criteria include excellent space-planning skills, knowledge of CAD, and an understanding of the bid process. Interior designers working at an office furnishings dealership also must be comfortable working as part of a team, as design solution presentations are often done in tandem with the sales staff.

For the most part, interior designers in office furnishings dealerships are compensated by salary. Some companies also allow a small commission related to the sale of a certain type of product. For example, the office furnishings dealer may pay the designers a commission based on the value of accessories purchased by the client.

Office Furnishings Dealer

JANE COIT, IIDA ASSOCIATE MEMBER
DIRECTOR OF DESIGN
VANGARD CONCEPT OFFICES
SAN LEANDRO, CALIFORNIA

What led you to enter your design specialty?

> It paid more than if I went into an A&D (architecture and design) firm. I also wanted to work in a corporate environment.

What is the most important quality or skill of a designer in your specialty?

> I have two: attention to detail without compromising productivity and the ability to communicate and work with a team.

How is your specialty different from other specialties?

> We specialize in specifying furniture and creating space plans for corporate environments.

What are your primary responsibilities and duties in your position?

> Creating systems furniture specifications and AutoCAD drawings for the project. Meeting with our project team and clients to understand end users' needs and desires and create a furniture solution as well as a furniture space plan. Working with our team to meet the client's budget within the time frame given.

What is the most satisfying part of your job?

> Seeing the project after it installs is quite satisfying, especially when the client is really happy. I enjoy space planning and the problem solving aspect. I look on it as advanced Legos.

What is the least satisfying part of your job?

> There are days that all you do is specify furniture and do not leave your desk. We also do a lot of reconfigures, which can be difficult.

Who or what experience has been a major influence in your career?

> Going to Europe while I was in university was the beginning—it really opened up my world of design. Living in Chicago was a huge influence as well, and my first few jobs working in residential design and at Luminaire. After working in this residential firm, I knew I wanted to work in commercial design because it is less personal.

What has been your greatest challenge as an interior designer?

> Catching all the details. There are so many details, and so much that can go wrong. Every project has a new challenge. It is another part that I love about the job. I am always learning.

What advice would you give to someone who wants to be an interior designer?

> They need to know that it is not just picking out fabrics and finishes. Interior design is not as glamorous as most people think. I would also advise them that they probably won't make a lot of money, but can make a decent living. It has its good and bad days like any career. I would also advise them to talk to a few designers to understand what a typical day is like.

Interior Design on a Global Stage

As you read this book, you will see examples of design work done outside the United States. It is quite common for some design firms to obtain projects outside their home location or state. For the most part, only the larger design firms will have the opportunity to design projects on the global stage. Often these interior designers are affiliated with architectural firms who have had the opportunity to design the building. Some highly specialized smaller firms also obtain work outside the United States after many years in their specialty. The Internet gives any size firm at least the opportunity to be noticed on the global stage.

Interior designers who do projects outside the United States must be prepared to do many tasks differently. For example, code requirements in the United States might not apply in foreign countries, as other countries may have more stringent requirements. Foreign countries utilize the metric measuring system rather than the common ordinal system used in the United States. Cultural differences can affect color choices, materials specification, and even space planning choices.

Although English is a common language worldwide, the designer wanting to perform design work in a foreign country may find it useful to learn some of that country's language. It is critical for the designer to realize that the seller—that is, the American interior designer—must adapt to the cultural needs of the client. It is also critical in international business for the designer to learn and observe local customs in business and social situations. This helps bridge cultural relationships with the client.

Designing projects in other countries can be very exciting and challenging. It will also be very demanding. If you are interested in working in foreign environments, you will want to be sure you have gained language skills in college. You will also want to try having informational interviews with interior design and architecture firms that provide design services outside the United States. That can easily be determined by Web searches of firms. These discussions can help you decide on class requirements that might go beyond the normal academic requirements of the school you attend. That will help you position yourself for the opportunity to join firms that provide interior design services on the global stage.

Commercial: Education, Government, Corporate, Healthcare

MARY G. KNOPF, ASID, IIDA, LEED AP

PRINCIPAL/INTERIOR DESIGNER

ECI/HYER, INC.,

ANCHORAGE, ALASKA

What led you to enter your design specialty?

❯ Working in a small city with a population of 280,000, designers tend to be generalists rather than specialists that you would find in larger city firms. This requires an interest in continuing education, research, and an awareness of current trends in many different areas. The benefit is the variety of constantly meeting new challenges and the broad spectrum of clientele.

What is the most important quality or skill of a designer in your specialty?

❯ Designers in smaller communities must address several specialty areas to be able to survive in the business. You need to have a thirst for knowledge and the discipline to constantly listen, observe, research, and learn. It is also important to understand when you need to call in other disciplines to augment your capabilities.

How is your specialty different from other specialties?

❯ To work as a commercial designer in a smaller demographic area, a designer must enjoy new challenges and have a thirst for knowledge. The required skill set includes the full gamut of expertise: space planning, detailing, color and finish selection, product research and specification, and—probably most important—communication and people skills.

What are your primary responsibilities and duties in your position?

❯ As a working principal in a smaller–scale firm, I continue to enjoy providing design services while managing other staff members and projects as well as searching for new projects and clientele. Our firm is an architecture and interior design firm with 12 architects and three interior designers. Our management consists of four principals—three architects and one interior designer. We split the management responsibilities and rely heavily on

High school: library, South Anchorage High School, Anchorage, Alaska. Mary Knopf, ASID, ECI/Hyer, Inc., Anchorage, Alaska.

PHOTOGRAPH: CHRIS AREND PHOTOGRAPHY

three fantastic support staff. We utilize the skills of both disciplines in all of our projects.

What is the most satisfying part of your job?

❯ Commercial design is not all glamour and art. Many projects require cognitive creativity to enjoy the geometry in an efficient space plan or to make the most of a limited budget tenant improvement. The most satisfying experiences are the appreciation our clients have for what we create. Their excitement about a fresh new look shows they understand and appreciate the skills, education, and experience required to create the end result that they were searching for.

Who or what experience has been a major influence in your career?

❯ When I graduated from college the economy was in a recession and my calls to inquire about employment were mainly met with regret. Firms were in the process of layoffs; they weren't hiring new staff. Many of my classmates had never practiced interior design, so they were forced into finding work in other fields due to the economy. I was persistent and therefore fortunate to find a position with the federal government in the General Services Administration. GSA was in the process of downsizing agency real estate holdings. After some test projects my manager was willing to give a young designer a great deal of responsibility. The position included cross training in leasing and facility management, both of which have been invaluable to me in working with property managers. The position honed my space planning skills and allowed me to travel throughout a four-state region, including Alaska, where I finally decided to make my home.

What has been your greatest challenge as an interior designer?

❯ There are many challenges in the field of interior design. I would say one of the greatest

High school: stairway, South Anchorage High School, Anchorage, Alaska. Mary Knopf, ASID, ECI/Hyer, Inc., Anchorage, Alaska.
PHOTOGRAPH: CHRIS AREND PHOTOGRAPHY

is to overcome the perception of being an "interior decorator" and educating other design professionals and clients about the difference. On the other end of the spectrum are people who mistakenly refer to me as an architect. Since I am part of an architectural firm and am at a senior level in experience, I constantly have to correct these misunderstandings. With a little levity this is an opportunity to advance the field by clarifying the differences and attributes of these complementary professions.

Facility Planning and Design

Another type of work environment is within the planning and interior design departments of large corporations. Best Western, Microsoft, Bank of America, and many other corporations employ facility planning and management personnel as in-house interior designers. In this work environment, interior designers are responsible for the space planning and interior design of the facilities for the corporation. When the corporation has multiple locations, the facility planning and design staff is generally involved in all the locations of the corporation. In some situations, they might work with an outside independent designer. These jobs might even have an international flavor, as so many large corporations have offices and facilities outside the United States.

Entry-level designers are rarely hired into this work environment. Most often, these companies need experienced interior designers. A broad range of design skills is required for facility planning, and interior designers are skilled in all phases of the design process. However, interior designers working for corporations are not often responsible for the actual ordering of merchandise because the company's purchasing department does it.

Working for a corporation can mean a higher salary and better health insurance, retirement, and vacation benefits than can be obtained working for independent interior design firms. Corporate interior design jobs often require considerable travel. Depending on your point of view, this is a positive or a negative aspect of working for a corporation. Frequent-flyer miles can add up for interior designers who are responsible for corporate projects throughout the United States—or around the world.

Sole Practitioner Work Environments

After working for someone else, many interior designers decide to start their own design practice. These interior designers are commonly called *sole practitioners*, indicating that they work alone. Interior designers start their own practice for the same reasons as many entrepreneurs: They are looking for the opportunity to be their own boss and reap the rewards (and suffer the consequences) of business ownership.

The sole practitioner commonly specializes in only one design specialty. It is difficult for a sole practitioner to offer services in multiple specialties of interior design since he or she is working alone. Depending on the design specialty and skills of the sole practitioner, he or she may find it necessary to outsource certain tasks to other interior designers or professionals. For example, a sole practitioner might outsource CAD services when construction drawings are required. Of course, sole practitioners also contract with vendors and tradespeople for the purchase of goods and to install items such as wall coverings and flooring.

Sole practitioners must be prepared to engage in all the activities of an interior design practice—that is, they must market their services to obtain clients, develop contracts or agreements for services, prepare necessary drawings and specifications of required goods, and recommend or arrange for the goods to be delivered to the client. In addition, sole practitioners are responsible for all the bookkeeping and paperwork that sustains a business. They must prepare all the paperwork involved in purchasing merchandise or services for the project, billing, and paying vendors.

The salary sole practitioners earn is drawn from the revenues of the firm—that is, they can pay themselves if revenue exceeds all the other expenses of operating the interior design practice. Of course, a solo practice operated out of a home office incurs minimal business expenses. However, making enough profit on a project requires excellent business control and management. Many sole practitioners find that the number of hours that must be worked to secure new clients, provide interior design services, and manage the business leaves them with less salary per hour than they made working for someone else. It can take several years for the sole practitioner to start to show profits and a satisfying income level.

The location of the solo practice varies with the owner's business goals. Solo practices are most commonly located in a home office. Some sole practitioners lease space in an executive office complex. In this case, the interior designer shares a receptionist and conference room with other firms while renting an appropriate amount of private office space. This is less expensive than renting an office suite and means that the hiring of additional staff can also be delayed. Other practitioners locate in a commercial office or retail location. Any type of commercial location for the interior design practice gives it a more substantial appearance than a home office does. It is, however, readily acceptable in this profession in today's marketplace for practitioners to work out of a home office or studio.

Eventually, sole practitioners discover they have enough business to require assistance. The first person hired by a sole practitioner is usually a part-time bookkeeper or some other part-time office administration assistant. Sometimes a business can grow to need additional design staff. At this point, it is generally necessary to move the firm to a commercial office location, as most cities do not allow home-based businesses to function in a residential area when they add on-site employees.

Interior designers who decide it is time to start their own firm must realize that the endeavor is a *business*. To be successful and grow—even though that growth is only in terms of total annual revenue—the solo practice must be planned and operated like a business with employees. The practice owner must use the same good business techniques of planning and structure that every firm uses. Not to do so can mean financial disaster as well as harm to the interior designer's reputation should a client file a lawsuit.

Interior designers can find career opportunities in numerous other places of business. "Alternate Careers in Interior Design" (see page 126) describes several of these that are not purely interior design operations.

High-End Residential

GRETA GUELICH, ASID

PRINCIPAL, PERCEPTIONS INTERIOR DESIGN

GROUP LLC

SCOTTSDALE, ARIZONA

What led you to enter your design specialty?

❯ Although my education was geared toward the commercial market and I always felt I would be a commercial designer, I just fell into a job at a residential design firm and really enjoyed the more creative aspects of the position.

What has been your greatest challenge as an interior designer?

❯ The greatest challenge has been relying on others to bring their part of the project in on time. Suppliers always promise on-time delivery but deliver late.

What are your primary responsibilities and duties?

❯ As a business owner, I wear many hats. I meet with clients, design the space, find the products, present the project, order the products, and supervise the installation. I find I spend too much time running the business versus doing the business.

What is the most satisfying part of your job?

❯ The most satisfying part of the job comes at the end, when I've done all the work, it looks beautiful and functions well, and the client loves it.

TOP Private residence: living room. Greta Guelich, ASID, Perceptions Interior Design Group LLC, Scottsdale, Arizona.
PHOTOGRAPH: MARK BOISCLAIR

RIGHT Private residence: sitting area. Greta Guelich, ASID, Perceptions Interior Design Group LLC, Scottsdale, Arizona.
PHOTOGRAPH: MARK BOISCLAIR

Who or what experience has been a major influence on your career?

❯ My internship with an architectural firm during my senior year at the University of Nebraska was a major influence on my career. The partners of this firm introduced me to real-world experiences in the field of design. They allowed me to attend meetings with their clients as well as work on drawings and perspectives for their presentations and projects.

How important is interior design education in today's industry?

❯ It is very important to be prepared and trained for a specific job, no matter what the position. With licensing just around the corner, education is even more critical for the interior designer.

What is the least satisfying part of your job?

❯ The least satisfying is what I call running my business—all the office paperwork that is necessary to keep the business going, such as sales tax, payroll tax, quarterly tax, and income tax reports.

What is the most important quality or skill of a designer in your specialty?

❯ In residential design, the most important quality is listening. It is extremely important that the designer listen to the clients and interpret what they want in the design. Being able to sketch a thought or design idea is very important to make sure the designer is thinking the same thing as the client.

ALTERNATE CAREERS IN INTERIOR DESIGN

Developers: Builders who develop residential properties have staff consultants that assist home buyers with the selection of interior materials. Developers of commercial properties are less likely to have a staff designer since the tenants or purchasers of commercial properties generally hire their own interior designer to assist with selections.

Product design: Interior designers might create custom designs that are executed as part of projects for clients. The designer may also at some point have the opportunity to work for a manufacturer creating new products.

Government agencies: The federal government has agencies that are involved in the planning and design of government offices and facilities. State governments may also have design staff who assist in the design of facilities for the state.

Independent agencies: There are several organizations or agencies such as the U.S. Green Building Council and professional associations such as ASID and IIDA that hire interior designers for some staff positions.

Journalism and the media: Some interior designers find alternative employment reporting and writing for newspapers, magazines, and other media on issues concerning interior design.

Teaching: Post–high school institutions hire interior design professionals to teach the classes of the interior design program. Generally an advanced degree is required for full-time teaching.

Historical sites and museums: Interior designers interested in history might find employment opportunities at a historical site such as Williamsburg in Virginia or museums. For positions at these types of locations additional course work in history or museum studies is required.

Residential Remodeling

SHARMIN POOL-BAK, ASID, CAPS, LEED-AP

OWNER, SHARMIN POOL-BAK

INTERIOR DESIGN LLC

TUCSON, ARIZONA

What led you to enter your design specialty?

❯ The market where I am located tends towards residential design. I do feel I have adapted well, and have a personality that works with the residential client. I guide them and want them to feel that the end product is something they identify with—yet I have to be able to tell them when something will not work functionally or within their budget. The client doesn't always understand *no,* but it is my responsibility to alert them to when their expectations will differ from what reality will provide.

What is the most important quality or skill of a designer in your specialty?

❯ There is a large balancing act between the homeowner and a contractor/builder. I end up

dealing with both sides in my work. I have a large vocabulary and understanding of the construction process. The ability to problem solve with both the clients and the vendors is ongoing, and requires the ability to reach a decision and back it up, sometimes with research, and sometimes on the spot.

How is your specialty different from other specialties?

❯ I have a small practice. I am often on the job site. And not in the office. More balancing again. Keeping track of current projects and preplanning for upcoming ones happens simultaneously. In addition to the planning and design work, business concerns are also part of the daily routine—bookkeeping, specifications, ordering, and tracking of orders.

What are your primary responsibilities and duties in your position?

❯ I am the sole provider of most activities in my office. I am the sole practitioner/designer/business owner. I do oversee all activities. I do the initial client visit, work to determine the scope of the project, coordinate the appropriate vendors for the project, and specify the products to be used. I coordinate my design vision with the expectations of the clients—and try my best to communicate to the client what will be the end product. I also do the ordering, tracking of orders, pay vendors, and invoice clients. I do job out some bookkeeping work, tax work, and drafting.

Private residence: master suite.
Greta Guelich, ASID, Perceptions Interior Design Group LLC, Scottsdale, Arizona.

PHOTOGRAPH: MARK BOISCLAIR

What is the most satisfying part of your job?

❯ Of course, the best part is finding the "aha" solution. Sometimes it is the perfect product to specify, sometimes it is the last detail or trim that brings the entire item to completion. The best for me, though, is finding a solution to a difficult space planning problem that solves all the problems that I was hired to solve.

What is the least satisfying part of your job?

❯ Delays in progress and not meeting the client expectation are by far the hardest for me to deal with. I have tried to increase my communication process to head these problems off. I deal with many different vendors and subcontractors on a job—if one of them is delayed or has a problem, then others get backed up. When that happens, the entire job sometimes seems to grind to a halt, and the clients look to me to get it back on track. It is frustrating when it is something that is out of my control such as a product being backstock or another vendor's schedule that I cannot immediately offer a solution to. These delays cause more problems in client well-being than almost anything else I can think of. The clients get worn down and tired of having endless work going on—in their eyes, they sometimes lose sight of how long a remodel can take.

Who or what experience has been a major influence in your career?

❯ I still think back to one of my favorite professors in college. Robert L. Wolf, IIDA, was an instructor when I was at Iowa State. I still remember a day we were in his class and he assigned a large project. It was due the same day as an assignment in another interiors class. As we all began to voice our opinion that that was too much to load on us in one short period (actually—probably at least three to four weeks!), we were so sure it should never be loaded on the shoulders of students all at once. He made a very short, concise point that has lasted to this day: "Your clients will not care if you have other deadlines, you must make them think that theirs is the most important project—because it is to them."

What I do to make sure I never, ever tell anyone that "I can't work on your project, deal with your problem, and the like, because I am too busy with something else."

What has been your greatest challenge as an interior designer?

❯ I try to balance everything—as a sole practitioner. I must learn to let more go and rely on others. Yet the client assumes and depends on me to know what is happening and keep tabs on the process. I continue to try and make sure the business end of the business does not suffer because of the time constraints.

Job-Seeking Tools

Opportunities in interior design require certain tools and strategies that every potential job candidate—and first-time employee—must utilize. A professional job requires an attitude different from getting those part-time positions during high school and college. Specific and key information must be conveyed in cover letters and résumés as the entrée to a job interview. Since interior design is a creative profession, the applicant's creative abilities must be conveyed via a portfolio of work that represents what has been mastered and how the applicant's skills can be used by the design firm.

The next sections survey drafting your résumé and assembling your portfolio. Tips on how to prepare the cover letter, résumé, and portfolio provide crucial basics about what content to include as well as format and presentation. The reference resources at the end of this book list several selections to help you with the details. The comments provided by interior design professionals that you find here will alert you to what designers look for in hiring a design employee.

COVER LETTERS AND RÉSUMÉS

Two documents necessary to begin the process of applying for a job in interior design are the cover letter and résumé.

A cover letter accompanies the résumé and introduces you to the potential employer. It is the first thing the employer reads before turning to your résumé. The cover letter should convey your interests and abilities to work in interior design in such a manner to create interest in you. The cover letter, however, must not be a lengthy document, no more than one page.

Cover letters usually consist of three to four paragraphs. The first provides a quick explanation as to why you are contacting the employer. It also needs to have a sentence that creates interest in you. The second and possibly third paragraphs highlight your experience and skills. These paragraphs should not contain everything about you. Detailed content goes into the résumé. The last paragraph creates a way for you to obtain a response or ask for an appointment.

The most effective cover letters are personally addressed rather than "To whom it may concern." Take the time to find out whom you must contact. The letter must be well written with perfect spelling and grammar. It should be typed—never handwritten—using standard business letter formatting. Interior design, of course, is a creative field and this allows for some creativity in the layout and design of your cover letter and résumé. Consider two things: (1) you do not want to be *too creative* (get a second opinion, say, from a teacher or an interior designer) and (2) you want to keep your cover letter and résumé standard letter size so that they can be properly filed or scanned for online application.

A résumé is a summary of your work and personal experience relevant to employment in the interior design profession. In combination with a cover letter, the résumé provides a quick glance at your experience and skills in interior design that might be of use to the employer. Because it is a *summary*—often no more than one or two pages—information related to work experience, education, special skills, and certain personal information must be presented concisely.

Whether you are a student or professional, your résumé will contain specific items:

Personal contact information

Career objective (for students)

Career summary (for professionals)

Education summary

Work experience summary

You should use your personal phone numbers or e-mail addresses for the job search—not your work phone number or e-mail address even if your current job is unrelated to the interior design field. Other personal information such as marital status, service records, religion, and community service involvement should not be included, as this information can unwittingly allow an employer to discriminate against you.

For entry-level designers, the career objective statement placed at the top of the résumé is a focal point. It states what you want to offer an employer and achieve for yourself. It entices the potential employer to read the rest of the résumé. You would use a few dynamic sentences to show how you can add to the firm or what you want to do in interior design. If the statement is too general, employers may feel you don't know what you want to do; if it is too specific, you may exclude yourself from consideration for a position.

Professionals use a career summary rather than a career objective. The summary is a brief statement that explains what you have done and how you can be a benefit to the employer. It is a snapshot of the professional's experience.

Of course, you need to list your educational information. Students may want to briefly list courses taken to help the employer understand the quality of your educational preparation. This is especially helpful if you are applying in a location where the employer may not be familiar with your school. Professionals should emphasize work experience over education and place the work experience section before education.

Résumés for entry-level designers will need to be simple while including key information. Work experience is most often shown in reverse chronological order (the current or most recent position first). This format is called a *chronological résumé* and is the most common style of résumé. Each position generally is shown with the dates of work indicated, the name of the company, location, your job title, and a brief description of duties. This description should be a very short narrative that clarifies your accomplishments and responsibilities in the position. Be sure you include terms that relate to skills that are needed in the interior design position for which you are applying. Always remain honest in what you can do, as dishonesty in a résumé can be discovered. Again, for refining the format and content of your cover letter and résumé, refer to "Interior Design References" (page 310), visit your local bookstore, and consult the many Web sites available on constructing job application materials. Information can be obtained from the ASID and IIDA Web sites as well as www.careersininteriordesign.com—a site specifically created to provide interior design career information. Another site that provides career information is www.Monster.com.

Public Assembly/Hospitality, Corporate

BETH HARMON-VAUGHN, FIIDA,
ASSOCIATE AIA, LEED-AP
OFFICE DIRECTOR, GENSLER
PHOENIX, ARIZONA

What led you to enter your design specialty?

❯ I had an interest in the design of spaces and objects. I was an art student in high school and knew I wanted to pursue a career in design.

What is the most important quality or skill of a designer in your specialty?

❯ The most important quality to be a successful interior designer is empathy—understanding the client's needs, worldview, and environmental/space needs.

How is your specialty different from other specialties?

❯ I am an interior designer but a generalist. However, I feel that the design of interior environments is the purview of the interior designer—not any other discipline. We design from the inside out, from the needs of the individual or group of individuals; we best understand how people use, move through, live, and work in space.

What are your primary responsibilities and duties in your position?

❯ I run a medium-size business inside a very large design firm—hire and develop staff, market for new work, establish strategies for growth and continuous improvement of our practice, address the daily financial/fiscal concerns (billings, collections, contracts), and focus our efforts on design excellence through our office culture.

What is the most satisfying part of your job?

❯ The most satisfying aspect of my job is working with my team and our clients—helping them define their vision for their future and seeing these come to reality.

Who or what experience has been a major influence in your career?

❯ Continuous education has expanded my horizons. Travel has expanded my world view. Membership in IIDA has expanded my understanding of our profession. Experience in practice has honed my client relationship and design and management skills.

What has been your greatest challenge as an interior designer?

❯ Continuously working with team members from other design professions and helping them understand the unique value that the interior designer brings to the client and our projects.

INTERIOR DESIGN PORTFOLIOS

Another necessary job-hunting tool for any interior designer is the portfolio. The portfolio is a visual record of the design skills you possess. The goal in having and presenting a portfolio is to show you have the skills necessary to do the job for which you are applying. What to include is a very important decision as it is not possible to include every item that a student or professional has concerning skills and experience.

For students, items should focus on the needs of the firm while showing a breadth of skills. For example, if you are applying to a residential firm, the majority of items should be related to residential projects. However, examples of other work can be included, especially if they show skills not evident in your work on residential projects.

A portfolio must be organized to show the best work you have done or are capable of doing. For a student seeking a first job in the profession, everything in the portfolio should be the very best work he or she can do. These items are commonly included in a portfolio:

Sketches

Space plans

Furniture layout plans

Color boards

Working drawings and specifications

Perspectives

Photos, slides, or publication reprints of projects

Private residence: living room. Greta Guelich, ASID, Perceptions Interior Design Group LLC, Scottsdale, Arizona.
PHOTOGRAPH: MARK BOISCLAIR

Designers who have been working for some time should present completed projects in their portfolio. Employers want to see both photographs of completed projects and examples of design documents, which illustrate the designer's mastery of technical skills.

Portfolios must be well organized. Over the course of an hour-long interview, an interviewer may spend only 10 or 20 minutes looking at an applicant's portfolio. Organize the items to tell your story as effectively as possible. Start with items that specifically relate to the job opening. If you have done your homework and know something about the firm and what they are looking for, your portfolio will be better organized and you will look organized yourself.

A portfolio should never be considered finished. As your skills improve or you produce more exciting or interesting work, replace less important pieces with those items. Professionals constantly document projects by having photos taken of completed work for their own marketing purposes and to have portfolio items should an opportunity to seek a new place of employment occur. Thus, it is important to get the highest-quality photos you can afford. Although digital photos are common today, when possible, have project photos taken by a professional architectural photographer.

Can You Describe the Optimum Portfolio for a Job Applicant?

❯ A good portfolio contains samples of a number of types of projects that relate to my target market (offices, small medical offices and facilities, and nursing homes), samples of one or two color and finish boards, some CAD drawings, some hand drawing and lettering, rough sketches, and perhaps something to show the applicant's creativity and problem-solving skills. The format should be easy to view and handle, and be self-explanatory in case I have to ask the applicant to leave it until I have time to look through it.

Terri Maurer, FASID

❯ If just out of school? Then enough to show their communication, technical, and design skill.

Bruce Goff, ASID

❯ An optimum portfolio includes examples of all aspects of their talents, including drawings, plans, sketches, perspectives, color boards, and photos of completed projects in a 9-inch by 12-inch portfolio. The job applicant could bring in their best color board along with this portfolio or include a color photo of the color board in their portfolio. The 9-inch by 12-inch size is less cumbersome for the interview.

Greta Guelich, ASID

❯ The best portfolio shows me a wide range of the applicant's skills. I enjoy seeing early projects that have not been touched up and then later projects to see the development. Fabrics, finishes, and furniture selections are also important. Organization in the portfolio tells me a lot about the applicant. Basically, a portfolio should just be a simple but solid presentation of the skills of the young designer.

Charles Gandy, FASID, FIIDA

❯ A portfolio should represent the best work that a person has done, with examples of construction documents, drawings, renderings, client programs, and photos of completed projects. In other words, keep it simple.

Sandra Evans, ASID

❯ Variety, good, clean work, accurate drawings, logical layouts (not cutesy), sketching ability, architectural printing a must.

Pat McLaughlin, ASID

❯ A portfolio should include examples of work that detail the designer's role on the project, a brief description of the project scope, and digital photos or actual examples of color boards. Also, letters of referral are an added benefit when they document the designer's credibility and ability to work with people.

Leonard Alvarado

❯ Several quick sketch items, several space-planning and concept design items, and several sets of drawings. Color and material boards that are either actual boards or photos.

Melinda Sechrist, FASID

❯ Projects on which the designer has been a participant, honesty in describing his or her personal role on the project, understanding of and responsiveness to the client's objectives in developing the design solutions evidenced by the projects.

Marilyn Farrow, FIIDA

❯ Most applicants arrive with a poor portfolio that has few senior projects and a lot of flotsam and jetsam—an eclectic group of assignments that provide little insight into the designer's or architect's abilities in a real-world situation. I like to see a substantial senior project that isn't b—s—, one that really demonstrates the person has

done some research, intellectually thought about the solution, and portrayed it in an aesthetically beautiful manner. Excellent presentation skills are important.

Jain Malkin, CID

❯ The optimum portfolio has hand-drawn sketches, a rendering, photos of school projects and/or actual work, AutoCAD drawings, a set of construction drawings and specifications, and a brief explanation of what part the designer had in putting together each of the projects submitted.

Linda Santellanes, ASID

❯ A portfolio should demonstrate your problem-solving process and logic. We are more interested in understanding your approach to problems then we are in pretty pictures. Focus on the results you created in completing a project. If you have a particular specialty that you excel in—for example, drawing or presentation development—we would like to see that as well. Show a small range of projects that demonstrate your approach to both small and large projects.

Sari Graven, ASID

❯ The portfolio is not the number one thing to me. The optimum portfolio is neat, organized, and shows diversity as well as most aspects of the design process.

Donna Vining, FASID, IIDA, RID, CAPS

❯ We look for quantity, diversity of project type, technical experience, sketching, references, and organization.

Fred Messner, IIDA

❯ A combination of work with an explanation of what was successful and what might have been improved.

Sally Nordahl, IIDA

❯ I look for creative thinking, for a broad knowledge of multiple areas of practice. I look for basic presentation skills, particularly in the applicant's ability to present ideas. I look for a passion for the profession.

Linda Elliott Smith, FASID

❯ The portfolio should be a concise expression of the job applicant's skills with a focus on the type of work needed by the design firm.

Linda Sorrento, ASID, IIDA, LEED-AP

❯ A good balance of aesthetic and technical skills. AutoCAD and examples of documentation skills are essential, along with good examples of design presentation techniques and a polished résumé.

Robert Wright, FASID

❯ A portfolio that presents beautifully and creatively and that indicates pride in the work. Although a range of basic skills is the minimum requirement, I tend to put more emphasis on how a person explains her or his portfolio than its actual contents.

Suzan Globus, FASID, LEED-AP

❯ Experience in a variety of types of projects. Experience in CAD. Attractive and/or exciting projects in the portfolio (you did say "optimum," right?). Good recommendations from previous employers. Good education from a reputable institution.

I think graduating students should do whatever they can to acquire experience—and perhaps intern at more than one type of firm.

Linda Kress, ASID

❯ For an entry-level position, combine artistic schoolwork (freehand work) with technical documentation abilities (CADD and handwork drafting). For positions beyond these, present a broad spectrum of project work responsibilities: hand drafting, freehand sketches, trace work, materials boards/selections, programming documents, completed project photos, etcetera. These must be professionally organized in a manageable size. Not all examples need to be originals, but they need to be professionally photographed.

David Stone, IIDA

❯ The portfolio should show a range of skills, not just pretty pictures.

Rosalyn Cama, FASID

❯ No. I'm sorry, but it can be so many things. For entry level, I like to see original design work and an interesting presentation—CD-ROMs or Web sites are fine. For an experienced person, I want to see images of their finished work and any unbuilt projects they may have, preferably in an interesting format.

Beth Harmon-Vaughn, FIIDA

JOB INTERVIEWS

As you might expect, the job interview is a critical hour in which you can make a good impression and convince the employer that *you* are the only person right for the job he or she is trying to fill. In that hour, it is up to you to build on the impression you made with the résumé that preceded your appearance at the office or studio. Remember that you have only one chance to make a first impression. That means everything about those first few minutes, from how you greet the receptionist to what you wear and how you shake hands can add or subtract from your interview opportunity.

Do not think of the interview as an isolated interaction with the potential employer. The interview is a process that begins with preparation. For a position in professional interior design, you need preparation even before you show up for the actual interview in order for you to make it a positive experience and opportunity. First, reconfirm your appointment and make sure you know how to get to the office. Review your homework on the employer to be clear about what the firm needs, what they do, and how you can fit into the company. Then check your portfolio and rearrange it if necessary for the upcoming interview. Finally, prepare yourself mentally by going over the questions you anticipate the interviewer may ask you.

Even though the interior design profession is a creative one, the job interview is not a time to be too trendy or casual about your interview appearance. Even if you know the firm is casual in its business dress code, your apparel should be on the conservative side, meaning suits and ties for men, business suits or a dress with a jacket for women. Of course, residential firms are more accepting of trendier dress, while commercial firms are generally more conservative.

A job interview is a stressful situation for most people. Everyone is nervous before an interview. However, your preparation should help you relax as you wait for the interviewer. Some firms actually keep you waiting on purpose. This may seem kind of cruel, but the idea is to see how you react to pressure. The receptionist reports later on how nervous or fidgety you were. So relax. Read a magazine and try to refrain from fidgeting with your portfolio or handbag. Entry-level designers are even more nervous as they try to get that first great job. One more thing: When the potential employer greets you, stand up and be prepared to shake hands, but wait for him or her to shake your hand.

Some firms use team interviews or multiple interviews. In a team interview, one person leads the interview and then passes you to another member of the firm for additional questions. Team interviews are most common in large firms. You may experience multiple interviews instead. This means the firm may interview several potential employees on one day and then call back a few for more in-depth interviews at a later time. Multiple interviews can also be the pattern of large firms. If you apply to a small design firm, you will most likely be interviewed by the owner and not meet any other employee (other than the receptionist) unless the interview is going well and they are likely to offer you a position.

While you are being interviewed, don't bring up personal problems, argue, or sound like you are begging for the job. If you are asked if you have ever been fired, however, you need to be honest and say so if it is true. Briefly explain the circumstances without making it a focus of the interview. Some interviewers ask tough questions to see how you react under stress. The temptation might be to argue, but do not let that happen. Keep as cool as you can and focus on your strengths as they relate to the job.

Questions you are likely to be asked are:

Why do you want to work for ABC Designs, Inc.?

What do you know about our company?

Tell me about the qualifications you have for this position.

Tell me about yourself.

How does your previous experience relate to this position?

What are your strengths and weaknesses?

As the interview draws to a close, you will want to ask your questions about salary and benefits. If you understand the firm is interviewing several people for the position, be sure to ask when they will make a decision. If you are given an offer, be prepared to say yes. If the salary level of the offer or the type of job is quite different from what you were expecting, it is okay to ask for a day to decide. However, don't make the employer wait longer than overnight when you have been offered a position. If you like the job, but have another interview and want to wait until that interview, ask for overnight to decide. If you like this offer, call and cancel the next appointment. Follow up all your interviews with a brief thank-you note. This is a courtesy that far too few people extend even though they should.

Many other strategies are involved in navigating interviews. Several of the books in the reference section can help you with specific questions.

ELECTRONIC JOB-HUNTING STRATEGIES

It has become increasingly common for large interior design firms to use electronic means to seek or prequalify potential employees. Firms also post job openings on company Web sites and Internet job sites. Job applicants can surf Web-posting locations for information on potential positions. Students and professional members of ASID, IIDA, or other organizations can check the association's job bank or job service for potential openings or post their résumé there.

Electronic résumés need to be simple in style and format. Fancy typefaces, boxes, graphics, and other formatting methods that are appropriate to a printed résumé can be disastrous on an electronic résumé. Keep the file simple so the résumé will be read correctly by the receiving company. Use the key words of the industry as appropriate so the résumé will be picked out if the company (or job bank) uses a scanning program.

If you e-mail your résumé, include it in the body of the e-mail rather than as an attachment. Many firms are afraid of the viruses that may accompany attachments. Because of the profusion of spam mail, many receivers will not open e-mail from people they do not know. It is a good idea to contact the design firm to clarify if they will accept an e-mailed résumé with an attachment.

Whether you use e-mail or fax, be sure to send a cover letter or note with your résumé. Blind mailing or spamming of your résumé will not get you in the door. You would not send a résumé by postal mail without a cover letter; the same goes for electronic mail.

What Do You Look for in Hiring a New Designer?

> Passion, professionalism, talent, personality.
Janice Carleen Linster, ASID, IIDA, CID

> I look for designers with the innate ability to see the big picture and to make decisions within that framework. The pretty or different solution to the problem is not nearly as creative as the solution based on a balance of function, value, and aesthetics.
M. Joy Meeuwig, IIDA

> Education, people skills, and a good design eye. How well they will blend with the staff.
Debra May Himes, IIDA, ASID

> I look for someone with exceptional creative and technical skills. Someone who is willing to learn and can well represent my firm.
Linda Santellanes, ASID

> For almost 30 years, I have been with design and architectural firms where a team approach has been the norm for projects. As a consequence, when hiring interior designers, I have always given consideration to the skills and experience of my existing staff and sought new hires who offered complementary skills so that we had a balanced team to work on projects. For example, if the current staff was detail-focused, then I might need a big-picture individual. If current staff was weighted on space-planning skills, then I might seek an individual with a gift for color, materials, and finishes. If the current staff lacked good presentation or public speaking skills, then good verbal communication skills might be foremost in mind when interviewing. My focus was to have a well-rounded team whose members worked well together and could learn from one another.

Notwithstanding the need for a great team, competency in design, document execution, computer use, and problem solving are mandatory.
Barbara Nugent, FASID

> I automatically assume graduates of reputable schools know the process of design. Portfolios (of new graduates and practitioners) demonstrate their level of creativity relative to our firm's and our clients' expectations.
Jennifer van der Put, BID, IDC, ARIDO, IFMA

> Someone who has successfully completed design education. Some of the traits are talented, innovative, self-made, dedicated, energetic, communicative, bold, and disciplined. Often someone with an interesting background is also considered—for example, someone who is well traveled and has many types of interests.
Alicia Loo, CID

❯ I look first for design talent and technical skill. However, I look most for the willingness to learn and to be a team player.

Beth Kuzbek, ASID, IIDA, CMG

❯ I look for education first and foremost, involvement in a professional association, ability to market themselves, and someone on the path to take NCIDQ. Professional appearance and an organized and well-presented portfolio are also important. CAD knowledge and 3D design are getting more and more important.

Juliana Catlin, FASID

❯ Common sense—and an ability to communicate well, a great attitude, positive, and a real focus on customer service. Presentation, polish, maturity, and a sense of humor.

Lisa M. Whited, IIDA, ASID, IDEC, Maine CID

❯ Ability to communicate graphically and verbally. Passion.

Neil Frankel, FAIA, FIIDA

❯ Good communication skills in the interview, a good portfolio, good intelligence, and competence in AutoCAD. Because I like to teach, I don't mind inexperience right now. But my firm hired me because I was older and had a lot of experience—they needed someone who could handle the client-relationship thing—not just put together pretty finish boards (not that finish boards aren't important—we just received a nice compliment today from a commercial client who has truly enjoyed using the finish boards we prepared for them to promote the work they are about to do on their theological seminary). And sometimes our firm is looking for a computer graphics expert—the verbal communication skills don't matter as much as a portfolio and competence. So the answer is: It depends on the needs of the firm at that time.

Linda Kress, ASID

❯ Basic CAD skills, personal and design presentation skills, a strong work ethic, technical knowledge, and enthusiasm. It is also good to see experience (internship) within the profession.

Fred Messner, IIDA

❯ Four-year degree; FIDER accreditation.

Teresa Sowell, ASID, IFMA

❯ Empathy (for client's needs), thoroughness (accuracy is *extremely* important), team player (with fellow employees and project team members), communication skills (oral and written), and, of course, the prerequisites: high level of basic design skills (space planning, material and finish selection, detailing, drawing, sketching, and CAD).

Jeffrey Rausch, IIDA

❯ The ability to define the problem, articulate a solution, and execute it. Problem solver. Someone who is willing to challenge the status quo and is open to new ideas and ways of doing things. Flexibility and humor.

Sari Graven. ASID

❯ The ability to communicate well and think logically. AutoCAD is a prerequisite.

Suzan Globus, FASID, LEED-AP

❯ When hiring, first we look for design talent, but of almost equal importance is the ability to communicate—and not only graphically. The most important communication skill is verbal communication.

M. Arthur Gensler Jr., FAIA, FIIDA, RIBA

❯ Someone with good communication skills and a willingness to learn and work hard will always contribute, but specific skills are needed for specific positions. For instance, a CAD manager will need different skills than a project manager or project designer.

Rita Carson Guest, FASID

Office: media presentation room. Terri Maurer, FASID, Maurer Design Group, Akron, Ohio.

PHOTOGRAPH: DAVID PATERNITE PHOTOGRAPHY

❯ Someone who is willing to listen and learn and take initiative.
Sally Nordahl, IIDA

❯ Intelligence, passion, design excellence, sketching skills, and CAD skills.
Nila Leiserowitz, FASID, Affiliate AIA

❯ I look for designers with an open mind who are willing to learn, flexible, and willing to do whatever it takes to get the job done.
Greta Guelich, ASID

❯ Attitude and a willingness to go the extra mile.
Donna Vining, FASID, IIDA, RID, CAPS

❯ Personality. How well the person interacts with me. A solid sense of good design—no gimmicks, just solid design. But personality is the real key.
Charles Gandy, FASID, FIIDA

❯ First, I look for a good attitude. I can teach people skills, but it's very hard to correct a bad attitude. Nirvana for me is finding someone who already has healthcare experience, but this is very rare.
Jain Malkin, CID

❯ Leadership skills first, then talent.
Rosalyn Cama, FASID

❯ We look for someone with technical skills and a strong work ethic—a team player.
Linda Isley, IIDA

❯ I look for commitment to professionalism, which consists of a degree in interior design. I look for someone who, if not currently certified by examination, is on the path to examination. And I look for good interpersonal skills.
Linda Elliott Smith, FASID

❯ College degree from a FIDER-accredited institution, preferably one where the interior program was in a college of architecture and five years, internship with a good firm or person, travel or work experience abroad, and something else. "Something else" can be a lot of things. I have worked with a world-class mountain climber, an artist, a chef, a pilot—the "something else" usually gives the person balance and dimension beyond their design education and experience.
Beth Harmon-Vaughn, FIIDA

> As a sole practitioner, I am kind of out of the hiring process. But if I were hiring new designers, I'd be looking for people who can do many things, not just design a project. The more they can do to help keep the business moving smoothly, like creating contracts and documents, ordering and expediting product, and that type of thing, the more valuable they would be to the firm. If you think about it, hiring a new designer who wanted only to design projects would do little for me as a small business owner beyond doubling the amount of paperwork and operational tasks I have to do. I'd be looking for someone to share the load and have the ability to cover all the bases in my absence.

Terri Maurer, FASID

> I look for three basic skills: the abilities to communicate, to work with others, and to be creative.

Linda Sorrento, IIDA, ASID, LEED-AP

> Talent, people skills, and a desire to improve— and to enjoy the journey.

William Peace, ASID

> Energy, enthusiasm, and a passion for design. But that doesn't go very far unless you add excellent written and oral skills, a sense of responsibility and thoroughness, and a strong design portfolio. How an individual performed in college can pretty much tell you how he or she will be in the professional world. Did the person attend class? Complete work on time? Participate in extracurricular activities? Travel? Work? I want to talk to someone who knew him or her in school— perhaps a professor or other students.

Robert Wright, FASID

> Education, experience, creativity, and ability to sell themselves and their ideas to others in the organization.

Leonard Alvarado

> I want someone who is creative, of course. I am also most interested in their training and life experiences. I look for someone with a degree from a FIDER-accredited program and someone who has traveled or had other experiences to expand that educational base. Work ethic is also important, as the person must contribute to the business revenue.

Sally Thompson, ASID

> Enthusiasm for design and people first, with skills in AutoCAD, creative design, color, and organization.

Sandra Evans, ASID

> Self-motivation.

Pat Campbell McLaughlin, ASID

> An educated designer with a four-year degree who can draw (both sketch freehand and CAD), has a good attitude, and is willing to do whatever needs to be done.

Melinda Sechrist, FASID

> Ability to talk with me, a responsibility to the profession to always want to know more, ability to relate to my clients in a way that reflects well on my work and my firm.

Michael Thomas, FASID

> Communication skills, tech skills, design skills— in that order.

Bruce Goff, ASID

What Do You Enjoy Most About Working in the Firm You Are in Right Now?

❯ The clients. Working in high-end residential jobs means that, for the most part, I work with interesting and creative individuals who are usually decisive yet respectful of the designer's role.
Charles Gandy, FASID, FIIDA

❯ I own it and because I am a small business owner, my schedule can be somewhat flexible, which allows me to be involved in outside organizations.
Greta Guelich, ASID

❯ I like the independence of setting my own pace and schedule and not having to ask for clearance to proceed with a concept or to explore other avenues.
Terri Maurer, FASID

❯ I enjoy collaboration across our firm on projects and on topics of importance to our society such as sustainability.
Beth Harmon-Vaughn, FIIDA, Assoc. AIA, LEED-AP

❯ Of course, owning my firm helps in the enjoyment of going to work each day, but I also try to create a happy atmosphere for my staff and clientele. Perhaps one of the best things about what I do—besides being creative—is that I am building something. I guess that is what I am all about. I love building good projects, good clientele business relationships, and building my businesses.
Debra May Himes, ASID, IIDA

❯ I work in a large architectural firm. The eight partners, all architects, view interior design as a completely separate discipline. They respect the full process of interior design and recognize its value and importance in complementing architectural work.
Jennifer van der Put, BID, IDC, ARIDO, IFMA

❯ The opportunity to meet great clients and to work with great people. I find the collaborative team process the most enjoyable part of any project.
M. Arthur Gensler Jr., FAIA, FIIDA, RIBA

❯ I own it. I am involved with an interesting variety of projects and enjoy working with most of my clients.
Melinda Sechrist, FASID

❯ I loved being part of Associates III for 27-plus years, a dynamic woman-owned firm that continually makes a difference in the field of residential interior design.

Today, and as I move forward with my next venture, I love nurturing my entrepreneurial spirit on my own, following my own dreams—the possibilities are infinite.
Annette Stelmack, Allied Member ASID

❯ I have a good group of people who support me and my work for clients.
Michael Thomas, FASID, CAPS

❯ As a senior design professional, I enjoy the high-level decision makers with whom I generally work. It is likely you will see projects realized when you have the ability to talk to the true leaders of the firm or corporation.
Marilyn Farrow, FIIDA

❯ I enjoy the laughter the most. It appears in the creative energy and camaraderie of the staff, and members of the design teams that we partner with, and the trust, loyalty, and delight of the clients.
Suzan Globus, FASID, LEED-AP

Church furniture: tabernacle at Saint Charles
Borromeo, Kettering, Ohio. James Postell, Associate
Professor, School of Architecture and Interior Design,
University of Cincinnati, Cincinnati, Ohio.

PHOTOGRAPH: JAMES POSTELL

❯ I enjoy the ability to collaborate and solve
problems as a team. I work in a small firm with
four architects and two interior designers. When a
deadline is imposed we all step in and help out our
colleagues to get the project finished in time. I have
observed that small firms appear to collaborate
more while larger firms invariably assign specific
duties to each employee and crossover does not
occur as much. I reference my preference for team
work in relation to sports and athletics. I preferred,

as a youth, playing team sports such as volleyball
or basketball far more than cross-country running.
Laura Busse, IIDA, KYCID

❯ The scale of the projects.
Teresa Sowell, ASID, IFMA

❯ Respect for the profession.
Nila Leiserowitz, FASID

❯ What I like the most about working in the firm
I am in today is the professional environment
created by the partners and employees. I contract
at a small firm that is extremely organized. The
environment is respectful of employees and clients
alike. Not only have they managed to achieve a
large workload from repeat business but also they
enjoy their work. The partners convey a sense of
great pride in what they have achieved and an
understanding of where they came from.
Linda Santellanes, ASID

❯ I am proud of the work we produce and the
success we are experiencing. I enjoy watching our
new designers finding themselves and building
their confidence. There is so much for them to
learn.
Robert Wright, FASID

❯ I enjoy the inspiration given by the people I
work with and the environment where I work.
Linda Sorrento, ASID, IIDA, LEED-AP

❯ The opportunity to work with outstanding
clients.
Rita Carson Guest, FASID

❯ It is my own firm; this gives me independence
and the freedom to specify exactly what my
client needs, not what someone might require
me to specify in order to meet a quota or sales
requirement.
Sally Thompson, ASID

❯ I love that I can work as hard as I want to and still spend as much time with my family as I need to without asking my boss for time off.
Maryanne Hewitt, IIDA

❯ I really enjoy the client interaction and problem solving.
Lisa Slayman, ASID, IIDA

❯ I am a solo consultant. I can live in Puerto Vallarta, serve ASID in Washington, do my work in Hong Kong and China, all the time working with design team members in Seattle, Paris, Los Angeles, Malibu, Beijing, and Hong Kong. What's not to like?
Bruce Brigham, FASID, ISP, IES

❯ Coming to work most days is really a high. We have an extraordinary work environment and many clients who provide numerous opportunities for creative, cutting-edge design.
Jain Malkin, CID

❯ At Hixson, we have a strong team environment, and with that, there is much we can learn by working together in our specialties of architecture, interior design, and engineering. With a good team, you can come to some great solutions by working together and sharing "both sides of the brain." In addition, our firm has a "continuous improvement" commitment, which makes education important to the individual, and which, in turn, gives back to the firm and to our clients.
Colleen McCafferty, IFMA, USGBC, LEED-CI

❯ Since it is my own firm, I enjoy it a lot. My goal to create a firm that does great design work, can handle technical projects, is good to work with, and is fun to work at.
Jo Rabaut, ASID, IIDA

❯ My firm is basically me at this point because I have leveraged my business experiences into another avenue: writing and presenting educational programs. I still maintain long-standing clients and work with them as their needs arise.
Linda E. Smith, FASID

❯ The firm's international presence allows for exposure to a variety of project types in a wide array of locations from local, small governmental jobs all the way to large, international, full-service projects—as well as the ability to work on a regional airport, local casinos, an upscale bank roll-out, a pediatric cardiothoracic ICU hospital wing, a corporate office build out in China, and a university campus in Central Asia. This project variety combined with the diversity of my coworkers, both in the local office and throughout the firm, provides a wealth of interest to keep an "old dog" happy.
David Stone, IIDA, LEED-AP

❯ I teach at Colorado State University. I have incredibly wonderful, hardworking students to teach. I love being in the classroom and learning from them. That is what I enjoy most.
Stephanie Clemons, Ph.D., ASID, IDEC

❯ One of the best things about the profession of interior design is that you can branch out to other industries, and the principles you have gained in both your education and experience can help you flourish and excel in any area of endeavor. I currently am employed with a manufacturer working with interior designers and architects throughout the country seeking specifications of our products on their projects. The work keeps me in the A&D community and allows me to be involved with hundreds of projects and dozens of interesting and exciting architects and interior designers.
Beth Kuzbek, ASID, IIDA, CMG

Office furnishings dealership: Collaborative Idea Neighborhood, Arbee Associates Headquarters, Gaithersburg, Maryland. Interior design by Gensler, Washington, D.C., in collaboration with Arbee Associates.

PHOTOGRAPH: KEVIN BESWICK

❯ I absolutely love the team of designers assembled here. I also like the upscale niche we have moved the firm into in the last few years. It is a natural fit for this team.

Jeffrey Rausch, IIDA

❯ Oh, I am having so much fun. I work for intelligent, funny, hard-working architects who have great integrity. They also all have a great sense of humor, which makes a pleasant working environment. Although they tease me by calling me the decorator, they have learned to value and appreciate what I can do to enhance and complete their projects. But what I like most is the variety of work I do. Sometimes I am doing the expected thing—furniture, finishes, equipment, furniture schedules, finish schedules, and so on. Other times I am meeting with clients—meeting the challenge of making sure the clients are happy to be working with Lotti, Krishan & Short. Other times I am on marketing trips or making presentations with our marketing principal. That's the excitement of competition. Often I am drawing interior elevations—I learned AutoCAD when I was 50 years old. I love it. Sometimes I use AutoCAD's 3D features combined with Photoshop to make little computer studies of a space so we can help the client understand something better. I also meet with subcontractors and manufacturers' representatives. And attend seminars—there's always something interesting to learn. I guess I enjoy almost all of the aspects of my work.

Linda Kress, ASID

❯ Designers are well rounded if they are given the chance to participate in different phases of a project in order to enhance their skills. I enjoy my job because every day is different, and I am consistently challenged to enhance my skills in different areas. It is good not to become pigeonholed or stuck doing the same type of task routinely.

Leonard Alvarado

❯ The freedom and flexibility I have to make decisions about my future.

Sally Nordahl, IIDA

❯ I enjoy the freedom that comes from owning my own practice. However, along with the freedom comes the responsibility to my clients, my employees, and my vendors.

Juliana Catlin, FASID

❯ I am involved in high-end hotel projects that are diverse in terms of geography, locality, and type of project, which can vary from a historic landmark hotel to a highly urban business hotel or a resort hotel.

Alicia Loo, CID

❯ I have to say that it is the thrill of challenge. Every day is a challenge in our firm. We have a multidisciplinary staff of approximately 85 people, including architects, interior designers, civil and structural engineers, and traffic and land use planners. It is a fast-paced, multitask environment where client demands require an extreme sense of urgency and responsiveness. Our clients' needs present daily challenges related to design, budget, or schedule goals. I enjoy meeting the challenge.

Susan B. Higbee

❯ Operating as a subgroup, with a unique culture and the brand identity of an interior design practice, while taking advantage of the deeper resources of a full-service multidisciplinary firm.

Janice Carleen Linster, ASID, IIDA, CID

❯ I enjoy the variety: the interaction between architecture and interiors, and our consultant engineers and landscape architects. I am fortunate to work in a small city with a unique mix of government and private sector large-scale projects. Our firm has also had the opportunity to team with many well-known international firms, including NBBJ, Perkins & Will, HDR, and ZGF. These outstanding learning experiences have served to confirm my desire to stay with the uniqueness and variety that a small city and small-sized firm offer.

Mary Knopf, ASID, IIDA, LEED-AP

4 Design Specialties

Most people think of interior design specialties in terms of two large categories: residential and commercial. Residential interior design focuses on private living places such as freestanding single-family dwellings, condominiums, and apartments. This area of interior design most likely comes to mind since it gets so much attention from the media. Commercial interior design addresses a large range of business- and government-owned facilities such as hospitals, hotels, schools, government office buildings, and corporate offices.

These two broad categories comprise a large number of targeted specialties. In fact, it is possible to say that any kind of specialty space can become a career niche. A niche is a highly specialized, even unique part of the total built environment industry. For example, the design of family practice medical office suites is a niche within the commercial specialty of healthcare design. Second homes and resort homes are a niche within residential interior design.

Despite the specialization, most interior designers and interior design firms do not focus narrowly on a single type of space. Many residential interior designers occasionally design professional offices. A hospitality designer can switch from hotel rooms to designing corporate offices, and an interior designer for an office furnishings dealer will often have the training and vision to design an employee cafeteria or even a private residence.

Economics can affect how interior design professionals move between specializations and actually cultivate more than one. When the economy is robust, as it was in the late 1990s, highly specialized designers and firms rarely work outside of their area of expertise and focus their business model on that specialty to further its success.

When the economy slows, however, the strategic-thinking design firms and individual designers often widen their practice into two or more related specialties. Most of the professional interior designers interviewed in this chapter (and throughout this book) primarily design in one or two specialty areas and can apply that experience to a variety of interior types such that they can adapt to the market and change like any other well-run business.

Since the first edition of this book was published, some design specialties have gained emphasis in the profession. Sustainable design, senior living facilities such and aging-in-place concepts for private residences, and residential kitchen and bath design—which are specialties unto themselves—have a new prominence in the industry and our narrative.

Residential Design

It is quite possible that you became interested in interior design and purchased this book because of your exposure to and interest in the design of spaces in your home or houses in general. Responsibility for designing the interiors of private residences is an interesting challenge. Residential interior designers bring their expertise and knowledge into the development of concepts that meet the family, social, and functional needs of the client as well as create beautiful spaces. The professional interior designer also recognizes and applies applicable building codes and addresses safety issues that affect the residential space. The successful residential interior designer knows how to expertly examine and understand the needs and wants of the client so as to help the client make the decisions that move the project to conclusion. A private residence is so special and personal a project that many clients have a difficult time making necessary decisions. Assisting them in making decisions is one aspect of residential interior design that attracts professionals to this specialty.

When specializing in residential interior design, the professional may work on projects involving the entire house, perhaps from the initial planning stage, in conjunction with the architect or custom home builder. Large residences can take several months, if not years, to complete. Less complex in size but not necessarily in concept are remodeling projects such as a new kitchen or family room. Residential design projects can also involve the more straightforward redecorating of a residence. A remodeling project can involve moving nonload-bearing walls, replacing cabinets, relocating plumbing fixtures, and other mechanical elements. Remodeling might also lead to adding a room to the house. In some jurisdictions, it is important to point out that these projects must be done with an architect. Redecorating involves changing architectural finishes on walls, flooring, and ceiling. It can also extend to replacing window treatments and planning new furniture items.

The interior designer is responsible for determining client preferences and the planning and specifications of the interior spaces to ensure the design meets the needs of the client. Depending on the size of the project, the interior designer may provide space planning options, furniture layouts, color palettes, and finish specifications for all interior architectural elements, accessories, and other elements outlined in the design process discussed in Chapter 5. Local laws might allow the interior designer to prepare the construction drawings for the remodeling or require him or her to work with an architect to prepare the documents.

Typical residential specialties include:

- Single-family dwellings
- Condominiums
- Townhouses
- Model homes
- Apartments
- Senior housing
- Kitchen and bathroom design

- Home theaters
- Residential historical restoration
- Colorizer for homebuilders
- Home office design
- Residential children's spaces
- Renovation for physically challenged
- Private yachts and houseboats

High-End Residential

CHARLES GANDY, FASID, FIIDA
PRESIDENT, CHARLES GANDY, INC.
ATLANTA, GEORGIA

What has been your greatest challenge as an interior designer?

❯ My greatest challenge as an interior designer has been to learn to listen to my clients, making sure I understand their needs and desires so I can help them achieve the best results.

What led you to enter your design specialty?

❯ I saw the need for a businesslike approach to residential design. I enjoy people, and this seemed like the best place to use my skills in business and design.

What are your primary responsibilities and duties?

❯ Being the president of my company means I set the pace for design solutions and direct my associates to see that those solutions are carried out.

What is the most satisfying part of your job?

❯ Seeing a happy client at the end—that special smile when they walk into a space.

Private residence: residential stairs. Charles Gandy, FASID, FIIDA, Charles Gandy, Inc., Atlanta, Georgia.
PHOTOGRAPH: RON RIZZO

Private residence: living room. Charles Gandy, FASID, FIIDA, Charles Gandy, Inc., Atlanta, Georgia.

PHOTOGRAPH: ROGER WADE

What is the least satisfying part of your job?

❯ The least satisfying is dealing with the day-to-day small problems that arise—but that's just being in business, I guess.

Who or what experience has been a major influence on your career?

❯ I have studied and written about the masters of design—those who came before. I have learned from them and been inspired from them. More recently, 30 years ago, Jack Lenor Larsen came to a school event and inspired me when he told us that he was successful because he "went to work." I have tried to do that my entire career, starting each day with "What am I going to accomplish today?"

How important is certification by examination and the licensing of interior designers today?

❯ Vitally! We have to make sure the public is protected. Qualified interior designers have a major impact on the health, safety, and welfare of those we come in contact with. We therefore should—must—be examined and licensed.

Private residence: dining room. Charles Gandy, FASID, FIIDA, Charles Gandy, Inc., Atlanta, Georgia.

PHOTOGRAPH: RON RIZZO

Aging in Place

The baby boomer generation—those born between 1946 and 1964—began turning 60 in 2006. These adults face numerous decisions and unprecedented freedom in choices of lifestyle, living place, and purchasing power. A huge decision for many is where to live as they age and face the "empty nest" or children having left to be on their own, retirement, and health issues. Many choose to stay in the homes they have always lived in, which can lead to creating a need for remodeling. That remodeling need may be by choice to change an older home's appearance or necessity due to health issues.

The concept of aging in place is not new, of course. It has received unprecedented attention in the late 20th century as the mature generation—the parents of the baby boomers—began to choose to stay in their homes into retirement and beyond. Of course, as health issues overtake these homeowners, some will make the transition into assisted living facilities where nursing care is available for otherwise independent adults. Others will realize that health issues and limitations require moving into long-term care facilities, where they will receive daily nursing care.

Designing or remodeling homes for adults who wish to age in place brings many challenges to designers. For example, materials specifications need to be made with safety in mind, as the polished stone floor used in a home for younger adults can be especially hazardous for the mature and senior adult. Door handles and faucet handles that require grasping can be very difficult for the person with moderate to severe arthritis. Door widths and thresholds can impede movement for someone in a wheelchair or who must use a walker. But these design changes, although often necessary, must be done subtly as healthy baby boomers often do not want to be reminded of potential health issues. But do any of us?

Residential interior designers must become sensitive to the needs of homeowners who wish to remain in their homes as they age. It is important for residential designers to learn as much as they can about the needs and issues of designing residences for mature adults. The American Society of Interior Designers (ASID) has research material available to members and nonmembers through its Web site, www.asid.org. Seminars are also available at national and many local chapter meetings that can be attended by any interested interior designer.

Aging-in-place residence: powder room. Patricia Rowen, ASID, CAPS, Rowen Design, Hillsdale, Michigan.

PHOTOGRAPH: BLUE SKY PHOTOGRAPHY COURTESY OF THE AMERICAN SOCIETY OF INTERIOR DESIGNERS

Another option chosen by many designers is to become a Certified Aging-in-Place Specialist (CAPS) through the National Association of Home Builders (NAHB). According to the NAHB, the CAPS program "teaches the technical, business management, and customer service skills essential to competing in the fastest growing segment of the residential remodeling industry: home modifications for the aging in place."[1] This program is of great value to interior designers who wish to specialize in working with clients who wish to age in place.

High-End Residential: Primary and Secondary Resort and Aging in Place

MICHAEL THOMAS, FASID, CAPS
PRINCIPAL, DESIGN COLLECTIVE GROUP, INC.
JUPITER, FLORIDA

What has been your greatest challenge as an interior designer?

❯ Trying to keep the balance of work, projects, income, and cash flow on an even keel.

What led you to enter your design specialty?

❯ Moved to Florida, where this specialty exists.

What are your primary responsibilities and duties?

❯ As principal, keeping the work flowing through the staff to accomplish the design specifications that we've established for the project.

What is the most satisfying part of your job?

❯ I enjoy the work the most when I am presenting our solutions to a client and it all seems to be clicking with them.

What is the least satisfying part of your job?

❯ Tracking down subcontractors who fail to show, do inferior work, won't return phone calls promptly; chasing around to make sure it all happens before the client kicks the bucket. Don't laugh. It happens.

Private residence: master suite. Michael Thomas, FASID, DESIGN Collective Group, Inc., Jupiter, Florida.
PHOTOGRAPH: CARLOS DOMENECH

What is the most important quality or skill of a designer in your specialty?

❯ Much better than average communication skills, including the ability to sell the solution to the client.

Who or what experience has been a major influence on your career?

❯ I guess nothing in particular stands out, but I have been provided with numerous opportunities to hone a number of skills, so I am broadly rather than narrowly experienced. This makes me deadly when I know a little something about everything I must ultimately be responsible for.

What advice would you give to someone who wants to be an interior designer?

❯ Establish criteria in depth with the client. Believe that the solution you are offering is the right one for the criteria. Don't be afraid to sell the solution you believe in.

Can you describe the optimum job applicant?

❯ Someone who has real-world experiences, and I find those people are over the age of 30. In fact, for a long time I employed only people who were older than me. Now I'm older, and so are they. But I still like employing someone who is not just out of school—at any price.

TOP RIGHT Private residence: living room. Michael Thomas, FASID, DESIGN Collective Group, Inc., Jupiter, Florida.
PHOTOGRAPH: CARLOS DOMENECH

RIGHT Private residence: guest suite kitchen. Michael Thomas, FASID, DESIGN Collective Group, Inc., Jupiter, Florida.
PHOTOGRAPH: JIM ROBINETTE, NOTHING NEGATIVE PHOTOGRAPHY

Commercial

Commercial interior design involves the design of public spaces for the purpose of private and nonprofit business. It is generally agreed that public spaces are interiors where the general public may enter, although, of course, there may still be some restrictions. Examples of for-profit businesses are movie theaters, hotels, restaurants, stores, and medical suites, while government buildings are nonprofit business facilities. Any type of business can restrict entry by the general public into certain areas of the business facility. For example, many corporate offices limit entry to employees. A restaurant does not generally allow customers into the kitchen.

All of commercial interior design, regardless of specialty, has certain common considerations. Commercial interior design projects must be executed with adherence to strict building, fire safety, and accessibility codes. Codes are "systematic bodies of law created by federal, state, and local jurisdictions to ensure the safety of the public."[2] These codes help the owner of the property, the architect, and the interior designer create safe places for employees to work and the public to enjoy.

Depending on the type of interior facility, the interior designer is challenged in meeting the needs of multiple groups. Of course, the owner of the property is always important in the design decision making, as the owner sets the budget and often the direction of the design project. Commercial facilities have employees, and their satisfaction with the design of the space can be key to the success of a business enterprise. A third group that must be satisfied are the customers, clients, guests, and other users of the space. A poorly designed restaurant will not succeed with some customers even if the food is very good.

Commercial interior design is an exciting area of the profession. Fast-paced, even stressful, commercial projects can be far larger and more complex than residential projects. The responsibility for creating a safe environment for the general public can be considerable. Clients are generally budget-conscious, and the concept of "cheaper, better, faster" is common for commercial projects. However, it is a challenge that interior designers in the profession accept. "Commercial Interior Design Specialtes" (facing page) provides a partial list of specialty areas in which interior designers focus depending on their market and economic reality. The rest of this chapter introduces you to a selection of both residential and commercial interior design specializations as well as many interior design professionals who work in a number of them.

COMMERCIAL INTERIOR DESIGN SPECIALTIES

Corporate and Executive Offices

Any size office for any kind of business other than those listed below

Professional Offices

Law

Accounting

Stockbrokers

Real estate brokers

Healthcare

Hospitals

Assisted living facilities

Medical and dental suites

Psychiatric facilities

Outpatient services

Medical laboratories

Veterinary clinics

Pediatric facilities

Hospitality and Entertainment/Recreation

Hotels, motels, and resorts

Restaurants

Health clubs and spas

Park facilities

Country clubs

Museums and galleries

Sports complexes

Convention centers

Retail Facilities/Merchandising

Malls and shopping centers

Department stores

Specialty stores

Gift shops

Visual merchandising for trade shows

Trade showrooms

Institutional

Government offices and facilities

Financial institutions; banks, credit unions

Elementary and secondary schools

Universities and colleges

Day care centers

Churches and other religious facilities

Industrial Facilities

Manufacturing facilities

Training facilities

Transportation

Airport terminals

Tour ships

Custom and commercial airplanes

Recreational vehicles

Sustainable Design

Sustainable design reaches into all types of commercial spaces as well as private residences. Clients are increasingly demanding healthy environments and products that do as little harm to occupants as is possible. There is great opportunity for interior designers—regardless of their specialty—to become engaged in design philosophies that embrace sustainable design theories and practices. Chapter 1 features an overview about sustainable design.

Corporate Interiors, Sustainable Design

COLLEEN MCCAFFERTY, IFMA, USGBC, LEED-CI
CORPORATE INTERIOR TEAM LEADER
HIXSON
CINCINNATI, OHIO

What led you to enter your design specialty?

❯ The challenge of interior design in the corporate entity does not let you down. There are always new challenges, new things to learn. Every company has its own fingerprint that needs to be understood in order to provide the right solution. The field itself has so many pieces to it that it takes more than a lifetime to perfect it all, and it is constantly changing. It is not boring.

What is the most important quality or skill of a designer in your specialty?

❯ I would answer this with two skills, not one. It is highly important to be a great listener, and then, a great problem solver.

How is your specialty different from other specialties?

❯ I think that the corporate entity is different because every corporate client brings its own culture and way of doing business. Solutions

Corporate: Lexmark café. Colleen McCafferty, IFMA, LEED-CI, Hixson Architecture, Engineering, Interiors. Cincinnati, Ohio.
PHOTOGRAPH: JIM CROTTY

are not cut and pasted: They evolve through the process of understanding the corporation, the users, and the people that you are working with. It is less restrictive in space planning and the use of materials, unlike healthcare and institutional design sectors. It is more about supplying the right solution through a discovery system and team collaboration. It's not about ego or trying the latest trend; it's about doing what is right for that company, listening to who they are, and finding creative solutions that help them get to where they want to be. It takes a high degree of understanding what the client is telling you and channeling that information into an environment that is conducive to that particular company.

ABOVE Corporate: Lexmark company store. Colleen McCafferty, IFMA, LEED-CI, Hixson Architecture, Engineering, Interiors. Cincinnati, Ohio.
PHOTOGRAPH: JIM CROTTY

BELOW Floor plan: Lexmark café. Colleen McCafferty, IFMA, LEED-CI, Hixson Architecture, Engineering, Interiors. Cincinnati, Ohio.
PHOTOGRAPH: JIM CROTTY

What are your primary responsibilities and duties in your position?

❯ As a team leader on a project, there is a project responsibility that includes the discovery process, a "Voice of the Customer" review, programming, space planning, finish selections— and the orchestration of a team of people for cost estimating, scheduling, client relationship development, engineering, architecture, production, and construction administration.

As a team leader for the interior design department, my responsibility is to make sure we are on the leading edge in our field, knowing what is new, what is being talked about, and sharing that information. I need to be sure our other designers are informed and on track for departmental and personal goals.

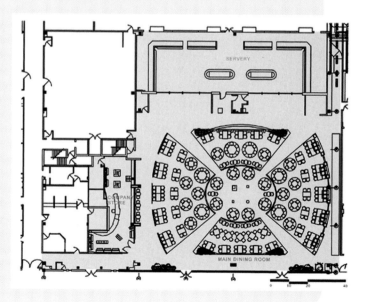

What is the most satisfying part of your job?

❯ The most satisfying part of my job is when a plan comes together, working as a team to create a solution, present it, implement it to the satisfaction of the client, and having them pleased with the result. People, by nature, do not like change. When you are able to work with the leadership group on a vision, implement *change management* with great communication tools, and create a new environment that is successful from a work process standpoint, as well as pleasing the user group and creating a great new aesthetic, that is sheer joy.

What is the least satisfying part of your job?

❯ When a client pays for your expertise, yet does not trust your opinion to do the right thing for them, that is the least satisfying part of my job. It becomes a loss for them.

Who or what experience has been a major influence on your career?

❯ The co-op experience at Herman Miller in the early 1970s has been a major influence. Because it was in its infancy, I got to be exposed to this company and others from early on, tracking the progress of the furniture industry that has had a powerful influence in the corporate world today. The furniture industry has had a commitment to research that has shaped the design trends of Corporate America.

What has been your greatest challenge as an interior designer?

❯ I suppose that the greatest challenge is the same as the reason I am still in this field: There is so much to learn and to keep on top of, with ever-changing information. It takes a commitment to become an expert.

What Do You Feel Is the Impact of Sustainable Design or Design for Seniors on the Profession?

❯ Huge! As I am heavily involved in the design for seniors area, I know how great the impact will be in a few years. If we use the sustainable, energy-efficient universal design standards in new construction from now on, there will be no need for aging-in-place modifications, as we would have already accommodated for all people. Sustainable design just makes sense; however, I do not believe product manufacturers are working hard enough to make it affordable for all.
Patricia Rowen, ASID, CAPS

❯ Regarding designing for an aging population, it will also be woven into our project solutions. Good design needs to include invisible, seamless solutions to address all accessibility, independent living, and universal design solutions for everyone.
Robert Wright, FASID

❯ Interior designers need to embrace both as a standard business practice. They're invaluable for human health and the fundamental value proposition for the interior design profession.
Linda Sorrento, ASID, IIDA, LEED-AP

❯ In just a few years, these issues will no longer be options or "fashion." They will each simply become an integral part of the way we do our ID business.
Bruce Brigham, FASID, ISP, IES

❯ The age wave and green wave are just now rolling down the highway and have not yet reached the tipping point; however, in 10 years, these trends in design will just be a daily part of what we all do.
Michael Thomas, FASID, CAPS

❯ Sustainable design and senior design are just a result of an improved awareness of our responsibility as human beings who care for all and our environment. We need to be ever conscious of how not to harm our physical environment in all that we construct and deconstruct. We need also to be ever conscious that at any age people have challenges and need our foresight to design universally for all capabilities.
Rosalyn Cama, FASID

❯ Both sustainability and designing for seniors need to become so intrinsically part of any design that it becomes rote on all design projects.
Patricia Campbell McLaughlin, ASID, RID

❯ With the first baby boomers now becoming seniors, interior designers need to understand how to design for four generations working together.
Rita Carson Guest, FASID

❯ Universal design is needed and interior designers need to show clients the benefits. When clients are presented with the options and understand the concept, they readily accept universal as part of their design plan.
Sue Norman, IIDA

❯ Hopefully, the impact is positive in that designers are addressing more socially responsible sectors of design for the good of society. Expanding the knowledge base corresponds with developing new definitions of aesthetics, strengthening the familiar "form follows function" dictum, and understanding that good design should be the norm not the exception for everyone everywhere. The impact on the profession and design education is that there is increasingly more to know and more to teach. Additionally, more critical thinking is required to evaluate the concepts and their application to projects—that is, what works and what doesn't, what can we believe or trust versus marketing and advertising campaigns, and what continuing education is required for professionals and what is taught to students for their prospective careers.
Carol Morrow, Ph.D., ASID, IIDA, IDEC

❯ The impact is definite. Without resources we cannot build and design, so it is essential that we pay special attention to sustainable products, services, and resources. As the population ages, design will change to accommodate the special needs of special people.
Charles Gandy, FASID, FIIDA

❯ As far as designing for seniors is concerned, our firm is proof that this is a growing field. With all of the baby boomers retiring, the demand for more active communities is increasing. The days of "nursing homes" are dwindling due to the fact that more people are becoming concerned with active lifestyles and finer living. Retirees over the next few generations are going to demand more community-based homes with more activities, fine dining, and an overall better quality of living in older age populations.
Shannon Ferguson, IIDA

❯ I believe that both sustainability and designing for all abilities (including all ages) is not so much something that is an impact as they are issues that should be fundamentally considered in all aspects of design.
David Hanson, RID, IDC, IIDA

> These are two design criteria no longer in the future but necessary disciplines now.
Mary Knott, Allied Member ASID, CID, RSPI

> I believe it has a strong impact. I think all projects regardless of type or size should have sustainable and universal design principles.
Donna Vining, FASID, IIDA, RID, CAPS

> Hopefully sustainable design will be what the Americans with Disabilities Act (ADA) was. It will just become a no-brainer for all to do. Design for seniors will continue to grow as we live longer and the boomers continue to age.
Jo Rabaut, ASID, IIDA

> I feel that sustainable design will be extremely important to help the planet and design professionals must begin to be educated about it. I also feel as the baby boomers age, there will be a very high demand for environments that affect seniors and their lifestyles.
Lisa Slayman, ASID, IIDA

> We have an imperative to correct the spiral of negative influence humans have exerted on our planet, and to make responsible choices that improve the environment, at the very least that do it no further harm.
Katherine Ankerson, IDEC, NCARB Certified

> Both areas are becoming more and more important, even if not specifically requested by the client. Our natural resources and overall health are dramatically affected by our ability to embrace and incorporate the basic principles of both aging in place and environmentally sensitive design solutions. We have less from which to build (sustainable design), and we are all using our facilities much longer (aging). Whether we realize it or not, both are now fundamental aspects in all design solutions, even if they are not LEED-certified or age specific.
David Stone, IIDA, LEED-AP

> Of course these are both important contemporary issues. There is a high learning curve for both areas of expertise, and one that all of us should be working on. We as a profession should be part of the process of preserving the resources of the planet we live on. We achieve that by understanding the materials that we choose for our projects and in continuing education to keep up with the ever-changing demands of this product knowledge. The baby boomers are a large part of our population and have a great influence on product design and environmental design.
Debra Himes, ASID, IIDA

> Universal design is also very important in today's society. Our population is living longer and working longer before retiring. The design of both residential and commercial spaces that can be universally enjoyed is a requirement rather than an option. There is growing need for senior living facilities that improve the quality of life as we live longer. Enhancing access, easing mobility, and creating a healthy, stimulating environment are key roles of the designer in this expanding market. Medical advances will likely create even more complex design solutions for this aspect of design.
Mary Knopf, ASID, IIDA, LEED-AP

> Very great as it affects the way you design, the products you specify, and the way you look at design. Especially as we state that we affect the "health, safety, and welfare" of the consumer. But I would caution us to be sure we truly research and have a strong set of facts and knowledge behind us before just jumping on the wagon.
Drue Lawlor, FASID

❯ Universal design is better design for all people. As a philosophy and practice, it should be treated and viewed the same way as sustainable design and threaded completely throughout the design curriculum.

Stephanie Clemons, Ph.D., FASID, FIDEC

❯ I like to think of it in reverse. Interior design has a tremendous contribution to make to both sustainable design and design for the aging population because interior design provides for the most intimate exchange between human beings and their environment. These comparatively new areas of expertise require additional study by all practitioners and create opportunities for new practice specialties.

Suzan Globus, FASID, LEED-AP

❯ Design for seniors is and will continue to be a strong market in the U.S. as the numbers of retiring baby boomers increase. Their needs are diverse and much more demanding than their parents' generation. This is going to be an active generation of seniors that won't fit any one mold. There will be many still working into their 70s while others change to a leisurely lifestyle at an early age. They will be driving many changes in how we design for retirement, life care centers, and even death due to the large segment of the population they represent and their spending power.

Robert J. Krikac, IDEC

❯ Interior designers have the strongest impact on the environment and what ends up in the landfill. New isn't always the best. Healthcare will revolve around designing for the aging population for the near future. Learn it and become knowledgeable.

Linda Isley, IIDA, CID

❯ Both are growing markets and will draw designers to new products and opportunities. The aging community will continue to increase

Sustainable residence: master bath, Lake Pines. Annette Stelmack, Allied Member ASID. Inspirit-llc, Louisville, Colorado; formerly with Associates III. Architect: Doug Graybeal, Graybeal Architects (formerly with CCY Architects).

PHOTOGRAPH: DAVID O. MARLOW

worldwide as healthcare improves. This growing demographic bubble should keep a spotlight on the changing needs of the elderly. The trend toward aging in place, adapting your home to accommodate the physical limitations that come with old age, will drive an industry of products that can adapt to a wide variety of physical challenges. The increased need for elderly accommodations will force new levels of safety and security in everyday products.

Sally D'Angelo, ASID, Affiliate Member AIA

❯ The latest "green" advancements are affecting the entire design community. I am seeing more and more products that have a very long life, yet can be recycled and come full circle.

Design for the senior housing sector is unique because clients are striving to provide the right balance between a luxurious resort and permanent housing for seniors at varying levels of independence. Above all, clients who create senior living communities really want great design. There are many small details involved in design for seniors such as lighting, flooring, width of hallways and entrances, but overall feel is critical too. I love incorporating this through bright colors, textures, and materials.

Trisha Wilson, ASID

❯ I have recently added certification in both these processes. I see myself dealing with the integration of design for all into almost all of my projects on a regular basis. Now my next step is to fully bring the contractors I work with to the same level of implementation.

Sharmin Pool-Bak, ASID, CAPS, LEED-AP

❯ Both of these areas require increased education on the part of designers and have specific product requirements. Sustainable design will become an integral part of how a designer specifies a project. In the same way 60-inch turnaround in a public restroom has become standard since the addition of the American with Disabilities Act, so will sustainable products. Designing for seniors in multiple capacities (independent living homes, nursing, dementia, and other care facilities) is one of the biggest segments of the market and is only growing because of the population dynamic right now. As more and more designers focus on senior design, I believe the education and experience gained from these products will lead to more universal design in general. While I am not a residential designer, I believe this will affect the residential house building market more substantially than the commercial market.

Laura Busse, IIDA, KYCID

❯ Planning and designing for seniors is a no-brainer. I essentially tie this tenet to universal design: making all spaces accessible to all people without having to provide special accommodations that single out one person (or group) from others.

Lisa Whited, IIDA, ASID, Maine Certified Interior Designer

❯ I believe that interior designers have the opportunity to affect these aspects of our lives more than others. I also do not believe it is possible to do sustainable design without integrating universal design at the same time. To use our resources wisely, we have to design in such a way that our designs will suit the broadest population segments. In other words, design must be proactive in preparing for the future of an aging population so that when special needs arise, it does not mean tearing out and rebuilding. Good design spans all generations and abilities and avoids wasting natural resources, which ultimately leads to less impact on our environment.

As our population matures—and our society is an aging population—we must be more informed than ever before regarding accessibility issues and universal design. In fact, we should never have to say: this project will be designed on universal design and accessibility principles. It should be a standard of practice that *all* our designs are executed in such a way that they apply to the broadest parameters. To not do so, is to design built-in obsolescence and thus abrogates sustainability. In other words, we are creating art, not design.

Linda E. Smith, FASID

Desert Palms Presbyterian
Church, Sun City West,
Arizona. Sandra Evans, ASID,
Knoell & Quidort Architects,
Phoenix, Arizona.

PHOTOGRAPH: JIM CHRISTY

❯ Sustainable design has finally hit our profession in a big way after some years of being nothing more than a topic for discussion over lunch. More resources are becoming available for designers to use in completing projects, which allow us to better educate and engage our clients in responsible design solutions. With the 76-millon-strong baby boomer generation entering retirement, the sheer numbers will demand that interior designers deal with design for seniors, whether it be in offices, hospitals, nursing homes, educational institutions, or residences. Aging in place will become a key factor for residential designers as boomers refuse to spend their retirement in nursing home facilities like their parents did.

Terri Maurer, FASID

❯ Both have a major impact on design today. Sustainable design is the foundation of LEED (Leadership in Energy and Environmental Design), which is now the standard in any government facilities you work on. In the Washington, D.C., area, government jobs are about 75 percent of your design work. In the D.C. area, sustainability is no longer an impact but a requirement, and designers must be cognizant of sustainability design methods.

Designing for the aging population is also important. Building codes today have taken into account physically disabled aspects and many of these factors pertain to the aging populations issues. Also, healthcare design is the fastest-growing segment in interior and architectural design—due in part to the growing aging population of our society.

Robin Wagner, ASID, IDEC

Corporate and Professional Offices

If you are interested in the economic impact of the interior design industry related to commercial interior design, a source of information that is available to the public and trade is *Interior Design* magazine. In January, it publishes an extensive report on the 100 largest design firms. Besides finding out who these firms are, you can also read information on the dollar value of design fees, amount of square footage designed in several commercial specialties, and through photographs, gain a glimpse of the type of work these large firms produce.

In the January 2007 edition of this research study, the office design specialty led the way in revenue generation with the top 10 firms earning over $359 million in interior design fees.[3] The corporate and professional office specialty is plainly the largest of the commercial interior design specialty areas.

An interior designer specializing in office design might design the office of the *chief executive officer* (CEO) of General Motors. Then again, he or she might be responsible for the offices of a group of employees in an advertising agency or even a neighborhood real estate office. A corporate interiors project might address the space planning and specification of office systems for thousands of employees at a corporate headquarters. Of course, the project might be for any size business that primarily uses office spaces to conduct business.

There are a few key factors to consider in the design of corporate offices. An important factor to effective planning is work patterns and communication patterns within the business. Work flows from one individual or group to others. The interior designer must understand this work flow in order to successfully prepare the floor plans and locations of individuals and work groups. Another factor is understanding what kinds of equipment each person in each job requires. Of course, everyone needs a desk—or do they? Some jobs may require large layout desks such as are used in advertising offices. Other jobs require space for multiple computers and monitors. Most workers need a desk and space for computers in today's business offices. Some also have brief meetings in their work space, while others only meet in groups in a conference room. Obviously, this is only a small amount of the differences that must be considered in the planning of corporate offices.

The design of corporate offices involves considering the hierarchy of the office; it is common practice for higher-level employees to have larger and more elaborately designed offices than lower-level employees. This is true whether the office project is for the CEO of a technology industry giant or your neighborhood tax preparer. Status differences are indicated by the size and location of offices as well as the quality of the furniture items in them.

Office facilities are often mixed-use structures. Spaces for conferences and training, employee cafeterias, healthcare areas, retail stores, or even a nursery may be located in a large corporate building. Thus, the corporate interior design specialist must be familiar with design codes and constraints for many types of commercial spaces or hire consultants for assistance. The element of mixed use makes the corporate and professional office design specialty very exciting. They must also be familiar with the types of products used in an office. As was pointed out, not everyone needs the basic desk. For the last 40 years, many office projects have employed office systems furniture consisting of freestanding panels and other components rather than private offices with standard desks. Designing with this product by correctly determining communication and work interaction patterns as well as space planning and component specification continues to be an important part of corporate design. All these factors make the design of corporate and business offices an exciting challenge for the interior designer who decides to specialize in this area of interior design.

Corporate Interiors

NILA R. LEISEROWITZ, FASID, ASSOCIATE AIA
MANAGING DIRECTOR/PRINCIPAL,
GENSLER
SANTA MONICA, CALIFORNIA

What led you to enter your design specialty?

❭ I enjoy designing corporate interiors because it involves design, strategy, and business.

What is the most important quality or skill of a designer in your specialty?

❭ Design talent and listening skills.

How is your specialty different from other specialties?

❭ My specialty combines strategy and design. I work with clients who are transforming their work environment.

Commercial: common area, ENMAX, Calgary, Alberta, Canada. Nila Leiserowitz, FASID, Gensler, Santa Monica, California.

PHOTOGRAPH: MICHELLE LITVIN

Commercial: company café, ENMAX Café, Calgary, Alberta, Canada. Nila Leiserowitz, FASID, Gensler, Santa Monica, California.

PHOTOGRAPH: MICHELLE LITVIN

What are your primary responsibilities and duties in your position?

❯ My primary responsibility is to balance the design and business goals of the client.

What is the most satisfying part of your job?

❯ Client interaction.

What is the least satisfying part of your job?

❯ Outside consultants that do not understand the design process.

Who or what experience has been a major influence in your career?

❯ ASID.

What has been your greatest challenge as an interior designer?

❯ Establish the value of our expertise.

Commercial: corporate reception area, McCann Erickson, Los Angeles, California. Nila Leiserowitz, FASID, Gensler, Santa Monica, California.

PHOTOGRAPH: MICHELLE LITVIN

Corporate and Hospitality

BRUCE GOFF, ASID, IES
PRINCIPAL, DOMUS DESIGN GROUP
SAN FRANCISCO, CALIFORNIA

What has been your greatest challenge as an interior designer?

❯ Keeping up with new products and solutions.

What led you to enter your design specialty?

❯ Corporations and hospitality people understand and value the use of designers.

What are your primary responsibilities and duties?

❯ As design director, I oversee all projects, set direction for concept, meet with clients, and supervise design staff.

What is the most satisfying part of your job?

❯ Client interaction.

TOP RIGHT Commercial: entrance to a hotel suite. Bruce Goff, ASID, Domus Design Group, San Francisco, California.

PHOTOGRAPH: JOHN SUTTON

RIGHT Commercial: corporate office lunchroom. Bruce Goff, ASID, Domus Design Group, San Francisco, California.

PHOTOGRAPH: JOHN SUTTON

What is the least satisfying part of your job?

❭ Managing people.

What is the important quality or skill of a designer in your specialty?

❭ Communication skills: written, math, oral. Great ideas are only great if someone pays you for them.

How important is interior design education in today's industry?

❭ Don't try this at home without an education—not unless you want to work for a small residential decorator or in a retail setting where selling, not tech skills, is the key.

Commercial: corporate office alternative office seating area. Bruce Goff, ASID, Domus Design Group, San Francisco, California.
PHOTOGRAPH: JOHN SUTTON

Law Office Design

RITA CARSON GUEST, FASID
PRESIDENT, CARSON GUEST INTERIOR DESIGN
ATLANTA, GEORGIA

What is the most important quality or skill of a designer in your specialty?

❭ The ability to communicate well and understand client needs, along with design talent.

What has been your greatest challenge as an interior designer?

❭ The greatest challenge has always been meeting unrealistic deadlines—the result of client needs and expectations—while still doing excellent design work.

What led you to enter your design specialty?

❭ As a young designer, I worked for a firm and was assigned work on a law office. The design was successful, and my clients recommended us to other law firms. The repeat work led to many more law office design projects. Over the years, I started studying law office design and became an expert in the field. Law offices are set up differently than corporations. It has been fun to grow with the practice of law as technology continues to change it.

What are your primary responsibilities and duties?

❭ I am president of my company and director of design. I work closely with our clients, set the design direction of our projects, make all major presentations, and maintain close contact with our clients from programming through the installation. I especially enjoy working with my clients on their art collections, selecting, framing, and supervising the installation of the artwork.

What is the most satisfying part of your job?

❯ The most satisfying part of my job is seeing space that we design built, and seeing how their new environment makes our clients happy and adds to the success of their business.

What is the least satisfying part of your job?

❯ The least satisfying part of my job is dealing with management problems with young designers.

What advice would you give someone who wants to be an interior designer?

❯ Understand that this is not a nine-to-five business. There are always deadlines to meet and after-hours installations to handle. If you want a nine-to-five job, select another profession.

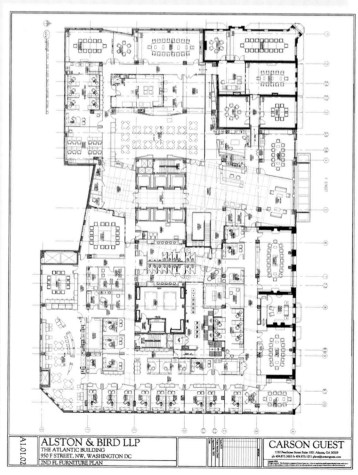

TOP: Law office: Alston & Bird LLP, elevator lobby. Rita Carson Guest, FASID, Carson Guest, Inc., Atlanta, Georgia.
PHOTOGRAPH: GABRIEL BENZUR

RIGHT: Law office: Floor plan Alston & Bird LLP. Rita Carson Guest, FASID, Carson Guest, Inc., Atlanta, Georgia
PHOTOGRAPH: GABRIEL BENZUR

Law office: Alston & Bird LLP, conference room. Rita Carson Guest, FASID, Carson Guest, Inc., Atlanta, Georgia.

PHOTOGRAPH: GABRIEL BENZUR

Can you describe the optimum portfolio for a job applicant?

❭ Provide a variety of work showing all your skills. Orient your portfolio to the type of work you want to do.

Who or what experience has been a major influence on your career?

❭ My first boss taught me.

Universal Design, Aging in Place, Seminars

DRUE ELLEN LAWLOR, FASID
OWNER, DRUE LAWLOR INTERIORS,
AND PRINCIPAL,
education-works, inc. (ewi)
SAN GABRIEL, CALIFORNIA, AND DALLAS, TEXAS

What led you to enter your design specialty?

❭ Forming education-works, inc. came from mutual involvement in ASID's national training programs—"mutual" meaning my business partner and other members of our team—and our strong belief in lifelong learning.

As far as entering the specialty area of universal design and aging in place, I became aware early in my design career that residential and commercial spaces can be limiting for those challenged by ability limitations. My extremely active mother was diagnosed with multiple sclerosis when she was in her 50s and eventually ended up in a wheelchair for nearly 30 years. My father adapted and remodeled their homes to work for my mother rather than against her. Though I helped, he was a natural problem solver and in many instances created solutions that had not been thought of before. I certainly learned from both of my parents that if spaces were created in their original design to welcome all ages and abilities, life would be much less stressful for everyone. I also began to realize that good design can have a positive effect on the function and physical part of their lives, of course, but also on the mental and spiritual. As we lose some of our abilities, the spaces we are in make an even stronger impact, I believe.

What is the most important quality or skill of a designer in your specialty?

❭ Listening and constantly learning. This applies to both ewi and my design specialty. Every person is different (thank goodness!) and we are often trying to help them plan for the future (as we are trying to plan the ewi business to meet the future needs of the people and organizations with which we work). Though I can't foretell the future, I need to think of what might be of help to each individual. The best way to do this is to truly listen to the client and to always be learning new approaches, new ideas, and about new products.

How is your specialty different from other specialties?

❭ As far as ewi is concerned, we are focused more on helping companies and organizations build their business, rather than performing interior design for them. And though we also offer

education to the consumer, we are not marketing our interior design skills when doing so. Rather we are marketing professional interior designers so we are often seen as a third-party marketer. The same can be true with some of the companies and organizations with whom we work.

As to the universal design and aging-in-place specialty, I don't view it as much as a specialty as a focus that every designer should have.

What are your primary responsibilities and duties in your position?

❭ With ewi, it would be marketing, writing, producing and presenting seminars, speaking engagements, strategic planning for organizations and companies, as well as working with our team on scheduling and setting the calendars.

What is the most satisfying part of your job?

❭ Researching and learning new information to share in seminars, presenting and speaking, and meeting new people.

What is the least satisfying part of your job?

❭ Often the travel can be wearing, as can the detail work.

Who or what experience has been a major influence on your career?

❭ For ewi, it would be the experiences as part of the ASID national training and being chair of a council. My parents would be the "who" because of their unfailing support and wise counsel. Also one of my first interior design instructors, Ann Vonn, ASID, who became my mentor and so strongly encouraged me to take the NCIDQ and to get involved in ASID. Also, Charles Gandy, FASID, though he may not remember, as he "opened a window" a little wider for me and gave me a little extra confidence.

Hospitality

One branch of hospitality interior design is lodging facilities. Examples are hotels, motels, resort facilities, bed-and-breakfast inns, and other places where guests stay for a few days to a few weeks. Many include recreational facilities such as golf clubhouses, spas, resorts, and casinos in this category because many lodging facilities include some form of recreational space. The other main branch of hospitality design is food and beverage facilities. Restaurants, cafés, coffee shops, cocktail lounges and bars, fast-food restaurants, and elegant dining rooms and lounges are the most common examples. Hospitality facilities owned by large chains—Hyatt Hotels and Chili's Restaurants, for example—are usually designed by interior designers working at the corporate headquarters. Many restaurants—for simplicity—and small lodging facilities such as a bed-and-breakfast inn are designed by independent interior design firms.

The design of hospitality facilities starts with a carefully researched and developed design concept that clarifies both the problem presented by the client and the expected solutions. The design concept provides an overall idea that unites the project elements into a cohesive whole. The wrong design concept in the wrong location will fail—even if the actual design is well done. Design concepts, by the way, are common documents prepared by interior designers during the initial stage of the project called programming for many kinds of commercial projects.

Lodging facilities is the all-encompassing term for rooms and related interiors in which a guest stays or uses for a short-term vacation, for a business conference or meeting, while traveling, or as a temporary residence for business or out of some other necessity. Interior designers who specialize in this type of facility are hired primarily to design the lobby, the ballroom and other meeting rooms, the guest registration area, the guest rooms, and the hotel offices.

Careful attention must be paid to the design of guest rooms, which constitute the primary revenue-producing area of the lodging facility. Of course, guest rooms must be attractive and meet expectations in terms of the price charged to stay there. Yet the planning and specification of products in the rooms is critical with respect to housekeeping and maintenance as well because costs associated with these essential functions are large. A fragile fabric on chairs in the guest rooms of a family resort facility, for example, will present difficult, even expensive, maintenance problems. This kind of consideration—and similar ones related to other public areas of the lodging facility—is critical for the hospitality interior design professional.

A hotel is a mixed-use space as well. It commonly has food and beverage areas, retail stores, and, perhaps, service shops such as beauty salons. Other spaces may include specialty businesses, workout rooms, spas, and play areas for children, to name the most common. As with a corporate headquarters, one design firm may have the expertise to design all these spaces, or a team of designers may be involved.

The interior planning and design of a restaurant or other food and beverage facility also begins with the development of the overall concept. A restaurant is an expensive business to open and careful consideration of competition, expected revenues, and the target guest are important before any actual interior design decisions are made. As the reader no doubt has observed, a food and beverage facility includes space planning for dining, locations of service areas, the kitchen, and other support spaces. The design and specification of furniture items, architectural finishes, lighting design, and accessories are all important, even critical, to the success of a food and beverage facility. These items, in combination with the menu, fulfill the concept envisioned by the owners. Commercial kitchens are quite complex and are usually designed by individuals who specialize in kitchen design. The interior designer is responsible for areas customers will use and coordinates traffic flow issues with the kitchen designer.

Hospitality: Hotels, Restaurants, Clubs, Spas, and Casinos

TRISHA WILSON, ASID
PRESIDENT, WILSON ASSOCIATES
DALLAS, TEXAS

What has been your greatest challenge as an interior designer?

❭ Managing employees.

What led you to enter your design specialty?

❭ I studied design at the University of Texas in Austin. On graduation, I went to work for a department store chain in their home furnishings department. From there I started doing residential design, then moved on to restaurant design through a residential client. My first hotel design project was the Anatole Hotel in Dallas, which I landed by making a gutsy phone call to the developer.

Lodging: tea lounge, Yokohama Royal Park Hotel Nikko, Yokohama, Japan. Trisha Wilson, ASID, Wilson Associates, Dallas, Texas.
PHOTOGRAPH: ROBERT MILLER

TOP Lodging: guest suite, Las Ventanas al Paraiso, Los Cabos, Mexico. Trisha Wilson, ASID, Wilson Associates, Dallas, Texas.

PHOTOGRAPH: PETER VITALE

ABOVE Lodging: lobby, Atlantis Resort, Paradise Island, Bahamas. Trisha Wilson, ASID, Wilson Associates, Dallas, Texas. Architect: Watg Architects & HKS, Inc.

PHOTOGRAPH: PETER VITALE.

What are your primary responsibilities and duties?

> Overall management of the firm, which includes employees, clients, and vendors. I read financial reports, look over contracts, and talk on the phone endlessly. Our six offices span the globe and are in different time zones. Because of this, there is never an hour in the day when the office is closed. I do still work on the design of several projects each year.

What is the most satisfying part of your job?

> The most satisfying is the accolades my team receives when we install a beautiful project. A satisfied client and appreciative public are really gratifying.

What is the most important quality or skill of a designer in your specialty?

> Communication. Of course, a designer needs to have talent, but if you cannot communicate your ideas or vision, you are ineffective.

Who or what experience has been a major influence on your career?

> My first major influence was developer Trammel Crow in the early 1970s in Dallas, Texas. He took a huge risk in hiring me (an unknown designer) to design his hotel convention center, the Anatole. It was a daunting project. But with his support, I just jumped right in and figured it out. A second influence was developer Sol Kerzner in South Africa in the early 1990s. He approached us to design his Palace of the Lost City hotel in Sun City, South Africa. It was another daunting project in a country that was extremely underdeveloped regarding the decorative arts and suppliers. With his encouragement and support (and a ton of hard work), we turned out a spectacular hotel.

Commercial: Office, Hospitality, Medical, Elderly Care, and Retail

DAVID F. COOKE, FIIDA, CMG
PRINCIPAL, DESIGN COLLECTIVE INCORPORATED
BALTIMORE, MARYLAND

What has been your greatest challenge as an interior designer?

❯ Planning for change in business (including economy, architectural community, and dealerships selling interior design services).

What led you to enter your design specialty?

❯ A mentor-boss named Chuck Nitschke.

RIGHT Restaurant: bar/lounge, The Ocean Club, New Albany, Ohio. David Cooke, Design Collective, Inc., Columbus, Ohio.

PHOTOGRAPH: MICHAEL HOUGHTON, STUDIOHIO

BELOW Restaurant: floor plan, The Ocean Club, New Albany, Ohio. David Cooke, Design Collective, Inc., Columbus, Ohio.

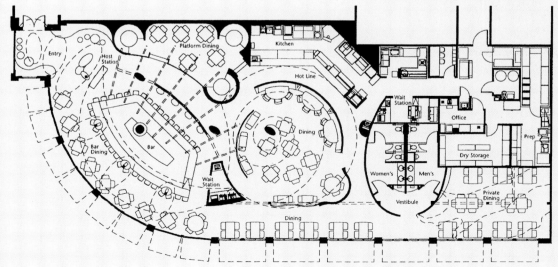

What are your primary responsibilities and duties in your position?

❯ After 30 years, you name it! Marketing, design, planning, staff relations, forecaster.

What is the most satisfying part of your job?

❯ I love the creation of a good idea into a real project and client interaction.

What is the least satisfying part of your job?

❯ I dislike staff reviews!

What is the most important quality or skill of a designer in your specialty?

❯ Communication skills: Can you talk *and* draw?

Who or what experience has been a major influence on your career?

❯ I cannot think of just one. Some have been the great clients, the IBD (Institute of Business Designers, now IIDA) national presidency, industry participation such as NCIDQ, FIDER, CMG, trips to manufacturers, and so on.

Commercial Office Design, Retail, and Restaurants

MARYANNE HEWITT, IIDA
OWNER, INTERIOR DESIGNER
HEWITT INTERIOR DESIGN GROUP, LLC
JACKSONVILLE BEACH, FLORIDA

What led you to enter your design specialty?

❯ My education influences at the University of Florida allowed me to develop the skill set needed to be able to effectively design in the commercial market. I enjoy commercial office space because I can have an impact on a larger group of people in a space they typically spend most of their time in. Commercial clients are also typically less emotional about their spaces than residential clients and I prefer that.

What is the most important quality or skill of a designer in your specialty?

❯ It is hard to pinpoint the single most important quality or skill for my field. It is equally important that the designer has a thorough knowledge of how the building systems go together, how to effectively draw and detail their design ideas so they can be priced and built, a sense of local project budgets,

and the ability to translate a client's conversations about their project into a reality.

How is your specialty different from other specialties?

❯ There are many differences between a commercial and residential designer. Specific to a commercial office design, commercial office space is becoming more of a universal design experience where businesses are offering office perks to compete for high-quality employees. The incorporation of fitness centers, daycare facilities, locker rooms, cafés, and food service vendors provide an employee with a convenience factor that is attractive in today's fast-paced society. This means that the commercial office interior designer now has to have competency in areas expanded beyond traditional office space design to be able to offer full-service design for these clients.

What are your primary responsibilities and duties in your position?

❯ My primary responsibilities as owner of my company are to ensure a steady inflow of design projects, ensure that our product is consistent in quality, that our bills are paid, our clients are happy, and our employees are enriched in their careers, respecting their own personal priorities and availability. Piece of cake!

What is the most satisfying part of your job?

❯ The most satisfying part of my job is working through the puzzle of forming a new space from the outline of requirements and then seeing it unfold during construction. I have two children and I associate the construction process with the birth of a child. Sometimes it is just as painful.

Who or what experience has been a major influence on your career?

❯ My experience at HOK Tampa was the most influential to my design career. The company is amazing. They are a well-oiled machine with the top creative talent. Their professionals know their stuff and I was honored to be one of them. I learned a lot from my colleagues and with a firm that big, I was able to work on a wide variety of projects.

What has been your greatest challenge as an interior designer?

❯ My greatest challenge as an interior designer is holding my tongue when I am called a decorator. I am constantly negotiating with myself how to (and even whether or not to) correct and educate people on the difference.

Remodeling: finished elevator lobby. Maryanne Hewitt, IIDA, ASID. Hewitt Interior Design Group, LLC, Jacksonville, Florida. Architect: PBV Architecture.

PHOTOGRAPH: SUE ROOT BARKER

Entertainment and Recreation

These facilities are challenging specialties of commercial interior design since they are multi functional spaces and involve many specialties in interior design. The planning and design is complex, often involving offices, food service at some level, possibly lodging such as a ski resort, and the entertainment or recreation activity itself. In some cases the activity may be multiplied by numerous activities such as golf, tennis, other racket sports, workout areas, and so on.

We go to places of entertainment and recreation to forget our troubles and have fun for a few hours. Perhaps we are vicariously transported to another land in movies and legitimate theater performances. Maybe we go to cheer our favorite sports team at a stadium. Other entertainment facility types are casinos, theme parks, golf clubs, ski resorts, and many types of small sports facilities. A more specialized area of entertainment interior design is the design of the sets and production spaces for television, radio, and movie studios.

The design of entertainment facilities requires strict adherence and attention to building and safety codes. The owners and designers must provide a safe environment for the large numbers of people who are welcomed into these facilities. There may be no compromises on safety issues in order to make the stadium or theater or studio somehow more attractive. The interior designer is challenged to design sports stadium skyboxes, casinos, and theaters safely as well as to attract consumers to the space.

As is true for most commercial projects, the interior designer is a member of a team in the design of entertainment spaces. Special considerations for lighting, acoustics, mechanical systems, and structural factors make entertainment spaces impossible for the interior designer to do alone. That is why most interior design firms who specialize in entertainment spaces work within architectural offices and hire experienced interior designers only.

Hospitality, High-End Residential

LISA SLAYMAN, ASID, IIDA
PRESIDENT, SLAYMAN DESIGN ASSOCIATES, INC.
NEWPORT BEACH, CALIFORNIA

What led you to enter your design specialty?

❭ When I graduated from college, I went to work for a very famous interior designer at the time that did high-end residential throughout the world. After I spent a few years with him, I left to work for a very well-known commercial firm because I wanted to see what commercial design entailed. After working for both these firms, I decided I wanted to get into specific parts of commercial and also stay in the exclusive high-end residential area.

What is the most important quality or skill of a designer in your specialty?

❭ Knowing how to work with very wealthy, demanding clients and also being able to create an environment that is not only well received, but fits their criteria. If you can accomplish this they will continue to send you work.

Sports arena: owner's box, Jobing.com arena, Glendale, Arizona. Lisa Slayman, ASID, IIDA, Slayman Design Associates, Inc., Newport Beach, California. Architect: HOK, Kansas City.
PHOTOGRAPH: PHILLIP ENNIS PHOTOGRAPHY

How is your specialty different from other specialties?

❭ You are working with very wealthy, successful, and demanding clients who need a designer whose work reflects their ego, along with creating something that people want to spend time in and come back over and over.

What are your primary responsibilities and duties in your position?

❭ My role as principal is working closely with the owner or person in charge communicating and presenting all proposed designs to clients, being responsible for all initial design concepts and relaying those to people in my firm who cannot only execute them, but add creativity, solutions, and any necessary details and drawings. I make sure that I am traveling and staying on top of all the new materials, furnishings, and any other new products that we can potentially use to make our design better. From an administrative side, I am overseeing all financial issues, employee issues, and making sure my firm is successful in all aspects.

What is the most satisfying part of your job?

❭ The most satisfying part of my job is when a project gets completed and looks outrageous, along with people who experience the spaces for the first time and love how it looks, feels, and functions. You could not ask for a better outcome on all the hard effort and time put into it.

What is the least satisfying part of your job?

❭ The least satisfying part of my job is dealing with all the unknowns that you cannot anticipate and the stress that goes along with fixing them.

Who or what experience has been a major influence on your career?

❭ Having a client for whom I did his beach house come to me and ask if I would like to do all the interiors for the new sports arena of the Phoenix Coyotes, the professional ice hockey team that he owned in Glendale, Arizona.

What has been your greatest challenge as an interior designer?

❭ Working on my first sports arena that was 800,000 square feet and knowing that there was no room for any mistakes, being responsible for millions of dollars and achieving my goal of creating an arena interior that would be one of the best in the country.

What do you enjoy most about working in the firm you are in right now?

❭ I really enjoy the client interaction and problem solving.

TOP Sports arena: Coyotes team store, Jobing.com arena, Glendale, Arizona. Lisa Slayman, ASID, IIDA, Slayman Design Associates, Inc., Newport Beach, California. Architect: HOK, Kansas City.

PHOTOGRAPH: PHILLIP ENNIS PHOTOGRAPHY

LEFT Sports arena: Lexus lounge, Jobing.com arena, Glendale, Arizona. Lisa Slayman ASID, IIDA, Slayman Design Associates, Inc., Newport Beach, California. Architect: HOK, Kansas City.

PHOTOGRAPH: PHILLIP ENNIS PHOTOGRAPHY

Retail Facilities

Consider a few of the stores that you have visited in the last few weeks. What drew you to any of these stores? Was it that you knew the merchandise you wanted was sold there? Was it a display of merchandise in the storefront? Was the interior design of the space in keeping with the merchandise sold in the store?

The interior design of retail facilities addresses these issues and more as the designer helps the retailer sell merchandise—regardless of the store's size or the type of merchandise sold to consumers. Department stores and specialty stores in shopping malls, freestanding stores, and specialty stores located in neighborhood open strip malls are included in this area of commercial interior design. Examples of projects are an independently owned apparel store in a shopping area, the interiors of a department store, and everything in between.

Merchandising is a familiar term to the retail facilities designer. It involves all the functions needed to effect the selling of merchandise, including advertising, the mix of merchandise, one-on-one selling, product displays, and the interior design and specification of the store itself. Because the total merchandising concept is so important to the success of a store, the interior designer working in this specialty must understand the business of retail.

The floor plan of the retail store is very important. The cabinets and bins—called *fixtures*—that display and store the merchandise are planned to draw the customer into the store and to encourage the customer to explore the items offered for sale. Have you ever wondered why, in a department store, the clothing items are placed on the sides of the store space while items such as cosmetics, jewelry, and accessories are often placed right near or adjacent to the entry? You might come to a department store to buy a shirt or a skirt, but placing high-demand (and often high price-point) items such as cosmetics near the entry creates additional sales. Those small items displayed at the cash register in a grocery store, referred to as *impulse items* in the retail business, are placed there to encourage quick, impulsive purchases, since customers rarely enter a grocery store in the 21st century to buy a package of gum.

In retail design, what is being sold has a critical impact on the plan and design of the store interior. Customers must be induced to visit all parts of the store so that spontaneous sales do occur. The planning and interior design is meant to give customers the opportunity to see a large number of merchandise items. The type of merchandise obviously affects the way the merchandise is displayed. Many store fixtures—the equipment used to display merchandise such as jewelry cabinets and clothing racks—are custom designed by the interior designer. Security measures intended to inhibit shoplifting are also important.

The independent interior design firm has more opportunity to work with the owners of small independent retail stores than with chain stores. Many department stores and franchise or chain specialty stores have in-house interior design teams that design new facilities. Corporate planners and interior designers as well as merchandising staff most often have the responsibility for the interior design of these stores.

Retail Design and Brand Development

BRUCE JAMES BRIGHAM, FASID, ISP, IES
PRINCIPAL, RETAIL CLARITY CONSULTING
SAYULITA, NAYARIT STATE, MEXICO

What led you to enter your design specialty?

❭ Retail and hospitality design are the most
intensely creative and experiential of the design
fields, in my opinion. Retail work requires rigorous
knowledge of brand development, interior design
and specialty planning, lighting design, graphic
design, not to mention strong knowledge of
interior architecture and storefront design. I can't
understand why anyone would want to practice
any other specialty.

What is the most important quality or skill of a designer in your specialty?

❭ Strategic planning. In the final analysis, that is
what brand development and experiential design is
all based upon.

How is your specialty different from other specialties?

❭ Store planning is a specialty art and science.
Fixture design is also a specialty, and critical to the
success of a store. There is also understanding of
traffic flow, sightlines, display development, the
creation of "an unfolding story," extremely precise
knowledge of lighting design, and the ability
to seamlessly integrate graphic designs into an
interior environment.

Pretty stores come and go with the wind;
strategically designed, functionally planned, and
meaningfully branded stores are what a great
designer creates. These are the stores that thrive
and do the two things a client is interested in:
making money and building a brand.

My work can literally double the sales of a
store overnight. So my clients who are true retailers
and understand what I do really appreciate me
and understand why we must make the capital
investments into the store environment that we do.

Commercial retail: TSL
Jewellery, Ltd., Hong Kong.
Bruce Brigham, FASID,
ISP, IES, Retail Clarity
Consulting, Laredo, Texas.
PHOTOGRAPH: BRUCE
BRIGHAM

What are your primary responsibilities and duties in your position?

❯ As an independent consultant I do everything in terms of the development of a prototype design.

What is the most satisfying part of your job?

❯ Conceptual design is the best.

What is the least satisfying part of your job?

❯ All that paperwork.

Who or what experience has been a major influence in your career?

❯ Getting a chance to prepare a worldwide design brief for Cartier in 1997. We visited 45 stores in 20 countries, and then wrote 600 pages with illustrations for them. And being able to spend the last seven years working on projects in Hong Kong, China, and Macao.

What has been your greatest challenge as an interior designer?

❯ Learning how to develop great strategies and store experiences in a country as foreign as China.

TOP RIGHT Commercial retail: STA Travel Store, San Francisco. Bruce Brigham FASID, ISP, IES, Retail Clarity Consulting, Laredo, Texas. Architect: Planet Retail Studios.

PHOTOGRAPH: MUSTAFA BILAL

RIGHT Recreation: Supersonics courtside club. Bruce Brigham, FASID, ISP, IES, Retail Clarity Consulting, Laredo, Texas. Architect: Planet Retail Studios.

PHOTOGRAPH: MUSTAFA BILAL

Healthcare

As the population ages, the design of healthcare facilities of all types is increasingly important. Healthcare facilities include medical office suites, hospitals, dental offices, and senior care facilities. Other types are freestanding medical facilities such as physical therapy centers, diagnostic imaging (radiology) practices, laboratories, residential facilities for Alzheimer's patients, and other nursing care facilities. Another subspecialty in the healthcare category is veterinary clinics. Designers who love animals may enjoy this specialty.

Many interior designers who design other kinds of office suites are knowledgeable about the design of medical office suites. However, to be successful, the interior designer must understand the medical specialty that will be housed in the suite. A medical office suite is not just another project. Each medical specialty has specific functional needs and requirements. Continually changing technology in the healthcare field also means that a designer who wishes to design medical office suites must maintain a level of medical technical knowledge to be sure that the spaces, products, and materials specified are matched to the technology necessary for the medical practitioner. Interior design planning and specification of a suite for a cardiac specialist is different than that for a pediatrician or a surgeon. The interior designer must know enough about the medical specialty to be sure the spaces and specifications will support the functions of the medical suite. Aesthetic decisions must be made after careful planning for the medical and functional needs of the facility.

Hospitals of various kinds are more complex and difficult to design satisfactorily than a medical office suite. Functional requirements, codes, and health department regulations are strict with respect to the interior design of hospital departments. The interior designer must work closely with hospital administration and staff as well as with the architect and other consultants. Knowledge of the workings of the medical departments and the technology involved is important to the successful design of hospital spaces. The interior designer might be hired to design public spaces such as the lobby, cafeteria, and patient floor lounges, or medical spaces such as patient rooms, nursing stations, and specialized medical areas. Designers with this highly specialized knowledge can assist the hospital staff and architect in the planning and specification of areas such as the laboratory, emergency department, diagnostic imaging, pediatrics department, and other departments as well as patient rooms.

Designing general practice dental offices and dental specialties such as orthodontics requires knowledge about how the doctor provides service to patients. Although specialty manufacturers supply the necessary medical equipment, interior designers often lay out the interiors of the operatories (that part of the office where dental services are rendered) and provide aesthetic treatments for architectural finishes and furnishings. The aesthetics and acoustical planning for interiors of this type of medical space must be made with care, as few patients enjoy dental visits. Thus, the interiors must function effectively for the dental practitioner as well as create a psychologically comfortable environment for the patient.

The design of medical facilities is an exciting and fascinating way to work in commercial interior design. It is not a specialty that one enters without gaining knowledge of the many specialized concerns of the medical practitioners and patients that use those facilities. If you are interested in medical facility design, it is a good idea to consider taking a course that covers an introduction to the medical field as part of your educational training as well as obtaining a grounding in office facility design.

Healthcare Interior Architecture

JAIN MALKIN, CID

PRESIDENT, JAIN MALKIN, INC.

SAN DIEGO, CALIFORNIA

Healthcare: Ethel Rosenthal Resource Library, Scripps Breast Care Center, La Jolla, California. Interior architecture and design: Jain Malkin, Inc., San Diego, California.

PHOTOGRAPH: GLENN CORMIER

What has been your greatest challenge as an interior designer?

❯ My greatest challenge as an interior designer has been to acquire the education that I needed, because these courses were simply not available when I went to school. I had to do a great deal of on-the-job learning and also embarked on a lengthy process of self-education.

What led you to enter your design specialty?

❯ When I moved to California from Chicago, I started fresh, with no clients, and I decided to specialize in an area that was underserved. In 1970, this was certainly the field of healthcare. I decided I would take a year off and read everything I could get my hands on in order to learn the field. But after two weeks at the library (this was way before the Internet), I had read both books written on healthcare architecture or design and just about every relevant article in the *Reader's Guide to Periodical Literature*. In short, there wasn't much there. I spent the rest of the year on-site in hospitals doing research. Actually, my degree in psychology prepared me better than anything else could have in order to do this

research, and it gave me a unique focus for the rest of my professional life, which was to be able to see the environment through the patient's eyes.

I came to the field with a research focus that few interior designers have, and this has led me to the books I have written that have become principal references in the industry. After spending that year doing on-site research, I started writing articles for magazines on the psychological aspects of being a patient, and I proposed environment design changes. Because little was being written on this subject, every article I wrote was published, and I became an expert in the field before I had any practical healthcare design experience under my belt. A few years later, after I had gained experience, I decided to write a book to help other designers acquire this information without such a laborious course of study. This was the first edition of my medical and dental space planning book, the third edition of which was published in April 2002. The book has been continuously in print

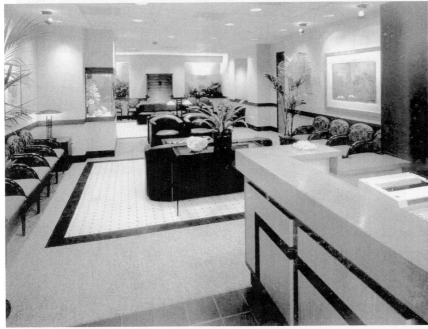

TOP LEFT Healthcare: waiting room, Smotrich Center for Reproductive Enhancement, La Jolla, California. Interior architecture and design: Jain Malkin, Inc., San Diego, California.
PHOTOGRAPH: GLENN CORMIER

LEFT Healthcare: waiting room, neurosurgery suite. Interior architecture and design: Jain Malkin, Inc., San Diego, California.
PHOTOGRAPH: STEVE MCCLELLAND

for over 20 years and is still the only book on the topic. It makes me feel good to know I've been able to contribute to others, and to the profession, in this manner. In 1992, I wrote *Hospital Interior Architecture*, which is a research-based approach to hospital design.

What are your primary responsibilities and duties?

❯ As the head of an interior architecture firm employing 20 individuals, I am responsible for running the firm, for marketing, for financial liability, and for inspiring and encouraging the talented people who work in my organization, and I oversee the creative direction of most projects. In addition, I bring research to the projects.

What is the most satisfying part of your job?

❯ The most satisfying part of my job is the incredible thrill I experience when a project has been constructed and it meets—even exceeds—my expectations. Better yet, seeing the impact it has on patients and staff is very satisfying. Nothing can compare to this exhilaration, and each time it happens I think I must be the luckiest person in the world to be able to do this kind of work.

What is the least satisfying part of your job?

❯ The least satisfying part of my job is managing employees. If one could clone the handful of employees who are creative, competent, have a good personality, positive attitude, and emotional maturity, this would be nirvana. The reality is that it is a challenge for me or any employer. Many other parts of running a business are simply not fun, such as billing. It's very important to have a tight rein on finances and constantly stay close to it in order to be financially viable. Preparing proposals and reviewing lengthy contracts is also drudgery—but, of course, necessary for any professional consulting firm.

What is the most important quality or skill of a designer in your specialty?

❯ The field of healthcare design requires many skills, most of which center around technical competence—understanding codes, knowledge of materials appropriate for healthcare, understanding life safety issues. In this setting, as compared with corporate interior design, the wrong selection or a design that fails can actually be harmful to a patient. It's a big responsibility, and clients will hold your feet to the fire if something you've specified or designed fails.

Who or what experience has been a major influence on your career?

❯ There have probably been many influences on my career. But I would have to say that the individual who gave me my first job, while I was a student in college, got me interested in the field. I lied about my age and experience and was able to convince him (there it is again, that quality of persuasiveness) to hire me. By the time he found out I didn't know much, I had already learned a great deal in his architectural firm, and it set me on a new career path. Incidentally, after a speaking engagement some years ago, someone in the audience came up to ask me a question. He said that for years there had been a rumor in his office that I used to work there many years ago, and he wanted to know if this was true. He took delight in knowing that the kid they had hired who didn't even have basic drafting skills became a successful healthcare designer.

Healthcare

ROSALYN CAMA, FASID
PRESIDENT, CAMA, INC.
NEW HAVEN, CONNECTICUT

What led you to enter your design specialty?

❯ It was a quirk that, in the recession I graduated into, there were no design jobs to be had. So I thought I'd go to graduate school. As I prepared for my GREs, I took a job at a local hospital as a draftsperson and, well, the rest is history. I was asked to stay on for a six-year, $173 million building project, and I learned hospital operations and the art of decision by committee. I also worked with two outstanding healthcare architectural firms. When the project was complete, I started my own practice and called on the alumni of that project, who helped build my healthcare design practice.

What has been your greatest challenge as an interior designer?

❯ Realizing I was not practicing an art but rather operating within a social science. We affect the lives of so many and are proving in our professional research that all we do does affect human behavior.

What are your primary responsibilities and duties?

❯ Some 20 years later, I am responsible for my firm's project marketing and development. I remain active in the design of our projects. I find it crucial to vision with our clients at the inception of a project. Their active leadership and clear view of what their facility will accomplish allows us to apply our best knowledge. We are then able to present the best solution for their project. This early groundwork allows me to manage my very talented team with a realistic end goal.

Healthcare: multispecialty waiting area. Rosalyn Cama, FASID, CAMA, Inc., New Haven, Connecticut. Architect: KMD, San Francisco, California.
PHOTOGRAPH: MICHAEL O'CALLAHAN

What is the most satisfying part of your job?

> I believe that in healthcare design we affect lives at critical times. When we create an interior that reduces the stress one goes through during a medical procedure, I have great satisfaction.

What is the least satisfying part of your job?

> I am most frustrated by the lack of appreciation this profession has. To too many, we are still the icing on the cake and are not called to the table when we can make the most difference.

How important is interior design education in today's industry?

> Three states in the United States are actually recognizing the impact design has on life as a whole. They are instituting pilot programs that will incorporate the topics of this profession throughout their K–12 curriculum. I applaud those efforts and say it is about time.

What is the most important quality or skill of a designer in your specialty?

> The ability to stay ahead of your client on the trends in the healthcare industry. Building flexibility into our projects is what makes them viable and lasts the length of time between renovations.

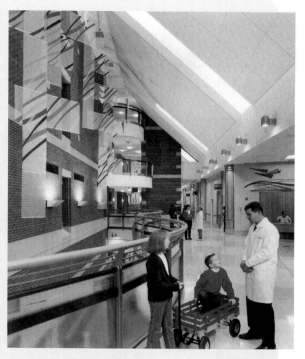

TOP RIGHT Healthcare: lobby. Rosalyn Cama, FASID, CAMA, Inc., New Haven, Connecticut. Architect: KMD, San Francisco, California.
PHOTOGRAPH: MICHAEL O'CALLAHAN

RIGHT Healthcare: ambulatory surgery waiting. Rosalyn Cama, FASID, CAMA, Inc., New Haven, Connecticut. Architect: KMD, San Francisco, California.
PHOTOGRAPH: MICHAEL O'CALLAHAN

Senior Living

Senior living facilities are also often placed with the healthcare specialty. This is because many provide specialized nursing care for residents who need short-term or long-term skilled nursing care in addition to ordinary living spaces such as apartments or condominiums for adults who can care for themselves. However, most of a senior living facility combines apartments with common spaces for active and healthy seniors. This specialty will continue to be an important part of interior design as the baby boomers (people born between 1946 and 1964) continue to make decisions about moving from their single-family dwellings to group living facilities.

Common areas and areas for nursing care are designed by the commercial interior designer who specializes in this area, while the resident apartments are often designed by residential designers or the residents themselves. The interior design of this type of facility involves specification of materials and products to facilitate residents who use wheelchairs or walkers or have other special physical needs. Materials and color specification must consider reduced visual acuity to enhance safety as residents move through common spaces. Space planning must also adhere to accessibility standards such as the Americans with Disabilities Act throughout the facility. The Americans with Disabilities Act (ADA) is federal legislation that provides for design guidelines to make public facilities of all types accessible to those with disabilities. All states have adopted this legislation.

Senior Healthcare, Corporate Interiors, Churches

LAURA C. BUSSE, KYCID, IIDA
INTERIOR DESIGNER
REESE DESIGN COLLABORATIVE
LOUISVILLE, KENTUCKY

What led you to enter your design specialty?

❯ Initially, I was drawn to commercial design because I was fascinated by the impact of the work environment on employees both from a work productivity standpoint and employee satisfaction standpoint. Within the commercial design arena, my area of expertise has evolved from corporate office design to healthcare design.

What is the most important quality or skill of a designer in your specialty?

❯ Commercial interior designers must be skilled at negotiating the different personalities of a CEO or an administrative assistant. The ability to wear many hats and juggle several projects at once is critical. Every day is different and you must be able to adapt to the challenges.

What are your primary responsibilities and duties in your position?

❯ In the course of a week, I typically complete a range of tasks. I often meet with manufacturer representatives to stay informed about products. I participate in a staff meeting where we distribute and go over the projects that are most critical. I almost always meet with clients, and the length of the meeting is very dependent upon the stage of the

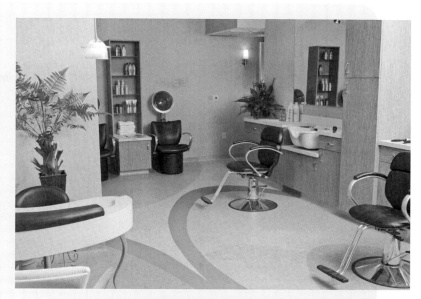

Senior living: hair salon, Buckingham Place Senior Friendly Apartments. Laura Busse, IIDA, KYCID, Reese Design Collaborative, Louisville, Kentucky.
PHOTOGRAPH: STEVEN G. PORTER

Senior living: lobby, Buckingham Place Senior Friendly Apartments. Laura Busse, IIDA, KYCID, Reese Design Collaborative, Louisville, Kentucky.
PHOTOGRAPH: STEVEN G. PORTER

design process at the moment. From a paper and computer perspective, I utilize spreadsheets, draft letters, prepare budgets, make presentations, space plan on AutoCAD, and use the Web to research.

What is the most satisfying part of your job?

❯ The most satisfying part of my job is the very beginning and the very end. The programming phase where I am gathering information about the client and begin to formulate ideas about how the space could work is exciting and therefore enjoyable. I also receive a lot of satisfaction after the client is working in their new space. Often the timeline of a project can span several years and by the close of the project you have developed a significant relationship with the client. Sharing in their joy of the new space make me feel very proud.

What is the least satisfying part of your job?

❯ The least satisfying part is keeping track of all the paperwork associated with this job and keeping it organized.

Senior living: apartment kitchen, Buckingham Place Senior Friendly Apartments. Laura Busse, IIDA, KYCID, Reese Design Collaborative, Louisville, Kentucky.

PHOTOGRAPH:
STEVEN G. PORTER

Who or what experience has been a major influence on your career?

❯ I have several influences. From a study and research perspective, I gained a lot of knowledge from the director of my thesis committee. I researched color in the work environment for nearly two years and five years later I am still utilizing methodology and research that I learned during this time. I am a stronger presenter, designer, and businesswoman after having worked for my current boss. He continually takes the time to explain the process, the nitty-gritty of the design, and always provides opportunities for me to expand my design knowledge and try something new. He is a mentor in the best way. Guiding me,

assisting me, but also making sure I do things on my own. Finally, I am influenced by my father. At a young age he exposed me to museums, cultural festivals, travel, and other creative endeavors. He taught me to be imaginative and also provided me the opportunity to observe lots of government work environments.

What has been your greatest challenge as an interior designer?

❯ My greatest challenge as an interior designer is separating my own personal self-esteem from a project. It is significantly easier for me to handle the rejection of my design ideas now than it was three or four years ago.

Institutional

Many types of facilities owned by government agencies or other public sector organizations are under the institutional specialty umbrella. Among these are educational facilities, museums, libraries, government offices at the local, state, provincial, and federal levels, and churches, synagogues, mosques, and other religious facilities. The category of institutional design also includes prisons. Commercial institutions such as banks, credits unions, and post offices are often placed in the institutional category though they are not public sector organizations per se—they are private corporations and businesses—but they do serve a similar public purpose in the way they deliver their services. As you can see, this category covers a wide range of facility types.

To help you understand why these types of facilities are considered institutional, let's look at a definition of the term. According to the dictionary, an institution is "an established organization, or corporation, especially of a public character."[4] With this definition in mind as well as the kinds of facilities commonly placed in this category, it is easy to see that an institutional facility is one that is publicly funded rather than privately owned. Obviously, not all institutional facilities are publicly funded, but this is generally the case.

This wide range of facility types is extraordinarily diverse in client needs. Interior designers who specialize in any of these areas must design for at least four groups of stakeholders. Taking a county office building as an example, the first stakeholder to consider is its owner or the government entity responsible for it. Another stakeholder group that must be acknowledged and satisfied is the employees who will work in the building. These might include elected county officials, a wide variety of office workers, and even judges. A third group is the people who have business in the county building. A fourth stakeholder group that, to some degree, must be satisfied is the taxpayers who actually fund the construction and finishing of the facility. This last group may not have decision-making power in the development of drawings and documents, but its members certainly air their opinions when the facility is completed.

Because varied activities take place in an institutional facility, the interior designer must be sensitive to the part emotions play in the design. For example, although learning takes place in all kinds of schools, the age of the students using a particular school must affect the selection of furniture, colors, signage, even the mechanical systems. Each religious denomination has different requirements for the design of the place of worship. Even churches within the same denomination and located in the same city can have different design treatments based on the wishes of the congregation. These examples are merely to show how important it is for the interior designer to be sensitive to the stakeholders' wishes and needs in the design of institutional interiors.

Government Design: State, County, Municipal, and Military

KIMBERLY M. STUDZINSKI, ASID
PROJECT DESIGNER
BUCHART HORN/BASCO ASSOCIATES
YORK, PENNSYLVANIA

What has been your greatest challenge as an interior designer?

❯ Awareness of all disciplines involved in a project team is essential. Understanding of all of a building's systems—structural, architectural, electrical, plumbing, and HVAC (heating, ventilating, and air conditioning), data and telecommunications, site, and security—is necessary in order to create a successful space. Designers need to be cognizant of budgets, scheduling, site and construction constraints, historical aspects, phasing logistics, and in the realm of government design, sensitive to public funding issues, politics, and community needs. Although it can be challenging to weave all of these elements together, it is the designer's job to make it appear seamless.

What led you to enter your design specialty?

❯ Geography and chance. Some people decide upon doing a particular thing and go wherever it takes them. Others decide where they want to be and then make it work. I belong to the latter group. I have made a personal choice not to live in a major urban area. Since many commercial interior design firms are located in higher density urban areas situated near a large client base, my employment options are more limited. I also enjoy working for a firm where I can focus on design more than marketing. Although I have tried to remain flexible about particular design specialization, I have had to search more intensely for the right fit within these parameters.

Fortunately, I have discovered wonderful opportunities in my backyard. Although my company is a large architectural and engineer firm with a diverse mix of clients, I have been able to focus on where the need has been—mostly with our government clients. Although it was not my purposeful intention, it happens to be an excellent fit.

Institutional: commissioner's hearing room, county administration building. Kim Studzinski, ASID, Buchart Horn, Inc./Basco Associates, York, Pennsylvania.

PHOTOGRAPH: BRYSON LEIDICH

Institutional:
commissioner's office,
county administration
building. Kim Studzinski,
ASID. Buchart Horn, Inc./
Basco Associates, York,
Pennsylvania.

PHOTOGRAPH: BRYSON
LEIDICH

What are your primary responsibilities and duties in your position?

❯ No two jobs are identical, so the actual tasks vary each time. Some of the more common tasks:

Programming: Develop a summary of personnel, space, and FF&E (furniture, fixtures, and equipment) needs through client interviews, walk-through of existing spaces, and inventories of existing furnishings.

Space planning: Design and create floor plans diagramming the organization of space. Preliminary designs are often sketches.

Client proposals and presentations: I create and present proposals for professional services or design presentations of work created for a client. Presentations that are more formal sometimes occur during public meetings. Oftentimes, I sketch and render three-dimensional views to illustrate designs.

Furniture layouts and specification: I make selections of furniture for projects including modular workstations, case goods, seating, and conference room furnishings. Depending on the job requirements, I may be assisting the client to procure, utilizing purchasing contracts with manufacturers or through competitive bidding. I also have been involved with negotiating leasing on behalf of clients. Most clients utilize some furniture they already own, so I coordinate this as well.

Finish specification: I select appropriate finishes and colors for interior materials. This is generally translated into a finish schedule, a matrix for identifying materials by room. I also coordinate with a technical writer who prepares a specification of each project. Specifications are written legal documents that outline important requirements such as what materials should be, how they should be applied or finished, and performance guidelines. In most cases, finish boards are created to present selection samples to the client.

Quality control: I review drawings and specifications to check for accuracy and consistency with design intent.

Drafting: Although I enjoy drafting, I do not typically do as much drafting as I used to. It is usually delegated to a junior member of the design team, utilizing computer-aided design (CAD) software.

Working on the computer: Most of the tasks above are executed at least in part using a computer. I work with a whole host of software programs for word processing, spreadsheets, project scheduling, databases, and CAD, including both two- and three-dimensional drawings.

What is the most satisfying part of your job?

❯ I enjoy having the opportunity to improve people's environments. In many cases, I am designing a place where people work—a place where some people spend a third of their lives. In areas that are more public, I have the opportunity to create places that foster civic pride.

What is the least satisfying part of your job?

❯ Occasionally a project is designed in its entirety only to have funding cancelled or direction drastically changed. It can be very frustrating to design something wholeheartedly and never see it come to fruition.

What is the most important quality or skill of a designer in your specialty?

❯ I always try to remember that the project is not for me, but for the client. Therefore, I try to set my own ego aside and listen to what the client truly needs and desires. In addition, in most government design projects, the client is the public community. Decision makers are often elected officials whose terms may not span the duration of a project. I strive to create solutions with broad appeal to eliminate as many revisions as possible.

Being flexible and adaptive is also very important. My approach is to develop the most appropriate solution possible. Designs are not created within a vacuum, but within specific parameters defined by all the building systems, budget, ultimate use, and aesthetics. Moreover, sometimes late in the game, these parameters may change due to unforeseen circumstances. Therefore, what is the most suitable design in the end is not necessarily the *ideal* design.

Who or what experience has been a major influence on your career?

❯ When I was younger, my family owned a small local hardware store. As I worked beside my father, he taught me, so I could in turn show our customers, how to do many things. I learned about plumbing, electrical, carpentry, hardware, building, and finish materials—how to use them, install them, fix them, and buy them. He also allowed me free rein with the merchandising and store layout. As our business grew, we added a kitchen and bath design center. A designer was born.

I remember the day I decided to pursue becoming an interior designer. I met a designer who, after finding out a little about me, told me about himself. Until that day, I knew what I liked to do, but did not fully realize it to be a bona fide career choice—for which one could go to school, earn credentials, and get a "real job." On that day, I told myself, "That's what I'm going to do."

Liturgical Design

JAMES POSTELL
ASSOCIATE PROFESSOR OF INTERIOR DESIGN
UNIVERSITY OF CINCINNATI
CINCINNATI, OHIO

What led you to enter your design specialty?

❭ I believe an important aspect of interior design knowledge is rooted in human factors research (theories of anthropometrics, ergonomics, and proxemics) along with the inclusion of behavior psychology relating spatial composition, material quality, and programmatic needs. This body of knowledge formulates a significant aspect in understanding the vocation of interior design. The premise behind this perspective is that interior design places emphasis on the human components (perceptually, functionally, and culturally) within the built environment.

I have designed a range of liturgical spaces and in most cases have designed the furniture, selected the materials and the equipment for the spaces. Over the years, the ability to design furniture and millwork in tandem with coordinating mechanical, structural, and lighting aspects for liturgical projects has in itself become bipolar foci—one delivers a specialty in furniture design and draws upon the human body to do so, while the other is occupied with the general need to integrate multiple systems and a range of spatial and material aspects through design.

What is the most important quality or skill of a designer in your specialty?

❭ The most important quality of a designer is to think and imagine with discipline and rigor without losing sight of the desire that comes from developing and evolving design ideas. Further, in the development of design—the knowledge of "making"—construing and constructing are codependent ways of understanding the production of design. One leads to a better

Liturgical interior: assembly room, Tiffin St. Francis Chapel, Tiffin, Ohio. James Postell, Associate Professor, School of Architecture and Interior Design, University of Cincinnati, Cincinnati, Ohio.

PHOTOGRAPH: JAMES POSTELL

Liturgical interior: altar, ambo, and presider chairs, Immaculate Heart of Mary Catholic Church. James Postell, Associate Professor, School of Architecture and Interior Design, University of Cincinnati, Cincinnati, Ohio.

PHOTOGRAPH: JAMES POSTELL

understanding of the other. Technique often allows the designer a means to reveal intentions and generate connections between ideas and built-form. And so, an important quality of a designer is to be able to think and imagine but also to have the ability to execute and realize their vision.

Liturgical spaces: model, Sisters of Mercy Belmont Chapel. James Postell, Associate Professor, School of Architecture and Interior Design, University of Cincinnati, Cincinnati, Ohio.

PHOTOGRAPH: SCOTT HISEY

Applied skills are necessary in order to develop, test, and refine design ideas. In this regard, computer modeling skills, physical modeling skills, and hand drawing skills are important skills in day-to-day practice. Collectively, a broad range of qualities and skills comes with experience. Experience surfaces as the valuable ideal—often the positive result of learning from success and failure encountered in practice and along the path of design.

How is your specialty different from other specialties?

❯ For years, the majority of my design commissions were liturgical in nature. These projects included chapels and synagogues and in nearly every commission, I was asked to design or renovate the spaces and include furniture in my scope of work. Nearly all of the furniture pieces were custom designed and fabricated. Liturgical commissions often have a significant degree of importance placed upon the furniture. The interrelationships between furniture and space are what differentiate liturgical design from other specialties.

What are your primary responsibilities and duties in your position?

❯ Design.

What is the most satisfying part of your job?

❯ The design process and collaborative efforts are both satisfying.

What is the least satisfying part of your job?

❯ The stress that comes with practice is the least satisfying part of my job. Stress was once explained to me as the feeling you get when there is not enough time to do what needs to be done.

Who or what experience has been a major influence on your career?

❯ Professors that maintained extensive practices and were able to find time to write about their work and in doing so, contributed substantially to the design disciplines.

What has been your greatest challenge as an interior designer?

❯ The range of skills involved in designing from composing spatial organizations to refining details in furniture.

Restoration and Adaptive Use

Residences and commercial buildings that have significant historical value are important to maintain in order for a community to understand its roots. Some interior designers specialize in the restoration of existing structures, working to preserve the past if the structure has historical significance, or rehabilitating the structure rather than see it destroyed. *Restoration* means "to carefully return a structure to its original appearance and integrity."[5] Restoration project team members include an architect trained in historical construction, the interior design specialist, historians, archaeologists, and specialized craftspeople. Research by the interior designer and other team members determines a structure's original design, finishes, and furnishings. Original work and reproductions (or even authentic antiques) are returned to the interior to make the restoration as authentic as possible.

Restoration of interiors and, of course, exteriors is precise and highly specialized work. Design professionals in this specialty often obtain additional educational background in architecture, art and architectural history, and even archaeology. In addition, the restoration of a historic building for contemporary use—not all become museums—involves special concerns for building code applications, safety, and the integration of modern materials with a structure built before the advent of modern codes and construction methods. The condition of the structure, what should and should not be restored, the availability of products and furnishings, and budget limitations are only a few of the issues that must be explored and resolved by the interior designer and design team engaged in restoration design work.

Adaptive use is a related specialty that involves modifying a structure or its interior from one use to a relatively different or even totally different use—for example, a residence that is redesigned as a bed-and-breakfast inn or a fast-food franchise outlet as a real estate office. In many cases, the original exterior design remains the same or similar while the interior changes dramatically. Adaptive use projects by interior designers are often done in conjunction with an architect, as structural design work is often needed to complete the modification.

Adaptive use allows neighborhoods and historic districts to change with the modern needs of the community while maintaining their original appearance. The exteriors look the same while the interiors serve new purposes. For example, many communities change the zoning of older residential areas to allow businesses to use the former homes. Adaptive use helps maintain the appearance of the neighborhood while allowing professional offices, service companies, and perhaps hospitality businesses to operate in the area.

Related Career Options

As you can see from this discussion thus far, you can choose among many exciting types of interior design specialties for your career focus. A wonderful aspect of the interior design profession is that designing and planning interiors is only one of the career paths it offers. The following descriptions explain many other career options affiliated with interior design that a trained individual might find fulfilling. Some require specialized training or several years of experience in interior design but are open to anyone interested in pursuing these alternative career opportunities in the interior design profession.

TECHNICAL SPECIALTIES

Acoustics design: Many kinds of commercial interiors require special attention to acoustic design. Theaters, large open office projects, hospitals, and restaurants are just a few of the interiors that often need the special services of an acoustician.

Kitchen and bath design: High-end residential kitchen projects are often very complex. Bath spaces in high-end residences—especially the bath space in the master suite—can also be complex in material and space planning design. Specialists working as consultants to residential interior designers or directly with homeowners often design residential kitchens. Commercial kitchens in hotels and restaurants, for example, are almost exclusively designed by kitchen design specialists.

Lighting design: An important part of any interior is proper lighting. Many complex interiors require a specialist to consult with the interior designer to ensure that the lighting is appropriate for both function and aesthetics.

Home theaters: High-end residential projects often include a specialized room to accommodate wide screen or projection quality television and sound presentation. The design of home theaters requires technical knowledge in terms of location of the screen, projector system, soundproofing of the space, and the sound system itself.

Wayfinding: Finding one's way in large facilities such as schools and hospitals can be difficult. Specialists in wayfinding create graphics and signage to help visitors and employees to stay "found" and to locate the exact part of the facility they are looking for.

Codes specialist: Interior designers who become especially proficient in the application of building, fire safety, and accessibility codes may choose to become consultants to other design professionals in this area. Such specialists review drawings prepared by other practitioners and make recommendations to improve code compliance in the design.

Kitchen Design and Space Planning

MARY FISHER KNOTT, ASID, RSPI, CID

OWNER, MARY FISHER DESIGNS

SCOTTSDALE, ARIZONA

What has been your greatest challenge as an interior designer?

❯ My greatest challenge is managing my time correctly. I am known for wanting to take too much on. I am still learning how to say no.

What led you to enter your design specialty?

❯ I love to cook and have cooked since I was a child. I feel the family is the most important part of life and building a home that nurtures the family is very important. The kitchen has always been the center of family life. I like designing spaces that meet family needs.

What are your primary responsibilities and duties in your position?

❯ My primary responsibility is working with the client and designing the space. I am also the primary draftsman on each project.

What is the most satisfying part of your job?

❯ When my clients invite me to their homes after the project is finished and tell me how much they love their new space.

Private residence: custom kitchen designs. Mary Knott, Allied Member ASID, RSPI, CID, Mary Fisher Designs, Scottsdale, Arizona.

PHOTOGRAPH: ROGER TURK, NORTHLIGHT PHOTOGRAPHY

Private residence: custom kitchen design. Mary Knott, Allied Member ASID, RSPI, CID, Mary Fisher Designs, Scottsdale, Arizona.

PHOTOGRAPH: ROGER TURK, NORTHLIGHT PHOTOGRAPHY

What is the least satisfying part of your job?

❯ Collection of past due accounts from some clients.

What is the most important quality or skill of a designer in your specialty?

❯ The ability to listen to the client and take good notes. It is the designer's responsibility to be a problem solver.

Who or what experience has been a major influence on your career?

❯ My mom and dad. They encouraged me to follow my love for art and home. At the time I began my career as a kitchen designer and space planner, there were very few designers specializing in this field.

Educator

JAN BAST, FASID, IIDA, IDEC
DESIGN INSTITUTE OF SAN DIEGO
SAN DIEGO, CALIFORNIA

Why did you become an interior designer?

❯ I had always loved reading floor plans, even as a child; I had worked for several developers—one in the architectural department—and had always been interested in space planning. And then the

social worker in me also liked the idea of working with people to create living environments that functioned well.

What advice would you give someone who wants to be an interior designer?

❯ Attend the best school possible, take a well-rounded group of general education classes, including psychology and sociology, and always maintain the highest standards in both schoolwork and your dealings with people.

What is the purpose of your program?

❭ From our mission statement: "To teach, preserve, and expand the knowledge of design which is essential to the quality of life in the diverse society it serves, and to educate individuals capable of assuming significant roles in the interior design profession. Our objective is to educate interior designers who are prepared for the professional world they will enter upon graduation."

What are a few characteristics of a good student?

❭ Attends class and participates in the class discussions; pushes herself to create the best work possible; asks questions; is involved in the design

community, whether in a student chapter of ASID or IIDA or as a volunteer or participant in design community events.

How do you prepare students for the workforce?

❭ Students must complete 135 hours of internship with an approved design or architectural firm.

What is the single most important skill a designer needs to be successful?

❭ Empathy and intuition and honor.

How important is certification by examination and licensing of interior designers today?

❭ Very important.

TENANT IMPROVEMENT

Interior designers who specialize in tenant improvement generally work with building managers, real estate brokers, or directly with clients seeking to move into an existing building to determine if the space will accommodate the tenant's needs. Tenant improvement specialists also can help select architectural finishes but are less often involved in the actual specification of furniture products for the tenant.

PROJECT MANAGEMENT

Interior designers who are excellent project managers have created consulting businesses that offer project management services. Such consultants may be hired by clients to act as their agent. Others provide project management consulting to smaller interior design firms that need expertise beyond their in-house resources. Of course, project managers are employees in many interior design firms.

MODEL HOMES

Interior design firms may work with a custom home builder to help make the interiors of a spec home as exciting as possible to entice potential buyers. A spec house is built on speculation rather than for a particular client. Developers of large residential housing tracts hire interior designers to help the buyer with materials and color choices for the architectural finishes. These professionals are often called colorizers or interior specifiers.

CAD SPECIALIST

Interior designers who wish to work independently but not necessarily through all phases of projects may specialize in CAD. These specialists offer their services to designers who do not have the skill or time to prepare CAD drawings themselves.

Restaurant: BluWater Café, Newburyport, Massachusetts. Corky Binggeli, ASID, Corky Binggeli Interior Design, Arlington, Massachusetts.
PHOTOGRAPH: DOUGLAS STEFANOV

PRODUCT DESIGNER

Most product designers are actually trained in industrial design and work for major furniture and other product manufacturers. However, interior designers also find creating custom designs challenging after creating custom furniture products for their clients. Some make the transition to working for a manufacturer while others start their own custom furniture business.

MODEL BUILDER

Models are most associated with architectural firms, but occasionally interior design firms prepare them. Scale models are another way to help the client understand what the finished project will look like. Model builders might work independently or for a design firm.

RENDERER

Renderers prepare three-dimensional perspective drawings and other orthographic drawings to help explain design concepts. Many renderers use computer software that allows them to prepare these drawings from an almost unlimited number of viewpoints. Renderings are often completed in color using a variety of media such as markers and watercolor as well as pen and ink. Like model builders, renderers may work independently or for an interior design firm.

MARKETING SPECIALIST

Marketing specialists have strong sales skills or strong communications skills along with thorough knowledge of the interior design process. Most often they work for large design firms, prospecting and otherwise obtaining new work for the firm. Others form a consulting business to provide marketing services to a variety of sizes and kinds of interior design firms.

SALES REPRESENTATIVE

Sales representatives work for retail stores and office furnishings dealers. They sell directly to the end users of residential or commercial interior projects. Many sales representatives are former interior designers who have a greater comfort zone with selling rather than doing space planning and specification. Some individuals are attracted to work as a sales representative because of the potential for higher income.

FURNITURE AND INTERIOR PRODUCTS MANUFACTURERS

The manufacturers of furniture and other products used in interiors offer yet more employment opportunities for interior designers. Some manufacturers have an in-house interior design staff whose members work on projects for the company headquarters and showroom locations. Another position is manufacturer's representative, or *rep*. Reps are the people who sell the product for the manufacturer. They help interior designers, architects, and clients by providing information about the products; their goal is to get the products they represent specified and purchased by the end user.

TRANSPORTATION

Transportation interior design comprises two subspecialties: the interior design of terminals at airports, train depots, and the like, and the interior design of transportation vehicles themselves—airplanes, ships, yachts, train cars, and so on. Because terminals are generally multiuse areas, the interior designer must be

Sports arena: Lexus lounge, Jobing.com arena, Glendale, Arizona. Lisa Slayman, ASID, IIDA, Slayman Design Associates, Inc., Newport Beach, California. Architect: HOK, Kansas City.
PHOTOGRAPH: PHILLIP ENNIS PHOTOGRAPHY

Public library: retrofit/adaptive use of 1970s department store. W. Daniel Shelley, James DuRant, Matthews & Shelley, Inc., Sumter, South Carolina.

familiar with many kinds of commercial space design. Most frequently, terminal spaces are designed in conjunction with an architectural office.

The design of transportation vehicles is highly specialized, as all design and specification decisions must be carefully considered in terms of the safe total engineering of the vehicle. If the wrong weight and size of furniture item is placed in the wrong location on a yacht, for example, the ship will not float and move through the water correctly, yielding an unsafe environment.

MUSEUM WORK

Historic sites, such as Colonial Williamsburg and the White House, and various kinds of museums, such as art, natural history, and presidential libraries, can be career venues for interior designers interested in museum cutorial work or this very specialized area of interior design. This career option requires advanced degree work in the field or even in archaeology or museum science.

JOURNALISM

A career with a trade or consumer magazine that focuses on interior design or architecture is an interesting option for people who enjoy writing. Many interior designers have articles published in magazines via contributing author status as a way to further market their design practices.

Children's area,
W. T. Cozby Public
Library, Coppell,
Texas. Barbara
Nugent, FASID,
F&S Partners, Inc.,
Dallas, Texas.
PHOTOGRAPH:
JAMES F. WILSON

TEACHING

Interior designers often teach part-time at community colleges and universities. Practitioners with advanced degrees may teach full-time in two-year or four-year programs. Teaching is a very fulfilling alternative career for interior designers who have gained several years of experience in one or more design specialties.

GOVERNMENT

In the United States, the General Services Administration (GSA) provides interior design services for a wide variety of federal facilities. These interior designers might design the new office for a senator or a large office project for an agency such as the Federal Aviation Administration. Many states, provinces, and local governments have facility planners and designers who do the actual design work or coordinate with outside design firms whenever government-owned public buildings are built or remodeled.

Numerous other niches in interior design and the built environment industry are related to interior design. Almost any aspect of the profession and any type of facility or portion of a facility can be a design specialty and career option—if there are enough clients to support the business.

Design and Manufacture of Furniture for Hospitality, Contract, and Residential Interior Design

PAT CAMPBELL MCLAUGHLIN, ASID, RID
PRESIDENT, STEEL MAGNOLIA
DALLAS, TEXAS

What has been your greatest challenge as an interior designer?

❯ Finding my niche.

What led you to enter your design specialty?

❯ I always enjoyed opportunities to provide custom pieces on interior design jobs. Then, all of a sudden, that was all I was doing—and I loved it.

What are your primary responsibilities and duties?

❯ Design, overseeing the manufacturing process, developing new products, and marketing.

What is the most satisfying part of your job?

❯ Every aspect.

What is the least satisfying part of your job?

❯ Accounting.

What is the most important quality or skill of a designer in your specialty?

❯ Attention to detail; producing the best product.

Who or what experience has been a major influence on your career?

❯ Being laid off and coming to the realization that it is always a positive rather than a negative. It is a time to reevaluate what your goals really are and how to get there. Then just go with the flow.

BELOW, LEFT TO RIGHT

Product design: Milan game table. Patricia McLaughlin, ASID, RID, McLaughlin Collection, Dallas, Texas.
PHOTOGRAPH: BRAD KIRBY

Product design: deco chair. Patricia McLaughlin, ASID, RID, McLaughlin Collection, Dallas, Texas.
PHOTOGRAPH: BRAD KIRBY

Product design: tulip table. Patricia McLaughlin, ASID, RID, McLaughlin Collection, Dallas, Texas.
PHOTOGRAPH: BRAD KIRBY

Working as an Interior Designer with a Product Supplier

CAROLYN ANN AMES, ALLIED MEMBER ASID
INTERIOR DESIGNER, COLOR MARKETING
AND DESIGN DEPARTMENT
GRADUATE, COLORADO STATE UNIVERSITY
DESIGN SPECIALTY: COMMERCIAL INTERIORS
SHERWIN-WILLIAMS COMPANY
CLEVELAND, OHIO

How did you obtain your education in interior design? What degree do you possess?

❯ I went to Baldwin-Wallace College for one year studying English and art when I realized I had a desire to work as an interior designer. Baldwin-Wallace did not offer interior design as a major, only a handful of classes. My adviser recommended the University of Akron as a top choice for its FIDER-accreditation and reputation. From there I earned a Bachelor of Interior Design with a minor in Studio Art.

What was your greatest challenge as a student?

❯ I worked nearly full-time as a server and went to school full-time. I paid for almost my entire college education on my own. It was a challenge, but such a rewarding one that I would never replace. It taught me, quite literally, the value of education.

Are you planning to take the NCIDQ exam if you have not already? Why or why not?

❯ I am in the process and passed the first section thus far!

How did you choose the firm that you are working for?

❯ Sherwin-Williams is a world-renowned company that offers outstanding paint products. We are headquartered in Cleveland, Ohio, and this is the only location of my department: Color and Design. This department handles everything from color trend and color theory studies to partnerships with commercial clients to full-scale interior design for our offices and stores. I chose this job because I absolutely love the challenges it presents and the different pacing of every single workday. I feel that this job presents growth in design training and knowledge and in career as a whole.

What has been your greatest challenge in your first years of employment?

❯ The greatest challenge in these first years of employment is to find a job in which my talents are best utilized and developed and in which I find the most satisfaction. It takes time, and possibly a couple of different jobs or work experiences along the route—do not be discouraged. The road leads to a great place.

Did you join the student chapter of ASID or IIDA at your school? Why?

❯ Yes, I was a member of the ASID Student Chapter. I also held the leadership roles of student president and student representative to the board (SRB). It was a tremendous experience for me—I forged terrific relationships with fellow classmates and professional networking experiences in the field.

How important do you feel an internship is to a student's educational experience?

❯ An internship is absolutely crucial. I had two internships, one at a high-end residential furniture showroom, and one at a commercial furniture dealer. The internship process demonstrates the real world to students, and by becoming an active member of the team, you learn many aspects of this job that you can simply not acquire from the classroom setting.

What Advice Would You Give Someone Who Wants to Be an Interior Designer?

> It is important to have a passion for this work. It's hard work and if you have a passion for it, you'll love it.
Beth Harmon-Vaughn, FIIDA, Assoc. AIA, LEED-AP

> I can't stress enough the importance of researching schools and making sure you get an education that is preferably CIDA-accredited and at a minimum is one that gives you the credentials to write the NCIDQ exam.
David Hanson, RID, IDC, IIDA

> I would advise them to first understand themselves and then to understand as much as possible about others. Interior design, as do many careers, involves a great understanding of personal behaviors as well as the overall body of knowledge.
Linda E. Smith, FASID

> Each designer must have basic three-dimensional skills and a sense of color, proportion, and scale, which I don't believe can be taught if you don't innately have them. However, if you do have them, then taking the necessary courses and programs provided by an accredited college is a great way to start your career.
M. Arthur Gensler Jr., FAIA, FIIDA, RIBA

> Know what an interior designer is and does. Find out what is required of you to become an interior designer that goes well beyond coordinating carpet, draperies, and wall coverings, and prepare yourself for where our profession is going. This means a degree from a FIDER-accredited institution, work experience, and passage of the NCIDQ examination as your basic requirements. Then, if you live and practice in

a jurisdiction that has regulations on the books regarding who can practice or use the name *interior designer*, be sure you are registered as an interior design professional.
Terri Maurer, FASID

> Talk with a variety of practicing professionals about the profession; ask questions about their specialty and how they came to it. Visit a number of different types of working offices to see how people really work. It's not anywhere near what TV portrays. And then focus on an accredited education that provides your foundation and helps you achieve your goals.
David Stone, IIDA, LEED-AP

> Go for it! It can be tremendously demanding and tremendously rewarding. Get the best education you can and never stop learning. Be involved in the community; give back to the community.
Jan Bast, FASID, IIDA, IDEC

> Don't do it because you think you have a flair for design. Millions of people have this. Do it because you understand that designers, by their work, are in the vanguard of the fight against the world's natural march toward chaos, decay, and entropy. Because of this, designers create beauty. What we do matters for this reason alone. All people can throw together one sort of design or another. Skilled designers alone have the ability to find order, structure, rhythm, and therefore beauty within the chaos of nature's entropy.
Jeffrey Rausch, IIDA

❯ Study, look, listen, and be passionate about design in all aspects of the built environment.
Sandra Evans, ASID

❯ Being an interior designer is an entire lifestyle—not just a job. Beginning designers must be willing to give interior design 100 percent for several years before they can put their arms around it. Be patient with your career path, and be flexible. Successful designers must be willing to adapt to outside forces like economic fluctuations, industry changes, new subspecialties, and new technology, and to their own personal growth.
Robert Wright, FASID

❯ Develop great people skills.
Sally Nordahl, IIDA

❯ Pursue your dream. Give yourself as many experiences as possible and work for a variety of firms. The first phase of one's career is a time to build a foundation and a time to travel, read, make things, and develop skills. By all means, don't be afraid to make mistakes. Research can draw positive lessons from mistakes. Practice can also draw positive lessons from mistakes. The advice is not to go out and make mistakes while you are young, but rather to not be afraid of making mistakes and to learn from both the successes and the failures encountered early in your career.
James Postell, Associate Professor, University of Cincinnati

❯ Learn as much as you can about the profession. With the availability of the Web, it is easier than ever to do preliminary research. Ask around and find practicing designers who will let you shadow them for a day. It is often surprising to a high school graduate or young design student all of the avenues a design degree may lead you. Even if you think you want to be a residential designer, shadow a commercial designer or spend the day with a textile manufacturer's representative. If you are able, find summer employment that has some relationship to the design profession. Answer phones in a design or architecture firm, help with inventory in a warehouse for furniture, or work in a retail environment that is related. Finally, I recommend taking as many art, computer, and business classes as are available to you prior to college.
Laura Busse, IIDA, KYCID

❯ Make sure you are passionate about design because it will seem dull, redundant, and trying at times. But when the rewards arrive, they come in glimmering packages.
Pat Campbell McLaughlin, ASID, RID

❯ Develop strong presentation and relationship building skills; each skill is critical to selling yourself and your ideas to potential clients and employers. Quickly accept the fact that a good design may never be realized unless it can be sold to the customer. Then learn to sell conceptually.
Leonard Alvarado

❯ Look at everything around you; realize that someone had to imagine it first and then had to draw it so someone could build or make it.
Melinda Sechrist, FASID

❯ Spend a week with a designer that practices in the specialty that you are interested in. Then, it is vital that you attend a CIDA-accredited program.
Annette Stelmack, Allied Member ASID

❯ Get a good education, look at the qualities you possess, and see if that fits with what you want and what you want to be. A most important thing is to love what you are doing.
Laurie Smith, ASID

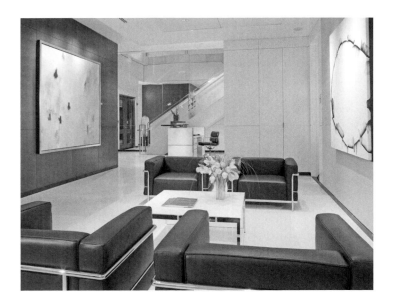

Law office: Alston & Bird LLP, office. Rita Carson Guest, FASID, Carson Guest, Inc., Atlanta, Georgia.

PHOTOGRAPH: GABRIEL BENZUR

❯ Work in the field for a summer to make sure you know what you are getting into.

Fred Messner, IIDA

❯ Get a great education (from a FIDER-accredited school) and find a good mentor. Active involvement in a professional organization has been my way of staying current with trends and getting the leadership training needed to be a great consultant.

Rosalyn Cama, FASID

❯ Try a variety of fields to find work that best suits your personal talents.

Marilyn Farrow, FIIDA

❯ It is a lot of hard work but can be very rewarding. Be open to new ideas, continue to embrace learning, and intern with a few companies before you step out on your own.

Greta Guelich, ASID

❯ Get the best design education you can and also take business courses. Expect to work many years before gaining enough on-the-job experience to feel competent and able to perform efficiently in any situation. This field has one of the longest learning curves of any profession.

Jain Malkin, CID

❯ Literacy, both within the profession and external to the industry.

Neil Frankel, FIIDA, FAIA

❯ Quality education and training will set you apart from all the wannabes. In addition to the usual design curriculum, focus on technical training: lighting design, computer networking and technologies, basic construction techniques, and detailing. Learn computer programs such as AutoCAD, 3D illustration, Photoshop, and Microsoft Project in addition to the standard office programs. Learn and understand marketing and business management.

Suzanne Urban, ASID, IIDA

> Got the passion? That's what cannot be taught. If you've got it, and a little bit of creativity and drawing skill, then nothing will stand in your way.
Bruce Brigham, FASID, ISP, IES

> Get to a four-year accredited design program and learn all you can. I also highly recommend taking business, accounting, and marketing courses along the way.
Juliana Catlin, FASID

> Learn how to communicate orally and write very well. Be intensely curious; learn to love to solve problems.
Lisa Whited, IIDA, ASID, Maine Certified Interior Designer

> It is a very exciting time to be involved in this profession. Since interior design is an industry that is relatively young, the field is growing and changing everyday. It takes a lifelong commitment to learning, flexibility, and a real concern for people and their needs to be a great interior designer, and there are endless possibilities for people who possess these skills. Like any profession interior design has its share of challenges, but interior design truly is a hugely rewarding career choice.
Lindsay Sholdar, ASID

> Meet with interior designers and ask them about their careers, do an internship with a residential or commercial interior designer, and take an introductory interior design course.
Michelle King, IIDA

> Dismiss the public perception that interior design is all about glamour and spending other people's money frivolously. This image only represents a small percentage of practitioners.
Jennifer van der Put, BID, IDC, ARIDO, IFMA

> Get a four-year degree. Pay attention in all of your classes. If you are thinking of going far in your field at all, you will truly end up using all that knowledge they are making available to you. Get very good at all the computer programs related to your field. Without competent computer skills, you are limited in the sorts of jobs for which you are qualified. Jump at any chance you have to do those stand-up-in-front-of-a-group presentations. Become good at communicating your ideas orally as well as through your drawings; often, clients do not want to pay for elaborate drawings. That's when you need sketches and quick material displays and the ability to explain it all with energy and enthusiasm. Don't shirk business classes. Interior design is 90 percent business and 10 percent creativity. (I'm not the one who first said that, of course.) Plan to take the NCIDQ. Support your profession (and it is a profession) by joining ASID or IIDA. (One hopes they will soon become a single organization.) And don't get into this field unless you love it. Your customers can tell the difference.
Linda Kress, ASID

> The best advice I can give someone who wants to be an interior designer is to listen to your client, develop your ideas based on the information you've received combined with your expertise, and communicate your ideas and your client's desires effectively.
Linda Santellanes, ASID

> Know that the days of interior design being a fun job are over. Interior design is a profession requiring knowledge and commitment and hard work.
M. Joy Meeuwig, IIDA

❯ Make your education an open book. Look for nondesign-related sources of inspiration. Get a variety of work experiences within design. The perspective gained from a variety of experiences is priceless.
Sari Graven, ASID

❯ Study people, the way they live and work, and never overlook the building's architecture as a key element of your design. Use these elements to develop a unique and distinctive design that reflects your client's lifestyle or required work environment. Keep in mind with every design project that function is always part of an empty building or space.
Sally Thompson, ASID

❯ I would advise two things: First, be flexible in your pursuit of your initial professional jobs. There are so many, many types of jobs in the field of interior design, and they all yield great experience for the interior designer. Whether you work in an architectural or residential design firm or a furniture or carpet retail environment, you will learn essential skills for this field. In other words, I think I am saying, "Be willing to take baby steps" and don't expect your dream job right out of school. Each job will contribute significantly to your versatility as a designer.

Second, always be up for the challenge, be driven to excel at all times. The field of interior design offers many challenges. I believe meeting the challenge is what brings great satisfaction in this career.
Susan B. Higbee

❯ Take business management courses (accounting, finance). Although design and architecture are artistic pursuits, they are still a business. I have seen many talented individuals fail because they didn't have basic business sense or even the good sense to hire a business manager.
Trisha Wilson, ASID

❯ If interior design is your passion, allow yourself to enjoy the business and flourish without placing too much emphasis on monetary rewards. This industry seems to be in a constant state of transition, as it should be. Strive to be on top of and hopefully ahead of the game.
Janice Carleen Linster, ASID, IIDA, CID

❯ Get as much formal education as you can and continue seeking education after you have graduated. Become NCIDQ-certified and registered to practice in as many jurisdictions as are appropriate. Advocate for your profession and pave the way for those who follow.

Perhaps most important is to always act ethically and professionally.
Suzan Globus, FASID, LEED-AP

❯ This is probably true for many career choices and holds true for interior design: Do your homework. Seek guidance about possible career choices from those who know, such as professionals in the field. Ask a lot of questions about career opportunities, what they feel makes a successful designer, what they feel job prospects are in particular locations and specialties, and what they like and dislike about what they do. If possible, do an internship early on to get some firsthand exposure to the field.

A well-rounded education is an important foundation. Find a program that will allow you to focus on your particular interest but also develops broader skills. It's important to learn good business practices, including writing skills. Computer-aided design skills are also required for many design jobs.
Kimberly M. Studzinski

❯ Talk to working interior designers in various fields. (This book should be a great help.) Look at your own background, interests, and working style and try to get work experience or at least visit with designers who share your approach. For example, I tend to pay a lot of attention to people around me, so it is important for me to work in a quiet, isolated space. I also love the independence of having my own firm. However, I have a friend who can't imagine wanting to work by herself out of her home; she is much happier surrounded by friendly coworkers.

Corky Binggeli, ASID

❯ If you love to solve visual puzzles and bring all the pieces together—you are perfect for interior design. If you realize interior design is so much more than picking out furnishings and finishes, and want to create spaces that are functional, dynamic, and meet the needs of the end user, well, get the education, work two to three years with a certified designer, take the NCIDQ exam, and start enjoying your career in interior design.

Robin Wagner, ASID, IDEC

❯ Complete your degree at an approved college, study and complete the NCIDQ exam, then continue to study so that you will be able to keep up with research and progress in your chosen field. Never stop studying!

Patricia Rowen, ASID, CAPS

❯ Attend as many industry events as a student as possible. The best way to get your foot in the door is by networking, and word travels fast in the design community. Also getting to know sales reps and building relationships with them goes a long way in the industry with helping to get your name out there and providing the potential for superior job opportunities.

Shannon Ferguson, IIDA

Lodging: atrium, The Palace of the Lost City, Sun City, South Africa. Trisha Wilson, ASID, Wilson Associates, Dallas, Texas.

PHOTOGRAPH: PETER VITALE

❯ If you want to be challenged to stay above the curve, if you work well with people and like teamwork, this is a great field. This is not the kind of field that you can just go and do your own thing without a lot of collaboration and listening. If you are serious about a career, and not just a job, go to the best school, put the time and the money into it, get good exposure through your co-ops, and commit yourself to the things you like to do and the things you don't like to do. Respect those that can be your mentors, and *learn*. Don't think you know it already.

Colleen McCafferty. IFMA, USGBC, LEED-CI

Residence: bedroom. William Peace, ASID, Peace Design, Atlanta, Georgia.

PHOTOGRAPH: CHRIS A. LITTLE

❯ I would suggest contacting a local professional interior design organization to request a list of designers to visit and interview. The ideal situation would be to talk to several designers who practice in different fields or specialties to thoroughly understand what a professional really does in their course of work.

Mary Knopf, ASID, IIDA, LEED-AP

❯ Expect to work hard. Most every successful interior designer that I know is passionate about the field and what they can do to create spaces for people that will please them and solve their problems. If you are creative, artistic, like to analyze, and be exposed to new materials and ideas, I think ID is an ideal career. I have heard this more than once and I say it myself, "You will never be bored."

Carol Morrow, Ph.D., ASID, IIDA, IDEC

❯ Rarely does interior design have anything to do with your own personal taste. It has everything to do with the taste of your clients and how you translate their needs into a beautiful and functional space they can live with.

Darcie Miller, NKBA, ASID Industry Partner, CMG

❯ To become an educated and well-skilled interior designer, one should begin with going to a college that offers a good program in the interior design field. This is a great way to begin to find out if interior design is the right field for you. We are not "pillow fluffers" and "color pickers." This is a very important field and there is a lot of responsibility attached to the interior design position.

Debra Himes, ASID, IIDA

❯ I would make sure they understand it is not just picking out fabrics and finishes. It is not as glamorous as most people think. I would also advise them that they probably won't make a lot of money but can make a decent living. It has its good and bad days like any career. I would also advise them to talk to a few designers to understand what a typical day is like.

Jane Coit, Associate Member IIDA

❭ Find a school near the area where you live and take some classes in interior design to see if it's what you want to spend your life doing. This will also tell you if you have the talent and makings of becoming an interior designer.

Lisa Slayman, ASID, IIDA

❭ Do some research. Interview several professional interior designers from different specialties. Become familiar with CIDA and NCIDQ while you research appropriate and accredited educational programs.

Keith Miller, ASID

❭ Travel and get exposure to many different environments. Be open to new experiences and always be willing to step up and help steward our profession. Join a professional association and lobby for favorable interior design legislation. Make a point of talking to students and setting an example.

Lisa Henry, ASID

❭ Don't start your own business right after school. Use your internships as learning experiences, not just as scholastic requirements. Work in a firm after graduation and strive to continue learning. Just because you're not in school doesn't mean you can't keep learning. Remember that you do need to work your way up, and the money may not just flow like a river in the beginning. Patience and persistence will take you much further, and the money will come. Accept the fact that you may need someone to do your billing or you may need assistance with the business side of the design world.

Marilizabeth Polizi, Allied Member ASID

❭ Understand the importance of interior design to the built environment. Be proud of your contribution.

Nila Leiserowitz, FASID, Associate AIA

❭ Always plan on attaining your credentials and NCIDQ certification. It shows your future employers and your future clients that you "mean business."

Linda Isley, IIDA, CID

❭ They should consider the importance of the profession and their ability to contribute to the greater good of humanity.

Linda Sorrento, ASID, IIDA, LEED-AP

❭ First of all, this is a more complex field than you probably have imagined. While it looks fun, fast, and glamorous on television, you have to design responsibly for the inhabitants of the space. Your clients will expect you to be creative, but also want to be safe and get the project completed efficiently. Get the best education you can and don't forget the classes in codes, construction, and business along with the arts.

Second, consider your location and the time required to gain experience. If you don't live within commuting distance to a major hub city, local design firms tend to be smaller and fewer. You'll have to work a little harder to get yourself started. Resist going out on your own before learning the ropes.

Third, set your mind toward becoming a professional. Try to train at a firm that will give you a broad understanding of the requirements for planning and specifying products, one that will continue to educate you. Most designers will change design specialties over the course of a career. Good practices ingrained from the beginning may help you to make a successful move in future years.

Sally Howard D'Angelo, ASID, AIA
Professional Affiliate Member

❯ Learn to communicate effectively. Every step of the process is another challenge to interpersonal communication.

- You must sell yourself, as a productive and capable designer.

- You must sell the process or project to the client.

- You must have a vehicle/method to communicate what you want done to the next level of subcontractors, purchasing agents, assistants, and most importantly the client.

- You must be able to confront and diffuse awkward situations—finances, billing disputes, nonperformance of contractors, misinterpretations of client expectations. If these are not dealt with in a straightforward manner, trouble will continue and drag the process down.

Sharmin Pool-Bak, ASID, CAPS, LEED-AP

- Make sure you truly understand the nature of the profession and career by visiting related Web sites; by job shadowing a couple of professional designers; and by talking with interior design educators.

- Enroll at an institution that offers an accredited interior design program.

- Engage in as many internships or part-time jobs that relate to interior design. Attend any workshops or presentations that host professional designers. They will ignite your passion for the profession.

- Remember to think outside the box and pay attention to details.

- Care about the quality of your work, work hard, and love life.

Stephanie Clemons, Ph.D., FASID, FIDEC

❯ Be passionate and creative, but don't forget the details.
Sue Norman, IIDA

❯ Find a four-year, CIDA-accredited program and dive in.
Maryanne Hewitt, IIDA

❯ For most designers, success does not happen overnight. It takes an extreme amount of hard work and dedication; dues must be paid (literally). The day does not end at 5:00 P.M., especially for those who own their own practice. There are clients to meet with, budgets to be considered, drawings to be completed, selections to be made, proposals to be presented, products to be ordered, deadlines to be met, and the endless trail of paper that follows. The list goes on and on, but at the end of the day, whatever time that may be, there is a deep sense of fulfillment in knowing that you've played a part in making someone else's world a more satisfying and comfortable place to be.
Teresa Ridlon, Allied Member ASID

❯ People interested in becoming a designer should spend time in the environment of designers. Try to spend a summer in a design firm, even if you are just picking up the department head's lunches. Work at a construction site—to understand the most fundamental aspects of building and learn from those who actually have to put your design vision together with bricks and mortar. Visit museums and read books and magazines on design. Spend some time shadowing a designer for a day or more. Look at the built environment around you and try to figure out why certain places make you feel good and others do not.
Kristi Barker, CID

CAD rendering: conference room, CAT, Inc., Nashville, Tennessee. Derek Schmidt, formerly at Design Collective Incorporated, Nashville, Tennessee.

❯ Get experience, internships, or work-based learning as part of your educational experience to give you the necessary skills; understand the relevance of what you are learning in the classroom to the practice of interior design and to help you confirm that you really do want to be an interior designer.

Susan Coleman, FIIDA, FIDEC

❯ From my experience, it seems that interior design programs don't place enough emphasis on technology. All the designers in our office, regardless of specialty, have some computer experience; at a minimum, they must have experience with some kind of CAD software and other computer skills such as Microsoft Word and Microsoft Excel. Candidates with excellent design skills and no computer experience will have a lot of difficulty finding jobs in our increasingly computer-based field.

Derek B. Schmidt

❯ Research what interior designers do. Find a facet of the industry that suits you best and pursue it. If it is not what you imagined, then find another occupation. Life is too short to work in a field you do not care for. Stick to what works for you.

Travel and meet people from all walks of design and life. Your work and sense of fulfillment will benefit.

Alexis B. Bounds, Allied Member ASID

❯ My best advice is to get out there. Do not be intimidated to attend a professional function, or network with a certified designer. Step out of your comfort zone in school projects and with career experiences.

Carolyn Ann Ames, Allied Member ASID

❯ An effective interior designer needs to understand design concepts, of course, but also business strategy and social psychology, meaning you have to be able to relate to your clients and to fellow designers. "People skills" sounds so fuzzy. But it is one of the most important skills you can have. If you are a lone wolf who hates working in teams or isn't comfortable dealing with a range of personalities, you might not be happy (or successful) as an interior designer.

Charrisse Johnston, ASID, LEED-AP, CID

❭ Make sure you have plenty of patience and time.

Chris Socci, Allied Member ASID

❭ I would recommend they sit in on a studio class, or keep a running dialogue through e-mail or conversation with a current design student. It's hard work, but if you have the desire and passion to enter in to this profession, it is entirely worth it. There is nothing more reassuring than stepping off that stage after receiving your college diploma knowing you are going into the right line of work for you. The wonderful thing about our profession is that each day presents a new challenge. I have never gone to work and felt as if I was unfulfilled, and that is a wonderful feeling. As a potential design student, I would also recommend researching a bit on various avenues of interior design and the fields related.

Shannon Mitchener, LEED-AP, Allied Member ASID, Associate IIDA

NOTES

1. National Association of Home Builders. 2007. "What Is CAPS?" http://www.nahb.org/assets/docs/files/ CAPS_1162003102728AM.pdf.
2. Christine M. Piotrowski. 2007. *Professional Practice for Interior Designers,* 4th ed. (Hoboken, NJ: John Wiley & Sons), 69.
3. Judith Davidson. 2007. "Interior Design Giants." *Interior Design,* January, 130.
4. *Merriam-Webster's Collegiate Dictionary,* 10th ed. 1994. (Springfield, MA: Merriam-Webster), 606.
5. Rosemary Kilmer and W. Otie Kilmer. 1992. *Designing Interiors.* (Fort Worth, TX: Harcourt Brace Jovanovich), 283.

5 The Design Process

A well-designed interior expresses everything from the personality of a homeowner's gourmet kitchen to the exciting ambiance of a trendy restaurant. Designing the interiors of homes takes a special understanding of people and the ability to interpret the intangible ideas and feelings expressed by the homeowner into a tangible answer created of furniture, colors, textures, objects, and safe planning concepts. In a similar way, the commercial interior designer must interpret the needs of a business to provide a functional office, hotel, medical space, and dozens of other interiors while also making that space safe and aesthetically pleasing for the employees and users.

The process used by interior designers to satisfactorily accomplish the goals of the homeowner or business owner requires a number of tasks by the interior designer and his or her team (see "Design Team Members," page 227). They gather numerous pieces of information from a variety of sources. They make dozens, if not hundreds, of decisions. They develop drawings and documents to ensure the design concepts are properly turned into reality. They perform these tasks in an orderly fashion so as to avoid omitting any of the required tasks; in other words, their sequence of tasks defines the work. The sequence is called the *design process*.

The design process, regardless of the size of the project, falls into five phases. Each phase is important, as each builds on the previous step until the project is complete. The five phases are *programming*, *schematic design*, *design development*, *contract documents*, and *contract administration*. Each of these phases includes several tasks shown in "Key Tasks in Interior Design Projects" (page 225) that must be carried out for every interior design project. Before any project and its various phases actually begin, however, another important process must take place, which is referred to by many designers as *project development*. Project development involves those tasks required to prospect and secure projects—that is, to seek out clients, and obtain a signed a contract—between the provider of interior design services and a client. Although vital to the whole of the process, it is not considered a part of the project design process. A brief discussion on how projects are developed is presented to give you insight into this vital business practices activity.

Of course, projects do not really fit into five neat little packages of activities with precise beginnings and endings that do not overlap. At certain times, activities of one phase are still going on as the work of the next phase commences. In addition, some designers argue, not all projects go through all the phases. For example, perhaps a designer is hired by a client to select a few pieces of furniture and bedding for the master bedroom or to redesign a conference room in an office complex. These more simplistic projects would not involve the whole of the design process described in this chapter. However, every project, regardless of its complexity or its size, involves some of the activities of each design process phase.

This discussion will help you understand what is expected in the completion of a professional interior design project. The description of the design process in this chapter is presented as an overview of what is commonly done in either a residential or commercial design project. In many cases, many more tasks are necessary in any or all of the phases discussed. The design process discussed here is based on that defined by the National Council of Interior Design Qualification (NCIDQ), as the NCIDQ-defined phases are widely accepted. For further details about the design process and how it works, see "Interior Design References" (page 310).

Project Development

Joe Smith, one of the owners of an interior design firm specializing in corporate offices and small retail facilities, devotes time each week to making contacts with potential clients. He calls this time "prospecting" because he is looking for project work that might exist, but then again, it might not come through. It is one of the many common activities that are part of *project development,* undertaken by Joe and all interior designers before the design contract or other agreement between client and designer is finalized.

Project development comprises many activities thought of as business practices. The activities of this project phase include marketing and prospecting for a new client, researching by the design firm into basic client and project needs in order to develop an understanding of what the project will involve, and the preparation of the actual agreement or contract that outlines the work to be performed.

Liturgical interior: fellowship hall, St. Matthew's Episcopal Church, Louisville, Kentucky. Laura Busse, IIDA, KYCID, Reese Design Collaborative, Louisville, Kentucky. Architect: CoxAllen & Associates Architects.

PHOTOGRAPH: DAVID HARPE

KEY TASKS IN INTERIOR DESIGN PROJECTS

Programming

- Determine specific client needs, goals, and project objectives.

- Check existing site conditions.

- Review existing or in-development floor plans.

- Review need for consultants.

- Research and review code issues.

- Evaluate existing furniture, furnishings, and equipment (FF&E).

- Finalize project program using graphics and written methods.

Schematic Design

- Begin initial space planning and furniture planning.

- Develop other conceptual sketches as needed.

- Develop preliminary materials and products specifications.

- Update programming information as needed.

- Prepare preliminary budgets.

- Ensure proposed design solutions comply with codes and regulations.

- Meet with any needed consultants such as architect, contractor, and engineers.

- Present preliminary concepts to client.

Design Development

- Refine space plan and furniture plan.

- Refine materials and products specifications.

- Refine budgets.

- Verify all code issues as related to refined plans.

- Prepare other design documents needed to clarify design concepts such as lighting plans, elevations, perspectives, and sample boards.

- Provide presentation of concepts to client.

Contract Documents

- Prepare working drawings and specifications of approved plans and concepts.

- Obtain required permits and approvals.

- Consult as needed with architect, contractor, engineer, etc.

- Prepare and distribute bid documents.

- Communicate with project stakeholders.

- Review contractor schedules.

Contract Administration

- Issue necessary addenda.

- Collect bids and make recommendations to client.

- Provide for client review and acceptance of work in progress.

- Issue purchase orders, invoices, and payments as client agent.

- Conduct periodic site inspections.

- Review submitted shop drawings and samples.

- Track orders of FF&E.

- Conduct final walk-through.

The ways in which interior designers market their services and find new clients are detailed in Chapter 6. For now, marketing needs to be considered, for it is the many ways in which clients learn about an interior design firm and its services. For example, clients increasingly use the Internet to review interior design firm Web sites in order to learn about designers in their area. They also learn about a design firm when that firm actively seeks clients through public relations activities such as projects being published in a local newspaper or magazine. Designers also obtain new clients from referrals provided by existing clients.

Once a contact is identified, the interior designer sets out to determine if the project is one the firm should pursue. If it is, the interior designer will meet with the client or even give a presentation about the design firm. Part of this interview allows the designer to further investigate the client and project to determine what must be done. This is referred to as the *scope of the project*. Determining the scope of the project is necessary so the interior designer can develop a *proposal* (or *design contract*) to present in a second meeting. At the least, the second meeting involves a discussion about how the client will be charged for interior design services. The interior designer should be careful not to offer free design concepts at this initial meeting stage. It is unfortunate, but some clients interview several interior designers in order to obtain free ideas—and then hire none of them.

In commercial interior design, many clients use a process called *request for proposal* (RFP) to qualify several interior design firms for a potential project. The RFP is a document that explains many requirements of the project and the client's expectations of the interior designer. The RFP is sent to several design firms. If an interior design firm is interested in the project, it responds by preparing a proposal that addresses the client's stated needs. The client then decides which responding firms to interview.

As the interior design firm gains interest in a project, the designer must visit the project job site or review existing floor plans to get a handle on the site conditions of the potential project. When plans are not available, the interior designer will have to do a *site measure*. This involves measuring all the walls, door and window openings, and other features of the existing project spaces so a dimensioned floor plan can be prepared. In actual practice, some firms accomplish these activities in the next phase of the project rather than at this time.

During project development, the interior design firm assembles the team that will be responsible for the project (see "Design Team Members," facing page). In a small firm or for a small project, the "team" may consist of a single interior designer. Complex projects require a multimember team headed by an experienced senior interior designer. Consultants may be hired for some projects; for example, a commercial kitchen designer may be needed to design the kitchen areas of a new restaurant.

When all the information needed to understand the conditions and requirements of the project and client is in order, the next step is to prepare a *letter of agreement* or *design contract*. This document describes such elements as the project process and how the design firm will charge for its services. Design agreements and contracts are discussed in Chapter 6. After the client returns the signed documents, the designer is ready to begin the first phase of the project.

DESIGN TEAM MEMBERS

A&D community: Stands for architecture and design community. People engaged in architectural and interior design practice.

Designer: The job title usually associated with a midlevel interior designer. Depending on the firm, a "designer" has from 3 to 10 years of experience.

Developer: Provides financial resources to create building projects such as residential housing developments, large hotel properties, and shopping centers.

General contractor: A company or individual licensed to supervise the actual construction of all phases of a building project.

Intern: A student working for a limited period while completing academic course work. Interns are generally unpaid employees of a firm.

Junior designer: An interior designer with limited experience in the profession. Also called a *design assistant.*

Principal: The owner of an interior design practice. In some cases, a very senior-level interior designer with partial ownership of the design firm is also called a principal.

Project manager: An experienced interior designer whose responsibilities primarily involve the supervision of a project rather than its creative design.

Senior designer: Generally, an interior designer with 10 or more years of experience in the profession.

Sole practitioner: An individual who works independently as an interior designer. He or she may provide services in one or more design specialties.

Stakeholders: All the parties who have a vested interest in the project, including the interior designer, the client, and vendors.

Subcontractor: A firm or individual licensed to perform only specific portions of construction work, such as electrical, flooring, wall covering, or finish carpentry.

Vendor: An individual or company that sells goods or services to interior designers or the client. Also referred to as a *supplier.*

Other design team members are discussed in Chapter 1.

Residential and Commercial

MELINDA SECHRIST, FASID

PRESIDENT

SECHRIST DESIGN ASSOCIATES, INC.

SEATTLE, WASHINGTON

What led you to enter your design specialty?

❯ The projects that came in the door when my firm was younger. You get better and better at the same type of work, and then you become known for it.

How is your specialty different from other specialties?

❯ All design uses the same process. The only difference is in the final outcome. If we are designing a senior living environment, it needs to meet the functional, aesthetic, and budgetary needs of our clients, and if we are designing a single-family home, the same criteria apply. The difference is in the details of the design itself.

What has been your greatest challenge as an interior designer?

❯ Managing a design business and the staff that goes with it. Dealing with subcontractors and suppliers who don't follow through on promises. Having to justify design fees.

What is the most important quality or skill of a designer in your specialty?

❯ Communication of the design to the client, contractors, and so on by written, drawn, or oral methods.

How important is interior design education in today's industry?

❯ Extremely important. Without it, you could not compete in the marketplace or provide the services expected of a professional designer.

Apartment complex: lounge/ library. Melinda Sechrist, FASID, Sechrist Design Associates, Inc., Seattle, Washington.

PHOTOGRAPH: STEWART HOPKINS

Corporate office: reception desk. Melinda Sechrist, FASID, Sechrist Design Associates, Inc., Seattle, Washington.

PHOTOGRAPH: STEWART HOPKINS

What are your primary responsibilities and duties?

❯ Procure all work; develop letters of agreement and scope of work for projects. Develop design concepts and ideas, meet with clients, and manage the projects and staff to support them.

What is the most satisfying part of your job?

❯ Working with great clients and seeing a job that works well and is appreciated by the client or public.

What is the least satisfying part of your job?

❯ Working with a difficult client who does not appreciate my work. Having to justify design fees.

Who or what experience has been a major influence on your career?

❯ Probably being a member of ASID. As a young designer, I met many designers who helped me out with information and encouragement, and then I was given many opportunities to grow as a leader that have helped me build my own firm. I'm still learning, too.

Apartment complex: rotunda. Melinda Sechrist, FASID, Sechrist Design Associates, Inc., Seattle, Washington.

PHOTOGRAPH: STEWART HOPKINS

Programming

After the client has signed a contract with the interior designer, the designer begins the tasks that are part of the *programming* phase. It is easiest to think of this as the *information-gathering* phase. During programming, the interior designer goes about discovering exactly what the client wants to accomplish in the project and conducts necessary research. Some of this information was obtained during project development, as it is necessary to fully understand the project scope in order to prepare a design contract. In the programming phase, however, specific details about the project are clarified.

Detailed interviews are conducted between the designer and client who might be the homeowner or selected members of a business. These key individuals with a vested interest in the project are called *stakeholders* since they have an important interest—or stake—in the project. Information is obtained to determine specific needs such as space adjacencies, furniture, and color preferences. Alternatively, and for commercial projects, the designer may obtain this information via questionnaires rather than personal interviews. Of course, accurate scaled floor plans of the spaces involved in the project are also needed. If scaled floor plans of the project space were not acquired during the project development, the interior designer obtains them during programming. The designer might also evaluate existing furniture to determine if any of it can be used in the new project.

An important part of programming involves the research of codes, which are legal regulations that influence both the way the interior project is space-planned and built and the finishes that may be used. In some jurisdictions, codes also regulate the furnishings that can be used in many commercial interior projects. Building, fire safety, life safety, mechanical, and accessibility codes are those that most affect the work of the interior designer. To some degree, all of these codes can affect the manner in which an interior project is planned as well as the furnishings and materials specified.

During programming, the interior designer determines if any consultants are needed. Some projects call for the services of an architect, electrical engineer, or mechanical engineer. Although laws vary by state, consultants are most often needed when a building permit is required, as interior designers generally are not allowed to prepare permit drawings under their own name. This type of consultative teamwork ensures the project is designed within the laws of the jurisdiction and in the best interests of the client.

All of these activities and others in this phase provide the interior designer with the information he or she needs to begin the actual design and preparation of drawings. A project cannot be executed successfully without careful attention to the gathering of information during programming.

High-End Residential and Commercial Design: Custom Furniture and Product Design

DEBRA MAY HIMES, ASID, IIDA
OWNER, DEBRA MAY HIMES INTERIOR DESIGN &
ASSOCIATES, LLC
CHANDLER, ARIZONA

What has been your greatest challenge as an interior designer?

❯ Becoming established, getting name recognition, and finding the great jobs.

What led you to enter your design specialty?

❯ I like to create and provide individual pieces for my clients.

What are your primary responsibilities and duties in your position?

❯ I own the company. Therefore, I am responsible for everything, even taking out the trash.

What is the most satisfying part of your job?

❯ Creating a space or product that makes my client say "Wow!" is the best possible feeling.

TOP RIGHT Private residence: dining room. Debra May Himes, ASID, IIDA, Debra May Himes Interior Design & Associates LLC, Chandler, Arizona.
PHOTOGRAPH: DINO TONN

RIGHT Private residence: great room. Debra May Himes, ASID, IIDA, Debra May Himes Interior Design & Associates LLC, Chandler, Arizona.
PHOTOGRAPH: DINO TONN

What is the least satisfying part of your job?

❭ The paperwork is, of course, the least interesting for me.

What is the most important quality or skill of a designer in your specialty?

❭ People skills and being a good listener. It is most important to make the client happy.

Who or what experience has been a major influence on your career?

❭ My grandmother's work ethics probably influenced me the most.

Private residence: custom-designed wine room door. Debra May Himes, ASID, IIDA, Debra May Himes Interior Design & Associates LLC, Chandler, Arizona.

PHOTOGRAPH: DINO TONN

Schematic Design

The second phase of the project, *schematic design*, is where the creative juices of the designer really start flowing. The interior designer produces rough sketches and makes preliminary decisions on materials and colors. Preliminary design concepts, drawings, and other documents are developed during this phase. An obviously important drawing developed during the schematic design phase is the floor plan. Sketches showing rough space plans (where the partition walls will be) and furniture layouts are a common communication tool in this phase for all interior designers regardless of design specialty (see "Floor plan sketch," facing page, top). Other preliminary sketches include bubble diagrams, adjacency matrices, block plans, thumbnail perspectives, and cross sections, which might be needed to help explain the design concepts.

It is in the schematic design phase of a project where the interior designer must begin to apply building, life safety, and accessibility codes and regulations. In most jurisdictions the International Building Code will define regulations related to the space planning of rooms and structural features that might be the responsibility of the interior designer. One of these would be the locations and sizes of corridors in an office suite. Life safety codes affect some of the specifications of materials that would be used on the floors, walls, and windows as well as many other issues of safety. In the United States, the Americans with Disabilities Act provides many guidelines and regulations that help make commercial interiors accessible to individuals with disabilities. The various codes guidelines are further refined in the remaining phases of the design project.

The designer also develops preliminary selections for the many furniture and finish products that will be needed. Color and finish palettes are prepared to help the client visualize the completed spaces. Budgets are put together to help the client and designer clarify the costs involved in completing the design as it unfolds during this phase. If costs are too high, the client and interior designer must make compromises to be sure the client can afford the finished project (see "Traffic analysis sketch," center right).

The design work prepared during the schematic phase is vital, as it sets the stage for the refinement of the project in the next phase. For the most part, drawings are done quickly and loosely, with the time spent on generating the concept, not in preparing highly refined drawings. When the client approves the concepts, the interior designer can confidently move the project to the next phase (see "Furniture layout," bottom right).

TOP TO BOTTOM

Floor plan sketch: a typical sketch prepared in the schematic design phase. David Stone, IIDA, LEED-AP. Formerly with Sasaki Associates, Inc., Watertown, Massachusetts.

Traffic analysis sketch: This sketch helps the interior designer understand expected traffic flow in large projects and acts as an aid in development of the floor plan. Robin J. Wagner, ASID, IDEC, RJ Wagner Designs, Clifton, Virginia.

Furniture layout: in commercial design, sketches of the floor plan showing furniture layouts is used to convey design ideas early in the project. Notice changes from the "Floor plan detail" (top of page) David Stone, IIDA, LEED-AP. Formerly with Sasaki Associates, Inc., Watertown, Massachusetts.

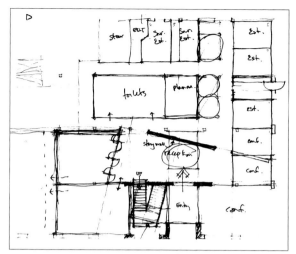

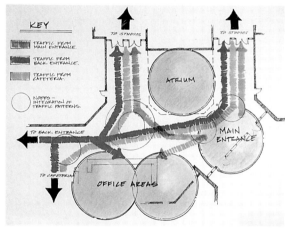

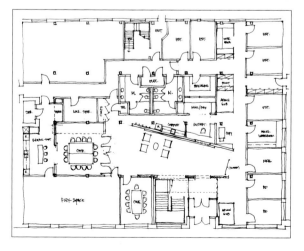

Corporate, Hospitality, Retail

DAVID D. STONE, IIDA, LEED-AP

SENIOR INTERIOR DESIGNER, LEO A. DALY

PHOENIX, ARIZONA

What led you to enter your design specialty?

❯ The first few offices that employed me focused their efforts on corporate work, which put me on the "conventional" office design track. These corporate clients, however, also have needs that fall into other realms with requests for food service operations, fitness centers, company stores, corporate apartments, and other specialties.

What is the most important quality or skill of a designer in your specialty?

❯ In any specialty, the ability to comprehend the hidden or unsaid client requirements and incorporate them into the solution produced is the most important skill a designer can have. The most important skill is to listen, really listen, to what the client says, and reinterpret that into the design solution.

How is your specialty different from other specialties?

❯ Corporate work can be a catchall project type, providing opportunities to work on project scales from the miniscule to the immense, and with a wide variety of specialty focuses thrown in. My experiences have been enlightening, fun, satisfying, and gratifying and have given me a broad-based experience that has allowed me to take on any new client, new project type, and even new employment with confidence and ease.

What are your primary responsibilities and duties in your position?

❯ I am responsible for everything from initial client meetings, through programming, design development, into construction documentation and field observation. I lead project teams in developing full design solutions including program documents and space plans, furniture layouts and product selections, and materials palettes and lighting solutions. I also get involved with responding to new project opportunities through proposals, interviews, and fee development.

What is the most satisfying part of your job?

❯ Developing a design solution that really excites the client—and me, too—is what I like most about my job.

What is the least satisfying part of your job?

❯ The project management aspects of our industry are what I hate most.

Who or what experience has been a major influence on your career?

❯ There have been a number of individuals with whom I've worked that have greatly influenced my career, some on the technical side, some on the project management side, but most on the design side. Two in particular were bosses; the first gave me great exposure to the design process, and the later let me lead the design process. Without the continued guidance of talented leaders and peers, I would not have grown into the designer I am today, nor hope to continue to evolve into in the future.

What has been your greatest challenge as an interior designer?

❯ To balance my desire to be a perfectionist with the realities of the design process—that is, fees, schedules, budgets.

Design Development

The *design development* phase of the project refines the concepts germinated in the schematic phase into the final approved plans and concepts. In this phase, the interior designer prepares drawings in a precise scale rather than sketches to ensure that the space plan and furniture plans actually fit the space (see "Final furniture floor plan," page 241). In today's practice, many interior designers prepare these drawings using *computer-aided drafting* (CAD) software. There are several examples of CAD-prepared drawings in the chapters. With CAD, needed changes are simple to achieve. CAD software also allows fully dimensioned drawings to be quickly produced, as the dimensions become another layer in the set of computer drawings. However, many small interior design firms prefer to use manual drafting techniques to prepare drawings. Thus, it is important for the prospective interior designer to learn both skills.

Other drawings at this phase might be lighting and electrical plans, elevations, and perspectives. Lighting plans (also called *reflected ceiling plans*) show the location of light fixtures for general and specific lighting. Appropriate lighting is important in both residential and commercial interior design projects to ensure functional use of the spaces. Electrical plans locate the outlets and switches that will control lighting fixtures and provide electrical service for the many other electronics components of interiors. Electrical plans also identify locations for dedicated circuits for computers, networking of computers in commercial facilities, safety features such as fire alarms, and other high-tech applications that are becoming common in both residential and commercial interiors. All of these drawings must be prepared accurately to prevent cost increases and other potential problems during the actual construction of the interior.

Perspective drawing: This drawing is used as a concept drawing of proposed interior. Kimberly M. Studzinski. Buchart Horn/Basco Associates, York, Pennsylvania.

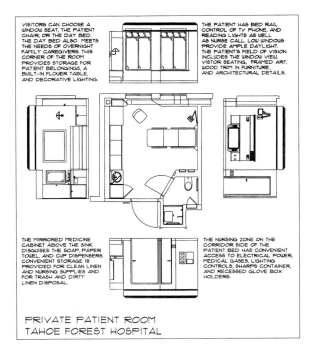

VISITORS CAN CHOOSE A WINDOW SEAT, THE PATIENT CHAIR, OR THE DAY BED. THE DAY BED ALSO MEETS THE NEEDS OF OVERNIGHT FAMILY CAREGIVERS. THIS CORNER OF THE ROOM PROVIDES STORAGE FOR PATIENT BELONGINGS, A BUILT-IN FLOWER TABLE, AND DECORATIVE LIGHTING.

THE PATIENT HAS BED RAIL CONTROL OF TV PHONE, AND READING LIGHTS AS WELL AS NURSE CALL. LOW WINDOWS PROVIDE AMPLE DAYLIGHT. THE PATIENT'S FIELD OF VISION INCLUDES THE WINDOW VIEW, VISITOR SEATING, FRAMED ART, WOOD TRIM IN FURNITURE, AND ARCHITECTURAL DETAILS.

THE MIRRORED MEDICINE CABINET ABOVE THE SINK DISGUISES THE SOAP, PAPER TOWEL, AND CUP DISPENSERS. CONVENIENT STORAGE IS PROVIDED FOR CLEAN LINEN AND NURSING SUPPLIES AND FOR TRASH AND DIRTY LINEN DISPOSAL.

THE NURSING ZONE ON THE CORRIDOR SIDE OF THE PATIENT BED HAS CONVENIENT ACCESS TO ELECTRICAL POWER, MEDICAL GASES, LIGHTING CONTROLS, SHARPS CONTAINER, AND RECESSED GLOVE BOX HOLDERS.

PRIVATE PATIENT ROOM
TAHOE FOREST HOSPITAL

ABOVE Floor plan: These drawings are sometimes "exploded" showing both the floor plan and the walls in elevation. M. Joy Meeuwig, IIDA, Interior Design Consultation, Reno, Nevada.

BELOW Rendered perspective sketch: Such sketches are often used at the end of the design development stage to help clients understand important elements of the proposed design. Robin J. Wagner, ASID, IDEC, RJ Wagner Designs, Clifton, Virginia.

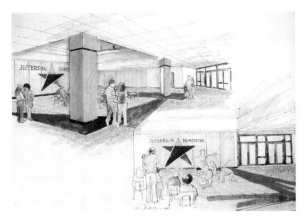

Elevations and perspectives are drawings that help explain design concepts in a form that clients can understand (see "Perspective drawing," page 235). An elevation is a drawing that shows no depth but gives the idea of appearance by depicting heights and widths. Some elevations are used for construction purposes and also provide dimensional information. Others are for presentation and may be highly detailed and even in color (see "Floor plan," top left). Perspective drawings provide a three-dimensional view of the interior. They are also called orthographic projections because they project a three-dimensional view on a two-dimensional plane (see "Rendered perspective sketch," bottom left). In all cases, the drawings are based on true scale so the projection accurately depicts what the interior will look like when actually built or finished.

This phase of the project is where the interior designer establishes refined specifications and budgets for all the construction work and goods required for the project. The furniture, furnishings, and equipment (FF&E) specifications are finalized and approved by the client in this phase. The FF&E specifications clarify the products required for the interior. All projects in some way begin with an FF&E list of requirements.

When the interior designer has prepared all the drawings, specifications, and budgets needed for the project near the end of the design development phase, a presentation is made to the client. The goal of this important presentation is to obtain approval by and as few changes in the project as possible from the client in order to move on to the fourth phase of the project, contract documents.

Hospitality and Residential

JULIANA CATLIN, FASID

PRESIDENT, CATLIN DESIGN GROUP, INC.

JACKSONVILLE, FLORIDA

What led you to enter your design specialty?

❯ I worked for an architectural firm and found myself working on hotel projects. Then I was hired by a developer in the resort industry, and so began a career in hospitality design.

What are your primary responsibilities and duties?

❯ As president of my own company, I basically do all the marketing and am involved in major client presentations. I have an excellent team of designers and support staff who do a lot of the day-to-day client contact, which allows me time to market and work on the big-picture part of our firm.

What is the most satisfying part of your job?

❯ The most satisfying is seeing a completed project. There is nothing like the thrill of seeing your initial design concepts become a reality.

TOP RIGHT Hospitality: restaurant interior. Juliana Catlin, FASID, Catlin Design Group, Inc., Jacksonville, Florida.

PHOTOGRAPH: DAN FORER

RIGHT Hospitality: restaurant interior. Juliana Catlin, FASID, Catlin Design Group, Inc., Jacksonville, Florida.

PHOTOGRAPH: THE HASKELL COMPANY

Hospitality: restaurant interior. Juliana Catlin, FASID, Catlin Design Group, Inc., Jacksonville, Florida.

PHOTOGRAPH: DAN FORER

What is the least satisfying part of your job?

❯ The least satisfying is dealing with all the subcontractors to make sure the project is carried out. Dealing with suppliers and schedules is the least gratifying job, but one of the most important in making a project hassle-free to our clients.

What is the most important quality or skill of a designer in your specialty?

❯ You need to have the ability to sell your concepts. In many ways, we are salespeople because we have to convince our clients that our solutions are the answer to their problems. Many talented designers fail in our industry because they cannot communicate their ideas well.

What advice would you give to someone who wants to be an interior designer?

❯ Get yourself to the best university that offers a FIDER-accredited interior design degree and plan on following the highest level of professionalism. I encourage all students of interior design to sit for the NCIDQ, the profession's two-day qualifying exam. Many states now require licensure to practice design, so make sure you have the proper education and experience.

Who or what experience has been a major influence on your career?

❯ My professor and the head of the design department at the University of Florida had a huge impact on my career. He gave me confidence in my design ability and made me realize that my people skills would help me succeed in our profession. He saw beyond just design ability and really instilled in his students that ethics, communication, business skills, and being a well-rounded human being would greatly affect their success. He also taught us how to quickly sketch our concepts, and I use that skill every day. He was a great man for making us realize that we help clients solve their life issues through design. He passed away several years ago, but he will always be remembered by his students for his lifelong impact on us as designers and people.

Contract Documents

Contract documents consist of accurately scaled drawings called *construction drawings* and other written documents called *specifications* that explain what the interior is to look like and how the look is to be achieved. A set of construction drawings includes the dimensioned floor plan, a lighting plan, electrical, plumbing, and other mechanical drawings, and construction elevations for built-in cabinets or other features. Depending on the project, large-scale detail drawings may be prepared that show how something is to be built; furniture plans (sometimes called *equipment plans*); schedules to clarify wall, floor, and ceiling treatments; and any other specialized drawings required for the specific project.

The most commonly recognized part of the construction drawings is the dimensioned floor plan (see "Dimensioned floor plan," below). The dimensioned floor plan shows the partitions, built-in cabinets, dimensional information, and other notations needed by a contractor to build or finish the interior. The interior designer must prepare highly accurate drawings so the interior nonload-bearing structural elements are properly completed and the furniture and equipment plans work. Inaccurate drawings and dimensioning can create problems during construction and other later phases of the project, leading to increased costs for the client. For example, an error in drawing the size of an alcove that is to receive a piece of furniture could mean the furniture does not fit. Thus, care in this stage of the project is very important.

The specifications are the written instructions that accompany the drawings and give complete information on project requirements. Interiors projects often have two sets of specifications, one for the materials and construction methods related to partitions and nonload-bearing building features such as cabinets, the other for the FF&E.

Dimensioned floor plan. Linda Santellanes, ASID, Santenalles Interiors, Inc., Tempe, Arizona.

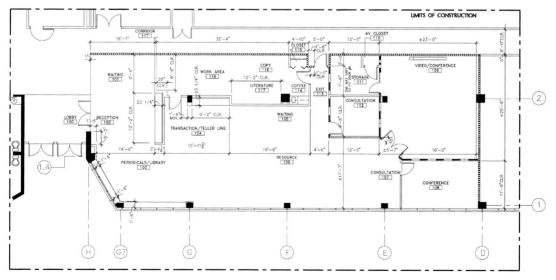

DIMENSIONED FLOOR PLAN
FIRST FLOOR
NTS

PLAN NORTH   TRUE NORTH

In many small commercial and most residential projects, the client and the interior designer (or perhaps just the designer) purchase goods and materials using the FF&E specification, often called an equipment list. For most large commercial projects, the interior designer must obtain prices (or *bids*) for the FF&E from more than one supplier. In this case, competitive bid specifications are prepared so the furniture and other movable products may be purchased from more than one company. Furniture specifications as competitive bids can be written so that a vendor (also referred to as a *supplier*) can offer to sell a product other than what was specified. If the vendor offers a different product, it must be similar to the original specification or the bid is not allowed. Competitive bid specifications are complicated but necessary for many commercial interior design projects.

Construction documents are issued to qualified contractors and bidders. The interior designer often advises the client on the selection of contractors and vendors needed. Some firms prefer to hire these companies themselves, acting as an agent for the client. Separate contracts are needed to purchase furniture and other goods as well as to hire the contractors and subcontractors that will perform construction work. The "end" of this project phase is when the documents are issued to receive bids or prices on the goods and construction.

Finding a Place in Residential Interior Design

CHRIS SOCCI, ALLIED MEMBER ASID
DESIGNER, BO UNLIMITED, INC.
GRADUATE: GWINNETT TECHNICAL COLLEGE
DESIGN SPECIALTY: RESIDENTIAL
ATLANTA, GEORGIA

How did you choose which school to attend to obtain your education in interior design? What degree(s) do you possess?

❯ I chose it based on how many years it would take me to complete the program. I already knew exactly what profession I wanted to do. I have a diploma from Gwinnett Technical College and also a diploma from Columbus Technical College in the Graphic Design Program.

What was your greatest challenge as a student?

❯ Working with others in groups, only to find out most were not as ambitious as I was.

How important do you feel an internship is to a student's educational experience?

❯ Very important—it was a very positive step for me as a studer   obtain the confidence.

How did you choose the firm where you work?

❯ After observing the style of work the firm produces, I felt like I could complement them. It was important to me to work with a small firm that has a high-end clientele.

What has been your greatest challenge in your first years of employment?

❯ Having the balance to understand others' opinions in the firm.

Are you planning to take the NCIDQ exam if you have not already? Why or why not?

❯ No. The school I went to wasn't FIDER-accredited.

Did you join the student chapter of ASID or IIDA at your school? Why?

❯ I joined ASID when I was a student. I joined because of the access it would give me to the profession. One important step for me was to meet professional designers.

Contract Administration

The last phase of the project is called *contract administration*. In this phase, the actual construction and the actual ordering and installation of FF&E occurs (see "Final furniture floor plan," below). As mentioned in the preceding section, the interior designer may be responsible for ordering the needed merchandise and hiring appropriate contractors to do the construction and installation work. For the design firm that does not sell furniture and other items all this administration is done by some other entity—possibly the client or a consultative project manager. Selling the FF&E is an additional revenue source for many interior designers. However, the additional legal responsibilities that must be undertaken when selling the merchandise lead some firms to design and specify the project without also selling the merchandise.

Supervising construction and installation of nonmovable elements in an interior often requires special knowledge and certification. Depending on local laws, the interior designer might not be allowed to supervise this type of work. However, the interior designer is often on the job site to ensure the work is executed according to the requirements spelled out in the contract documents. Discrepancies are discussed with the client and contractor so changes can be made.

When the interior designer sells the required goods to the client, he or she is an agent for the client. When this is the case, the interior designer is responsible for managing a variety of documents so the proper goods are ordered and delivered. Purchase orders are required to actually place orders with a furniture factory. The factory sends an acknowledgment to the designer indicating they can supply the required goods. When the furniture is ready for shipment, the factory sends the interior designer an invoice (i.e., the *bill*). The interior designer also sends invoices to the client for payment.

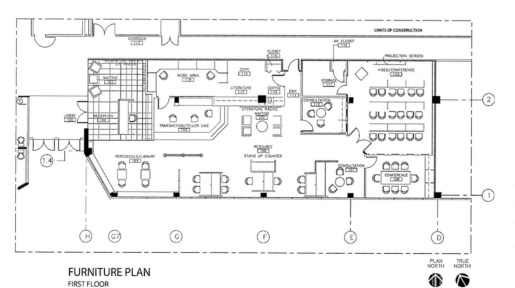

FURNITURE PLAN
FIRST FLOOR
NTS

Final furniture floor plan. Linda Santellanes, ASID, Santenalles Interiors, Inc., Tempe, Arizona.

When the construction work is done and all the furniture and other items are delivered, the client and designer do a *walk-through* to ensure the work is complete. This final project activity is done to note missing items or damaged goods. The interior designer or other appropriate company is then responsible for completing or repairing the work and ensuring that the missing items are delivered where required. Final payments of design fees to the interior designer and final payments to the contractors and vendors are also approved at this time to complete the interior design project.

Commercial: Offices, Restaurants, and Retail

DAVID HANSON, RID, IDC, IIDA

OWNER, DH DESIGNS

VANCOUVER, BRITISH COLUMBIA, CANADA

What led you to enter your design specialty?

❯ The experiences I had with various positions after I graduated exposed me to various design specialties and moved me towards focusing on the areas in which I continue to work.

What is the most important quality or skill of a designer in your specialty?

❯ It is hard to say that one skill is most important. The ability to gather and analyze information, space plan, and coordinate many different consultants and trades would be some of the most important.

How is your specialty different from other specialties?

❯ There are some aspects of design that are common to all interiors projects, but one of the unique aspects of commercial design is the large scale of many of the projects as well as the effects that current trends have, especially on restaurant and store design.

What are your primary responsibilities and duties in your position?

❯ Being a sole proprietor my duties include all aspects of design and project management as well as managing the affairs of running a business.

Corporate: reception area, Accenture. David Hanson, IDC, IIDA, DH Designs, Vancouver, British Columbia, Canada.

PHOTOGRAPH: ED WHITE PHOTOGRAPHICS

What is the most satisfying part of your job?

❯ The most satisfying part of the job is seeing the completion of a project when the client moves in and their work environment is dramatically improved.

What is the least satisfying part of your job?

❯ The least satisfying part is being the accountant, marketing director, and janitor.

Who or what experience has been a major influence in your career?

❯ An employer who mentored me and encouraged me to get involved in volunteering for organizations related to our profession was probably the most important influence on how my career has evolved.

Besides finding satisfaction in completing design projects, I have found great satisfaction in making a contribution to professional organizations such as the IDC, NCIDQ, and IIDA. When you volunteer for a local or national organization, you get back so much more than you give. You meet amazing people and learn so much more about the profession. It is important to the future viability of interior design as an independent profession that designers continue to volunteer to move the profession forward.

What has been your greatest challenge as an interior designer?

❯ Constantly having to educate people on what an interior designer does and the value of good design to their business.

TOP Corporate: general open office area, Accenture. David Hanson, IDC, IIDA, DH Designs, Vancouver, British Columbia, Canada.

PHOTOGRAPH: ED WHITE PHOTOGRAPHICS

ABOVE Corporate: staff lounge and meeting room, Accenture. David Hanson, IDC, IIDA, DH Designs, Vancouver, British Columbia, Canada.

PHOTOGRAPH: ED WHITE PHOTOGRAPHICS

Project Management

Properly and professionally managing an interiors project is a very important part of the project process. Many projects involve thousands of details that must be dealt with from the beginning of the programming through the completion of the installation. Research and practice has shown that a major reason clients hire professional interior designers is their knowledge of how to professionally manage all the tasks required to complete the project. The person responsible for the orderly management of these many tasks is commonly referred to as the *project manager*. Project management is the orderly control of all the tasks required in order for the project to be completed as designed and at a reasonable profit for the design firm. For a small project such as a residence, the project manager and interior designer are often one and the same. Large-scale projects such as casinos can have both an interior design team and a project management team. Obviously, the more complex the project, the more staff members are involved in both the interior design tasks and the project management tasks.

The project manager has many duties and responsibilities. The smaller the interior design firm, the more these responsibilities fall on one person—often the lead interior designer, who may also be the owner of the firm. Some key tasks of project managers are serving as the primary liaison of the client, the design firm, and contractors and vendors; preparing and overseeing project schedules; supervising the design team; establishing budgets; overseeing the project files and documents; and preparing status reports for the client and other stakeholders.

Interior designers learn to be good project managers through the work experiences they gain after their academic training is complete. Only certain components of project management can be included in a curriculum. By observing senior designers, participating in meetings, and working as part of a design team, entry-level interior designers learn most project management skills on the job. Excellent project management also requires understanding the working relationships of the various stakeholders in a project. Let's take a brief look at that in the next section.

PROJECT MANAGEMENT TERMS

Bidder: An interior designer or vendor who provides a price for goods and services required of the project.

Built-environment industry: All the professions and trades involved in the design, construction, and completion of a residence or commercial building project.

Contract documents: The drawings, specifications, and other documents, such as a design contract, needed for the completion of a project.

Construction drawings: Typical scaled drawings for an interior design or architecture project. Include dimensioned floor plans, elevations, sections, and detail drawings.

Equipment drawings: Scaled floor plans that show the location of furniture and other movable items. Also called *furniture plans*.

FF&E (Furniture, furnishings, and equipment): This abbreviation also identifies projects that involve minimal construction work.

Load-bearing walls: Walls designed to carry the weight (or load) of the roof, ceiling, and other structural elements.

Partition walls: Walls that divide spaces into rooms or areas. A true partition wall is not a load-bearing wall.

Project management: The process of organizing and controlling the design project from beginning to end.

Space plans: Scaled drawings that show the layout of the rooms and other areas within the building. They usually do not show furniture.

Specifications: Written instructions that explain the quality and kinds of materials as well as the methods of construction related to the designs shown in construction drawings.

Walk-through: A final inspection of the job site conducted by the client and interior designer to ensure that all required work has been completed and all specified products are in place.

Working Relationships

Obviously, the most important working relationship is between the interior designer and the client. Excellent rapport and professionalism is needed to maintain a strong working bond with the client. As is obvious from the previous discussion, interior designers frequently collaborate with other members of the built environment industry.

Often, interior designers work alongside architects as plans for a building are being developed. The architect focuses on the basic building, mechanical systems, and internal structural elements. The interior designer works with the client and architect with space planning of partition walls, furniture planning, and the specification of furniture and other decorative goods and treatments.

The interior designer also collaborates with building contractors, trade members, and vendors. The building contractor uses the plans developed by the architect and interior designer to construct the structural elements and fabricate the interior mechanical systems. One example of a trade member is a cabinetmaker who builds a custom cabinet. Vendors supply furniture, wallpaper, lighting fixtures, file cabinets, and other items necessary to complete an interior.

Good working relationships are essential, as dozens of vendors and other contributors are often

needed for an interior design project to be completed. Thus, it is important for the interior designer to get along with not only the client but also all the others involved in the project. Managing this team is a critical responsibility in project management.

The interior designer's knowledge and skills of the design process, project management, and building systems helps blend the contributions of many individuals and groups into the final completed project. A successful project is not achieved solely by virtue of a great design created by an experienced interior design professional. A successful project also comes about because the interior designer knows how to orchestrate the vital working relationships that contribute to its achievement.

Animal clinic: reception area, Loving Hands Animal Clinic. Jo Rabaut, ASID, IIDA, Rabaut Design Associates, Inc., Atlanta, Georgia.
PHOTOGRAPH: JIM ROOF CREATIVE, INC.

IT'S NOT JUST CREATIVE ABILITY

The media often portrays an interior designer as someone who is very creative. Many people interested in the profession who feel they are not creative or "artistic" feel they can't make it in this profession. Although creative ability is an important skill, there are many ways in which to be involved in the profession. That is something that the author has always felt was great about interior design.

One question that you might ask yourself as you consider a career in interior design is "Do you like to solve puzzles?" If you do, interior design might be for you after all. A design project is like a puzzle in that there are many pieces that must be put together to come to a successful conclusion. Some of those puzzle pieces involve finding out what the client really wants and needs. Other pieces are the plans that might need to be drawn and the selection of all the products and materials needed for the spaces.

The interior design profession does, of course, have a body of knowledge that is taught in school. And that body of knowledge includes much more than learning ways to put materials and colors together. Students learn how to sketch and draw precise drawings of floor plans. A concern for detail is important as there can be hundreds of details that must be designed into a residential project. Have you ever considered that a master bedroom could contain over 30 separate items to complete the plan and look of that space?

There are many ways to work and the many skill sets that are taught and used provide numerous options for someone interested in interior design. Your interest in professional interior design and dedication to learning the skill sets will give you entrée into many working opportunities that you will read about in this book. Here are what a few interior design professionals consider to be important skills for working in interior design.

What Is the Single Most Important Skill an Interior Designer Needs to Be Successful?

❯ To be able to converse intelligently with clients, really listen to them, and then be able to communicate a solution to them that they can understand is the single most important skill a designer can have. If you cannot convey your solution, especially verbally, it won't be realized.

   A side note is that I believe the lost art of the quick sketch, not computer drafting abilities, is one of the most valuable basic skills any successful interior designer must have.
David Stone, IIDA, LEED-AP

❯ I don't think there is a single skill, there are many that are needed. Patience, being able to think on your feet, sense of humor, ability to communicate well with all different kinds of people.
Laurie Smith, ASID

❯ A designer needs many important qualities and skills to be successful. Among them is the ability to be persuasive. Most clients have no idea what the design you've proposed is going to actually look like, and what they are buying is your enthusiasm

and your ability to convince them that this is the right direction and that it will meet their goals and objectives.
Jain Malkin, CID

> The ability to be creative and work as part of a team without being egotistical.
David Hanson, RID, IDC, IIDA

> Communication, good sense of color and proportion.
Rita Carson Guest, FASID

> The ability to listen to what is said and to understand the totality of the words is a skill the successful designers all seem to possess.
Fred Messner, IIDA

> I think different important skills apply to different designers in different job situations. As a sole practitioner, discipline and stick-to-itiveness are crucial to staying in business. However, perhaps teamwork is important in a large firm situation, or a high level of creativity could be important to an employee working in a firm doing high-end residential work. Different situations require different skills for success.
Terri Maurer, FASID

> Communication (oral, written, graphic)—if you can't effectively communicate your ideas, they'll likely never be built.
Beth Harmon-Vaughn, FIIDA, Assoc. AIA, LEED-AP

> Multitasking.
Sue Norman, IIDA

> People skills; design skills can be learned.
Jan Bast, FASID, IIDA

> The ability to communicate with all the different types of people you deal with. Not everyone communicates in the same manner, or requires the same amount or type of information. Yours is the goal to figure out all of the players in a project and what their expectation of information is, and then to provide it.
Sharmin Pool-Bak, ASID, CAPS, LEED-AP

> Besides talent, the ability to listen and interpret a client's needs and desires in a tasteful and efficient way is a critical skill.
M. Arthur Gensler Jr., FAIA, FIIDA

> It is important that the practitioner have great listening skills combined with extraordinary people skills.
Linda E. Smith, FASID

> I think the ability to convince or to sell your concept and ideas is a valuable part of your design abilities. Talent as a designer is important. But if you cannot convince your client of your abilities, you are unable to see them carried through. Many talented designers do not have successful careers because of their inability to verbalize their concepts, and, unfortunately, many untalented people do well in our industry because they can better convince clients to follow their advice.
Juliana Catlin, FASID

> Enjoying working with people. This is a people business, and if you don't enjoy being around and meeting new and interesting people, then this is not the business for you.
Charles Gandy, FASID, FIIDA

> Listening and really hearing what someone says.
Donna Vining, FASID, IIDA, RID, CAPS

Private residence: media room. Michael Thomas, FASID, DESIGN-Collective Group, Inc., Jupiter, Florida.

PHOTOGRAPH: CARLOS DOMENECH

❭ Listening and communicating are at the top of the list to be successful in producing creative interiors and bringing order out of chaos.
Sandra Evans, ASID

❭ Communication and listening skills rank very high in any service profession. I would rate these skill sets even slightly higher in importance than artistic talent. Many clients not only do not understand the profession, they do not necessarily know what they really want or need and have difficulty visualizing design solutions. Communication includes the ability to orally and graphically demonstrate ideas through clear and concise descriptions, sketches, or three-dimensional imaging.
Mary Knopf, ASID, IIDA, LEED-AP

❭ Integrity.
Keith Miller, ASID

❭ All aspects of project management skills.
Robert Wright, FASID

❭ Communication. Without good client communication, you will not be able to be successful in the long run. Good communication allows you to assure that your client's concepts will come to life and that the course of the project through to completion will be a success. Also, poor communication including grammar in oral communication as well as written (e-mails especially) will give your clients a negative impression of your abilities no matter how smart you are and regardless of your education and background.
Shannon Ferguson, IIDA

❭ The ability to communicate your designs to your potential clients or your design team, freehand sketch on a napkin is still important. Don't rely on the computer for everything.
Linda Isley, IIDA

❭ An open mind to experience the world and people around you which in turn brings depth and richness to your creativity and designs.
Annette Stelmack, Allied Member ASID

> There are so many that are important but first of all you need to be able to listen. Second, you need to be able to work as part of a team, as you will be working with a number of different experts in completing the design—including the client around whom it all revolves. And if you do not have strength in specific areas (business, drafting, sketching, etc.), then you need to be able to honestly admit this and bring in people to work with you who have these areas of expertise.
Drue Lawlor, FASID

> No single skill will make an interior designer successful; instead, an array of skills is needed. A successful designer is creative, knowledgeable, a good listener, dependable, and accountable.
Linda Santellanes, ASID

> Concept selling, which is making yourself valuable to your customers by being skilled at creating the customers' need. Concept selling is hard. Why? Because the designer is fighting *the way it is* with *the way it could be.*
Leonard Alvarado

> To know his or her value as a designer. The expertise we have has value; thus we have the right to charge for it.
Pat Campbell McLaughlin, ASID, RID

> The ability to connect the client's vision to the resources necessary to fulfill it. This seems obvious. But most designers don't really understand what the client wants, and more still lack the ability to source the necessary materials for the project. The Internet has made sourcing infinitely easier in the last few years.
Jeffrey Rausch, IIDA

> Ability to put logical design solutions on paper and communicate those designs to the client.
Melinda Sechrist, FASID

> Presentation skills are vitally important to getting your idea across to the client.
Greta Guelich, ASID

> Big-picture thinking coupled with the communication skills necessary to allow implementation of the vision.
Marilyn Farrow, FIIDA

> The ability to deliver the completed project.
Suzan Globus, FASID, LEED-AP

> The single biggest skill is persistence. If you are persistent, you will view learning and keeping abreast of the industry as part of the job; you will complete projects on time; you will earn respect from colleagues, bosses, and clients because you follow through. Being persistent also includes doing the work when it isn't fun, when you are frustrated beyond belief, or are losing your profit margin.
Laura Busse, IIDA, KYCID

> The ability to interview and interpret the findings into a three-dimensional solution that affects behavior.
Rosalyn Cama, FASID

> I think developing good people skills is extremely important.
Sally Nordahl, IIDA

> It is just being able to believe in the work and to communicate that to a client. Selling the concept is a must. Many great designs are not given the opportunity to come to life because the designer just isn't able to show the client that the solution is the best that can be created.
Michael Thomas, FASID, CAPS

> The desire to continually learn. The world is changing quickly, and it will continue to do so. As true professionals, we must all be committed to continuous learning. The issues, trends (and

I don't mean fads), consequences, products, and methodologies touching our profession are changing; it is imperative that we stay informed. Our clients look to interior designers to help them make better decisions, and a large part of intelligent decision making is to understand the broad issues as well as the consequences of our choices.

Barbara Nugent, FASID

❭ There isn't one single most important skill. That would simplify the profession too much. Important skills include eye for detail, creativity, hard work ethic, ability to communicate (graphically, orally, in writing). The latter could be one of the very top skills.

Stephanie Clemons, Ph.D., FASID, FIDEC

❭ Commitment to continuous learning and the ability to listen well.

Lisa Henry, ASID

❭ Confidence and risk taking.

Neil Frankel, FAIA, FIIDA

❭ Without a doubt, I would say listening is the most important skill an interior designer needs to be successful. Every assignment or project begins with developing and understanding the client's goals. With the client, the designer establishes the design vision for the project. It's all about listening and developing the right vision for your client. The most successful results are produced when the project goals are thoroughly understood, ensuring solutions that meet the client's intent. Clients are not happy when they are not heard or when the designer persists in his or her personal design goals over those defined by the client.

Susan Higbee

❭ A no-static, open-minded personality.

Derrell Parker, IIDA

❭ We often say listening skills, but I would add a passion for learning and giving back.

Linda Sorrento, ASID, IIDA, LEED-AP

❭ Whether residential or commercial, an interior designer must be a good listener. Even commercial clients remark on whether or not the architect

Corporate: reception area, Accenture. David Hanson, IDC, IIDA, DH Designs, Vancouver, British Columbia, Canada.

PHOTOGRAPH: ED WHITE PHOTOGRAPHICS

or designer really listens to them and responds to their needs.

Linda Kress, ASID

❯ A successful interior designer takes initiative. Initiative to get the required education, pursue the job they want, maintain their education, and striving to continue to grow throughout their career.

Lindsay Sholdar, ASID

❯ In order to be successful, an interior designer needs to know that the profession is a business and that time is as much a commodity as design outcome itself.

Jennifer van der Put, BID, IDC, ARIDO, IFMA

❯ Vision.

Marilizibeth Polizzi, Allied Member ASID

Library: custom display kiosks. Sandcastles. Toms River Branch of Ocean County Library. Suzan Globus, FASID, LEED-AP, Globus Design Associates, Red Bank, New Jersey.

PHOTOGRAPH: STEPHEN J. CARR.

❯ It is hard to limit this to one skill or trait. I might also suggest different skills depending on whether a designer chooses to focus more on the design or the management aspects of the project process. I would emphasize the importance of innate creative thinking and problem solving, honed visual and verbal communication skills, and a passion for the art and business of this industry.

Janice Carleen Linster, ASID, IIDA, CID

❯ Passion. Passion beats genius 9 times out of 10 in my book.

Bruce Brigham, FASID, ISP, IES

❯ Communication, both orally and through documentation of ideas and concepts.

William Peace, ASID

❯ Good people skills are mandatory for interior designers. They also should be solution driven.

Debra Himes, ASID, IIDA

❯ Presentation. Whether it is your own personal presentation or that of your project, if you want to be credible, you must be able to present yourself and your ideas well.

Patricia Rowen, ASID, CAPS

❯ The ability to critically think.

Robin Wagner, ASID, IDEC

❯ A strong commitment to design, and the overall design industry.

Nila Leiserowitz. FASID, Associate AIA

❯ You need a balance of art and design, business communication and people skills.

Sally D'Angelo, ASID, AIA
Professional Affiliate Member

❯ The ability to listen well and communicate with clients.

Teresa Ridlon, Allied Member ASID

6 Interior Design as a Business

Running your own interior design business requires knowing how to handle all the business decisions and the responsibility that ownership entails. The design employee has business responsibilities as well, since his or her work also affects the success or failure of the design firm. For that reason, all interior designers should have an understanding of business principles.

The interior design practice must deal with the same issues that challenge every business. The owner—or some employee assigned to do so—must keep a steady stream of new business and clients flowing to the firm. Decisions must be made about how to charge for services. If furniture and interior products are to be sold to the client, their markup or discount must be determined. The process of performing the work—and assigning responsibility for each required task—must be clarified. Employees must be hired, motivated, and rewarded. These are just a few of the issues that must be addressed, controlled, and managed by business owners and employees.

Planning and organizing the business of interior design are just as critical to the ongoing success of a firm as are the technical skills and creative competence of the owner and staff. If the practice does not conduct itself in a purposeful business manner, it cannot survive no matter how creative the staff is. Neglect the business, and the firm can suffer financial hardships and even legal complications.

This chapter surveys a number of key business challenges for the interior design practice owner. Its purpose is to give you a quick look at the business side of the interior design profession. Attention is focused on marketing, the importance of contracts, revenue generation, and legal issues. In addition, the selected key terms in "Business Practice Terms," page 254, will help you understand the business side of interior design.

BUSINESS PRACTICE TERMS

Billable hours: The time the interior designer works on tasks directly related to the completion of the design documents, specifications, and supervision on the job site.

Income statement: An accounting report showing revenues and expenses for a specific period. Also called a *profit and loss (P&L) statement.*

Letter of agreement: A simplified form of a contract for services.

Member: The term associated with the owner of a limited liability company (LLC)

Proposal: A response the interior designer makes to a *request for proposal* (RFP) offered by a client. It is not necessarily a contract for goods and/or services. Some designers also use *proposal* to mean the outline of products they are suggesting for the client.

Purchase agreement: The document used to clarify the furniture and furnishings that are going to be purchased for the client.

Referral: A positive recommendation from a client of an interior designer.

Request for proposal (RFP): Clients use this document to obtain specific information from a number of interior designers interested in designing the client's project.

Retail price: The price by value charged to the consumer. It is generally 100 percent higher than the wholesale price of the goods.

Retainer: Payments made by the client to the interior designer to cover future work by the professional in the interest of the project.

Scope of services: A description of what must be done by the interior designer to complete the project. It is listed within the body of the design contract or letter of agreement.

Wholesale price: A special price given to the interior designer by a manufacturer or other vendor that is lower than the price to the consumer.

Business Formations

There are many ways that a business can be legally formed. A *business formation* refers to the legal organization of the business. The type of business formation chosen by the entrepreneur affects managerial processes including income tax reporting and legal liabilities. The following two subsections discuss typical business formations used in interior design practice.

SOLE PROPRIETORSHIP AND PARTNERSHIPS

When someone starts a business, one of the first decisions that must be made is what type of business formation to use. One of these you have already encountered in Chapter 3: the *sole proprietorship*.

While a sole proprietorship is a business owned and operated by a single person, a partnership is a business owned and operated by more than one person. Two or more designers or others in combination with a designer (such as an architect) can organize a partnership. The partnership business formation requires that the people involved in the business determine who will be responsible for the various tasks of operating the business. They will also determine how much money each partner will invest in the business and how business profits or losses will be divided.

Partnerships allow two or more designers who have various skill and experience levels to work together to obtain business. For example, perhaps one designer has only been engaged in residential interior design but wishes to also branch out into hotels. A colleague might have experience in hotels and offices and might feel that this is the right time to begin working for his own interests and style of design rather than what a boss requires. The two colleagues could form a partnership form of business.

Partners need to be compatible in more than design skills and experience. Because the partners are working closely together and the success of the firm needs both people to be pulling together, business partners need to be compatible in business sense and responsibility. If one person is supposed to be responsible for obtaining new clients and the other taking care of all business paperwork, each will expect the partner to do his or her share. Or arguments might occur, problems that could affect professional work for clients might crop up, and the business could even fail.

LIMITED LIABILITY COMPANY AND CORPORATION

Another type of business formation that has become quite common is the *limited liability company* or LLC. This type of business formation is a sort of hybrid of a partnership or sole proprietorship and a corporation. Depending on state law, a limited liability company can have one owner called a member or several owner/members. It must be created based on the legal requirements of the state in which the LLC exists and will be somewhat more complex to organize than a sole proprietorship or a partnership.

The LLC has become a popular type of business formation for interior designers because this formation provides the legal liability protection of a corporation while maintaining a simpler

Private residence: kitchen. Susan Norman, IIDA,
Susan Norman Interiors, Phoenix, Arizona.

PHOTOGRAPH: PAUL BERKNER

organizational structure than a corporation. By legal liability protection, the member has no personal liability even if the company is sued or faces large debt. In a sole proprietorship, however, if the owner is sued, the person suing might be awarded funds from the owner's personal savings. This is not the case in an LLC or corporation as the business is sued, not the owner per se.

A *corporation* is another type of business formation. Because a corporation is created based on specific legal statues of the states, it is considered a separate entity from any of the owners or originators. It can exist even if the original owners cease to be involved—perhaps they sell the business to someone else—which is not the case of the other business formations.

An important advantage of the corporation business formation is the legal protection from a harmed party taking personal assets of the owners in a dispute. The corporation form of business in the interior design industry is more often utilized by only the largest design firms and firms that manufacture and sell products. The smaller design firms are more likely to use the partnership or LLC business formation upon start-up.

"Interior Design References" (page 310) lists several guides on how to select and set up a business formation that is suitable for the kind of interior design operation that you want to create. To learn about making this choice when it comes to companies larger than a sole proprietorship, read the following responses from designers who own their own firms.

What Motivated You to Start Your Design Firm?

❯ I've always been an entrepreneur, from the time I was six years old. I never even thought of working for someone else; it just seemed natural for me to start my own firm, and I did so at a very early age.
Jain Malkin, CID

❯ I had a baby and didn't want to go back to work full-time at the firm I was with and which did not allow me to work part-time. I was also bored with doing exclusively space planning for that company.
Melinda Sechrist, FASID

❯ I have been an employee, associate, sole practitioner, and now am in a partnership. Each has its own characterizations, strengths, and weaknesses. As an employee, the idea of working on my own and being my own boss sounded wonderful. However, the reality was that more time and investment was required to make a sole proprietorship profitable than anticipated. I missed the teamwork, growth opportunities, and access to larger projects that a midsized firm offered. After proving to myself that I could make it on my own, I opted for a paycheck and benefits. However, the experience gained from this adventure has been very valuable in future leadership roles and finally in accepting a partnership.
Mary Knopf, ASID, IIDA, LEED-AP

❯ I owned a practice in commercial corporate design and enjoyed the freedom it presented. I was motivated by the market demand for specialists in interior design.
Linda Sorrento, ASID, IIDA, LEED-AP

❯ Someone said to me, "Hey, wanna partner with me in creating a commercial design firm?" I said yes. Six years of answering to the powers-that-be in a 400-person firm was enough for me.
Bruce Brigham, FASID, ISP, IES

❯ Never thought of any other way.
Donna Vining, FASID, IIDA, RID, CAPS

❯ For me, it would have to be my lack of understanding of how hard it is to sustain a successful practice. There is an implied goal in our profession of being an entrepreneur, controlling your own destiny. Ego drives many of us to try our own business. There are many hard lessons to learn along the way.
Fred Messner, IIDA

❯ I used to have my own residential design firm. I operated out of a home office. The greatest part, besides low overhead, was that I could control my schedule and take time off to go play with the grandchildren. I enjoyed it very much, and I have good friends in ASID who are operating in this manner today. They are very successful and probably make more money than I do. When you own your own design firm complete with employees, overhead, and the like, that's another thing entirely. At this stage in my life and the state of today's economy, it's not what I want to do.
Linda Kress, ASID

❯ I didn't start it—I was hired as a draftsman and through hard work, diligence, and talent I now own it.
W. Daniel Shelley, AIA, ASID

❯ The thought that I had a better idea of how to operate a design firm and the desire to lead a team of people. Increased income potential also played a factor.
Jeffrey Rausch, IIDA

› Fell on my head one too many times. In reality, I thought I should do this my way if I were going to do it at all. Never worked for anyone, not even an internship. Stupid! But, oh well.

Bruce Goff, ASID

› My husband encouraged me to open my own business. I was afraid I would never have clients, but one successful project led to another and another.

Rita Carson Guest, FASID

› Authority and responsibility.

Neil Frankel, FIIDA, FAIA

› I was 27 years old and had just finished a project for which I was hired to work on all the interiors. The company was Jack Nicklaus Development, where I worked on a new golf community that he had developed. After I completed all the interior design projects for him, I had three choices: one was move to Florida and work on other country clubhouses with him, work for another firm. or start my own firm. I felt I had made enough contacts and relationships to venture out on my own. It was definitely a challenge at such a young age.

Lisa Slayman, ASID, IIDA

› I started my own business so that I would be solely responsible for my vision and to have a chance to express that vision in my own way. Having one's own business is not necessarily the thing to do for everyone, but for me it was.

Charles Gandy, FASID, FIIDA

› Self-expression is very important. It was the only way for me to reap the biggest professional and economic rewards.

Robert Wright, FASID

› We have exciting projects and great clients. The firm is an open studio that encourages the interaction of talented and professional persons who inspire each other.

Sandra Evans, ASID

› Insanity. I thought I knew it all. No, really, probably wanting to run things my way.

Jan Bast, FASID, IIDA, IDEC

› Having just taken a weeklong leadership training course, I've found that my risk-taking component is such that it was a natural outcome. I graduated from school and initially formed a partnership with an individual. Within 3 years, the partnership dissolved, and I formed my own design firm, which is now 17 years old.

Linda E. Smith, FASID

› The opportunity to practice as the owner of an architectural firm was always my vision. However, the size and complexity of our firm was never planned or dreamed of. But the opportunities this profession has provided me are certainly beyond my expectations. I love the opportunity to create spaces, to work with clients, and to be part of the design and construction profession.

M. Arthur Gensler Jr., FAIA, FIIDA, RIBA

› I hit the glass ceiling at a firm and because I did not want to purchase it, I started another one in such a way that it made sense for my existing clients to do business with me and stay with me over the long haul.

Michael Thomas, FASID, CAPS

› I loved what I was doing. And I thought—hey, why kill myself, working all of these hours for $12,000? Why not start my own company and make it on my own? Yes, the first year I didn't make much money. But after that I sailed onward and made a very decent living, the best year grossing $250,000. Not bad for a 23-year-old with a lot of gumption and a positive attitude.

Lisa M. Whited, ASID, IIDA, IDEC, Maine CID

❭ After starting a family, I needed more freedom than the large company where I was employed could offer me. As a mother of two children, I wanted more freedom in arranging my schedule to meet my family's and my clients' needs. I had many clients of my own. At that point, they were very willing to work around my family schedule. However, the corporate environment I was in was famous for 7:30 breakfast meetings, and that was very difficult with children. You must remember that a steady paycheck has advantages during tough economic times. So each person has to weigh his or her need for freedom with the lack of security you have when you work for yourself.

Juliana Catlin, FASID

❭ I do not have my own practice. However, three years ago I had an opportunity to start up an interior design division within an established architectural office.

Jennifer van der Put, BID, IDC, ARIDO, IFMA

❭ Economics, control, freedom to succeed or fail by my own actions.

Derrell Parker, IIDA

❭ It seemed like a natural progression to grow in my field without the limitations of a structured corporate environment.

Sally Nordahl, IIDA

❭ To use my skills effectively and enjoy the experience of providing a positive design experience for my clients.

William Peace, ASID

❭ I have my own design business but maintain a full-time contract with a cabinetry manufacturer. For five years, I was initially employed by a cabinetry manufacturer prior to branching off and starting my own firm. After that for the past four years, I have maintained a full-time contract with them. I did this to allow myself more flexibility with my time and to gain more control over the responsibilities I have with the projects that I am involved in. My motivation was to set my own schedule and to make more money.

Darcie Miller, NKBA, ASID Industry Partner, CMG

❭ There was no one out there doing what we do.

Rosalyn Cama, FASID

❭ My entrepreneurial nature and a desire to be completely comfortable with management's decisions motivated me to start my firm.

Suzan Globus, FASID, LEED-AP

❭ When I moved to the small town of Gainesville, Florida, 33 years ago, my only option was to start my own practice. I had worked for an independent design practice in Miami and wanted to continue to have the freedom to specify and design for my clients' needs. I did not want to meet the quotas or specific manufacturer sales required by a furniture store or office furniture dealership.

Sally Thompson, ASID

❭ While I have ownership in my firm, I am one of several partners and unfortunately cannot take credit for starting the firm.

Janice Carleen Linster, ASID, IIDA, CID

Marketing Methods

As you might expect with any business, an interior design business needs a steady stream of clients to remain financially healthy. In a sole proprietorship, the owner himself or herself must obtain referrals or engage in some form of marketing to raise awareness of the firm and obtain clients. In larger design firms, marketing might be done by individuals other than the owner. There are literally dozens of methods that can be used by the interior design firm to market. Which method to use depends on the goals of the firm and naturally, the funds available to try different marketing methods.

Regardless of whether or not a particular interior design firm sells furniture and other products to the client, the essence of interior design is the provision of interior design services to clients. Marketing professional interior design services, however, is different from marketing products. Services are intangible; they do not exist until they are performed. The positive satisfaction the client is looking for cannot be realized until the project is done. Therefore, the client has to choose an interior designer on faith, hoping that the selected interior designer will provide the quality and professionalism required to complete the project. The interior designer must sell the client on his or her ability to solve the client's problem and execute the requirements within budget. This is why experience in a particular area of interior design, technical skills, and the designer's reputation are so important in the marketing of professional interior design services.

A *marketing plan* helps the firm identify what the goals are for marketing activities and helps bring a focus on which marketing methods are best suited to achieve the marketing goals. The overall goals of the design firm, along with the marketing goals, affect how the firm will market itself. For example, if the company wishes to grow, it must find a constant stream of new clients. When this is the case, a greater number of marketing methods are needed. On the other hand, if the firm wishes to remain small, marketing for new clients will likely focus on low-cost marketing methods such as referrals. Should the firm want to seek work in other geographic locations, marketing decisions must first be made to create awareness and obtain clients in those new areas. Firms whose goal is to enter a highly specialized area of design will need to employ different marketing activities than a generalist firm. These are just a few examples.

Most small firms obtain the majority of their new clients from referrals by existing clients. A referral occurs when a client provides positive comments about a firm to a potential customer. Providing excellent service and building a relationship with the client are the best ways to get referrals. Missed appointments and unfulfilled promises do not constitute excellent service. Caring about what the client needs rather than dictating to him or her is critical in establishing a positive relationship. You must develop a positive connection with the client in order for that relationship to build. Developing a good relationship with a client brings you back to the point of providing excellent service.

Generating referrals is just one way to market an interior design firm. Various marketing tools are used by the professional interior designer (see "Marketing Tools and Strategies," below). Most marketing activities are used to attract attention to the firm or to provide information about the firm. Whether the design firm places an advertisement in a local magazine, develops a Web site, or convinces a magazine to publish information about a project, the objective is to gain exposure that translates into an interview with a client so that a contract for a new project is developed.

MARKETING TOOLS AND STRATEGIES

- Business stationery, including logo
- Company Web site
- Project photos portfolio
- Brochures
- Advertising
- Ongoing press release strategies
- Entering projects in design competitions
- Newsletters
- Direct mail letters and flyers

- Speaking at seminars
- Distributing premiums
- Preparing slides or CDs for presentations
- Participating at industry conventions open to the public
- Writing articles in local newspapers or other appropriate print media
- Networking at events to meet potential clients
- Multimedia marketing presentations

Kitchen, Bath, and Aging-in-Place Home Modifications

PATRICIA A. ROWEN, ASID, CAPS
OWNER/DESIGNER, ROWEN DESIGN
HILLSDALE, MICHIGAN

What led you to enter your design specialty?

❯ After completing my design program, we moved to the San Francisco area during the early 1990s, when California was experiencing a serious recession. I learned interior design was really a luxury for many people. However, no matter whether the economy is up or down or your geographical location, people will still spend money on their kitchens and baths.

I was also assisting with the care of a parent with cancer. This prompted me to learn more about aging-in-place design. I attended my first CEU (continuing education unit) for this type of design in 1991.

What is the most important quality or skill of a designer in your specialty?

❯ You must be able to sell. Your first challenge is to sell yourself. Your client must have complete confidence in your ability or you will never get to the next step, which is design. To be confident in selling you must know your field of design, the products available, and have a creative mind for problem resolution.

How is your specialty different from other specialties?

❯ It is very technical and unforgiving if you make a mistake. This specialty requires having current knowledge of the building codes, construction procedures, finish carpentry, plumbing codes, construction, and finish materials, as well as that of the various products necessary to complete the project.

Aging-in-place residence: project sketch. Patricia Rowen, ASID, CAPS, Rowen Design, Hillsdale, Michigan

Aging-in-place residence: kitchen. Patricia Rowen, ASID, CAPS, Rowen Design, Hillsdale, Michigan.

PHOTOGRAPH: PATRICIA ROWAN

What motivated you to start your own design firm?

〉 We moved to a rural county in Michigan of approximately 46,000 people with a median income of $40,000 per year. I needed to create my own work to be employed in this area of the state.

What are your primary responsibilities and duties in your position?

〉 Some of my responsibilities include CAD or hand-drawn plans, project management, bookkeeping, ordering product, unloading trucks, and constant study to keep up with technology.

What is the most satisfying part of your job?

〉 I've learned the key to a happy family may be found in the kitchen. It is very satisfying to find that I have been able to change the lives of a family for the better through good design.

What is the least satisfying part of your job?

〉 It is stressful and very detail oriented. My clients trust that I have made good decisions for them, so I am constantly working to maintain high standards from design and construction through to project completion.

Who or what experience has been a major influence on your career?

〉 My husband, who has encouraged me to study and work hard to reach my goals.

What has been your greatest challenge as an interior designer?

〉 It is challenging to keep up with my work and the necessary study to be one of the best in my field.

Contracts

A very important business strategy for any size interior design firm is to use written *contracts* or *agreements*. Written contracts protect the interior designer and the client in case of disagreements. One type of contract explains the services that will be provided by the interior designer. The other, often called a *purchasing agreement*, details the furniture and other interior goods the client has agreed to purchase from the designer. A contract signed by the client is the only legal recourse the designer has should the client not pay or otherwise try to get out of the project. If an interior designer begins design services without a contract or orders any goods before the client has signed a purchasing agreement, there is no way to ensure that the client will pay the invoices.

Contracts or letters of agreement do not have to be lengthy or confusing. Plain language helps both designer and client understand what needs to be provided. To be legally binding on the client, the document must contain these five elements (see also "Elements of a Design Contract for Services," facing page):

1. The date.

2. A description of the project location.

3. The scope of services (for a contract for services) or a description of the goods to be sold by the designer to the client.

4. The fee or price.

5. The signature of both the client—the party being charged—and the interior designer.

Contracts for services can be fairly simple letters when the project is not complex. When they take this form, they are often called *letters of agreement*. As long as the letter of agreement contains the contract agreement information listed above, it is a binding legal document. However, when a project is complex, requiring several months or even years to complete, more formal contracts are prepared. A detailed, formal contract generally has additional clauses that deal with other responsibilities—a clause concerning arbitration in case of disputes; charges for extra services; disclaimers of responsibility for specific situations; ownership of documents; and other appropriate clauses are a few examples.

Very important in all contracts for design services are the clauses used to describe the scope of services. This element describes what will be done and how it will be done. The scope of services must be detailed to clarify the required work. If the scope of services is vague, then the designer can be responsible for providing services without being fairly compensated. The design process described in "Key Tasks in Interior Design Projects" (page 225) mentioned many tasks that are included in a scope of services clause. "Elements of a Design Contract for Services" (facing page) explains several key clauses and sections of a contract for interior design services.

Designers who also sell goods must clarify in the design services agreement how this will be achieved.The contract for the sale of goods, however, is different from the contract for services. This is because the law regarding the sale of goods departs somewhat from basic contract law. The interior designer prepares a separate document—most often called a *purchase agreement*—that explains what is being sold and the terms and conditions of the sale. This type of agreement is similar in concept to any agreement that you sign when you special order something from a store. Just as with the contract for design services, the purchase agreement for the sale of goods must be signed by the client, include a description of what is being sold along with prices, and include the date the contract was offered to the client.

ELEMENTS OF A DESIGN CONTRACT FOR SERVICES

Date: Obvious, but necessary for the contract to be valid.

Description of project area: It is important to identify the project area. For example, "provide design services for your residence at 1237 New York Avenue N.W., Washington, DC" is appropriate when you are responsible for designing the entire residence. When the project involves a smaller area, a phrase such as "for the remodeling of the family room and kitchen" is appropriate. This is done so you are responsible—and compensated—only for the areas of the project described in the contract.

Scope of services: This section defines the services you will provide in order to complete the required work. Services are always listed in the order in which they will be executed relative to the design process (see Chapter 5); this helps the client understand how the project will progress. The scope of services varies considerably depending on the size, type, and complexity of the project.

Method of compensation: This critical element is a clear explanation of how the client will be charged and billed for the interior design services constituting the contract. (A few common fee methods are explained in "Fee Methods," page 272). Designers can bill at the end of each month or with respect to the phases of the project. A retainer is usually required upon signing the agreement and is used to partially cover services to be performed.

Purchasing of goods: If the designer intends to sell merchandise to the client, a clause is included that tells the client how this will be done. Relevant information includes terms of payment, pricing, and other details that clarify how the client will be charged for the merchandise sold by the interior designer.

Signatures: A contract is not valid until the client signs it. Beginning work before you receive a signed contract is not good business practice, as you have no legal recourse to exact payment.

Other clauses: Additional clauses can be included in a design contract. The more complex the project, the more complex the agreement. The items mentioned above, however, are the basic elements of every valid contract. See "Interior Design References" (page 310) for books that detail the other elements of strong, binding contracts for interior design services and the sale of merchandise.

Restaurant (Hospitality) and Residential

LINDA ELLIOT SMITH, FASID
PRESIDENT, SMITH & ASSOCIATES, INC.,
AND education-works, inc.
DALLAS, TEXAS

What has been your greatest challenge as an interior designer?

❯ I think one of the greatest challenges of an interior design practitioner is the multitasking that is constantly part of the interior design process. This multitasking can sometimes become a great source of stress to the practitioner.

What led you to enter your design specialty?

❯ I got into restaurant design as a result of an opportunity that was presented, and it turned into a 10-year commitment to restaurant design.

The residential aspect of my specialty actually was an outcome of an early opportunity for what I call contract/residential design, which involved the interiors of condominium/apartment developments throughout the Southeast.

What are your primary responsibilities and duties?

❯ I am the principal in charge of all design processes.

What is the most satisfying part of your job?

❯ Knowing that I have met the clients' needs and fulfilled their expectations.

What is the least satisfying part of your job?

❯ Dealing with people who have little respect for customer service and performance of project responsibilities.

Restaurant: franchise prototype, dining area. Linda Elliott Smith, FASID, smith & associates, inc., Dallas, Texas.
PHOTOGRAPH: BILL LEFEVOR

What is the most important quality or skill of a designer in your specialty?

❯ I think that in any specialty the most important skill is the ability to listen and then translate.

How important is interior design education in today's industry?

❯ The knowledge gained through structured interior design education is invaluable as the basis for any practitioner. However, because the interior design profession continues to evolve and expand, the interior design practitioner's education must not stop at graduation. With sources, processes, and code requirements in a constant state of evolution, the interior designer must make a commitment to lifelong education.

Who or what experience has been a major influence on your career?

❯ My involvement with the American Society of Interior Designers has provided me with skills and knowledge I could never have obtained out in the field. My association with other professionals nationwide has been one of the most enriching experiences of my life.

Restaurant: franchise prototype, counter. Linda Elliott Smith, FASID, smith & associates, inc., Dallas, Texas.
PHOTOGRAPH: BILL LEFEVOR

Restaurant: franchise prototype, floor plan. Linda Elliott Smith, FASID, smith & associates, inc., Dallas, Texas.

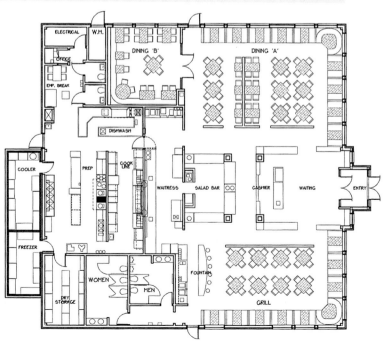

Hospitality, Municipal Government Facilities, Education Centers

KRISTI BARKER, CID

INTERIOR DESIGNER

HAYES, SEAY, MATTERN & MATTERN, INC.

VIRGINIA BEACH, VIRGINIA

What has been your greatest challenge as an interior designer?

❯ One of the greatest challenges of interior design is finding your niche. I was fortunate to work in several types of design firms. I was exposed to residential design and commercial design and was able to determine what area would best suit my skills, interests, and personality. It can become discouraging when you are working in

an environment where you do not feel successful. Continuing to explore your options and trying different project types until you determine where you can best apply your talent is the ultimate challenge.

What led you to enter your design specialty?

❯ After working in different environments with different personalities, you grow as both a designer and an individual. I found that my personality type was not suited for residential design, so I was able to avoid positions where that would be a focus. I learned in school that I was quite pragmatic, so commercial work was more suited to my interests and abilities. Projects where I could mix my pragmatic side with my desire for things to be creative, colorful, and fun has been my goal. Working on educational facilities like college student centers and hospitality-oriented projects like restaurants has enabled me to work on projects that meet my professional goals and enhanced my strengths.

What are your primary responsibilities and duties in your position?

❯ In my current position, I am responsible for the interior design on all our projects in the Virginia Beach branch office. I am tasked with developing an interior design department for our office, which means I am working to develop and enhance our drawing standards and operational procedures. I also participate in the marketing of our company at industry and community events and mentoring of younger employees.

Retail: store interior, Zie Spot, Norfolk, Virginia. Kristine S. Barker, CID, Hayes, Seay, Mattern & Mattern, Inc., Virginia Beach, Virginia.
PHOTOGRAPH: KRISTI BARKER

What is the most satisfying part of your job?

❯ The most satisfying part of my job is the feeling of accomplishment I get when I have created a unique and viable solution for a project and the client is thrilled with the result.

What is the least satisfying part of your job?

❯ The least satisfying thing is the frustration one can feel when a client just doesn't understand your design intent or is unwilling to release control over a situation and trust you to do your job to the utmost of your ability.

What is the most important quality or skill of a designer in your specialty?

❯ One of my favorite quotes is from architect I. M. Pei: "There are endless mysteries within discipline; infinite possibilities exist within a set of rules. It is not an individual act, architecture. You have to consider your client. Only out of that can you produce great architecture. You can't work in the abstract."

TOP RIGHT Food and beverage: Regattas Café & Market, Kingsmill Resort, Williamsburg, Virginia. Kristine S. Barker, CID, Hayes, Seay, Mattern & Mattern, Inc., Virginia Beach, Virginia.
PHOTOGRAPH: KRISTI BARKER

RIGHT Entertainment: lower level, University Center, College of William & Mary, Williamsburg, Virginia. Kristine S. Barker, CID, Hayes, Seay, Mattern & Mattern, Inc., Virginia Beach, Virginia.
PHOTOGRAPH: JEFF HOERGER

The client should come first and foremost in what you do. You must listen, even when you don't want to. You must bend a little, even when you don't think it's right. You must observe—even the most ridiculous things have a measure of value.

Who or what experience has been a major influence in your career?

❯ In my career, I have been most influenced by my coworkers. I learned that it doesn't become you to be bitter and dour, overly self-involved, or chaotically disorganized. Approach each new project as a new opportunity for learning, be friendly, educate yourself on current events, listen. As a young designer, finding a mentor you can emulate is very important. I was fortunate to work with a designer who was a confident and independent career woman. I learned from her to develop a sense of style to complement my strong technical skills. Her advice? Read all types of magazines, trade in your college wardrobe for one that conveys you have a sense of style, eat at fine restaurants, explore the world around you, and be open to new adventures. My first mentor had admirable people skills and was able to deal with clients with ease. She taught me when to talk and when to close my mouth and listen. It can be difficult to learn that when you are an eager young designer right out of college.

Interior Design Revenue

As can be discerned from the section on contracts, interior design firms can obtain revenue by two methods. Residential interior designers most commonly generate revenue from the sale of the goods that the client needs or by combining a design fee with the sale of merchandise. The most common method used by firms that specialize in commercial interior design is to charge the client a design fee for the required interior design services. Few professional interior design firms obtain their revenue solely from selling goods. This is more common in retail furniture stores and specialty stores that offer "free" interior decorating services.

Fees for professional interior design services can be calculated using several methods (see "Fee Methods," page 272). Because all designers have a limited amount of time to sell, an hourly fee is one of the most common ways for a designer to charge for services. In its simplest form, an hourly fee is charged for every hour or portion of an hour the interior designer works in the interests of the project as defined in the scope of services. The hourly fee approach is used by most service professionals, including attorneys, engineers, architects, and accountants.

How that hourly fee is determined is obviously an important question. It must be calculated to provide sufficient dollars to cover profit as well as the expenses of doing the work. Profit is the amount of money left over when expenses are deducted from what is charged to the client. Determining a fee amount for interior design services has three parts. The first is salary and benefits paid to employees. Next are operating expenses, which are overhead costs and other expenses not related to revenue production. The third factor is the desired profit. That profit can be realized only if the other two factors are accurately estimated.

The interior designer might also charge a fee for the project as a whole rather than by the hour. This is commonly called the *fixed fee* or *flat fee* method of determining fees for services. For example, after the scope of services is determined, the interior designer estimates how long it will take to complete the tasks, determines other costs of the project, such as printing scaled floor plans, adds a desired profit margin, and then sets a fee for the project.

Some interior designers also gain revenue from the sale of merchandise or goods to the client. Interior designers, of course, can purchase merchandise for less than the consumer would. Interior designers (and others in the built-environment industry) then mark up the merchandise in order to produce revenue from the sale of those goods. There is no set markup because the seller—in this case, the interior designer—can sell merchandise to the consumer at essentially any price they like. (The buyer doesn't have to buy at that price, of course.) The markup amount represents additional dollars to the designer to help cover the expenses of operating the business and likely yields a certain amount of profit for the overall project.

Inherent problems exist, however, for the interior design firm that sells merchandise. When the firm takes on the ordering of goods, additional paperwork is needed to process the orders. In addition, the design firm must monitor the order and shipment of the goods to the job site. The interior design firm also has various responsibilities related to damages or loss in transit from the factory to the job site. When the goods are obtained from a source out of state, freight charges must be considered. Finally, the interior designer probably will have to spend more time at the job site to ensure that the merchandise is delivered and placed or installed properly. All these additional costs and expenses must be considered in the determination of the markup and added to the cost of the merchandise in order for the interior designer to realize any profit from the sale of the goods.

Healthcare: West of the Moon Lounge, Scripps Breast Care Center, La Jolla, California. Interior architecture and design, Jain Malkin, Inc., San Diego, California.
PHOTOGRAPH: GLENN CORMIER

FEE METHODS

Hourly fee: This method is straightforward and similar to any professional service provider's primary fee method. The interior designer charges a set fee for every hour he or she works in the interest of the client's project. Interior design fees can range from $85 to over $200 an hour depending on the designer's reputation, experience level, and market competition. Due to competition, on average, it is common for the hourly rates of residential designers to be higher than those of commercial designers.

Fixed fee or flat fee: The interior designer estimates a total fee for all the interior design services required for the project. The client agrees to pay one flat fee rather than an hourly rate. Contracts rarely allow the designer to charge the client additional fees if the fixed fee is insufficient to cover all actual project time.

Cost plus: Using this fee method, the interior designer adds a percentage to the cost of the products needed for the project. Between 10 and 35 percent is usual, but the percentage can be higher. In most cases, the interior designer is also selling the required merchandise to the client or arranging for the purchase of goods in the client's name.

Retail: The retail fee method, like the cost plus method, is related to the products specified for the project. In this case, the client pays the retail price for goods. Retail, often marked up a minimum of 100 percent from cost, is the price manufacturers recommend sellers (i.e., the interior designer and stores) bill consumers. For example, if the seller can buy a lamp from a manufacturer for $50, the retail price would be $100.

Legal Issues

As is true in every business and profession, the interior design professional can be affected by legal ramifications when work is incorrectly executed or otherwise outside normal professional performance. Clients can sue interior designers when work is done incorrectly. The first line of defense is to take on only those projects you know you are capable of doing with the utmost professionalism. The two areas of legal responsibility that most often affect working relationships relate to negligence and breach of contract.

Negligence, for the purpose of our limited discussion in this chapter, is when an interior designer does not use appropriate care in executing the project for the client, and the lack of care leads to some sort of harm. This can most often be summed up in the term *professional negligence*. When the interior designer is sued for professional negligence, he or she is accused of not doing the work in a manner that the courts define as normal for a professional interior designer. Although negligence is very serious, many of these claims are negotiated to a resolution rather than going to court—unless, of course, serious injury has occurred.

Harm does not only mean physical injury. For example, if a business cannot open on time and the delay is due to a fault or error by the interior designer, then professional negligence has technically occurred. The interior designer can be accused of negligence if he or she specifies the project way over the budget or makes a mistake on the construction drawings such that construction work must be redone. For the most part, the interior designer is not literally sued by the client for these kinds of problems. Some compromise is usually worked out. However, this type of unprofessional work can lead to legal consequences that can harm the business and reputation of the interior designer.

Another legal issue that can involve the interior design professional is *breach of contract*. Once a contract between the interior designer and the client is signed, both parties have a responsibility to complete the tasks spelled out in the agreement. A breach of contract occurs when one of the parties to the contract does not do something agreed to in the contract. For example, if the interior designer is required to prepare the construction drawings and does not do so, he or she has breached the contract. If the contract calls for the client to pay design fees within 30 days of receiving the bill for those fees but the client does not do so, he or she has breached the contract.

Breach of contract between an interior designer and client seldom goes to court or requires the services of an attorney. In most instances, a compromise is worked out. Interior designers must be mindful of what they put into their design contracts and sales agreements. Whatever is stated must be done or provided—or, technically, the designer has breached the contract and the client may sue.

This discussion and the examples provided give you the very smallest explanation of legal responsibilities that affect the work of the interior designer. Several books listed in "Interior Design References" (page 310) have further information.

Libraries

SUZAN GLOBUS, FASID, LEED-AP
PRESIDENT, GLOBUS DESIGN ASSOCIATES
RED BANK, NEW JERSEY

What has been your greatest challenge as an interior designer?

❭ To keep focusing on how my work can enhance the lives of those using the space.

What led you to enter your design specialty?

❭ I told a client I was considering starting my own firm, and he suggested I talk about offering interior design services to a library director who was building a new library. I started my own business with the contract for that library. Soon after, the referrals began and a specialty was born. It felt like a good fit for a former journalist.

What are your primary responsibilities and duties?

❭ My primary responsibilities are obtaining new business, client communications, and managing staff.

What is the most satisfying part of your job?

❭ Hearing clients describe how a finished project has changed their lives is most satisfying because it reminds me how profound the effects of a well-designed space can be on its occupants.

Library: children's area, Ocean County Library, Little Egg Harbor Branch, Little Egg Harbor, New Jersey. Suzan Globus, FASID, LEED-AP, Globus Design Associates, Red Bank, New Jersey.
PHOTOGRAPH: DIANE EDINGTON

Library: reading area and staircase, Ocean County Library, Brick Branch, Brick, New Jersey. Suzan Globus, FASID, LEED-AP, Globus Design Associates, Red Bank, New Jersey.
PHOTOGRAPH: DIANE EDINGTON

What is the least satisfying part of your job?

❯ The least satisfying part is managing poor staff performance, and I have been very fortunate in that regard.

What is the most important quality or skill of a designer in your specialty?

❯ It is not specific to this specialty, but the ability to ask questions and listen to the answers has never failed to serve me well.

Who or what experience has been a major influence on your career?

❯ Carlos Bulnes, a college professor who taught me that human beings are not an accessory in the space.

How Important Is Certification by Examination and Licensing of Interior Designers Today?

❯ Certification is necessary to become a full professional in the two major interior design associations, as well as it is required to be registered in those states and provinces with interior design legislation.

David Stone, IIDA, LEED-AP

❯ In my opinion, now is the time for interior design as a profession. Rules and exams and licensing are part of that evolution from job to profession. It is time we admit and celebrate the difference between design and decoration.

M. Joy Meeuwig, IIDA

❯ I believe it is an accepted method by which professionals seek to establish a recognized baseline of skill and knowledge, and by which public entities seek to ensure the safety of the public.

Sari Graven, ASID

❯ We deal with too many areas of impact on HSW (health, safety, and welfare) to not be licensed.

Bruce Goff, ASID

❯ If interior design is to survive as a profession then interior designers must become professionals, not hobbyists. With professionalism comes responsibility for the protection of the public (users, clients).

Derrell Parker, IIDA

❯ It is vital. It will define and protect our right to practice our profession. Without it, our profession is vulnerable.

Suzan Globus, FASID, LEED-AP

❯ To encourage our profession to reach to the level the professional designer needs it to be is the best argument for certification or licensing.

Debra May Himes, IIDA, ASID

❯ It certifies the commitment of the individual to their profession. Those that don't certify either have an ego issue about their abilities or are happy with the "lot" in life and are not interested in increasing their opportunities.

Linda Isley, IIDA

❯ Very! It demonstrates a level of commitment the individual interior designer has to the profession. It legitimizes the profession for public consumption.

Jennifer van der Put, BID, IDC, ARIDO, IFMA

Commercial: Corporate Offices

JO RABAUT, ASID, IIDA
PRESIDENT/OWNER
RABAUT DESIGN ASSOCIATES, INC.
ATLANTA, GEORGIA

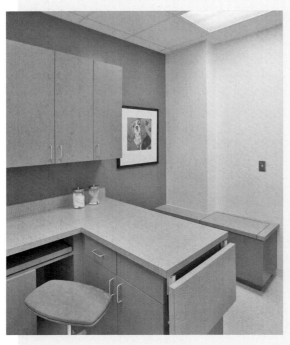

What led you to enter your design specialty?

❯ I grew up with a grandfather who was an architect, and at Sunday dinners we always listened to his stories. He actually understood what an interior designer did and supported it. This was in the 1950s. I think he was ahead of his time.

What is the most important quality or skill of a designer in your specialty?

❯ Ability to listen, problem solve.

How is your specialty different from other specialties?

❯ Since I do commercial work, we need to have a broad range of expertise, from codes and life safety to construction to finishes, details, and even accessories.

What are your primary responsibilities and duties in your position?

❯ As I own my own business, I tend to wear just about every hat available.

TOP LEFT Animal clinic: examination room, Loving Hands Animal Clinic. Jo Rabaut, ASID, IIDA, Rabaut Design Associates, Inc., Atlanta, Georgia.
PHOTOGRAPH: JIM ROOF CREATIVE, INC.

LEFT Furniture showroom: display space, Walter Wickers, Inc. Jo Rabaut, ASID, IIDA, Rabaut Design Associates, Inc., Atlanta, Georgia.
PHOTOGRAPH: CHRIS LITTLE PHOTOGRAPHY

What is the most satisfying part of your job?

❭ Mostly having a happy client—and taking clients who do not put much stock in the "value" of interior design and then turn them around to be one of your best supporters.

What is the least satisfying part of your job?

❭ Vendors who do not live up to lead times promised and bad contractors just wanting to slap the project up.

Who or what experience has been a major influence on your career?

❭ My grandfather. He was an architect, worked with firms and started his own. He became an FAIA. I listened to his stories about construction and design all the time. He only had architecture magazines at his house. I loved to sneak into his office and see what he was drawing.

What has been your greatest challenge as an interior designer?

❭ All advice given to me is to specialize into one area of expertise and I enjoy doing a multitude of different project types.

Corporate: reception lobby. Jo Rabaut, ASID, IIDA, Rabaut Design Associates, Inc., Atlanta, Georgia.
PHOTOGRAPH: JIM ROOF CREATIVE, INC.

Residential

KEITH MILLER, ASID
CERTIFIED INTERIOR CONSULTANT AND OWNER
MILLER & ASSOCIATES
INTERIOR CONSULTANTS, LLC
SEATTLE, WASHINGTON

What led you to enter your design specialty?

❭ I took two internships simultaneously in the summer before my senior year in college: one commercial and one residential. After listening to panel discussions with residential interior designers in student chapter ASID meetings, I swore I would never do residential or run my own business because the pressure seemed so daunting. I accepted an entry-level position at the commercial establishment where I took my internship, and kept in touch with the residential designer from the other internship. I started helping the residential designer on the side, and fell in love with the level of creativity and deep sense of reward solving unusual problems for so many unique people. In just a little over a year in the commercial position, I turned in my resignation, cleared out a corner in my home, and started my own residential interior design business.

What is the most important quality or skill of a designer in your specialty?

> Candor. My first big mistake running my own company happened when I failed to clearly communicate important cost information to one of my clients. She was extremely upset and demanded clarification, including all of my record keeping related to her project. My wife and I met with her and her husband, a lawyer. The mistake was clearly mine. Instead of taking me to the cleaners and after my wife helped me admit my wrong, these very kind people sent us away after a remarkably gracious lecture about discerning appropriate levels of honesty and openness in human relationships—candor.

How is your specialty different from other specialties?

> Residential interior design requires an enormous amount of tact, compassion, patience, flexibility, and even counseling skills, among other intangible abilities. Part of the reason I love working in residential is the joy that I find improving quality of life—the physical surroundings being just the start.

What are your primary responsibilities and duties in your position?

> Everything, including client and vendor relations, research, creative solution development, establishing, tracking, expediting work orders, problem solving, conflict resolution, and so on.

What is the most satisfying part of your job? The least?

> The most is exceeding client expectations; surprising them with solutions that delight and meet their specific requirements. The least is the paperwork and badgering vendors who fail to hold to their word.

Who or what experience has been a major influence on your career?

> Among many, I single out my continuing education. I have natural abilities, but without training, I wouldn't have been introduced to the invaluable tools of universal design. Without exposure to recent research developments in sustainable design, I wouldn't know to research and demand more responsibly manufactured products from my vendors.

What has been your greatest challenge as an interior designer?

> Time.

What Is the Greatest Business Challenge for Interior Design Firms?

> Considering that many interior design firms are small, I believe the greatest challenge is maintaining the business side of the enterprise. Many firms seem to sacrifice business operations in favor of creative operations. This unbalance can be a death knell.

Linda E. Smith, FASID

> I'd say that staying in a competitive mode during the ups and downs in the economy is the most difficult and challenging job facing any business owner today. The overall economy and the many directions it takes are a topic that all business owners need to keep a handle on if they want to remain in business. This takes planning and looking to the future so we are not blindsided by unexpected changes.

Terri Maurer, FASID

Liturgical interior: renovated sanctuary, St. Matthew's Episcopal Church, Louisville, Kentucky. Laura Busse, IIDA, KYCID, Reese Design Collaborative, Louisville, Kentucky.
PHOTOGRAPH: STEVEN G. PORTER

❯ Small firms? The need for the owner to be everything. Large firms? Keeping enough quality projects flowing in. Midsize? All of the above.
Bruce Goff, ASID

❯ To maintain design integrity and an ethical business practice on all projects.
Beth Kuzbek, ASID, IIDA, CMG

❯ To educate the public about what interior design firms do. The public needs to understand the value of good design—and the profession needs to understand the value of collaborating with other professionals (architects, engineers, landscape architects, and so on).
Lisa Whited, ASID, IIDA, IDEC, Maine CID

❯ Keeping a consistent run of projects coming in, in order to meet expenses. Using whatever marketing skills are needed to ensure referrals and interesting work. Taking on large and small designs to help even out the cash flow.
Michael Thomas, FASID, CAPS

❯ Creating value for the client.
Nila Leiserowitz, FASID, Associate AIA

❯ The greatest business challenge for most designers is simply being a good businessperson. Just because we are a creative bunch does not mean we should not also be good businesspeople. I think creative people often think they cannot be businesslike—but this is just not the case. The more businesslike one is, the more respect one commands, and thus the better a designer one is. To me, creativity and business go hand in hand.
Charles Gandy, FASID, FIIDA

❯ Finding the best partners, that is, the subcontractors who make your design a reality.
Donna Vining, FASID, IIDA, RID, CAPS

❯ Getting paid for the real value of our expertise and services.
Sari Graven, ASID

> The greatest business challenges for interior design firms are to maintain accurate records of time, to write contracts/agreements, and to keep qualified employees. Time is money, and we have to earn a living while fulfilling our creativity.
Sandra Evans, ASID

> Continuing to bring in enough fee revenue to pay our designers what they are worth.
Rita Carson Guest, FASID

> The greatest business challenge today is to be diverse and flexible in services provided so as to prosper in any economic situation.
Linda Sorrento, ASID, IIDA, LEED-AP

> First, there's a great deal of competition and people who are prepared to provide design services at unreasonably low fees. The greatest challenges are to recognize that interior design is a profession and a business and to be able to listen to clients and provide solutions for them—not just for the designer.
M. Arthur Gensler Jr., FAIA, FIIDA, RIBA

> Paperwork—keeping track of the minutiae inherent in design. And thank heaven for Design Manager software!
Jan Bast, FASID, IIDA, IDEC

> Identifying the right road to profitability.
Pat McLaughlin, ASID, RID

> Attracting and retaining experienced and talented designers in today's competitive workplace.
Leonard Alvarado

> Developing a good client base and remaining competitive.
Sally Nordahl, IIDA

> Making sure we stay within the scope of work for which we have contracted and that we are paid for all the work that is done. Keeping track of when the scope changes and communicating that to the client. Also, hiring competent staff and managing the staff you do have.
Melinda Sechrist, FASID

> Competitive fee structures in juxtaposition with real labor costs. Clients have been very successful in asking for the moon without expecting to pay for the level of professionalism we bring. We all need to respect our own abilities and agree that they are worthy of payment.
David Stone, IIDA, LEED-AP

> To reinvent ourselves because the architectural community and furniture dealers have reduced our value into nothing more than furniture specifiers. We need to use research to show that our value is in how we change behavior.
Rosalyn Cama, FASID

> Balancing the art with the business of design. Managing personnel time so as to facilitate good design executed in a timely fashion.
Marilyn Farrow, FIIDA

> Today, the greatest business challenges for interior design firms are identifying our target market and building a marketing plan that grabs attention and showcases our skills and imagination.
Greta Guelich, ASID

> Professional viability is the greatest business challenge for small interior design firms. We keep meticulous records of time spent on individual projects, and we have historical data for many years on fees expended for various types and sizes of projects that enable us to accurately price

new work. However, it's always difficult, if one is doing really creative design, to turn out a project at a profit. It takes tremendous effort to monitor productivity, keep billings current, and watch expenses. Work seems to come in clumps. On three occasions in the past 20 years, in a brief few months, every large project we had under contract was either abandoned or in abeyance. This type of loss is hard to recover from; one can't lay off employees who take years to train for healthcare design. At other times, so much work is coming in that it's like being on a treadmill that never stops. It never seems to be an even pace.

Jain Malkin, CID

❯ The greatest business challenge for interior design firms is to not lose sight of the company's goals and how to achieve them. It seems that in this busy world we can become immersed in what is happening today and not look out for the future. Having a business plan for your firm can make the difference between calculated survival and luck.

Linda Santellanes, ASID

❯ Finding clients; getting projects completed on time and on budget.

Debra May Himes, ASID, IIDA

❯ Knowing when the business is too large and complex to be treated like the family checkbook. Finally admitting that we became interior designers for the creative aspect, not the day-to-day running of a business.

Derrell Parker, IIDA

❯ Understanding how to charge effectively for the services we provide. Many times, designers go beyond the scope of their fees for a project. Because of our desire for the project to be fully complete, we get involved in many aspects not originally planned for. It is hard to stop the design

Healthcare: Sunga DDS Dental Suite. Linda Isley, IIDA, Young + Co., Inc., San Diego, California.
PHOTOGRAPH: LINDA ISLEY

process and say, "Hold on! This is not in our contract." We need to be more effective in charging and not giving away our design services.

Juliana Catlin, FASID

❯ Investment in new knowledge and research.

Neil Frankel, FAIA, FIIDA

❯ To educate the public about the talents and benefits of hiring an interior designer, and that we are worth the money.

Linda Isley, IIDA

❯ Reinventing the firm to meet the changing needs of the marketplace.

M. Joy Meeuwig, IIDA

❯ Staying competitive without undermining the profession's value. I find some of my peers price their design services so low that they project a perception to the public that devalues interior design.

Jennifer van der Put, BID, IDC, ARIDO, IFMA

> In small firms, too many designer/owners try to do it all themselves. We need to hire the right people instead. We are not office managers, draftspeople, or assistants. Do what you do best: Design and work with the client.

Robert Wright, FASID

> Either keeping up your marketing efforts constantly, and I mean constantly, or convincing people that interior design is as important as the architecture and the construction job. It seems that there is always a nonprofessional around who feels he has a knack for design, and a project committee is tempted to try to save money by eliminating the interior designer. Often, of course, this costs them money—because they have to redo a bad paint selection, or replace inappropriate floor coverings, or live with very bad lighting—all problems that can be avoided if a proper professional does the job. Or, perhaps, the greatest challenge today is getting interior designers changed over from selling stuff to charging for their professional services.

Linda Kress, ASID

> I would say developing core competencies that strengthen the firm for present and future needs. It is essential today to be versatile and flexible in the services offered in order to be able to meet all your clients' needs and to stay competitive with other designers. Over the years, Group Mackenzie Interiors has evolved with the needs of our clients. It is important to continue growing into new markets by developing and maintaining a diversified range of client types.

Susan B. Higbee

> Educating the public about the value of using interior designers.

Suzan Globus, FASID, LEED-AP

> To be successful economically while treating clients fairly, meeting their needs and expectations. A designer must be able to work both *on* the business and *in* the business.

Sally Thompson, ASID

> I imagine the challenges of an interior-design-only firm may vary from those of a multidisciplined architectural, interior design, and engineering firm. Speaking on behalf of all design disciplines within our industry, I believe our biggest challenge is the lack of recognition as a valued profession in comparison to other professions. Our profit margins pale in comparison.

Janice Carleen Linster, ASID, IIDA, CID

> Being professional in your business practices, which results in respect from clients, vendors, and others.

William Peace, ASID

> I would say the slow economic climate is the greatest challenge facing design practices today. Because design is a want and not a need, clients can live without the expense until the climate changes.

Naomi Anderson

> Business practices and keeping up with changing technology. We are taught design, and that is what we are good at. However, if we are to grow and sustain our businesses we really need to continue to educate ourselves and take the time to work *on* our businesses rather than *in* them. I read at least 6 to 10 books a year on business, economics, and history. This has a big impact on how I run my business, how I think about design, and how I affect those around me.

Melinda Sechrist, FASID

Finding a Place in Interior Design

ALEXIS B. BOUNDS, ALLIED MEMBER ASID
ASSOCIATED GROCERS, INC.
BATON ROUGE, LA

How did you choose which school to attend to obtain your education in interior design? What degree do you possess?

❭ Louisiana offers programs to help students afford college at state schools. It was best for me to take advantage of this opportunity. Coincidentally, Louisiana State University (LSU) offers a well-recognized design program as well. May 2006, Bachelor's of Interior Design.

What was your greatest challenge as a student?

❭ The greatest challenge was balancing school, a part-time job as a junior designer at a local architecture firm, my roles as ASID South Central Chapter's Student Representative to the Board and as the ASID Student Chapter President at LSU, and being a fiancée.

How important do you feel an internship is to a student's educational experience?

❭ Extremely! You learn things at an internship that you do not have the opportunity to experience in school. Learning the ropes of Microsoft Office, working with people, and getting familiar with general office etiquette are a huge advantage.

Are you planning to take the NCIDQ exam if you have not already? Why or why not?

❭ Absolutely. I'm studying to take it in October 2008. This is the next step in completing my education. I would not miss out on the opportunity for anything.

What has been your greatest challenge in your first years of employment?

❭ My greatest achievement was learning the best ways to communicate with clients and coworkers. I quickly learned the benefits of using programs such as Microsoft Outlook to manage my time and projects.

Did you join the student chapter of ASID or IIDA at your school? Why?

❭ I was a student member of IIDA and ASID. I was Student Representative to the Board for ASID's South Central Chapter. I was the Student Chapter President for Louisiana State University.

I joined the organizations because I saw the value of being able to network with designers outside of the university environment. I joined both because the student membership fee is so affordable, and I felt it could have been a potential disadvantage had a not been a member of one when it came time to look for a job.

How did you choose the firm that you are working for?

❭ The opportunity presented itself to me. I researched the company, its benefits, and the position. I interviewed and accepted the job.

7 The Future

The many interior designers who consented to be interviewed for this book responded to a final question in this last chapter, a question that faces everyone in this profession as well as those who contemplate a career in interior design and its related fields.

What Do You See as the Future for the Interior Design Profession?

❯ The tide of design—in all its forms and manifestations—is ever-rising. More and more people are understanding design and learning to appreciate it and refusing to live without good design in their lives. The future is design. As Tom Peters says in *Re-Imagine: The Essence of Design*, "Design is the 'soul' of new enterprise." And to quote Anna, age 11, "If there was no design, there would be nothing to do, and nothing would progress or get better. The world would fall apart."
Bruce Brigham, FASID, ISP, IES

❯ The shifts that have taken place since the early 20th century, when interior design was called "interior decoration," have been enormous for the field and its development as a profession. Affected by technology, a changing and broader clientele, by gendering and then degendering of the field, and with aesthetic and sociocultural paradigm shifts, the profession has become increasingly complex and diverse in its knowledge and skill base. A possible future is to more consciously promote specialization in order to distinguish professional expertise and to provide diversified programs of study in order to prepare the next generations of students adequately for the workplace.
Carol Morrow, Ph.D., ASID, IIDA, IDEC

❯ The profession is just beginning to be recognized as critical to a business.
Nila Leiserowitz, FASID, Associate AIA

❯ The future for the profession is bright because of the greater importance given to the human experience in the environment.
Linda Sorrento, ASID, IIDA, LEED-AP

❯ The future of the profession lies in our ability to continue to be the "go to" problem solvers for our clients. By being the profession that deals with the most tactile aspect of the design world, we will continue to have the most influence on how people live, play, and work.
David Stone, IIDA, LEED-AP

❯ More and more, clients comprehend the value that we bring to their projects, within all sectors of the market and specialties. Sustainability will be an integral part of all design projects as in applying the codes, regulations, standards, and practices that protect the health, safety, and welfare of the public. We must all take responsibility for our actions, and the decisions we make every day. Our choices actively affect market transformation.

Annette K. Stelmack, Allied Member ASID

> Our profession is growing and maturing at a very rapid rate. The importance of what we do and how we affect the built environment is expanding and being recognized by the public. Every project we work on, no matter how small, affects the lives of those who live, work, and play in the environment we design. What we do affects the health, safety, and welfare of the public. The level of responsibility for designers is rising as well, so we must prepare to shoulder this additional responsibility through our education, work experience, and qualifying examination. Regulation of our industry will be the norm, as will a first-rate education and a strong qualifying examination.

Terri Maurer, FASID

> With the growing awareness of the importance of design in our society, I believe the interior design profession is poised to be a significant force in the design of our environment, to bring leadership to and perhaps reinvent the way we think about interior environments. Environmental sustainability as well as social equity and economic viability are becoming key issues in defining design problems. The redefinition of these problems will lead to new and innovative solutions. Interior design is a relatively young profession and may be the most open to looking at new ways to redefine and solve problems.

Beth Harmon-Vaughn, FIIDA, Associate AIA, LEED-AP

> The profession is going to continue to evolve, with opportunities arising in heretofore unidentified areas. Interior designers are problem solvers and as such bring much-needed skills to a wide variety of specialty areas and associated fields.

Linda Elliott Smith, FASID

> The future of the profession is very strong. The field is still in its infancy, and as it gains in recognition and respectability, consumer demand will grow.

Dennis McNabb, FASID, IDEC

> The future is bright if we take the initiative to regulate legally the practice of interior design. We must build consensus on the body of knowledge and advance it, supported by research and theory. Our profession is much more complex than it was 20 or even 10 years ago. Research is the key to understanding how to improve the human condition through design.

Denise A. Guerin, Ph.D., FIDEC, ASID, IIDA

> First, interior designers must find an effective way to quantify the fiscal impact the workplace has on individual performance to counterbalance the financial pressures owners often put on the design team.

Businesses need the workforce to be innovative as well as productive. The workplace must support people to do their best. A well-designed workplace is one of the best ways for companies to support the human capital that is the real source of their prosperity and growth.

The workplace must support the creative process so teams can be innovative. Managers, who do not consider the effects that changes to workplaces may have on professional productivity, may look superficially as though they are doing well for their firm in terms of reducing space consumption, but in reality they could be doing irreparable damage in terms of lowering productivity and morale.

Second, interior designers can bring great value to the business culture in helping clients understand the design studio process.

When teams are called on to create new products, services, and experiences, their innovation process brings them closer to the design studio than the traditional workplace. Some argue that business challenges are so like design problems that traditional "business logic" and methods of analysis don't work anymore. All of which means that right-brain types, those who think like artists and designers, are coming into their own in the workforce.

Third, as interior designers, we can reinvent our future once we effectively show the value we bring to clients and their businesses in tangible ways.

Rita Carson Guest, FASID

> Interior design will only get better and stronger. Technology will play an even greater role in the future of our world, and design is not an exception.

Charles Gandy, FASID, FIIDA

> I think that interior designers lead the way in planning and implementing corporate design. I learned in the early 1970s, when I was in school, that you design "from the inside out." This is still not completely done—we create buildings and then try to fit people and rooms into the building, instead of understanding the corporation and the work first, then building around that information. It's not a numbers game: It's a game of understanding the effects of an environment on people and the work process.

Colleen McCafferty, IFMA, USGBC, LEED-CI

> Education will play a key role in the profession as technology and global issues become more complex. I am seeing other professions such as engineering and architecture increase both their course and continuing education requirements. I believe that the interior design profession will need to follow suit to keep up with changes in the marketplace. Specialization will likely increase as certain sectors of the market become even more complex.

Mary Knopf, ASID, IIDA, LEED-AP

> The future is limitless. As we document and understand the effect on human behavior of the environments we create, this profession will continue to grow and deliver tremendous value to the people it serves.

Suzan Globus, FASID, LEED-AP

> The future should be bright for the field of interior design. We have become a more educated, technical, and respected team member that also brings important product knowledge and specific expertise to our projects.

Debra Himes, ASID, IIDA

> More value placed on what we have to offer and more income produced from that value rather than from sale of product. This is a realization by many in our field already, thank goodness. But we need to sell our value every chance we get in order for it to be recognized.

Drue Lawlor, FASID

> I believe the future is very promising for interior designers. I see more and more states realizing our role in protecting the public and passing more stringent interior design legislation. I also see us working more closely with other design professionals.

Jan Bast, FASID, IIDA, IDEC

Private residence: kitchen. Debra May Himes, ASID, IIDA, Debra May Himes Interior Design & Associates LLC, Chandler, Arizona.

PHOTOGRAPH: DINO TONN

❯ I am certain that interior designers will always be in demand and that the consumer will realize the value in working with a designer. We will be expected to know more technically as well as be more aware of building systems and codes that govern them. The interior designer of the future will be expected to appropriately work with the limited resources that our earth has to offer and help curb our country's enormous consumption habits.

Robert Wright, FASID

❯ Applied research design. As the profession continues its growth to qualification and certification, the need for people to be able to apply research methods to design solutions is becoming essential. Additionally, businesses are searching for people with the ability to look at a problem both analytically and creatively.

Robin Wagner, ASID, IDEC

❯ Interior design is going to continue to grow and there will be more specialties in the field. I am hoping that the environmental aspect of our jobs keeps gaining speed and becomes a factor in every project we work on. I worry that many corporations are using LEED certification as the buzzword "du jour" rather than as a principle.

Jane Coit, Associate Member IIDA

❯ I look upon interior design's relationship with architecture as the imprint upon the frame, where architecture constitutes the frame and interior design embodies the imprint. The idea of "imprint" embodies human needs and behavior responses in the built environment, which is a conceptual focus in interior design. My focus in both teaching and practicing is to nurture the relationships between the frame and its imprint. I see the future of interior design engaging the living component or imprint of architecture for years to come.

James Postell, Associate Professor, Interior Design, University of Cincinnati

❯ As professions go, we are a toddler and as such all of us must be the best we can be, setting the stage for the future. We must not only preach the talk, but walk the walk in light of the three Es: education, experience, examination.

Donna Vining, FASID

> It must become a united front that stands on the foundation of one professional organization. With all of us working together, interior design will gain stature and provide a rewarding profession for all who practice.
Mimi Moore, ASID, CID

> Own the definition of the human experience in the built environment and be poised to measure it so that you will push innovation in an informed way and pull your colleagues and clients to an enlightened state about how to design and build the interior environments we inhabit.
Rosalyn Cama, FASID

> I think the future of interior design will continue to evolve with new technology and green influences. There will have to be a more integrated design approach to combine function, aesthetics, and a user-friendly experience.
Trisha Wilson, ASID

> I am disappointed in our legislative efforts throughout the U.S. I believe it is important that we are considered a design professional and not just a decorator. Of course, this requires education and the passage of the NCIDQ exam.
Patricia Rowen, ASID, CAPS

> I am very excited to be a part of the interior design industry right now. I feel with legislation around the country enacting practice acts, our profession is becoming more legitimized and will have a great effect on what it really means to be an interior designer.
Kristin King, ASID

> Great things! I started in the early 1980s and keep getting reinvigorated by this profession. As the body of knowledge and documented research about interior design grows, we are carving a wonderful path to the profession for future interior designers. We will continue to fight the misperception of what constitutes interior design, but the best way to do that is through excellent educational programs, solid mentoring by seasoned professionals, and a high-caliber examination process. In addition, creating functional spaces that support—and enhance—the human condition will be the best indication of what comprises interior design.
Lisa Whited, IIDA, ASID, Maine Certified Interior Designer

> I think the future is good for the profession but changing rapidly with technology and the Internet. It creates a knowledgeable client who has the ability to gather just as much information as you can.
Laurie Smith, ASID

> Through all areas of the interior design profession—residential, commercial, hospitality, retail—the list goes on and on, with both large and small projects, there are unlimited opportunities, but success will come only to those prepared to make the commitments to time and education and dedicated to creating great environments and wonderful places.
M. Arthur Gensler Jr., FAIA, FIIDA, RIBA

> I think that the public as well as other trade professions such as architects and contractors will continue to have a better understanding of interior design and how important licensing is for the profession. With all of the state legislations that are working on licensing I think we will eventually

have most states with some sort of requirements for interior designers which will bring a better awareness of the interior design profession.

Shannon Ferguson, IIDA

❯ I am very optimistic about the future of interior design and I think that we will see increasingly focused specialization in the various areas of design.

David Hanson, RID, IDC, IIDA

❯ A strong future for designers who focus on specialty areas and who provide expertise in workplace productivity, sustainable interiors, energy conservation, and health and safety. All of these disciplines affect an organization's bottom line, and that is the driving force for hiring a consultant or professional today.

Leonard Alvarado

❯ Defining interior design as a profession is more important than ever; the field is challenged from all sides. Our specific area of expertise, based on education, internships, and continuing education, must be defined in a title act or a practice act.

Pat McLaughlin, ASID, RID

❯ The future of interior design will be more important than ever as people realize how important good design is for everyday human interaction and function. Also designers will be called upon to create environments that will be very green minded as the planet's resources dwindle away and populations increase.

Lisa Slayman, ASID, IIDA

❯ The design process is applicable as a creative problem-solving approach to a wide variety of situations and problems. Our ability to gather and organize large amounts of information; channel it into a working, cohesive concept; and then implement it is what every business is looking for

today. Our education has never been more relevant to the issues we face today in business as well as our personal lives.

Sari Graven, ASID

❯ The future is as a service industry, providing plans and specifications for interior architecture. Interior designers need to get out of the business of selling furniture or, at a minimum, separate the two activities into separate businesses. Our ideas are our most valuable assets.

Tom Witt

❯ The future is not clear. The media aspect of our profession implies that what we do is all about vision and touch. There is a clear threat from architecture to severely limit what an interior designer can do without being legally subservient to architects. Last, we have too many professional organizations, a fractured voice that inhibits our ability to effectively deal with these challenges.

Robert Krikac, IIDA

❯ Just as it has been to date: improving quality of life; increasing productivity; protecting human health, safety, and welfare. Furthermore, the growing mature life population (age 65 and over) in America, and exciting new solutions for the way things are made (read *Cradle to Cradle: Remaking the Way We Make Things* by Michael Braungart and Bill McDonough) will continue to place stringent demands on the problem-solving design skills of tomorrow's interior designer.

Keith Miller, ASID

❯ I believe two significant changes will occur in the design profession and are already occurring. As states pass legislation leading to licensure for interior designers, the profession becomes more like architecture and, therefore, I think greater collaboration occurs for the client. When interior designers are involved at the start of a project, the client certainly benefits. There is also greater opportunity for cohesive, packaged design instead of interior design becoming a choppy afterthought. The second change is environmental. The Midwest is known for being time delayed from the coasts for all major design or product movements. I believe that within five years specifying green or environmentally friendly materials will not be so unusual. In fact, I think it will be the norm.

Laura Busse, IIDA, KYCID

❯ Until architects accept us for the talents, knowledge, and value we bring to the project, we will stay where we are. Architects need to value our abilities and stop trying to cheapen what we do by hiring students (cheap labor) to do the work we should be doing.

Linda Isley, IIDA, CID

❯ The intimate relationship between the human animal and his or her little piece of the built environment just keeps becoming more important. The interiors specialist needs to become an integral part of the A&D team. It isn't just knowledge about interior finish materials and use of space but also about how people perceive their surroundings. People are adaptable, but wouldn't it be wonderful if interior spaces supported people rather than people having to adapt to the spaces?

M. Joy Meeuwig, IIDA

❯ An expanded role in the strategic decisions our clients are facing. Interior designers are going to be called upon to have expansive knowledge of branding and an understanding of the full design experience and sustainability in a world with limited resources.

Juliana Catlin, FASID

❯ The future of the profession, in my thinking, is strong. The field has matured and has many support vehicles in place. A central need of societies is interiors; thus the designer is in a central position as well. The stewardship needed in relation to architectural interior environments is similar to that of the natural environment. We'll continue to see new means of working with technology. We will see an increasing interest in and attention to custom design. The social consciousness and ecological concerns related to the built environment will become increasingly understood and acted upon. Designers with such knowledge will emerge with a stronger voice and will be able to see the gestalt of a project, providing translations for clients.

Joy Dohr, Ph.D., FIDEC, IIDA

❯ The interior design profession has and will continue to have immense responsibilities. Interior design will carry the burden of educating the public on how the decisions they make regarding their home and workplace affect the environment. Interior design will need to answer the call for spaces that allow the population to grow older in comfortable, accommodating surroundings. Interior design will continue to be responsible for removing obstacles in the spaces we create that allow for the ease of use by all.

Lindsay Sholdar, ASID

❯ In a very few short years, the interiors profession will become the point position for a variety of projects, bringing together and coordinating architecture, engineering, landscape architecture, and subspecialties such as sound engineering, lighting, green and sustainable design, and include the principles of universal design and aging-in-place into a complete picture. Designers may also be included in such business issues as staff retention, business branding, and land development.

Michael Thomas, FASID, CAPS

❭ An interior designer today and in the future will be required to know more about everything. An example is sustainable design. This area is now offered in maybe a couple of classes at most interior design programs. In the future all interior designers will be well versed in the vocabulary of green design as well as design strategies to incorporate into their projects. I see a lot more collaboration with other professionals in projects and interior designers becoming involved much sooner in a project. I also see the interior designer in the future becoming a lot more knowledgeable about the return on the investments their clients make in design. The conversations they have with clients will be focused more on the value-added payback for implementing changes in their current work environment to help drive the client's business results.

Lisa Henry, ASID

❭ Interior design will continue to grow as a profession. It will be more necessary for the professional interior designer to translate technology in livable terms of our personal surroundings.

Mary Knott, Allied Member ASID, CID, RSPI

❭ I see interior design being universally recognized in North America as its own profession.

Jennifer van der Put, BID, IDC, ARIDO, IFMA

❭ I believe that the interior design profession will continue to gain acknowledgment and greater respect, as it has in the last decade. Our job becomes more and more essential every year to create healthful living environments. Rising issues in ergonomics, worker productivity, sustainability, and so on can no longer be ignored. Our role is critical in the creation and success of healthful interior environments.

Susan B. Higbee

❭ I see my profession becoming more important as we serve as consultants with architects and engineers, working as a team, to create better living and working environments.

Sally Thompson, ASID

❭ I hope the future includes an understanding by the general public that we don't just hang curtains and pick colors. I have to say that the industry has inspired a vast array of product developments and helped facilitate the conversation on environmental impact of our design decisions. I can see that with the continued momentum of these things, our earth will be healthier and what we think is creatively impossible now will not be in the future.

Maryanne Hewitt, IIDA

❭ Changes will continue to move in the direction of a more defined and encompassing field. Education, accreditation, and examination issues will have to be assessed and changed as issues are identified.

Sue Kirkman, ASID, IIDA, IDEC

❭ It's still a young profession, fighting for respect among the building professionals. We've made tremendous progress in the last 20 years in the areas of education and professional recognition. I can only see the profession becoming stronger and more widely ingrained in society and business. The U.S. Department of Labor projects the interior design field to grow 17 percent by 2010.

Sally D'Angelo, ASID

❭ I believe our profession is rolling through a fluid metamorphosis. While the changes that have taken place in the last 20 years are exciting, I believe the growth and transition of our profession will continue. Because we most often design environments to be experienced by people, I think our business in the future will require us to be much more knowledgeable about our human instincts, our feelings, our health, our learning process, and so on. There is also much to be gained from understanding the developments in the world around us that directly affect our clients' business and therefore our design solutions. This does not imply that we ourselves have to know everything there is to know; however, we will need to know how to partner, how to collaborate, and how to engage outside resources.

Janice Carleen Linster, ASID, IIDA, CID

❯ The interior design industry seems to be working on developing a unified voice so the goal of passing certification and regulation laws in all 50 states can be achieved. With regulations in place, there can be more control over who can call himself an interior designer. Interior designers are responsible for implementing design solutions that affect the safety and welfare of the public in an interior environment. Certification would let the public know that the designer they hire understands current codes, regulations, and standards for interior environments. Those who call themselves

interior designers should be educated at approved institutions of higher learning and pass rigorous exams. Those who do not meet these requirements should not be able to call themselves interior designers. I think we will see more action from lawmakers on regulation of our industry.

Kristi Barker, CID

❯ I see the continuing trend towards specialization. There are so many segments of the market that one designer cannot have the expertise required to deal with everything from residential remodeling to medical office design or any offshoot.

Sharmin Pool-Bak, ASID, CAPS, LEED-AP

❯ I believe the future of the interior design profession is incredibly strong and viable. The profession of interior design rests in the people we serve and for whom we design. Their stories of how good design reshaped their lives succinctly capture the value of the profession.

Stephanie Clemons, Ph.D., FASID, FIDEC

Lodging: guest room. Hilton Kuala Lumpur, Kuala Lumpur, Malaysia. Trisha Wilson, ASID, Wilson Associates, Dallas, Texas. Architect: KKS Tokyo.

PHOTOGRAPH: PETER MEALIN PHOTOGRAPHY

Law office: dining room, Alston & Bird LLP. Rita Carson Guest, FASID, Carson Guest, Inc.
PHOTOGRAPH: GABRIEL BENZUR

❯ I believe that our profession will continue to grow and strengthen in the future. As technology continues to advance, new products will be invented that will need to be integrated into private residences. The renewed interest in a healthy planet as well as healthy people has created new products for residential living.
Teresa Ridlon, Allied Member ASID

❯ I think the demand for interior designers will increase as state legislation becomes more defined. I have noticed that a general awareness of what designers do increases where licensing or certification is required. I also anticipate that designers will be utilized more as the design/

build approach becomes more popular. Also, the hierarchy of designers, depending on experience level, will become more universally defined.

I find more clients demanding flexibility in design. Meeting rooms are becoming multipurpose rooms with furniture that can be reconfigured. Workstations need to be adaptable to workplace personnel churn. This requires interior designers to be more creative.

I also believe that further development and increased availability of wireless technology and battery-operated equipment will change the landscape of spaces, enabling desired flexibility. Computers won't be tethered to a wall or cubicle by wires. The approach to furnishing and space planning will change, just as the development of the powered workstation panel changed layouts decades ago.
Kimberly M. Studzinski, ASID

❯ There is currently a movement towards educating the public about what interior designers do. I think that once there is a clear understanding of our work there will be a greater acceptance of interior designers. In turn, this will mean a greater demand for our work not only by the general public but also by other design professionals.
Leylan Salzer

❯ Although the profession continues to raise its standards and define itself through a growing body of knowledge, accreditation of interior design programs, and demonstration of professional competency through testing, there are many challenges that our profession faces. Some of the most challenging aspects, from my point of view, are the loss of entry-level jobs to offshoring, turf wars with the architecture profession, practitioners who oppose competency testing, and the ability to retain experienced designers.

There is a gradual change in the way some firms are producing their contract documents by using offshore labor sources. These sources communicate well in English and produce accurate documents at a fraction of the cost of producing them in-house. The accuracy, reduced cost, and ability to send the documents across the globe to work 24/7 is very enticing to firms looking to be more competitive. But it is going to eradicate the traditional entry-level positions our graduates fill in design firms. In order to provide students with skills and knowledge necessary for entry-level positions, we need to strengthen the design management aspects of our curriculums. Although graduates will still need to have a thorough understanding of the design and production of contract documents, I see the entry-level needs of practice shifting away from the production of contract documents to leadership in design and management of firms, projects, and clients.

The architecture profession continues to challenge the interior design profession's ability to provide interior design services. There are also growing numbers of designers opposed to testing for competency who are taking action against title and practice acts. In states where designers are working to get title or practice acts legislated, these organizations are heavily involved in lobbying to deny such acts. Where acts exist, the groups are working to deem them as unconstitutional because they limit an individual's right to work. In all instances, the reason for the acts remains: that interior designers affect the health, safety, and welfare of the general public through the decisions they make in their designs. It is not "Wallpapering with Red Tape," as George Will noted in a recent editorial column after being lobbied by a group paid to fight interior design legislation. Legislation is merely trying to reinforce the fact that persons not qualified by experience, education, and examination are more likely to make decisions that have a negative effect on the users of their spaces.

There are other instances of groups working to limit interior designers' ability to practice by changing the wording of building codes. Most international model building codes currently in use by jurisdictions allow any "registered design professional" to submit plans for building permits. Working at a local level, groups opposed to the registration of interior designers have been able to get this changed to "licensed architect and engineer," thereby restricting an interior designer who has been registered to practice interior design and requiring them to seek the services of a licensed architect or engineer in order to obtain a permit.

The point is that the profession must become much more unified and diligent about protecting its ability to execute design services without being subservient to another profession.

Lastly, the profession needs to find ways to keep its members from having to choose between family and career. Too often, the career loses out and our profession loses some of its most talented people. This situation is not a unique one for interior design, but other professions have been able to make accommodations so that they can keep these valued employees. If we are going to retain the best and brightest to meet our challenges, we need to be more supportive and creative in giving women the environment and tools they need to have both a family and a career.
Robert Krikac, IDEC

❯ The profession continues to mature and grow. We have a hand in most all of the built environment. Designers get the opportunity to help design and create interiors where people heal, grow, learn, eat, are entertained, work, pray, and dream. Who could ask for a better career?
Melinda Sechrist, FASID

Commercial retail: SAXX
Jewelry store. Bruce Brigham,
FASID, ISP, IES, Retail Clarity
Consulting, Laredo, Texas.
PHOTOGRAPH: BRUCE BRIGHAM

❯ This is the century of design—the possibilities are endless.
Rachelle Schoessler Lynn, CID, ASID, LEED-AP, IFMA, Allied Member

❯ Amazing.
Katherine Ankerson, IDEC, NCARB Certified

❯ The design profession, in my eyes, is transcending into the new "fashion" design. You see companies such as Maharam partnering with fashion designers like Paul Smith to create apparel for upholstery. I think that for a long time, interior design followed fashion. Now I can see interior design starting to set the style trends for itself and, perhaps, sparking the trends for the fashion apparel industry.
Carolyn Ann Ames, Allied Member ASID

❯ Good design goes beyond aesthetics to quality of life and social responsibility issues. So, interior designers will be required to understand and work with many more disciplines than we do today—not only engineers, craftsmen, and architects but also gerontologists, urban planners, environmentalists, material and product designers, and others.
Charrisse Johnston, ASID, LEED-AP, CID

❯ I see that the profession is only going to become more noticeable. People now understand why interior designers are needed.
Chris Socci, Allied Member ASID

INTERIOR DESIGN RESOURCES

INTERIOR DESIGN ORGANIZATIONS

American Society of Interior Designers (ASID)
608 Massachusetts Avenue NE
Washington, DC 20002-6006
202-546-3480
www.asid.org

Council for Interior Design Accreditation (formerly FIDER)
146 Monroe Center #1318
Grand Rapids, MI 49503-2822
616-458-0460
www.accredit-id.org

Interior Design Educators Council (IDEC)
7150 Winton Drive
Indianapolis, IN 46268
317-328-4437
www.idec.org

Interior Designers of Canada (IDC)
Ontario Design Center
260 King Street East #414
Toronto, Ontario, Canada M5A 1K3
416-964-0906
www.interiordesignerscanada.org

International Facility Management Association (IFMA)
1 East Greenway Plaza #1100
Houston, TX 77046-0194
713-623-4362
www.ifma.org

International Furnishings and Design Association, Inc. (IFDA)
150 South Warner Road, #156
King of Prussia, PA 19406
610-535-6422
www.ifda.com

International Interior Design Association (IIDA)
222 Merchandise Mart Plaza, Suite 1540
Chicago, IL 60654-1104
312-467-1950
www.iida.org

National Council for Interior Design Qualification (NCIDQ)
1200 18th Street NW #1001
Washington, DC 20036
202-721-0220
www.ncidq.org

National Kitchen & Bath Association (NKBA)
687 Willow Grove Street
Hackettstown, NJ 07840
908-852-0033
www.nkba.org

INTERIOR DESIGN CAREER AND JOB INFORMATION

American Society of Interior Designers
www.asid.org

Bureau of Labor Statistics
www.bis.gov

Career Resource for Interior Design Industry
www.interiordesignjobs.com

Careers in Interior Design
www.careersininteriordesign.com

International Interior Design Association
www.iida.org

ALLIED ORGANIZATIONS

American Institute of Architects (AIA)
1735 New York Avenue NW
Washington, DC 20006
202-626-7300
www.aia.org

American Society of Furniture Designers (ASFD)
144 Woodland Drive
New London, NC 28127
910-576-1273
www.asfd.com

Building Office & Management Association International
(BOMA)
1201 New York Avenue NW, Suite 300
Washington, DC 20005
202-408-2662
www.boma.org

Business and Institutional Furniture Manufacturer's
Association (BIFMA)
2680 Horizon Drive, SE, #A-1
Grand Rapids, MI 49546
616-285-3963
www.bifma.org

Color Marketing Group (CMG)
5904 Richmond Highway, Suite 408
Alexandria, VA 22303
703-329-8500
www.colormarketing.org

Construction Specifications Institute (CSI)
99 Canal Center Plaza, Suite 300
Alexandria, VA 22314
703-684-0300
www.csinet.org

Illuminating Engineering Society of North American (IES)
120 Wall Street, 17th Floor
New York, NY 10005
212-248-5000
www.iesna.org

International Code Council
500 New Jersey Avenue NW, 6th Floor
Washington, DC 20001-2070
1-888-ICC-SAFE (422-7233)
www.iccsafe.org

Institute of Store Planners (ISP)
25 North Broadway
Tarrytown, NY 10591
914-332-1806
www.ispo.org

National Trust for Historic Preservation
1785 Massachusetts Avenue NW
Washington, DC 20036
202-588-6000
www.nationaltrust.org

Organization of Black Designers (OBD)
300 M Street SW, Suite N110
Washington, DC 20024-4019
(202) 659-3918
Contact: OBDesign@aol.com

U.S. Green Building Council (USGBC)
1015 18th Street NW, Suite 805
Washington, DC 20036
202-828-7422
www.usgbc.org

CIDA-ACCREDITED INTERIOR DESIGN PROGRAMS IN THE UNITED STATES AND CANADA

This list is current as of the publication date of this book. For more information, go to the Council for Interior Design Accreditation Web site: www.accredit-id.org.

ALABAMA

Auburn University, Auburn
Interior Design Program
College of Human Sciences
Web site: www.humsci.auburn.edu

Samford University, Birmingham
Department of Interior Design
School of Education and Professional Studies
Web site: www.samford.edu

University of Alabama, Tuscaloosa
Interior Design Program
Clothing, Textiles, and Interior Design
Human Environmental Sciences
Web site: www.ches.ua.edu

Southern Institute School of Interior Design at Virginia
College, Birmingham
Interior Design Program
Division of Virginia College
Web site: www.vc.edu

ARIZONA

Arizona State University, Tempe
Interior Design Program
Department of Interior Design
College of Design
Web site: www.design.asu.edu/interior

Art Center Design College, Tucson
Interior Design Program
Web site: www.theartcenter.edu

Art Institute of Phoenix
Interior Design Program
Web site: www.aipx.edu

Mesa Community College, Mesa
Advanced Interior Design
School of Design
Web site: www.mc.maricopa.edu

Scottsdale Community College, Scottsdale
Interior Design Program
Web site: www.sc.maricopa.edu

ARKANSAS

University of Arkansas, Fayetteville
Interior Design Program
School of Human Environmental Sciences
Web site: www.uark.edu

University of Central Arkansas, Conway
Interior Design Program
Department of Family and Consumer Sciences
Web site: www.uca.edu

CALIFORNIA

Academy of Art University, San Francisco
Interior Architecture and Design
Web site: www.academyart.edu

American InterContinental University, Los Angeles
Interior Design Department
Web site: www.la.aiuniv.edu

Brooks College, Long Beach
Interior Design Department
Web site: www.brookscollege.edu

California College of the Arts, San Francisco
Interior Design Program
Web site: www.cca.edu

California State University, Fresno
Interior Design Program
Department of Art and Design
Web site: www.csufresno.edu/artanddesign

California State University, Northridge
Department of Family and Consumer Sciences
Web site: www.fcs.csun.edu

California State University, Sacramento
Interior Design Program
Department of Design
School of the Arts
Web site: www.csus.edu/design

Design Institute of San Diego
Interior Design Program
Web site: www.disd.edu

Interior Designers Institute, Newport Beach
Interior Design Program
Web site: www.idi.edu

San Diego State University, San Diego
Interior Design Program
School of Art, Design, and Art History
College of Professional Studies and Fine Arts
Web site: www.sdsu.edu

UCLA Extension, Los Angeles
Interior Design Program
Department of the Arts
Web site: www.uclaextension.edu/arc_id

University of California, Berkeley Extension, San
Francisco
Interior Design and Interior Architecture
Department of Art and Design
Web site: www.unex.berkeley.edu

West Valley College, Saratoga
Interior Design Department
Web site: www.westvalley.edu/wvc/careers/
interiordesign.html

Woodbury University, Burbank
Department of Interior Architecture
School of Architecture and Design
Web site: www.woodbury.edu

COLORADO

Art Institute of Colorado, Denver
Interior Design Program
School of Design
Web site: www.aic.artinstitutes.edu

Colorado State University, Fort Collins
Interior Design Program
Department of Design and Merchandising
College of Applied Human Sciences
Web site: www.cahs.colostate.edu/dm

Rocky Mountain College of Art and Design, Denver
Interior Design Program
Web site: www.rmcad.edu

DISTRICT OF COLUMBIA

George Washington University at Mount Vernon Campus,
Washington, DC
Interior Design Program
Fine Arts and Art History Department
Web site: www.gwu.edu

FLORIDA

Ai Miami International University of Art and Design, Miami
Interior Design Department
Web site: www.ifac.edu

Art Institute of Fort Lauderdale, Fort Lauderdale
Interior Design Department
School of Design
Web site: www.aii.edu/fortlauderdale

Florida International University, Miami
Interior Design Department
School of Architecture
Web site: www.fiu.edu/~soa

Florida State University, Tallahassee
Department of Interior Design
College of Visual Arts, Theatre, and Dance
Web site: interiordesign.fsu.edu

International Academy of Design and Technology, Tampa
Interior Design Program
Web site: www.academy.edu

Ringling School of Art and Design, Sarasota
Interior Design Department
Web site: www.ringling.edu

University of Florida, Gainesville
Department of Interior Design
College of Design, Construction, and Planning
Web site: www.web.dcp.ufl.edu/interior

GEORGIA

American Intercontinental University, Atlanta
Interior Design Program
Web site: www.aiuniv.edu

Art Institute of Atlanta, Atlanta
Interior Design Program
Web site: www.aia.artinstitutes.edu

Brenau University, Gainesville
Interior Design Program
Department of Art and Design
School of Fine Arts and Humanities
Web site: www.brenau.edu

Georgia Southern University, Statesboro
Interior Design Program
Department of Hospitality, Tourism, and Family and Consumer Science
College of Health and Human Sciences
Web site: www.georgiasouthern.edu

University of Georgia, Athens
Interior Design Program
Lamar Dodd School of Art
Web site: www.art.uga.edu

IDAHO

Brigham Young University—Idaho, Rexburg
Department of Interior Design
College of Performing and Visual Arts
Web site: www.byui.edu/interiordesign

ILLINOIS

Columbia College Chicago, Chicago
Art Design Department, Interior Architecture Program
Web site: www.colum.edu/undergraduate/artanddesign/interior/index.html

Harrington College of Design, Chicago
Web site: www.interiordesign.edu

Illinois Institute of Art at Chicago
Interior Design Department
Web site: www.ilic.artinstitute.edu

Illinois Institute of Art at Schaumburg
Interior Design Department
Web site: www.ilis.artinstitutes.edu

Illinois State University, Normal
Interior and Environmental Design Program
Department of Family and Consumer Sciences
Web site: www.fcs.ilstu.edu/

International Academy of Design and Technology, Chicago
Interior Design Department
Web site: www.iadtchicago.com

Southern Illinois University, Carbondale
Interior Design
School of Architecture
College of Applied Sciences and Arts
Web site: www.siu.edu/~arc_id/id.html

INDIANA

Ball State University, Muncie
Interior Design Program
Family and Consumer Sciences Department
College of Applied Sciences and Technology
Web site: www.bsu.edu

Indiana State University, Terre Haute
Interior Design Program
Department of Family Consumer Sciences
Web site: www.indstate.edu/interior

Indiana University, Bloomington
Interior Design Program
Apparel Merchandising and Interior Design
College of Arts and Sciences
Web site: www.indiana.edu/~amid

Indiana University—Purdue University Indianapolis, Indianapolis
Interior Design Technology Program
Purdue School of Engineering and Technology
Web site: www.iupui.edu/academic

Purdue University, West Lafayette
Interior Design Program
Department of Visual and Performing Arts
Division of Art and Design
Web site: www.purdue.edu

IOWA

Iowa State University of Science and Technology, Ames
Interior Design Program
Department of Art and Design
Web site: www.design.iastate.edu/ID

KANSAS

Kansas State University, Manhattan
Interior Design Program
Department of Apparel, Textiles, and Interior Design
College of Human Ecology
Web site: www.humec.k-state.edu/atid

Kansas State University, Manhattan
Department of Interior Architecture and Product Design
College of Architecture, Planning, and Design
Web site: www.capd.ksu.edu/iapd

KENTUCKY

University of Kentucky, Lexington
School of Interior Design
College of Design
Web site: www.uky.edu/design

University of Louisville, Louisville
Interior Architecture Program
Hite Art Institute
College of Arts and Sciences
Web site: www.art.louisville.edu

LOUISIANA

Louisiana State University, Baton Rouge
Department of Interior Design
College of Art and Design
Web site: www.id.lsu.edu

Louisiana Tech University, Ruston
Interior Design Program
School of Architecture
Web site: www.latech.edu/tech/liberal-arts/architecture

University of Louisiana at Lafayette
Interior Design Program
School of Architecture and Design
College of the Arts
Web site: www.arts.louisiana.edu

MASSACHUSETTS

Boston Architectural College, Boston
Interior Design Program
Web site: www.the-bac.edu

Endicott College, Beverly
Interior Design Program
Department of Interior Design
School of Art and Design
Web site: www.endicott.edu

Mount Ida College, Newton
Interior Design Program
Chamberlayne School of Design
Web site: www.mountida.edu

Newbury College, Brookline
Interior Design Program
School of Arts, Science, and Design
Web site: www.newbury.edu

New England School of Art and Design at Suffolk
University, Boston
Interior Design Program
Web site: www.suffolk.edu/nesad

Wentworth Institute of Technology, Boston
Interior Design Program
Department of Design and Facilities
Web site: www.wit.edu

MICHIGAN

Eastern Michigan University, Ypsilanti
Interior Design Program
School of Engineering Technology
College of Technology
Web site: www.emich.edu

Kendall College of Art and Design of Ferris State
University, Grand Rapids
Interior Design Program
Web site: www.kcad.edu

Lawrence Technological University, Southfield
Interior Architecture
Department of Art and Design
College of Architecture and Design
Web site: www.ltu.edu

Michigan State University, East Lansing
Interior Design Program
School of Planning, Design, and Construction
College of Agriculture and Natural Resources
Web site: www.msu.edu/spdc

Western Michigan University, Kalamazoo
Interior Design Program
Family and Consumer Sciences
Web site: www.wmich.edu/fcs/itd/index

MINNESOTA

Dakota County Technical College, Rosemount
Interior Design and Sales Program
Web site: www.dctc.edu

University of Minnesota, St. Paul
Interior Design Program
Department of Design, Housing, and Apparel
College of Design
Web site: www.cdes.umn.edu

MISSISSIPPI

Mississippi State University, Mississippi State
Interior Design Program
College of Architecture, Art, and Design
Web site: www.caad.msstate.edu/id

University of Southern Mississippi, Hattiesburg
Interior Design Program
Department of Art and Design
Web site: www.usm.edu/interiordesign/

MISSOURI

Maryville University of St. Louis
Interior Design Program
Art and Design Department
Web site: www.maryville.edu

University of Missouri, Columbia
Interior Design Program
Department of Architectural Studies
College of Human Environmental Sciences
Web site: www.missouri.edu/~arch

NEBRASKA

University of Nebraska, Lincoln
Interior Design Program
Department of Architecture
College of Architecture
Web site: www.archweb.unl.edu

NEVADA

University of Nevada, Las Vegas
Interior Architecture and Design Program
School of Architecture
Web site: www.unlv.nevada.edu

NEW JERSEY

Kean University, Union
Interior Design Program
Department of Design
Web site: www.kean.edu

NEW YORK

Buffalo State, Buffalo
Interior Design Program
Interior Design Department
School of Arts and Humanities
Web site: www.buffalostate.edu/interiordesign/

Cornell University, Ithaca
Interior Design Program
Department of Design and Environmental Analysis
College of Human Ecology
Web site: www.human.cornell.edu/che/DEA/index.cfm

Fashion Institute of Technology State University of New York, New York
Interior Design Department
Web site: www.fitnyc.edu

New York Institute of Technology, Old Westbury
Interior Design Department
School of Architecture and Design
Web site: www.nyit.edu

New York School of Interior Design, New York
Interior Design Program
Web site: www.nysid.edu

Pratt Institute, Brooklyn
Interior Design Department
School of Art and Design
Web site: www.pratt.edu

Rochester Institute of Technology, Rochester
Professional Level Program
Department of Industrial and Interior Design
School of Design
College of Imaging Arts and Sciences
Web site: www.rit.edu

School of Visual Arts, New York
Interior Design Department
Web site: www.schoolofvisualarts.edu

Syracuse University, Syracuse
Interior Design Program
School of Art and Design
College of Visual and Performing Arts
Web site: www.syr.edu

NORTH CAROLINA

East Carolina University, Greenville
Interior Design Program
Department of Interior Design and Merchandising
College of Human Ecology
Web site: www.ecu.edu

High Point University, High Point
Interior Design Program
Department of Home Furnishings and Design
Earl N. Phillips School of Business
Web site: www.highpoint.edu

Meredith College, Raleigh
Interior Design Program
Department of Human Environmental Sciences
Web site: www.meredith.edu

University of North Carolina at Greensboro, Greensboro
Department of Interior Architecture
School of Human Environmental Sciences
Web site: www.uncg.edu/iarc

Western Carolina University, Cullowhee
Interior Design Program
Department of Art and Design
College of Applied Sciences
Web site: www.ides.wcu.edu

NORTH DAKOTA

North Dakota State University, Fargo
Department of Apparel, Design, Facility, and Hospitality Management
College of Human Development and Education
Web site: www.ndsu.nodak.edu/afhm/id

OHIO

Columbus College Art and Design, Columbus
Interior Design Program
Division of Industrial and Interior Design
Web site: www.ccad.edu

Kent State University, Kent
Interior Design Program
College of Architecture and Environmental Design
Web site: www.caed.kent.edu

Miami University, Oxford
Interior Design Program
Department of Architecture and Interior Design
Web site: www.muohio.edu/interiordesign

Ohio University, Athens
Interior Architecture Program
School of Human and Consumer Sciences
College of Health and Human Services
Web site: www.ohiou.edu/design/

Ohio State University, Columbus
Interior Design
Department of Industrial, Interior, and Visual Communication Design
Web site: www.design.osu.edu

University of Akron, Akron
Interior Design Program
School of Family and Consumer Sciences
College of Fine and Applied Arts
Web site: www.uakron.edu/colleges/faa/schools/fcs/interior

University of Cincinnati, Cincinnati
School of Architecture and Interior Design
Program of Interior Design
College of Design, Architecture, Art, and Planning
Web site: www.daap.uc.edu/said/

OKLAHOMA

Oklahoma State University, Stillwater
Interior Design Program
Design, Housing, and Merchandising
College of Human Environmental Sciences
Web site: www.okstate.edu/hes/dhm/

University of Central Oklahoma, Edmond
Department of Design
College of Media Arts and Design
Web site: www.camd.ucok.edu/design

University of Oklahoma, Norman
Interior Design Division
College of Architecture
Web site: www.id.coa.ou.edu

OREGON

Marylhurst University, Marylhurst
Interior Design Program
Art and Interior Design Department
Web site: www.marylhurst.edu/art/bfa-interiordesign.
php

University of Oregon, Eugene
Interior Architecture Program
Department of Architecture
Web site: www.architecture.uoregon.edu

PENNSYLVANIA

Art Institute of Pittsburgh, Pittsburgh
Interior Design Program
School of Design
Web site: www.aii.edu

Drexel University, Philadelphia
Interior Design Program
Department of Design
College of Media Arts and Design
Web site: www.drexel.edu

La Roche College, Pittsburgh
Interior Design Department
School of the Professions
Web site: www.laroche.edu

Moore College of Art and Design, Philadelphia
Interior Design Department
Web site: www.moore.edu

Philadelphia University, Philadelphia
Interior Design Program
School of Architecture
Web site: www.philau.edu

SOUTH CAROLINA

Winthrop University, Rock Hill
Interior Design Program
Department of Design
College of Visual and Performing Arts
Web site: www.winthrop.edu/vpa/design/

SOUTH DAKOTA

South Dakota State University, Brookings
Interior Design Program
Apparel, Merchandising, and Interior Design
Web site: www.sdstate.edu

TENNESSEE

Middle Tennessee State University, Murfreesboro
Interior Design Program
Department of Human Sciences
Web site: www.mtsu.edu

O'More College of Design, Franklin
Interior Design Program
Web site: www.omorecollege.edu

University of Memphis, Memphis
Interior Design Program
Art Department
Web site: www.people.memphis.edu

University of Tennessee at Chattanooga
Interior Design Program
Department of Human Ecology
Web site: www.utc.edu/Academic/InteriorDesign

University of Tennessee, Knoxville
Interior Design Program
College of Architecture and Design
Web site: www.arch.utk.edu

Watkins College of Art and Design, Nashville
Department of Interior Design
Web site: www.watkins.edu

TEXAS

Abilene Christian University, Abilene
Interior Design Program
Department of Art and Design
Web site: www.acu.edu/academics/cas/art.html

Art Institute of Dallas, Dallas
Interior Design Program
School of Interior Design
Web site: www.aid.edu

Art Institute of Houston, Houston
Interior Design Program
Web site: www.aih.aii.edu

Baylor University, Waco
Interior Design Program
Department of Family and Consumer Sciences
College of Arts and Sciences
Web site: www.baylor.edu/fcs/splash.php

El Centro College, Dallas
Interior Design Department
Arts and Sciences Division
Web site: www.ecc.dcccd.edu

Stephen F. Austin State University, Nacogdoches
Interior Design Program
Department of Human Sciences
Web site: www.sfasu.edu/hms

Texas Christian University, Fort Worth
Interior Design Program
Department of Design, Merchandising, and Textiles
AddRan College of Humanities and Social Sciences
Web site: www.demt.tcu.edu/demt/

Texas State University, San Marcos
Interior Design Program
Department of Family and Consumer Sciences
College of Applied Arts
Web site: www.fcs.txstate.edu

Texas Tech University, Lubbock
Interior Design Program
College of Human Sciences
Web site: www.hs.ttu.edu

University of the Incarnate Word, San Antonio
Interior Environmental Design Program
School of Interactive Media and Design
Web site: www.uiw.edu/ied

University of North Texas, Denton
Interior Design Program
School of Visual Arts
Web site: www.art.unt.edu/divisions/interiordesign.cfm

University of Texas at Arlington
Interior Design Program
School of Architecture
Web site: www.uta.edu

University of Texas at Austin
Interior Design Program
School of Architecture
Web site: www.ar.utexas.edu

University of Texas at San Antonio
Interior Design Program
School of Architecture
Web site: www.utsa.edu/architecture

UTAH

Utah State University, Logan
Interior Design Program
College of Humanities, Arts, and Social Sciences
Web site: www.interiordesign.usu.edu

VIRGINIA

James Madison University, Harrisonburg
Interior Design Program
School of Art and Art History
Web site: www.jmu.edu/art

Marymount University, Arlington
Interior Design Department
School of Arts and Sciences
Web site: www.marymount.edu

Radford University, Radford
Department of Interior Design and Fashion
College of Visual and Performing Arts
Web site: www.id-f.asp.radford.edu

Virginia Commonwealth University, Richmond
Department of Interior Design
School of the Arts
Web site: www.pubinfo.vcu.edu

Virginia Polytechnic Institute and State University,
Blacksburg
Interior Design Program
School of Architecture and Design
Web site: www.interiordesign.caus.vt.edu

WASHINGTON

Bellevue Community College, Bellevue
Interior Design Program
Arts and Humanities Division
Web site: www.bcc.ctc.edu/ArtsHum/interiordesign

Washington State University, Spokane
Interior Design Program
Department of Interior Design
Web site: www.idi.spokane.wsu.edu

WEST VIRGINIA

West Virginia University, Morgantown
Interior Design
Division of Family and Consumer Sciences
Davis College of Agriculture, Forestry, and Consumer
Sciences
Web site: www.cafcs.wvu.edu/majors/undergrad/id.html

WISCONSIN

Mount Mary College, Milwaukee
Interior Design Department
Art and Design Division
Web site: www.mtmary.edu

University of Wisconsin, Madison
Interior Design Major
Environment, Textiles, and Design Department
Web site: www.sohe.wisc.edu/etd/index.html

University of Wisconsin, Stevens Point
Interior Architecture Program
Division of Interior Architecture
Web site: www.uwsp.edu/ia

University of Wisconsin—Stout, Menomonie
Interior Design Program
Art Program Direction Office
Web site: www.uwstout.edu

CANADA

Algonquin College, Ottawa, ON
Interior Design Program
Web site: www.algonquincollege.com

Dawson College, Westmount, QC
Interior Design Department
Web site: www.dawsoncollege.qc.ca

Humber Institute of Technology and Advanced Learning,
Etobicoke, ON
Interior Design Program
School of Applied Technology
Web site: www.degrees.humber.ca/interiordesign.htm

International Academy of Design and Technology,
Toronto, ON
Interior Design Program
School of Interior Design
Web site: www.iadttoronto.com

Kwantlen University College, Richmond, BC
Professional Level Interior Design Program
Interior Design Department
Web site: www.kwantlen.ca/applied-design/site/idsn-
infopackage/

Mount Royal College, Calgary, AB
Department of Interior Design
Web site: www.mtroyal.ca/arts/interiordesign/

New Brunswick Community College—Dieppe, NB
Interior Design Program
Web site: www.dieppe.ccnb.nb.ca

Ryerson University, Toronto, ON
School of Interior Design
Web site: www.ryerson.ca

Sheridan College Institute of Technology and Advanced
Learning, Oakville, ON
Interiors Program
School of Animation, Arts, and Design
Web site: www.sheridanc.on.ca

St. Clair College of Applied Arts and Technology,
Windsor, ON
Interior Design Department
Web site: www.stclaircollege.ca

University of Manitoba, Winnipeg, MB
Department of Interior Design
Web site: www.umanitoba.ca

INTERIOR DESIGN REFERENCES

Abercrombie, Stanley. 1999. "Design Revolution: 100 Years That Changed Our World." *Interior Design,* December, 140–198.

American Institute of Architects. 2002. *The Architect's Handbook of Professional Practice.* 4th student ed. Hoboken, NJ: John Wiley & Sons.

American Society of Interior Designers. Web site information. www.asid.org.

American Society of Interior Designers. 1993. ASID Fact Sheet, "Economic Impact of the Interior Design Profession." Washington, DC: ASID.

———. 2000. *Aging in Place: Aging and the Impact of Interior Design.* Washington, DC: ASID.

———. 2001. "ASID: FAQs About Us." ASID, Washington, DC.

Ballast, David Kent. *Interior Construction and Detailing.* 2nd ed. Belmont, CA: Professional Publications, Inc. 2007.

———. 2002. *Interior Design Reference Manual: A Guide to the NCIDQ Exam.* 4th ed. Belmont, CA: Professional Publications Inc.

Baraban, Regina S., and Joseph F. Durocher. 2001. *Successful Restaurant Design.* 2nd ed. New York: John Wiley & Sons.

Barr, Vilma. 1995. *Promotion Strategies for Design and Construction Firms.* New York: John Wiley & Sons.

Barr, Vilma, and Charles E. Broudy. 1986. *Designing to Sell.* New York: McGraw-Hill.

Berger, C. Jaye. 1994. *Interior Design Law and Business Practices.* New York: John Wiley & Sons.

Binggeli, Corky. 2003. *Building Systems for Interior Designers.* Hoboken, NJ: John Wiley & Sons.

——— 2007. *Interior Design: A Survey.* Hoboken, NJ: John Wiley & Sons..

Birnberg, Howard G. 1999. *Project Management for Building Designers and Owners.* Boca Raton, FL: CRC Press.

Bonda, Penny, and Katie Sosnowchik. 2007. *Sustainable Commercial Interiors.* Hoboken, NJ: John Wiley & Sons.

Bureau of Labor Statistics. Web site information. www.bis.gov.

Campbell, Nina, and Caroline Seebohm. 1992. *Elsie de Wolfe: A Decorative Life.* New York: Clarkson Potter.

Ching, Francis D. K. 2008. *Building Construction Illustrated.* 4th ed. Hoboken, NJ: John Wiley & Sons.

Cohen, Jonathan. 2000. *Communication and Design with the Internet.* New York: W. W. Norton.

Coleman, Susan. 2002. *Career Journey Road Map.* Costa Mesa, CA: Orange Coast College.

Davidsen, Judith. "100 Interior Design Giants." January 2007. *Interior Design,* January, 95–136.

Davies, Thomas D., Jr., and Carol Peredo Lopez. 2006. *Accessible Home Design: Architectural Solutions for the Wheelchair User.* Washington, DC: Paralyzed Veterans of America.

Farren, Carol E. 1999. *Planning and Managing Interior Projects.* 2nd ed. Kingston, MA: R. S. Means.

Foster, Kari, Annette Stelmack, and Debbie Hindman. 2007. *Sustainable Residential Interiors.* Hoboken, NJ: John Wiley & Sons.

Hampton, Mark. 1992. *Legendary Decorators of the 20th Century.* New York: Doubleday.

Harmon, Sharon Koomen. 2008. *The Codes Guidebook for Interiors.* 4th ed. New York: John Wiley & Sons.

Interior Designers of Canada (IDC). Web site information. www.interiordesignerscanada.org.

International Interior Design Association (IIDA). Web site information. www.iida.org.

Israel, Lawrence J. 1994. *Store Planning/Design*. New York: John Wiley & Sons.

Jensen, Charlotte S. 2001. "Design Versus Decoration." *Interiors and Sources,* September, 90–93.

Kilmer, Rosemary, and W. Otie Kilmer. 1992. *Designing Interiors*. Fort Worth, TX: Harcourt Brace Jovanovich.

Kliment, Stephen A. 2006. *Writing for Design Professionals*. 2nd ed. New York: W. W. Norton.

Knackstedt, Mary V. 2006. *The Interior Design Business Handbook*. 4th ed. Hoboken, NJ: John Wiley & Sons.

Lawlor, Drue, and Michael Thomas. 2008. *Residential Design for Aging in Place*. Hoboken, NJ: John Wiley & Sons.

Linton, Harold. 2000. *Portfolio Design*. 2nd ed. New York: W. W. Norton.

Malkin, Jain. 1992. *Hospital Interior Architecture*. New York: John Wiley & Sons.

———. 2002. *Medical and Dental Space Planning*. 3rd ed. New York: John Wiley & Sons.

Marberry, Sara, ed. 1997. *Healthcare Design*. New York: John Wiley & Sons.

Martin, Jane D., and Nancy Knoohuizen. 1995. *Marketing Basics for Designers*. New York: John Wiley & Sons.

McDonough, William, and Michael Braungrant. 2002. *Cradle to Cradle: Remaking the Way We Make Things*. New York: North Point Press.

McGowan, Maryrose, and Kelsey Kruse. 2005. *Specifying Interiors*. 2nd ed. New York: John Wiley & Sons.

McGowan, Maryrose. 2004. *Interior Graphic Standards*. Student ed. Hoboken, NJ: John Wiley & Sons.

Mendler, Sandra F., and William Odell. 2000. *The HOK Guidebook to Sustainable Design*. Hoboken, NJ: John Wiley & Sons.

Merriam-Webster's Collegiate Dictionary. 10th ed. 1994. Springfield, MA: Merriam-Webster.

Morgan, Jim. 1998. *Management of the Small Design Firm*. New York: Watson-Guptill.

Murtagh, William J. 2005. *Keeping Time*. 3rd ed. Hoboken, NJ: John Wiley & Sons.

National Council for Interior Design Qualification. 2000. *NCIDQ Examination Study Guide*. Washington, DC: National Council for Interior Design Qualification.

———. 2003. *Practice Analysis Study*. Washington, DC: National Council for Interior Design Qualification.

Pelegrin-Genel, Elisabeth. 1996. *The Office*. Paris and New York: Flammarion.

Pilatowicz, Grazyna. 1995. *Eco-Interiors*. Hoboken, NJ: John Wiley & Sons.

Pile, John. 1995. *Interior Design*. 2nd ed. Englewood Cliffs, NJ: Prentice Hall.

———. 2000. *A History of Interior Design*. New York: John Wiley & Sons.

Piotrowski, Christine M. 1992. *Interior Design Management*. New York: John Wiley & Sons.

———. 2008. *Professional Practice for Interior Designers*. 4th ed. Hoboken, NJ: John Wiley & Sons.

Piotrowski, Christine M., and Elizabeth Rodgers. 2007. *Designing Commercial Interiors*. 2nd ed. Hoboken, NJ: John Wiley & Sons.

Postell, Jim. 2007. *Furniture Design*. Hoboken, NJ: John Wiley & Sons.

Rutes, Walter A., Richard H. Penner, and Lawrence Adams. 2001. *Hotel Design: Planning and Development*. New York: W. W. Norton.

Stipanuk, David M., and Harold Roffmann. 1992. *Hospitality Facilities Management and Design*. East Lansing, MI: Educational Institute of the American Hotel and Motel Association.

Tate, Allen, and C. Ray Smith. 1986. *Interior Design in the 20th Century*. New York: Harper & Row.

U.S. Green Building Council. 2003. *Building Momentum: National Trends and Prospects for High Performance Green Buildings*. Washington, DC: U.S. Green Building Council.

———. 2006. *Commercial Interiors Reference Guide*. 3rd ed. Washington, DC: U.S. Green Building Council.

World Commission on Environment and Development. 1987. *The Brundtland Report: Our Common Future*. Oxford: Oxford University Press.

INTERIOR DESIGNERS

Leonard Alvarado
Principal
Contract Office Group
Milpitas, California

Kristen Anderson, ASID, CID, RID
Designer
Truckee-Tahoe Lumber/Home Concept
Tahoe City, California

Naomi Anderson
Owner
Rampdome Systems
Scottsdale, Arizona

Katherine Ankerson, IDEC, NCARB Certified
Professor, Interior Design
University of Nebraska–Lincoln
Lincoln, Nebraska

Kristine S. Barker, CID
Interior Designer
Hayes, Seay, Mattern & Mattern, Inc.
Virginia Beach, Virginia

Jan Bast, FASID, IIDA, IDEC
Interior Design Program Director
Design Institute of San Diego
San Diego, California

Corky Binggeli, ASID
Principal
Corky Binggeli Interior Design
Arlington, Massachusetts

Bruce James Brigham, FASID, ISP, IES
Principal
Retail Clarity Consulting
Laredo, Texas

Laura C. Busse, IIDA, KYCID
Interior Designer
Reese Design Collaborative
Louisville, Kentucky

Rosalyn Cama, FASID
President
CAMA, Inc.
New Haven, Connecticut

Juliana Catlin, FASID
President
Catlin Design Group
Jacksonville, Florida

Stephanie Clemons, Ph.D., FASID, IDEC
Professor, Interior Design
Colorado State University
Fort Collins, Colorado

Jane Coit, Associate Member IIDA
Director of Design
Vangard Concept Offices
San Leandro, California

Susan Coleman, FIIDA. FIDEC
Retired faculty
Orange Coast College
Costa Mesa, California

David F. Cooke, FIIDA, CMG
Principal
Design Collective Incorporated
Baltimore, Maryland

Sally Howard D'Angelo, ASID, Affiliate Member AIA
Principal/Owner
S. H. Designs
Windham, New Hampshire

Joy Dohr, Ph.D., FIDEC, IIDA
Professor and Associate Dean, Retired
University of Wisconsin–Madison
Madison, Wisconsin

Theodore Drab, ASID, IIDA, IDEC
Associate Professor
University of Oklahoma
Norman, Oklahoma

Sandra G. Evans, ASID
Principal
Knoell & Quidort Architects
Phoenix, Arizona

Marilyn Farrow, FIIDA
Principal
Farrow Interiors/Consulting
Taos, New Mexico

Shannon Ferguson, IIDA
Project Manager
ID Collaborative
Greensboro, North Carolina

Neil P. Frankel, FIIDA, FAIA
Design Partner
Frankel + Coleman
Chicago, Illinois

Charles Gandy, FASID, FIIDA
President
Charles Gandy, Inc.
Clayton, Georgia

M. Arthur Gensler Jr., FAIA, FIIDA, RIBA
Chairman
Gensler
San Francisco, California

Suzan Globus, FASID. LEED-AP
Principal
Globus Design Associates
Red Bank, New Jersey

Bruce Goff, ASID
President
Domus Design Group
San Francisco, California

Sari Graven, ASID
Director of Program and Resource Development
Seattle University
Seattle, Washington

Greta Guelich, ASID
Principal
Perceptions Interior Design Group LLC
Scottsdale, Arizona

Denise A. Guerin, Ph.D., FIDEC, ASID, IIDA
Professor
University of Minnesota
St. Paul, Minnesota

Rita Carson Guest, FASID
President
Carson Guest, Inc.
Atlanta, Georgia

David Hanson, RID, IDC, IIDA
Owner
DH Designs
Vancouver, British Columbia, Canada

Beth Harmon-Vaughn, FIIDA, Associate AIA, LEED-AP
Office Director
Gensler
Phoenix, Arizona

Lisa Henry, ASID
Architecture and Design Manager
Knoll
Denver, Colorado

Maryanne Hewitt, IIDA
Owner
Hewitt Interior Design Group
Jacksonville Beach, Florida

Susan B. Higbee
Director of Interior Design
Group Mackenzie
Portland, Oregon

Debra May Himes, ASID, IIDA
President and Owner
Debra May Himes Interior Design & Associates LLC
Chandler, Arizona

Linda Isley, IIDA, CID
Senior Project Designer
Young + Co., Inc.
San Diego, California

Kristin King, ASID
Principal/Owner
KKID
Los Angeles, California

Michelle King, IIDA
Interior Designer
Dekker/Perich/Sabatini
Albuquerque, New Mexico

Sue Kirkman, ASID, IIDA, IDEC
Dean of Education
Harrington Institute of Interior Design
Chicago, Illinois

Mary G. Knopf, ASID, IIDA, LEED-AP
Principal/Interior Designer
ECI/Hyer, Inc.
Anchorage, Alaska

Mary Fisher Knott, Allied Member ASID, CID, RSPI
Owner
Mary Fisher Designs
Scottsdale, Arizona

Linda Kress, ASID
Director of Interior Design
Lotti Krishan & Short Architects
Tulsa, Oklahoma

Robert J. Krikac, IDEC
Associate Professor
Washington State University
Pullman, Washington

Beth Kuzbek, IIDA, CMG
National Specification Manager, Healthcare
Omnova Solutions, Inc.
Fairlawn, Ohio

Drue Ellen Lawlor, FASID
Owner, Drue Lawlor Interiors
Principal, education-works, inc.
San Gabriel, California

Nila Leiserowitz, FASID, Associate AIA
Managing Director/Principal
Gensler
Santa Monica, California

Janice Carleen Linster, ASID, IIDA, CID
Principal
Studio Hive, Inc.
Minneapolis, Minnesota

Rachelle Schoessler Lynn, CID, ASID, IFMA, LEED-AP,
Allied AIA Minnesota
Partner
Studio 2030
Minneapolis, Minnesota

Lois Macaulay, Allied Member ASID
President
Lois Macaulay Interior Design
Toronto, Ontario, Canada

Jain Malkin, CID
President
Jain Malkin, Inc.
San Diego, California

Terri Maurer, FASID
Owner
Maurer Design Group
Akron, Ohio

Colleen McCafferty, IFMA, USGBC, LEED-CI
Corporate Interior Team Leader
Hixson Architecture, Engineering, Interiors
Cincinnati, Ohio

Patricia Campbell McLaughlin, ASID, RID
Owner
MacLaughlin Collection (formerly Steel Magnolia)
Dallas, Texas

John Mclean, RA, CMG
Principal and Design Director
John Mclean Architect/architecture and industrial design
White Plains, New York

Dennis McNabb, FASID, IDEC
Associate Chair, Fashion and Interior Design
Central College
Houston Community College System
Houston, Texas

M. Joy Meeuwig, IIDA
Owner
Interior Design Consultation
Reno, Nevada

Fred Messner, IIDA
Principal
Phoenix Design One, Inc.
Tempe, Arizona

Darcie R. Miller, NKBA, ASID Industry Partner, CMG
Design Director
Miller Design
Ashland, Alabama

Keith Miller, ASID
Miller & Associates Interior Consultants, LLC
Seattle, Washington

Mimi Moore, ASID, CID, IDEC
Professor
San Diego Mesa College
San Diego, California

Carol Morrow, Ph.D., ASID, IIDA, IDEC
Academic Director of Interior Design
The Art Institute of Phoenix
Phoenix, Arizona

Sally Nordahl, IIDA
Director of Interior Design
Leo A. Daly
Phoenix, Arizona

Susan Norman, IIDA
Principal
Susan Norman Interiors
Phoenix, Arizona

Barbara Nugent, FASID
Principal
bnDesigns
Dallas, Texas

Derrell Parker, IIDA
Partner
Parker Scaggiari
Las Vegas, Nevada

William Peace, ASID
President
Peace Design
Atlanta, Georgia

Marilizabeth Polizzi, Allied Member ASID
Owner
Artistic Designs LLC
Scottsdale, Arizona

Sharmin Pool-Bak, ASID, CAPS, LEED-AP
Owner
Sharmin Pool-Bak Interior Design, LLC
Tucson, Arizona

James Postell
Associate Professor of Interior Design
University of Cincinnati
Cincinnati, Ohio

Jennifer van der Put, BID, IDC, ARIDO, IFMA
Director of Interior Design/Senior Associate
Bregman + Hamann Interior Design
Toronto, Ontario, Canada

Jo Rabaut, ASID, IIDA
Principal
Rabaut Design Associates, Inc.
Atlanta, Georgia

Jeffrey Rausch, IIDA
Principal
Exclaim Design
Scottsdale, Arizona

Teresa Ridlon, Allied Member ASID
Owner/President
Ridlon Interiors
Tempe, Arizona

Patricia A. Rowen, ASID, CAPS
Owner
Rowen Design
Hillsdale, Michigan

Leylan Salzer
Instructor/Interior Designer
Washington State University
Spokane, Washington

Linda Santellanes, ASID
Principal
Santellanes Interiors, Inc.
Tempe, Arizona

Derek B. Schmidt
Project Designer
Design Collective Incorporated
Nashville, Tennessee

Melinda Sechrist, FASID
President
Sechrist Design Associates, Inc.
Seattle, Washington

W. Daniel Shelley, AIA, ASID
Vice President/Secretary
James, DuRant, Matthews & Shelley, Inc.
Sumter, South Carolina

Lindsay Sholdar, ASID
Principal
Sholdar Interiors
San Diego, California

Lisa Slayman, ASID, IIDA
President
Slayman Design Associates, Inc.
Newport Beach, CA

Laurie P. Smith, ASID
Principal
Piconke Smith Design
Downers Grove, Illinois

Linda Elliott Smith, FASID
President
education-works, inc.
Dallas, Texas

Linda Sorrento, ASID, IIDA, LEED-AP
Director, Education and Research Partnerships
US Green Building Council
Washington, DC

Teresa Sowell, ASID, IFMA
Principal Facilities Engineer
Raytheon, Inc.
Tucson, Arizona

Annette K. Stelmack, Allied Member ASID
Owner
Inspirit-llc
Louisville, Colorado

David D. Stone, IIDA, LEED-AP
Senior Interior Designer
Leo A. Daly
Phoenix, Arizona

Kimberly M. Studzinski
Project Designer
Buchart Horn/Basco Associates
York, Pennsylvania

Michael A. Thomas, FASID, CAPS
Principal
The Design Collective Group, Inc.
Jupiter, Florida

Sally Thompson, ASID
President
Personal Interiors by Sally Thompson, Inc.
Gainesville, Florida

Suzanne Urban, ASID, IIDA
Principal
STUDIO4 Interiors Ltd.
Phoenix, Arizona

Donna Vining, FASID, IIDA, RID, CAPS
President
Vining Design Associates, Inc.
Houston, Texas

Robin J. Wagner, ASID, IDEC
Associate Professor
Director of Graduates, Interior Design
Marymount University
Washington, DC
and Wagner Somerset, Inc.
Clifton, Virginia

Lisa Whited IIDA, ASID, Maine Certified Interior Designer
Principal
Whited Planning + Design
Portland, Maine

Trisha Wilson, ASID
President
Wilson Associates
Dallas, Texas

Tom Witt
Associate Professor
Arizona State University
Tempe, Arizona

Robert Wright, FASID
President
Bast/Wright Interiors, Inc.
San Diego, California

INDEX